FIVE MASTERS OF INTERNATIONAL LAW

This book consists of interviews with five distinguished international lawyers from the UK, USA, Uruguay and France, conducted by the editor, Antonio Cassese, between 1993 and 1995. Each interview is preceded by a brief 'intellectual portrait' of the interviewee. In the Preface, Cassese stresses that the interviews, all based on the same questionnaire, were intended to bring out not only the main ideas associated with each scholar in the fields of international law and international relations, but also his intellectual and philosophical background, his general outlook and his views of the prospects for the evolution of the international community. In his final essay, Cassese brings together the main threads of the interviews, and points to the parallels and divergences appearing from them.

This book offers a unique and important insight into the legal minds and outlook of a select group of prominent scholars of international law and legal institutions during the last years of the 20th century.

Five Masters of International Law

Conversations with R-J Dupuy, E Jiménez de Aréchaga, R Jennings, L Henkin and O Schachter

Antonio Cassese

• HART •
PUBLISHING
OXFORD AND PORTLAND, OREGON
2011

Published in the United Kingdom by Hart Publishing Ltd
16C Worcester Place, Oxford, OX1 2JW
Telephone: +44 (0)1865 517530
Fax: +44 (0)1865 510710
E-mail: mail@hartpub.co.uk
Website: http://www.hartpub.co.uk

Published in North America (US and Canada) by
Hart Publishing
c/o International Specialized Book Services
920 NE 58th Avenue, Suite 300
Portland, OR 97213-3786
USA
Tel: +1 503 287 3093 or toll-free: (1) 800 944 6190
Fax: +1 503 280 8832
E-mail: orders@isbs.com
Website: http://www.isbs.com

British Library Cataloguing in Publication Data
Data Available

ISBN: 978-1-84946-120-7

Typeset by Hope Services, Abingdon
Printed and bound in Great Britain by
Lightning Source UK Ltd

Preface

The unexpectedly favourable reception of my interview with BAV Röling,[1] set me thinking that I could repeat the experiment by preparing a series of questions which would serve as a blueprint for interviewing other distinguished international lawyers. True, for certain readers, an interview may prove less interesting than a fully-fledged academic paper. However, interviews have the advantage of allowing a lively and fresh exchange of views. They also vividly reproduce a person's train of thought. The ponderings of the interviewee run in a sort of fluid discourse, not having been crystallised yet in the immutable propositions of a paper. Hence, interviews also make easy reading. This was recently confirmed by a distinguished member of the International Court of Justice, who told me that he had enjoyed reading the interview with Röling while comfortably lying in a deck chair on the beach, without the constraints of sitting at his desk to take notes, pencil at the ready.

I therefore resolved to embark on this new enterprise. I was curious to ask a selected number of scholars not only to expound their thoughts on the current role of international law in the world community and venture some forecasts, but also to have them share the story of their initial steps as scholars, to understand whether they shared a common intellectual matrix and to see whether there had been a particular school of thought influencing them. I also planned to consider the interviewees not only as prominent professionals who had excelled in their careers, but also as human beings of flesh and blood. This, I acknowledge, finds its underpinning in my belief that it is not true what Hegel (followed by the Italian philosopher Benedetto Croce) held, namely that in the end what matters is not the private life of human beings but their works, that only their works remain and only by their works can one gauge the value of their authors. For Hegel, once men have fulfilled their tasks, they are similar to empty hulls that fall away from their kernel.[2]

[1] BVA Röling, *The Tokyo Trial and Beyond: Reflections of a Peacemonger* (A Cassese ed)(Oxford, Polity Press, 1993).

[2] '*Was sie [die Menschen] sind, ist eben ihre Tat gewesen; diese ihre Leidenschaft had den Umfang ihrer Natur, ihres Charakters ausgemacht. Ist der Zweck erreicht, so gleichen sie leeren Hulsen, die abfallen.*' ('What they are is nothing else than their work; their passion has determined the scope of their nature and of their character; once they have attained their purpose, they resemble empty hulls that fall off'): GWF Hegel, 'Vorlesungen über die Philosophie der Weltgeschichte', in GWF Hegel, *Sämtliche Werke*, vol VIII (ed Georg Lasson) (Leipzig, Verlag von Felix Meiner, 1920) at 78.

Instead, with respect, I think that their personal life is no less important, and once they have passed away much of that life remains in the minds as well as in the hearts of those who knew them. In a way they belong to the Lares and Penates of those who survive, together with the memory of our own personal ancestors.[3]

Thus, I decided to include personal questions about the interviewees' lives too. I wanted to understand to what extent their professional activities had sheltered them from disquiet in the face of so many tragedies afflicting the world. This—I must acknowledge—was not an easy task for me: somehow I felt like like Asmodée, the lame devil described by the French writer Lesage, who, once he was liberated from the corked phial in which a magician had kept him for long, in exchange for his delivery took his liberator, the student Cléofas Léandro, to a tower, heaved up the roofs of all the houses in downtown Madrid and, notwithstanding the darkness of the night, exposed their insides to his view.[4] Of course I lacked Asmodée's diabolical powers, I was not so inquisitive, and in addition the interviewees—perhaps unwittingly—tended to shelter behind a heavy protective armour.

Another issue which intrigued me was the extent to which these scholars had acted under the influence of positivism. Indubitably, legal positivism has represented great progress in the evolution of legal thinking, on two grounds. First, it has enabled scholars and practitioners to separate law from morality, 'the law as it is from the law as it ought to be'.[5] This is epitomised in the famous dichotomy between *lex lata* and *lex ferenda*. By the same token, the proponents of positivism also have rightly insisted on the need to distinguish between 'statements of fact' and 'statements based on values', and to exclude the latter from legal inquiries. Secondly, positivism has emphasised the need to distinguish between the legal analysis of rules and institutions, and sociological or historical investigations of the law. Legal analysis must use legal methods of interpretation, legal concepts and constructs, and refrain from relying on parameters proper to other disciplines. It usually suffices to open a legal treatise from the 19th century to realise that the uncritical mixture of historical, legal and sociological inquiry resulted in a fuzzy reconstruction of legal institutions and rules with a total lack of rigour. In a retort concerning this lack of compartmentalisation of the social sciences, Dionisio Anzilotti—indisputably one of the most eminent international lawyers of the 20th century and a very influential positivist—quoted an astute maxim by Kant at the beginning of his masterpiece, *Corso di diritto internazionale*[6] (*Textbook of International Law*), which reads 'one does not multiply science but rather

[3] The Lares and Penates, considered spirits of the dead, were the Roman gods who acted as guardians of the entire household.

[4] Alain-René Lesage, *Le Diable Boiteux*, first published in 1707 (Paris, Gallimard, 1984).

[5] HLA Hart, *Essays in Jurisprudence and Philosophy* (Oxford, Clarendon Press, 1983) at 50–53.

[6] D Anzilotti, *Corso di diritto internazionale (ad uso degli studenti dell'Università di Roma)*, 3rd edn (Rome, Atheneum, 1928).

ends up marring it if one merges the borders between the various scientific disciplines'.[7]

However, while deeply appreciating the merits of positivism, one should not overlook some of its striking limitations. Let me highlight two of them here. First, positivism's most conspicuous defect lies in the fact that its inherent methodological tenets may constitute an impediment to the evolution of law. To illustrate how problematic this is, one need only recall the objections the two American delegates to the Paris Peace Conference raised in 1919 against the inclusion of provisions banning crimes against humanity in a treaty, in the name of positivism.[8] The same kind of positivist objections were voiced in 1920 within the 'Advisory Committee of Jurists', appointed by the Council of the League of Nations to draft the Statute of the Permanent Court of International Justice. When the Belgian delegate, EEF Descamps, expressly relying on the celebrated 'Martens clause',[9] suggested the new Court should also apply 'the rules of international law as recognized by the legal conscience of civilized nations' in addition to treaties and custom, the American, British and Italian delegates invoked positive law to oppose the proposal.[10] The current formulation of the provision in

[7] '*Es ist nicht Vermehrung, sondern Verunstaltung der Wissenschaften, wenn man ihre Grenzen ineinenderlaufen lässt.*' Oddly, this maxim does not appear in the French translation of the *Corso* (*Cours de droit international*, translated by GC Gidel (Paris, Recuil Sirey, 1929)).

[8] 'As pointed out by the American representatives on more than one occasion, war was and is by its nature inhuman, but acts consistent with the laws and customs of war, although these acts are inhuman, are nevertheless not the object of punishment by a court of justice. A judicial tribunal only deals with existing law and only administers existing law, leaving to another forum infractions of the moral law and actions contrary to the laws and principles of humanity. A further objection lies in the fact that the laws and principles of humanity are not certain, varying with time, place, and circumstance, and according, it may be, to the conscience of the individual judge. There is no fixed and universal standard of humanity.' See R Lansing and J Brown Scott, 'Memorandum of Reservations Presented by the Representatives of the United States to the Report of the Commission on Responsibilities (April 4, 1919)', Annex II to Commission on the Responsibility of the Authors of the War and on Enforcement of Penalties, Report Presented to the Preliminary Peace Conference (Versailles, March 29, 1919), (1920) 14 *American Journal of International Law* 95, at 144.

[9] This was the celebrated clause adopted, at the instigation of the Russian jurist and diplomat Fyodor Fyodorovich Martens (1845–1909), at the Hague Peace Conference of 1899, and which became part of the preamble of the IVth Hague Convention. It stated that 'Until a more complete code of the laws of war has been issued, the High Contracting Parties deem it expedient to declare that, in cases not included in the [Hague] Regulations [on the Laws of War on Land] adopted by them, the inhabitants and the belligerents remain under the protection and the rule of the *principles of the law of nations, as they result from the usages established among civilized peoples, from the laws of humanity, and the dictates of the public conscience.*' (emphasis added). (The French original was worded as follows: 'En attendant qu'un Code plus complet des lois de la guerre puisse être édicté, les Hautes Parties contractantes jugent opportun de constater que, dans les cas non compris dans les dispositions réglementaires adoptées par Elles, les populations et les belligérants restent sous la sauvegarde et sous l'empire des principes du droit des gens, tels qu'ils résultent des usages établis entre nations civilisées, des lois de l'humanité et des exigences de la conscience publique.') On this clause see my paper 'The Martens Clause: Half a Loaf or Simply Pie in the Sky? (2000) 11 *European Journal of International Law* 187.

[10] The US delegate Root noted that 'Nations will submit to positive law, but will not submit to such principles as have not been developed into positive rules supported by an accord between all States', League of Nations, Permanent Court of International Justice, Advisory Committee of Jurists, *Procès-Verbaux of the Proceedings of the Committee, June 16th–July 24th 1920* (The Hague, van Langen-Huysen Brothers, 1920) 287. He subsequently asked: 'Was it possible to compel nations to submit their disputes to a Court which would administer not merely law, but also what it deems to be the conscience

question (whereby the Court can 'apply the general principles of law recognized by civilised nations') was a compromise following strenuous negotiations.

Positivism's second major weakness is that in certain circumstances it may be deemed to involve a logical and moral ban or impediment to lawyers in the fight against authoritarian regimes. Admittedly, in dark periods of dictatorships, positivism has enabled scholars and other experts to avoid getting enmeshed in political life, thus preserving a large measure of 'purity' in legal investigations. On the other hand, positivism has also provided a moral licence for eminent scholars to be subservient to authoritarian regimes on the assumption that jurists must only interpret the law, whatever its content and whether or not it is consonant with democratic principles. In other words, they should not go so far as to advance value judgements, or assess the merits or flaws of the authoritarianism of existing social and political institutions, which obviously would entail approving or disapproving them. The example that springs most easily to mind is one which I have already had the opportunity to recount elsewhere.[11] It concerns the distinguished Italian international lawyer, Tomaso Perassi, who, although a man of strong democratic ideals, had no qualms about his position as chief legal adviser to the Italian Ministry of Foreign Affairs under Mussolini, since he separated his official functions from his democratic ideals with the barrier of strict positivism. Perhaps it was only fair that his legal formalism ended up arousing the disdain of the fascist authorities (in 1939 the Foreign Minister Galeazzo Ciano scornfully labelled him 'a professional pettifogger' (*professionista del cavillo*)).

It is partly as a reaction to this intellectual trend that I have sought to show some flexibility throughout my own career. While substantially accepting the basic axioms of positivism in my own research, I have modestly attempted to make some circumspect forays into related disciplines. In particular, I have tried to draw upon history and political sciences whenever they could provide insight into the rationale behind a legal institution or rule. I have also critiqued legal concepts or institutions, and proposed how in my view they could be ameliorated in order for them better to respond to current demands.

I was therefore keen to understand how the eminent international lawyers I was to interview had come to grips with this problem, and in particular to what extent they had segregated law from other social sciences.

I initially planned to interview only European scholars and judges so as to highlight the commonalities of the European schools of thought, but also to identify the differences between the various branches of the European tradition. However, on reflection, such an approach seemed shallow, if not artificial, since it would not reflect the increasing intermingling and cross-fertilisation of ideas and approaches in the modern world. Not least, I realised

of civilized peoples?' (*ibid*, at 294). For the statements of the three delegates against the Belgian proposal, see *ibid*, 293–94, 308–10, 315–17, 318–25.

[11] A Cassese, 'Soliloquy' in A Cassese, *The Human Dimension of International Law: Selected Papers* (eds P Gaeta and S Zappalà) (Oxford, Oxford University Press, 2008) lix.

that non-European jurists should be included since they are no less influential than their counterparts operating in Europe. I thus cast my net wider than the Old Continent and selected those international lawyers whom I considered outstanding in their field but also representative of the different schools of thought. In the end, I chose two Europeans (René-Jean Dupuy and Sir Robert Jennings), one Latin American very close to the US and European traditions (Eduardo Jiménez de Aréchaga), and two leading US scholars (Louis Henkin and Oscar Schachter).

I also asked two prominent Italian international lawyers, Roberto Ago and Gaetano Arangio-Ruiz, to take part in the enterprise. The former kindly advised me that he was not really interested. This surprised me as I was convinced he would be keen to expound his ideas, discuss his career and highlight his many scholarly, diplomatic and judicial achievements. The latter (Arangio-Ruiz) accepted and gave a spirited if disjointed interview. Then, when he read the transcript, he expressed his dissatisfaction with his own answers (which were actually incisive and profound). After some time, he gave me a completely redrafted set of answers. This time, it was my turn to be discontented, for the interview had lost its freshness; his answers were lengthy lucubrations about international legal issues and in particular against the growing role of the UN Security Council. He of course sensed my hesitations, and after some time, asked me to return the transcript to him, promising to hand in a new draft. However, more than four years have passed since then, and I have not received any revised draft. I therefore deduced that he simply wanted to drop out in a gracious if tortuous manner. However, with his authorisation, a few pages of his interview were published, together with excerpts from the interviews of Jiménez de Aréchaga and Schachter, in a Symposium on Kelsen published in the *European Journal of International Law* in 1998.[12]

I prepared a tentative questionnaire for the (six, then five) interviewees, so as to ask each of them the same questions and then compare their answers and try to draw some sort of conclusions from them. The questionnaire is included in this book to provide an idea of the anticipated structure of the dialogues. The interviews themselves are printed in the chronological order in which they were conducted. However, they clearly expand upon some of the questions contained in the Basic Questionnaire, and do not use precisely the same headings. This explains some of the differences between the questionnaire and the interviews, and between the interviews themselves.

I thought it would be useful to provide readers (especially the younger ones) with a concise intellectual 'portrait' of each interviewee before his interview. I also felt it necessary to try to gather up the various threads at the end of the book, by highlighting the many significant ideas which emerged from

[12] See Gaetano Arangio-Ruiz, Eduardo Jiménez de Aréchaga and Oscar Schachter, 'Kelsen, Personal Recollections' (1998) 9 *European Journal of International Law* 386. The extract from the interview with G Arangio-Ruiz is *ibid* at 386–87.

the interviews and contrasting the varying responses on some crucial points. Furthermore, at the (right) request of the publisher, I added many footnotes, providing references to the writings or cases mentioned by the interviewees. I also briefly set out in footnotes the relevant dates (and, in some instances the salient features) of the numerous authors referred to by some interviewees. Although this job was time-consuming, I thought it would prove helpful to the younger generations, who often seem to ignore all (or most) scholars of the past. Thus, in the end, this book should also have some sort of pedagogical value for younger scholars.

This book has taken me almost 20 years to complete. I began the first interview in 1993 and conducted the last one in 1995. Then many other intellectual chores distracted me from the task of revising and editing the manuscript. Now that all the interviewees have passed away and the editor is also likely to set out on that eternal voyage soon, I thought it was high time to resurrect the project in order to avoid leaving this wealth of material lying forever in a dusty drawer. Luckily, Sandra Sahyouni helped me in the demanding task of editing the various sections of the book, and Valentina Spiga was of great assistance in sorting out all the numerous footnotes and double-checking references. I am most grateful to both of them.

I hope that the book will make interesting reading and that all the time-consuming efforts to bring it to completion prove worthwhile.

Antonio Cassese
September 2010

Summary Contents

Contents

Basic Questionnaire[13]

I. The Beginnings

(i) Initiation to scholarship

—Which international lawyer most influenced your thinking, at the beginning of your scholarly activity?
—Which international lawyer you met in your career has impressed you the most, and why?

(ii) The state of legal scholarship at the outset of your career

—By and large, what was the status of legal scholarship when you initiated your scholarly activity?

a) What were the areas of major interest of the legal literature in your country?
b) What were the major features of that literature? (In particular, did it take a pronounced positivist, or even legalistic approach? Did it draw upon other social sciences such as history, political science, sociology?)
c) How did the legal literature of your country compare with that prevailing in other European countries?

(iii) Law and philosophy

—Leaving aside legal scholarship, which philosophical or ideological schools influenced your intellectual development? Or did you instead stay impervious to any non-legal school of thought?

(iv) On being a public figure

—Have you been active or visible in the public arena? Have you written for newspapers, appeared on television or spoken on the radio?

[13] As mentioned in the comments to the Preface, clearly I have expanded upon the following basic questions in the interviews. The questionnaire merely formed the foundation for our discussions.

—Do you think international lawyers (or any lawyers, for that matter) should be socially active and involved in their communities? Or do you feel instead that they should concentrate exclusively on their activities as experts?
—Have you ever taken part in any political (or trade union) activity in your country or at the international level? Have you ever been a militant in an NGO?
—Do you perceive yourself merely as a 'technician' or as a fully-fledged 'intellectual'?

II. Scholar v Practitioner

—How have you considered your activity as a scholar separate from your activity as a practitioner (be it as judge, legal adviser, contributor to law-making, etc)? Or are they both mutually reinforcing, and part and parcel of each other?
—What impact did your activity as a practitioner have on your intellectual development?
—What primarily motivated you to undertake non-scholarly activities as a practitioner? Do you perceive the practice of law (as opposed to its study) as being mainly motivated by a real calling or vocation (*Beruf* in the Weberian sense)?

III. Contributing to International Law

—What would you consider your major contribution to international law

a) at the academic level?
b) at the level of law-making, adjudication or law-implementation?

—Do you feel that you have been able to create a 'school' by training and inspiring a number of disciples? If so, what are, in your view, the main features of this 'school'?
—Independently of the scientific value of your contribution to international law, in your view, which part of your activity is likely to have a lasting impact on the international community?
—Do you have any regrets about something that you might or should have done in your career as a scholar or practitioner?

IV. The Outlook for the World Community

—How do you perceive the current trends emerging in the international community? In your opinion, which values of traditional international law should be preserved? Which should be discarded?

—What values and features of the present international community do you think might potentially disrupt the present fabric of the world community?
—What values are instead indicative of a dynamic and positive evolution toward a better world community?
—Is there any means of bridging the present gap between normative values (human rights, *jus cogens*, repression of crimes against humanity, the notion of international crimes of States, etc) and the actual reality of international relations, still inspired by nationalist and sovereignty-oriented feelings?

V. Personal Matters

(i) Heeding the demon

—At the end of his essay on 'Science as a vocation', Max Weber wrote that each scholar should 'find and obey the demon (*daimonion*) who holds the fibre of his very life'. Do you feel that you have heeded the commands of your *daimonion*? Do you feel that you have met 'the demands of the day', in human relations as well as in your vocation?

(ii) Making life more bearable

—In his essay of 1930 on 'Civilization and its Discontent', Freud wrote that life 'is unbearable because of too much pain, disillusion, and tasks that cannot be fulfilled', adding that none of us can get through it without 'palliatives' (*Linderungsmitteln*), of which, according to him, there exist essentially three:

1. 'Powerful diversions' (*mächtige Ablenkunkungen*) that make us 'attach little value to our misery' (examples for Freud are scholarly activity or the gardening suggested by Voltaire in the last page of *Candide*);
2. 'Substitute gratifications' (*Ersatzbefriedigungen*) which 'lessen our misery' (one of them being art, which creates illusions that distract us from reality);
3. 'Drugs' (*Rauschstoffe*), 'that make us insensible to misery'.

To what palliatives have you willingly or unwillingly had recourse in your life?

René-Jean Dupuy

MOST ACADEMICS DISTIL the best of their intelligence and experience into their writings. There are a rare few, however, who shine best with their oral craftsmanship, through spoken words and skills of oratory which have the power to touch their interlocutors directly, and with the humanism of their teaching and the vivacity with which they communicate their knowledge. René-Jean Dupuy belonged to this latter category. His lectures were extraordinary. He addressed legal issues with rigour and clarity, never limiting himself to superficial analysis or being descriptive but placing issues in their proper historical and theoretical context. His intellectual heft and power of persuasion were extraordinary. His legal discourse was also underpinned by a vast culture. He would regularly draw on an eclectic array of writers, philosophers and essayists to inject his lectures with citations that gave colour and texture to his legal arguments. He would carefully handpick these references to support and advance each proposition in his argumentation, turning them into integral steps in his reasoning and never-gratuitous demonstrations of knowledge. This was inevitable perhaps, since his legal thinking was conditioned to such a degree by his readings of political and philosophical masters.

The care with which Dupuy chose his literary and political references was matched by the time he invested in preparing his lectures, and whoever sat next to him could sneak a peek at the meticulously prepared outline, written by hand and—in the last years of his life, when his eyes had grown weary—in large font. He continued with his speaking commitments well into old age, but the physical effort required for public speaking would be slightly more visible than during his youth, often causing him to pause for a few minutes in the middle of the lecture or to remove his sweater. Dinner-table conversations with him were an immense pleasure: he overflowed with wit and was always ready to dive into his repository of classic quotes, recount anecdotes or recall encounters with notable characters. It was during one of these conversations that he spoke to me at length about a French writer he loved and who was then unknown to me: Romain Gary. I later indulged in the novels of this fascinating writer, and transferred the discovery and newfound appreciation to my wife, thanks to Dupuy.

The strength and elegance of his oral delivery and the joy he took in it were such that, occasionally, listening to him, I would think of Plato's words on spoken discourse as being the only legitimate discourse—as compared to the written transmission of ideas, good only as an aide to memory.[1] I could not help but also observe that, just as Plato was not being entirely truthful in his dismissal of writing (because after all, unlike Socrates, he did commit most of his philosophy to writing), so too did Dupuy cherish the written word just as much as the spoken word, going to great lengths when penning his reflections – and indeed attaching enormous importance to his *écriture.*

In his human contacts, Dupuy radiated warmth and charm. He used to stress that he was 'a man from the South'. He was proud of his Italian origins and his childhood in Algeria, being born in Tunis to a French father from Algiers and a Neapolitan mother. The ease with which he built friendships was notable though not surprising, since he prized friendship as a great human asset. Boutros Boutros-Ghali rightly spoke of 'this luminous network of friendships that he had been able to create' (*ce réseaux lumineux d'amitiés*

[1] The historian of ancient philosophy Giorgio Colli (*La nascita della filosofia* (Milan, Adelfi, 1975) at 108–16) deserves to be credited for drawing attention to two passages in Plato's works. The first passage is in *Phaedrus* (274a–276a, translated into English by HN Fowler in *Plato in Twelve Volumes*, vol 1 (Cambridge, MA, Harvard University Press, 1982)). Socrates recounts to Phaedrus the story of Theuth who, presenting his inventions to the king of Egypt Thamus, praised the 'invention of letters', which 'will make the Egyptians wiser and will improve their memories; for it is an elixir of memory and wisdom that I have discovered' (274e). To this Thamus replies that 'this invention will produce forgetfulness in the minds of those who learn to use it, because they will not practice their memory. Their trust in writing, produced by external characters which are no part of themselves, will discourage the use of their own memory within them. You have invented an elixir not of memory, but of reminding; and you offer your pupils the appearance of wisdom, not true wisdom, for they will read many things without instruction and will therefore seem [275a] to know many things, when they are for the most part ignorant and hard to get along with, since they are not wise, but only appear wise' (*ibid*, 275b). And Socrates comments on this story as follows: 'Writing, Phaedrus, has this strange quality, and is very like painting; for the creatures of painting stand like living beings, but if one asks them a question, they preserve a solemn silence. And so it is with written words; you might think they spoke as if they had intelligence, but if you question them, wishing to know about their sayings, they always say only one and the same thing. And every word, when [275d] once it is written, is bandied about, alike among those who understand and those who have no interest in it, and it knows not to whom to speak or not to speak; when ill-treated or unjustly reviled it always needs its father to help it; for it has no power to protect or help itself.' (275e)

A stronger support of oral logos as opposed to written wisdom can be found in Plato's *Seventh Epistle* (generally regarded as authentic; I shall here use the translation by J Harward). After attacking Dionysios (the tyrant of Syracuse, who had hosted him) for having written down what he had heard from him, Plato notes that philosophy must be transmitted orally, '[f]or it does not admit of exposition like other branches of knowledge; but after much converse about the matter itself and a life lived together, suddenly a light, as it were, is kindled in one soul by a flame that leaps to it from another, and thereafter sustains itself. Yet this much I know—that if the things were written or put into words, it would be done best by me, and that, if they were written badly, I should be the person most pained. Again, if they had appeared to me to admit adequately of writing and exposition, what task in life could I have performed nobler than this, to write what is of great service to mankind and to bring the nature of things into the light for all to see?' (at 25). He then adds to it by stressing that 'no man of intelligence will venture to express his philosophical views in language, especially not in language that is unchangeable, which is true of that which is set down in written characters' (at 27). And later on he clinches the point by saying 'every man of worth, when dealing with matters of worth, will be far from exposing them to ill feeling and misunderstanding among men by committing them to writing. In one word, then, it may be known from this that, if one sees written treatises composed by anyone, either the laws of a lawgiver, or in any other form whatever, these are not for that man the things of most worth, if he is a man of worth, but that his treasures are laid up in the fairest spot that he possesses. But if these things were worked at by him as things of real worth, and committed to writing, then surely, not gods, but men "have themselves bereft him of his wits"' (at 30).

qu'il avait su créer). Dupuy was always at his friends' service, regardless of ideological or political affiliation, nationality or religion. The devotion he showed them was replicated in the way he interacted with his students. He proudly liked to say that his 'school' embraced persons from all parts of the political spectrum, to whom he was equally attached whether they belonged to the right or to the left, whether they were conservative or progressive.

René-Jean Dupuy (1918–97) had a stellar academic career. He became Professor of International Law in 1950, and taught at the universities of Algiers, Aix-en-Provence, Nice and Paris (Panthéon-Sorbonne). He was elected to the Collège de France in 1979, an august institution which is considered the apex of teaching and research in France, where he taught until 1990. His being granted a chair in international law there was all the more impressive and noteworthy since that branch of scholarship had never been taught before at the Collège, and had been created expressly in recognition of Dupuy's place in the pantheon of scholars in the field.

In addition to his professorial career, Dupuy could also boast of various para-academic achievements. He was a member of the European Commission of Human Rights (1974–81), Secretary-General of the Hague Academy of International Law (1966–84) and, from 1967 onwards, a member of the *Institut de Droit international*. He also took part in international judicial activities, acting as umpire in a few arbitrations, most notably in the famous case *Texaco Overseas Petroleum Company and California Asiatic Oil Company v The Government of Libyan Arab Republic.*[2] In this case he handed down an award which drew him much criticism.[3] In addition, he acted as legal counsel in a number of cases before the International Court of Justice.

Within the legal scholarship of the 20th century, Dupuy belonged to the European tradition. Although he was a leading figure of the French School, he stood out from his national peers because of some unique features. Unlike his colleagues, who embraced the positivist tradition (a group including such distinguished scholars and judges as Jules Basdevant, Suzanne Bastid, Paul Reuter, Gilbert Guillaume and Jean Combacau, to mention just a few), he did not confine himself to engaging in positivist research of existing law or nascent law (he did so in his many writings on the law of the sea); he also conceived great frescos of the world community, where he propounded new concepts which aptly captured the developing features of that community. In this respect, he continued the tradition of his professor and mentor, George Scelle.[4] Like Scelle, Dupuy cherished the grand historical–theoretical frescos

[2] See *ad hoc* award of 19 January 1977, published in (1978) *International Legal Materials* 3. Published in French in (1977) 104 *Journal du Droit international* 350.

[3] See F Rigaux, 'Des dieux et des héros—Réflexions sur une sentence arbitrale' (1978) *Revue critique de droit international privé* 435.

[4] G Scelle (1878–1961) was Professor of International Law at the Sorbonne and a leading French international lawyer. He was an imaginative and ground-breaking lawyer, able to open up new vistas for students of international relations. His major work is *Précis de droit des gens: principes et systématique*, 2 vols (Paris, Recueil Sirey, 1932–34), 2 vols. On his contribution to international law, see the various

and recognised the importance of proper contextualisation. He added, however, a profundity which is perhaps lacking in Scelle. Dupuy's legal culture was permeated with political philosophy. He was familiar with the writings of such thinkers as Nietzsche, Benjamin Constant and Proudhon, such philosophers as Bergson, and authors such as Peguy, Valéry and Camus; it is therefore no surprise that his own writings were salted with citations from their works. In addition, Scelle sometimes was impatient with new concepts he advanced: once he had proposed a new notion, he would stop short of fleshing it out in full, refining it or developing all its possible ramifications. In contrast, in Dupuy's writings, one can see the 'labour of the file'; he always took care to spell out all the implications of his concepts, and in addition relished polishing and re-polishing his writings, with regard to both substance and style.

Dupuy's essay on the two categories of custom, the 'wise custom' (*coutume sage*) and the 'wild custom' (*coutume sauvage*), illustrates his inclination to look at legal constructs not only from a historical perspective but also within a general conceptual framework.[5] On the one hand, he argued, there are traditional customary rules, born out of the combination of the two classical elements (*usus* and *opinio juris*) and having their foundation in the consensual or voluntarist origin (custom as *pactum tacitum*). He contrasted this category of custom with what he called 'wild' customary rules, or rules born in a short period of time out of the desire of a large group of States to impose their demands on the whole community. Here the voluntary element trumps the historical development, the repetition in time of the same behaviour accompanied by the awareness that it responds to a legal obligation. Wild customary rules are 'revisionistic' (*révisionnistes*) or 'challenging' (*contestataires*). As examples of these new rules born from 'wild' custom, Dupuy pointed to the rule on the 400-mile exclusive zone and the principle that a State bears responsibility for trans-boundary pollution originating from within its territory.

Dupuy's conceptual parameters for understanding the main features of the world community may seem too classificatory today, and indeed have not been adopted by subsequent writers. In reality, however, they are useful conceptual tools for better understanding the workings of the international community. Dupuy developed the most significant of his concepts in what can be considered his best scholarly work: his remarkable general course at The Hague Academy in 1979.[6] There, Dupuy first defined and discussed

papers published in (1990) 1 *European Journal of International Law* 193–249, which include a splendid paper by R-J Dupuy on his mentor, 'Images de Georges Scelle' (*ibid*, 235–39).

[5] See R-J Dupuy, 'Coutume sage et costume sauvage', in *Mélanges Rousseaux* (Paris, Pedone, 1974) 75–87. He returned to this concept in various other writings. See, eg, his essay, 'Égalité et inégalité des nations' in R-J Dupuy, *La Sélection, Cours général 1994–95* (Lausanne, Publications de l'Université de Lausanne, 1995) 84.

[6] R-J Dupuy, 'Communauté internationale et disparités de développement: cours général de droit international public' (1979-IV) 165 *Recueil des cours de l'Académie de Droit International de La Haye* ('*Recueil des cours*') 9

law relating to inter-State relations (*droit relationnel*) and law governing institutions (*droit institutionnel*), universal law (*droit universel*) and law relating to the specific situations of States (*droit situationnel*). The *droit relationnel* is the law of the old community, where what mattered primarily was to have a modicum of rules regulating inter-State dealings in order to facilitate such dealings; it was therefore essentially a procedural law (*droit de procédure*). The model of international community underpinning this kind of law is characterised by three factors:

a) the diffusion of power among legal subjects, and the simultaneous absence of individuals from the world community;
b) the fact that power was not regulated by any legal restraint, law being essentially a law of coordination and not of subordination; and
c) the fact that resort to force to protect one's interests and rights was lawful.

In contrast, the *droit institutionnel* is a substantive law, designed to impose obligations relating to the behaviour of States, particularly in such new areas as environment, outer space and human rights.[7] It is characterised by:

a) a concentration of power, States being now members of, and subject to, international institutions, where individuals also have a say;
b) the fact that the power of States is no longer unfettered but is regulated by international institutions; and
c) the circumstance that now States are no longer allowed to resort freely to force in international relations, but are bound by the imperatives of the UN Charter, notably the ban laid down in Article 2(4).

Dupuy then shows how the two models interact. He notes that States frequently endeavour to project the institutional model onto the traditional body of law which inspired the relational model. The role of the International Law Commission (ILC) is seen as such an attempt, the new majority of States trying, through the ILC, to update or expand the old law and make it more responsive to the demands of developing countries by helping create new law through an institutional mechanism.

Another set of concepts propounded by Dupuy is that of 'universal law' and 'situational law'. The former is the law of the old international community, where all States were put legally on the same footing, whatever their economic, military and political importance. All States were deemed to belong to the same abstract and homogeneous category, the law being a body of 'impersonal' norms which willingly ignored *de facto* differences. In contrast, the second model, that of 'situational law', intends to take account of the factual differences between States, and therefore makes allowance for new

[7] See R-J Dupuy, *Leçon inaugurale au Collège de France (faite le vendredi 22 Février 1980)* (Paris, Collège de France, 1980) 13.

classes of States, such as 'developing countries', 'least developed countries', 'landlocked States' and so on.

Dupuy suggested yet another set of conceptual constructs in his Hague lectures, delving into them more deeply in some of his subsequent writings. For one, he drew a distinction between a 'historical' notion of the international community' (*communauté historique*) and the community as a myth and a prophesy (*communauté mythique et prophétique*). The 'historical' community is, in his view, the traditional community, as it exists today and which evolved from the 17th century on; it is a community dominated by self-interest, where there is no collective value and State interests in economic, military and political matters override all other concerns while the individuals play no role whatsoever. The 'mythical' community, on the other hand, is a concept chiefly advocated by developing countries who wish to bring about a world society where solidarity and universal values prevail and the developed countries take care of the problems besetting the less-advanced countries. As Dupuy wrote in 1980, this notion

> is the constantly renewed source of permanent contestation within the historical community; it serves to steadily call into question the vested assets of the historical community, to prevent those that invoke those assets from clinging to them and refusing to move forward towards the building of a new economic international order.[8]

What remains of Dupuy for those who did not have the chance to meet him, listen to him or enjoy his friendship? Two sets of writings stand out from Dupuy's significant legal output: his publications on the law of the sea, and those he devoted to the structure and legal configuration of the international community. He kept a keen eye on developments in the law of the sea and wrote assiduously on the emergence of the new law in the 1980s. He looked carefully into new concepts such as the continental shelf, the exclusive economic zone and the common heritage of mankind, and analysed them comprehensively. Without doubt, these writings will eventually be superseded by newer works from other authors as new legislative or jurisprudential developments occur. This is the ineluctable fate governing our legal contributions: new legislative and jurisprudential developments are destined to render previous writings obsolete (as Julius Herrmann von Kirchmann once wrote, 'three amending words by the law-makers suffice for entire law libraries to be pulped').[9] Moreover, Dupuy's last books on law, perhaps rather too reliant on literature and philosophy, and somewhat over-indulging in elegant writing, are likely to fall into oblivion. Nonetheless, his general course at The Hague Academy and the splendid lecture he gave in

[8] *Ibid*, 26.

[9] '*Drei berichtigende Worte des Gesetzgebers und ganze Bibliotheken werden zu Makulatur*', in JH von Kirchmann, *Die Wertlosigkeit der Jurisprudenz als Wissenschaft: Ein Vortrag* (Berlin, Nachdruck der Ausg, 1848) (reprinted by Heidelberg, Manutius Verlag, 1988) 29.

1980 when entering the Collège de France will remain indispensable reading for any good international lawyer for years to come. The concepts of relational and institutional law, of universal law and situational law, and the contrast between a historical community and a mythical community are legal tools that will bear fruit on a par with better-known conceptual tools, such as the distinction between 'law of coordination' and 'law of cooperation' (Friedmann)[10] and that between the Westphalian model of the international society and the UN Charter model (Falk).[11]

[10] W Friedmann, *The Changing Structure of International Law* (London, Stevens, 1964). These concepts have been taken up by many authors, chiefly G Abi-Saab, 'Cours général de droit international public' (1987-VII) 207 *Recueil des cours* 9, at 319–27, and C Tomuschat, 'International Law: Ensuring the Survival of Mankind on the Eve of a New Century: General Course on Public International Law' (1999) 281 *Recueil des cours* 9, at 56–62. Wolfgang Friedmann (1907–72) a German scholar who had emigrated to the US, was professor at the Columbia University School of Law from 1955 to 1972. The aforementioned book is his major scholarly contribution to international law.

[11] R Falk, *Legal Order in a Violent World* (Princeton, NJ, Princeton University Press, 1968); R Falk, *The Status of Law in International Society* (Princeton, NJ Princeton University Press, 1970); R Falk, *Law in an Emerging Global Village—A Post-Westphalian Perspective* (New York, Transnational Publishers, 1998) esp at 3–45.

Interview with René-Jean Dupuy

June 1993

I. The Formative Years

A. The encounter with international law

Which internationalist would you say most influenced your education?

It was undoubtedly Georges Scelle, for the very simple reason that he was the one to reveal the existence of international law to me. I had pursued advanced studies in private law and wanted to become a professor of private law. Then one day, in Paris, when I was working on my Master's degree[12] in public law and planned to go on to a doctorate, I mixed up lecture theatres. I entered a hall where a professor was giving a class. I realised right away that this wasn't the course I had intended to take, because he was talking about the effect of treaties on the domestic legal order. It was Georges Scelle. I found him so brilliant, with such a dazzling command of rhetoric, that I had my revelation of international law via the intellectual appeal of this remarkable man.

I had had great scorn for international law until then, because, as I was a private lawyer, it seemed to me to lack rigour, to depend on voluntary compliance, on States, on their sovereignty, and that it was therefore impossible to build a real body of law at the international level. With Georges Scelle, however, this appeared possible thanks to his explanation which was based on legal monism and the primacy of international law, and in which he demonstrated that treaties apply immediately in the domestic legal order, that reception theories had to be set aside, and that it was the hierarchy of norms and legal orders that mattered. His intellectual appeal worked its magic on me immediately. At that precise moment, I converted to international law and thus became, at the very beginning, profoundly Scellian.

What year was that?

It was 1946, at the Law Faculty in Paris. I then wrote my thesis with Scelle on pan-Americanism's evolution toward federalism, a topic which he had proposed. It had nothing do with demonstrating that Bolivar's old dream of unity of the continent was effectively put into practice in the pan-American

[12] *Diplôme d'études approfondies.*

conferences, but rather of contrasting what was moving in the direction of federalism, and what was impeding it. You know that during the Second World War, a strong solidarity developed on the continent. I defended my thesis in 1948, right after the Bogotá Conference had taken place.

Did you remain in contact with Scelle until his death?

I always remained in contact with Scelle, who, at that time, was Secretary-General of the Academy of The Hague. Gidel was President.

Therefore, we could say that it was Georges Scelle who influenced your education, not only because you met him and discovered international law thanks to him, but later on as well, during your career.

While I was writing my thesis, yes. Later on in my career, in 1957, I wrote an article entitled 'L'organisation internationale et l'expression de la volonté générale'.[13] Gaetano Arangio-Ruiz[14] read this article a few years ago and told me: 'But, I don't understand why you no longer mention this article, why you've forgotten it. It's a seminal article.' The Scellian influence is clearly visible in this article. In it, I try to explain how the general will of Member States gradually emerges in an international organisation. I obviously relied to a great extent on the United Nations Charter. I demonstrated the application of a direct democracy in the General Assembly and of a representative democracy in the Security Council, an organ with restricted membership whose members are supposed to represent the system as a whole. Above all, I discussed the European Communities. I emphasised the influence of Saint-Simon and Proudhon, that is, of the intellectual masters of federalism in its original form.

But in the decade which followed my thesis defence, I evolved. I didn't betray Scelle's thinking, but I came to conceive of it differently. When you read Scelle's work, you always see that there is an opposition between what he calls '*la société interétatique*' and '*la société superétatique*'. Georges Scelle is one of those who were greatly disappointed by the League of Nations. His dream was to see a very effective international organisation capable of applying *Bundes-Execution* pursuant to the federalist technique. He would have dreamt of a League of Nations powerful enough to have crushed Hitler, the aggressor, in 1936. This was the idea of a superpower. This explains why he distinguished the inter-State model from the supra-State model. For my part, I came to think that this distinction had something overly static about it. It was a vision based

[13] (1957) 4 *Revue Générale de Droit International Public* 527

[14] Gaetano Arangio-Ruiz (Italian, *b* 1919) is Professor Emeritus of International Law at the University of Rome. He was a member of the International Law Commission (1985–96), where he presented elaborate and deeply thought-out drafts on State responsibility. Member of the *Institut de Droit international* since 1981. Currently is a Judge on the Iran–US Claims Tribunal. He is the author of many outstanding works on public and private international law.

on fixed, Aristotelian logic, as if one day, by who knows what means, we would suddenly pass from an inter-State society to a supra-State society.

It seemed to me that, with the world's transformation (already foreseen by Scelle) and the development of trade and communications, international cooperation and solidarity, and an increasing awareness of this cooperation and solidarity, were growing and moving in a certain federal direction. But at the same time, there was a whole series of phenomena which continued to perpetuate the inter-State society which Anzilotti[15] so masterfully studied. The idea eventually occurred to me that, in reality, these two models were not mutually exclusive, but rather had a dialectical relationship. When, in 1963, I wrote my little book for the *Que sais-je?* collection, I contrasted the two models which I respectively called '*la société relationnelle*' and '*la société institutionnelle*'. I set out to show that they are based on a differing logic. In the relational society, power is dispersed, unregulated—except when States willingly commit themselves—and violent, since the right to war is recognised. In contrast, in the institutional society, power becomes concentred and moves toward regulation (regulation by the Charter which supersedes other treaties), and we witness the emergence of a hierarchy of norms and a hierarchy of legal orders. Ultimately, if power is violent, it is repressed, as it was during the Gulf War—thanks to the end of the Cold War and the implementation of Chapter VII of the Charter.

But having contrasted these two models in the first two parts of the book, I insisted on their dialectical relationship in the third part. I explain that, in reality, these two models are entangled. On the didactic front, for the sake of clarity, they can be separated as two distinct models, but in the reality of international life, the two models are intertwined. It's a little like what Saint Augustine says of the City of Earth and the City of God. He wrote:

> Two cities have been formed by two loves. The earthly by the love of self, even to the contempt of God: the City of Earth; the heavenly by the love of God, even to the contempt of self: the City of God.

In reality this does not refer to the city which is in Heaven, but rather to the city *according* to Heaven, meaning, according to the spirit of love, of love of one's neighbour. Therefore, there is love of oneself and love of others. Saint

[15] Dionisio Anzilotti (1867–1950) was Professor of International Law at Rome University, and Judge (1922–46) and then President (1928–30) of the Permanent Court of International Justice (PCIJ). He became famous for his adherence to and magnificent development of the 'dualist' theory of relations between international law and national legal systems, as well as for voting against his own country (Italy) when sitting as a judge on the PCIJ (in the *SS Wimbledon* case (*UK, France, Italy and Japan v Germany*, with Poland as intervening party), decided in 1923. Anzilotti, joined by another great judge, the Swiss Max Huber, appended a dissenting opinion to the case (PCIJ, Series A no 1, judgment of 17 August 1923, 35–42)). It is notable that Anzilotti did express his dissent nine months after Mussolini had seized power in Italy becoming Prime Minister (16 November 1922). However, Anzilotti gave his best in many short writings, as well as in his masterpiece, the *Corso di diritto internazionale (ad uso degli studenti dell'Università di Roma)* (*Textbook on international law*), 3rd edn (Rome, Atheneum, 1928), translated into various languages except for English. On his contribution to international law, see the various papers published in (1992) 3 *European Journal of International Law* 100–62.

Augustine says that from the instant the Holy Spirit descends upon, the two societies are 'entangled until the end of time'. It's a dialectic of which obviously no one knows the outcome. It's reminiscent of the Marxist dialectic: for Lenin, in the first stage, communist society is still carrying the remnants of capitalist society and the failings of the bourgeois society which bore it. Therefore, these two societies are entangled until passage to the perfect society—the one without classes—has been achieved.

In my conception of this, there is no happy ending, there is no dialectic leading to a stage in which everything will be in order. On this Earth, there are good forces at work, not just evil ones.

In reality, there is this dialectic of violence and law, regardless of whether its source is religious or secular. Ultimately though, and contrary to Marx and Hegel, I don't foresee any possibility of future untangling if the two societies are indeed entangled. It is what I call the 'open dialectic'. It always remains open because Man is free and there is no determinism. If the dialectic is closed by determinism, Man is no longer free. Man is free; he is a reality which has not been completed yet but is in the ongoing process of either completing or undoing itself. There you have it, starting from Scelle, the passage to another vision of the world.

B. The state of legal scholarship at the start of Professor Dupuy's career

Let us now turn to the state of legal scholarship at the outset of your research activity. In France, in particular, especially in the area of international law, did the positivist approach prevail, apart from Scelle?

Apart from Scelle, there was an essentially positivist and very formalistic approach. There were a few natural law authors, such as Le Fur, Albert de La Pradelle, but they were not very innovative in my opinion. I don't have anything against the proponents of natural law, but they espoused a classical and minority view. Otherwise, positivist authors dominated.

Was French scholarship at the time influenced by German, Italian, or any other national school of thought? Was there a link with other areas of legal literature?

I think the literature was thankfully under Anzilotti's influence. There was more of an Italian influence than a German influence, likely because of of the hostility between France and Germany, but also because I believe Anzilotti had an immense talent for expounding legal notions. His thought process was very rigorous and admirably constructed. Gidel did a translation of Anzilotti's book.[16] I myself heard Scelle praising Anzilotti, notably on his theory of State

[16] *Cours de droit international* (Paris, Recueil Sirey, 1929).

responsibility, and saying that nothing had been understood about the international responsibility of States before Anzilotti.

The gurus of international law at that time were precisely Scelle and Gidel, or were there others?

The great legacy of Louis Renaud was still felt. At the beginning of the century, he was legal adviser to the Quai d'Orsay. We can't forget Jules Basdevant (1877–1968), who was essentially a practitioner since he too was legal adviser to the Ministry of Foreign Affairs, and then a judge and President of the International Court of Justice. He wrote relatively little. He did, however, leave the Academy of International Law in The Hague a general course which has always been cited in French doctrine as a model of the Positivist School. It is entitled 'Règles générales du droit de la paix'[17] and is considered, rightly so, a masterpiece.

As for Scelle, he really shook things up, but at the same time, he didn't receive the professional recognition that others did. First of all, we mustn't forget that Scelle was a man of the Left. There was that famous incident, around 1924. The Law Faculty of Paris always used to nominate two candidates during elections for a tenured professorship at the Faculty, one as the preferred candidate, the other as the second choice. Tradition dictated that the Minister appoint the first-ranked candidate. On this occasion, the first-ranked candidate was Le Fur and the second was Scelle. The Minister of Education was Édouard Herriot, who was head of the Radical Socialist Party and close to Scelle's ideas. He went against tradition and appointed Scelle. The students of the Right and Far Right, and the royalists of the *Action française* set off street protests in the Latin Quarter crying foul play and invoking the liberties, traditions and exemptions of the University. Scelle did not want to be imposed against their will. He later told me: 'I didn't want to teach my courses in front of the police.' He therefore returned to the Law Faculty of Dijon, where he used to teach, and to the University of Geneva. He only came back to Paris later, and was never given a course in international law to teach. He was assigned a doctoral course in 'General Public Law'; in other words, a course in jurisprudence. In reality, we see from photocopies of his course notes that his lectures always devoted a large place to public international law.

Who were Scelle's other students?

Reuter[18] was one of Scelle's students. He was influenced by him in numerous ways. Don't forget that Reuter he was the one who penned the draft treaty creating the European Coal and Steel Community (ECSC). It was the most

[17] (1936-IV) 58 *Recueil des cours* 471.
[18] Paul Reuter (1901–90) was Professor of International Law at Paris University.

supra-State, supranational treaty ever to have been established. More so than the Treaty of Rome of 1957. You can say that Scelle was somewhat in the same position as Moses, who died seeing the Promised Land. Scelle caught a glimpse of the Promised Land with the European Communities, because he died in 1961, just as the two treaties of the Community, the ECSC and the EEC, came out. He therefore was able to see the setting up of supra-State and supranational structures. No doubt the Cold War then blocked the coercive function from fulfilling its full potential. On the level of principles, Scelle was able to derive a certain degree of satisfaction in commenting on the United Nations Charter. But the Community treaties unmistakably displayed the Scellian influence. Men like Professor Pierre-Henri Teitgen,[19] who was Minister of Justice under De Gaulle after the Liberation, and a number of young law professors who went into politics, were all influenced by the thinking of Georges Scelle, notably by the idea that it was necessary to set up structures capable of subordinating States.

Note that Reuter was positivist as a lawyer, but politically, as a man of the Liberation, he was very drawn to the Communities. It must be said that he was very close to Robert Schuman,[20] who was his compatriot. Because of their birthplace, both took the destiny of France, Luxembourg and Germany to heart. I have always said, and I don't mean this in a derogatory way, that Robert Schuman's thought was situated within the triangle marked out by three cathedrals: Strasbourg, Aix-la-Chapelle and Metz. Both men were Lotharingians, hence their idea of bringing together coal and steel, so as to render war between France and Germany impossible. A constraining authority had to therefore be established to regulate the Community.

Were there any international lawyers who were close to De Gaulle or worked for him?

Cassin[21] went to London right away in June 1940. He was very brave. He had fought quite brilliantly during the war of 1914–18 and had been seriously injured. He entered the international political world as a militant of the International Veterans Association during the inter-war period. This group

[19] Pierre-Henri Teitgen (1908–97) was French Minister of Information in 1944, Minister of Justice in 1945–46 (in charge of the purges of the Vichy regime followers and collaborators with Nazi Germany) and Minister of Defence in 1947–48. In 1949, in the Consultative Assembly of the Council of Europe, he contributed to the drafting of the European Convention of Human Rights. He was later Overseas Minister in 1950 and a member of the Constitutional Committee in 1958. He was twice Deputy Prime Minister, in 1947–48 and 1953–54. In 1976 he was appointed a member of the European Court of Human Rights.

[20] Robert Schuman (1886–1963), born in Luxembourg, was a French statesman. Twice Prime Minister (1947–48), as well as Minister of Finance and Foreign Minister, he was instrumental in building post-war European institutions. He is widely and rightly regarded as one of the founders of the European Union, the Council of Europe and NATO.

[21] René Cassin (1887–1976) was Professor of Civil Law at Paris University, Vice-President of the French *Conseil d'Etat* (1944–60), and member (1959–65) and President (1965–68) of the European Court of Human Rights at Strasbourg. He was awarded the Nobel Peace Prize in 1968. His contribution to the drafting of the Universal Declaration on Human Rights (1948) was invaluable.

sought to reconcile war veterans. Aristide Briand appointed Cassin to the French delegation at the League of Nations, and that's how his career on the international scene began. So the question of knowing whether or not there were international lawyers close to General de Gaulle means: did any of them go to London? Reuter participated in the Resistance, but in occupied France, not in London. Teitgen played a heroic role in the clandestine struggle. I myself, from 1940 to 1945, participated in the military campaigns of the *Forces Françaises*.

To whom did General de Gaulle turn when he came to power here in France and became President of the Republic?

General de Gaulle was very attached to French sovereignty. He was of a positivist and voluntarist persuasion and, as you know, very reticent with regards to a supra-State Europe, a Community Europe. Finally, through his political skill, De Gaulle created the Common Agricultural Policy, which was advantageous for France, and at the same time played the Community game.

I recall a letter he wrote to Sartre, when Sartre wanted to organise the Russel Tribunal in Paris, to tell him that only one form of State justice exists, and that it was senseless to speak of a Tribunal of opinion. But De Gaulle surrounded himself with distinguished jurists, for instance R Cassin and J Basdevant

Basdevant was very close to De Gaulle. In 1940, when Marshal Pétain took power, Basdevant was still legal adviser of the Quai d'Orsay, a post he held under the Third Republic. When the Marshal decided to pursue a policy of collaboration with Germany, consecrated in the Montoire meeting of 24 October 1940 (between Marshal Pétain and Adolph Hitler), Basdevant courageously wrote him a letter of resignation, which constituted a magnificent act of resistance. One of Basdevant's sons, a brother of Madame Bastid, was shot by the Germans.

There were no international lawyers associated to the Vichy Regime, were there?

I am not well informed on this question as I was not in France during that period.

At the time of your education, did French legal scholarship have any links with English or American international law scholarship?

I don't believe American legal scholarship exerted much influence. For example, I don't believe Myres McDougal[22] had any influence in France.

[22] Myres McDougal (1906–98) was Professor of International Law at Yale University. He was President of the American Society of International Law and of the Association of American Law Schools.

Kelsen,[23] on the other hand, certainly had an impact on some of our colleagues. Georges Scelle himself had been influenced by Kelsen. He accepted Kelsen's theory on the hierarchy of norms. But for Kelsen, this was a formal theory only. For Scelle, the hierarchy of norms was linked to the hierarchy of orders, that is to say, to the hierarchy of social groups. According to him, the common interest of the international society is broader and thus superior to the interest of a national society. In turn, the common interest of a national society is broader than that of a provincial society, and so on. Scelle always based his reasoning on social fact. Kelsen, on the other hand, seemed to be a pure theoretician.

C. The major cultural trends

Which philosophical and ideological trends most influenced your intellectual development? I mean, on the meta-legal level?

I believe that on the philosophical level, I was affected by Henri Bergson, notably by his notion of *élan vital*, and by his distinction between open and closed societies. A book like *Les deux sources de la morale et de la religion*[24] made a strong impression on me as early as high school and university.

After the war, I leaned towards existentialism (like many of my generation) because it presented itself as a philosophy not of truth, but of reality. I must point out that, in this regard, I have always been closer to Camus than to Sartre. The author of *L'homme révolté*[25] really illustrated to me the meaning of justice and human rights.

On the social philosophy front, I was influenced by Proudhon, via a man who is not well known in France but who is nevertheless French, and who must be over 90 years old today. His name is Alexandre Marc. In the *Mélanges* published in my honour last year, Claude Nigoul wrote an article

[23] Hans Kelsen (1881–1973), born in Prague (then in the Austro-Hungarian empire), was Professor of Law in Vienna and subsequently in Cologne, then in Geneva and finally at the University of California at Berkeley. He contributed to the drafting of a new Austrian Constitution, enacted in 1920, and was appointed to the Constitutional Court, for a life term, but then removed in 1930. He emigrated to the US in 1940, to avoid persecution in Europe. Thus, the obtuse and senseless Nazi anti-semitism deprived Europe not only of Albert Einstein and Sigmund Freud, but also of the greatest law theoretician. His numerous works are impeccable logical constructions, not dissimilar in conceptual refinement and beauty of details to gothic cathedrals. However, one should also be aware of his flaws. They were sharply synthesised by Paul De Visscher as follows: '[L]a méthode casuistique et formaliste que prône Kelsen tend à faire du droit un instrument d'immobilisme et de conservatism. Elle ne rend pas compte de la fonction dynamique que le droit joue dans nos sociétés contemporaines en s'efforçant de réaliser ces transformations pacifiques et ordonnées qui doivent mettre ces sociétés à l'abri des révolutions violentes, négatrices de tout droit.' (P De Visscher, 'Hans Kelsen' (1973) 59 *Bulletin de la Classe des Lettres et des Sciences morales et politiques de l'Académie Royale de Belgique* 540) See also M Virally, 'Le juriste et la science du droit' (1964) 80 *Revue du droit public* 591 at 604.

[24] H Bergson, *Les deux sources de la morale et de la religion* (Paris, Librairie Félix Alcan, 1932).

[25] A Camus, *L'homme révolté* (Paris, Gallimard, 1951).

entitled 'RJ Dupuy et le fédéralisme: de Georges Scelle à Alexandre Marc',[26] in which he analyses my intellectual development. Alexandre Marc is one of Proudhon's great followers. He arrives at an idea of federalism which is different from that of Georges Scelle, who was fascinated by the idea of a super-State and a super-power. Proudhon, on the other hand, abhorred the State. Therefore, he's not a federalist who's interested in building a super-State. Scelle envisions federalism as an aggregate of component units which come to create a super-power. Alexandre Marc, in contrast, like Proudhon, envisions federalism by segregation. He doesn't believe federalism is possible with centralised States. To him, it's necessary first to federate within States, and in particular to allow treaties to be concluded between regions such as the Italian Piedmont and the French Savoie, and to encourage cross-border cooperation, so that it should not always be necessary to pass through Paris and Rome. True democracy is realised through agreements of this nature. Nowadays, the Council of Europe does encourage cross-border cooperation between neighbouring provinces.

II. Encounters with Other International Lawyers

Apart from Scelle, which international lawyers have made the biggest impression on you?

Charles de Visscher, undoubtedly. His book *Théories et réalités*[27] really struck me, because after a Scellian reading of international law, *Théories et réalités* provided a different and complementary approach in its concern for realism. Then, Roberto Ago,[28] notably by his introduction of the idea of spontaneous law. I was seduced by his talent, by his presentation of customary law. These phenomena had already been observed, but Ago and Giuliano's[29] merit lay in their having spoken of spontaneous law at a time of normative growth in international law, as the international community was developing and becoming increasingly integrated. It was a presentation of the growth process of the law of nations. In truth, spontaneous law stems from customary law, from the general principles of law as produced by the normative drive of an evolving international community.

[26] Published in *Humanité et droit international: Mélanges René-Jean Dupuy* (Paris, Pedone, 1991) 233. A Marc (1904–2000), born in Odessa to a Jewish family, moved to France and became a French national.

[27] *Théories et réalités en droit international public*, 4th edn (Paris, Pedone, 1970).

[28] Roberto Ago (Italian, 1907–95) was Professor of International Law at Rome University. He was a member (1956–79) and chairman (1964–65) of the UN International Law Commission, President of the Vienna Conference on the Law of Treaties (1968–69), and member of the International Court of Justice (1979–95). He was also a member (1932–95) of the *Institut de Droit international*, over which he presided in 1992–93. His scholarly writings on State responsibility, as well as his elaborate reports on the matter to the UN International Law Commission, constitute his enduring legacy.

[29] Mario Giuliano (Italian, 1914–90) was Professor of International Law at Milan University.

You therefore have the impression that the novelty of these theories is related to the time period during which they were elaborated. That is, to an era in which custom played a more important role. I would say, on the contrary, that the 1950s were the period in which one began to give greater importance to the codification of international law. It was the Third World which was keener to enact codifying treaties in order to restructure international law than it was to emphasise customary practices.

You're absolutely right. It was the era in which codification, for which Roberto Ago played an essential role, developed. However, you also know that at that time a phenomenon emerged of which I have often spoken (especially in the 1970s) and which I called 'declaratory law': the Third World, seeing that treaties did not come to life easily and that, when they did, they were not ratified, directed normative strategies at the General Assembly by having resolutions brought to the vote. In and of themselves, and from a formal point of view, the resolutions did not have any binding legal value. But, through repeated voting, which the Third World was able to ensure because of its automatic majority, these resolutions ended up being considered custom. Classical customary law gives greater importance to repeated behaviour, repeated legal facts and repeated reactions of legal subjects. For the Third World countries, it was the repetition of words and ideas that was seen as causing new reactions. And sometimes they won. For example, take the rule according to which nationalisation of foreign properties is legal in international law—I recognised it myself in the *Texaco* arbitral award. It was a new principle which emanated from General Assembly resolutions.

Yes, but this declaratory law, as you call it, has nothing to do with spontaneous law, if I understand correctly.

What interested me about spontaneous law at the time, was that it was at a turning point. Ago, Giuliano and the others were aware that something was happening, but—maybe because of their generation, their way of thinking, or their education—they continued to apply the notion of spontaneous law when it was already out of date. They weren't discussing the dynamism of the General Assembly, which would slowly emerge in the decade to come.

Which other international lawyers most affected you on a personal level?

I have to mention a man whom I loved very much and whose memory I worship: Paul Rügger. I met him in the Curatorium of the Academy of International Law in The Hague. He lived and died in Florence, and I kept close ties with him. He was an exceptional character. A man who carried out different missions. He began as a young Swiss diplomat close to Max Huber. When the latter was elected judge and then President of the Court in The Hague, Rügger was the Court's Deputy Registrar. The Registrar at the time was Hammarskjold, Dag Hammarskjold's cousin. Rügger was heavily influenced by Max Huber and by Hammarskjold, then he embarked on a diplomatic career. There was no Swiss Ambassador in Italy before the war. He was Switzerland's diplomatic representative in Rome; and when Italy entered the war, it was in this capacity that he managed the interests of 40 States. He met with the *Duce* and Foreign Minister Ciano several times. He was a man of great experience. He had the manners of a diplomat of the Vienna Conference of 1815 and seemed to have just left a dinner at the court of Franz Joseph. His physical appearance combined the look of an English lord (his mother was English) with that of a prince from the Central Empires, from where it seems that he actually did originate. He had extraordinary class and he displayed a disarming sense of humour. People who knew him only superficially might have taken him for a small-time diplomat, but when you got to know him well and had long conversations with him (we used to '*tutoyer*' each other in French, even though he was my senior) you were struck by his in-depth knowledge of international life. He often confided in me, and his judgement of men he had known, amongst whom were several heads of State and government, was admirable in its lucidity.

He also had surprising physical courage. Although he appeared to be the quintessential man of the world, he was at Count Bernadotte's side when the latter was assassinated in Palestine. Rügger actually stood with the Red Cross flag (he was President of the International Committee of the Red Cross at the time) in the middle of Arab and Israeli crossfire, in order to enforce a cease-fire. He was also the one who initiated the small-step diplomacy during the Cuban Missile Crisis. He told me how he had been the one to propose that the Red Cross be given the authority to inspect the cargo of Soviet ships heading toward Cuba while they were still on the high sea. President Kennedy had demanded that Americans be able to conduct these inspections. But on the high sea, this would have been contrary to international law. This is when Rügger had the unexpected idea of throwing the Red Cross into the ring, which showed how it would have taken a strong personality to propose such an intervention, given the organisation's usual prudence. The Americans didn't accept at first, but Rügger continued the negotiations and played a considerable role in helping Dean Acheson and Zorin reach an agreement. He multiplied the initiatives, thanks to his diplomatic imagination.

During the Biafran War, he found himself on a Red Cross plane full of medical supplies he was taking to Biafrans. The plane arrived at night, and the Biafrans thought it was an enemy plane and turned off the runway lights. Rügger gave the order to the commander on board to land all the same, even though they were being shot at. This man was fearless, he had the qualities of a valiant knight.

Who else has really left their mark on me? I must tell you that there is one person whose death left me inconsolable: Wolfgang Friedman, a wonderful man, a private lawyer by training. He wrote his thesis on unjust enrichment. He left Germany in 1933 and became a British citizen, and then pursued his career, as you know, in the United States. He was assassinated one afternoon while leaving Columbia University. He was a very dear friend. We used to play music together. He was a very good pianist, he used to accompany me while I sang *Lieder*, notably when we were working at the Villa Serbelloni in Bellagio, at the time when Friedman was presiding over the Study Group in charge of reforming The Hague Academy. It was this group which introduced the external programme and many new activities. When, in 1966, the Ford Foundation gave a substantial grant to the Academy, it was decided that a working group would be established composed of external scholars. It was presided over by Friedman, and consisted of Jennings, Van Panhuis, Boutros-Ghali, Shigeru Oda and myself. The conclusions of the Study Group, notably concerning the external programme, were discussed for a long time in the Curatorium before being accepted. The Group set up workshops and modernised the Academy. I was elected Secretary-General when Charles Chaumont left. The Study Group worked for two years, meeting either in The Hague or in the Rockefeller Foundation's Villa Serbelloni. As a legal scholar, Friedman was also a very interesting man because he had a real sense of the changes occurring in the world. You are surely familiar with his book, *The Changing Structure of International Law*,[30] which at the time I found to be very stimulating and original.

I see that the people who most impressed you are all jurists who were not positivists.

It's true, they weren't positivists. Although they were perfectly capable of being positivists for the sake of resolving a particular case. I do not look down on positive law at all. In the course of my life, I acted as arbitrator several times, and I pleaded. Therefore I practised positive law. I was also a lawyer in my youth. I am very attached to law. In the end, on the application front, positive law must prevail. But on the scientific front, from an intellectual point of view, I was always very attracted to meta-legal analysis. I like the different approaches to law. That's what amuses me on both a critical and didactic level, and I have written more or less in this perspective, except on the law of the sea. Obviously, I studied positive law of the sea. I studied it above all, of course, during the Third UN Conference.

I'm captivated by reality in the making. You know that here in the Collège de France, it's the grand tradition in the various sciences studied here. Ernest Renan, who played a very important role in the evolution of the Collège, advocated this approach. The Collège was created by François I in 1540 to respond to the need for knowledge during the Renaissance. But in the 19th century, Ernest Renan was brought in to head this institution. He said that the Collège was open to sciences 'in the making', thus to ideas which were still in development. And when I was elected to the Collège, I was obviously encouraged in this direction. Even the scientists take a certain amount of distance from their discipline in an attempt to foster critical reflection upon it.

[30] W Friedman, *The Changing Structure of International Law* (London, Stevens and Sons, 1964).

Did you ever meet Röling?[31]

Yes, I met Röling—in The Hague of course and in various colloquia at the Institute of International Law. I also met him once in Florence during a lunch at Rügger's house, who respected him a lot. Their friendship was all the more remarkable since Rügger was a great realist and Röling was regarded as a great utopian, as a person with a generous mind, but who, in the eyes of his critics, was cut off from the international world. Ridiculous criticisms. Rügger had great esteem for Röling because he himself was a great intellectual, and he had perfectly understood that Röling's alleged utopianism was really a perfectly lucid view of the world. His vision was both that of a great moralist and a specialist in political science and law. Röling actually castigated the international world. In addition to his high intellect and moral stature, he also had a great deal of charm and truly glowed when he spoke.

Do you think Röling was a moralist rather than a jurist?

I believe he was a jurist. Without a doubt. But the reputation of a jurist is always a rather cold one. When we say that someone is 'a great jurist', it means he's a good legal technician. But when a jurist has a great deal of prestige and personal aura, it's for other, loftier reasons. Either because he has a critical view of law, or because he has a critical view of society in general and because his judgements have a philosophical dimension. Law itself gives us a reason to admire those who are very clever, those who know how to manipulate it and apply it in difficult cases. We admire professors who know how to capture the interest of their audience in a lively way during a lecture, even though the subject seems technical and off-putting. We admire great masters who can clearly present complex issues. But this doesn't go beyond a certain level of esteem. Whereas for Röling, I believe there was an admiration which was more than just an admiration of his qualities as a jurist, which were undeniable and stemmed from his personal brilliance.

Would you say that he had an effect on the international scene?

He didn't have influence on the international scene, which belongs largely to Machiavellians and does not willingly pay much attention to prophets. He had a great deal of influence on many students and, through them, on the evolution of thought.

[31] BVA Röling (Netherlands, 1906–85) was Professor of Criminal Law. He was appointed a judge on the Tokyo Tribunal (1946–48). Back in The Netherlands, he moved to international law, polemology and peace research. He was professor at Groningen University. He is the author of a seminal booklet: *International Law in an Expanded World* (Amsterdam, Djambatan, 1960), in which he propounded a new vision of the world community as the gradual development of a community consisting of Christian nations (1648–1955), to one made up of 'civilized nations' (1956–1940s), to end up finally with a community of peace loving nations (1945 onwards). He forcefully argued for a community more alert to the demands of developing countries and strongly focusing on the question of war and the issue of armements. On his contribution to criminal law, international law and international criminal law, see the various papers in (2010) 8 *Journal of International Criminal Justice* 1071–1152.

Of course.

I know a woman who had a great deal of influence on me and on her generation: Elisabeth Mann-Borgese. I have been working with her for over 25 years now. She is not a jurist but a sociologist, a geo-political scientist, a philosopher and also an economist. She has acquired, through the course of events, a knowledge of law, especially of law of the sea. She is also a great idealist. She had decisive influence, for example, on Arvid Pardo[32] when, in 1967, he asked the question 'To whom does the seabed belong?', to which he himself provided the answer: it is the common heritage of mankind. He had developed this idea with Elisabeth Mann. This idea was also advanced within the United Nations by the Director of Scientific Issues, a Jesuit priest who was a high-ranking civil servant, Emmanuel Seguès de Breuverie. He was a friend of Teillard de Chardin and, like him, had a global vision of humanity.

Elisabeth Mann is not religious, but she identifies herself with this current of universalist ideas. She created the *Pacem in maribus* movement, which began as a huge conference bringing together representatives from all political areas, from all countries, from the Eastern, Soviet and Communist blocks, the capitalist world and the Third World. She obviously deeply sympathised with the Third World. This *Pacem in maribus* is a remarkable achievement which she renews every year, focusing each time on interesting problems concerning the sea and humanity from a planetary perspective. She fought staunchly during the Conference on the Law of the Sea. Although she's an American citizen, she succeeded in getting herself hired as an adviser to the Austrian delegation and played a very active role in the meetings since she could attend them as a delegate. She is a woman with an uncommonly skilful imagination. In 1970, she conceived a whole scheme whereby all the sea belonged to humanity and States were only its custodians on behalf of humanity. This even included the territorial sea or the continental shelf, or what would later become the economic zone. All of it had to belong to the common heritage of mankind. The powers of coastal States were simply to be seen as powers delegated to them by humanity and which they were to exercise on behalf of humanity.

[32] Arvid Pardo (Maltese, 1914–99), from 1964 was Permanent Representative of Malta to the United Nations. From 1967 to 1971 Pardo was also Malta's Ambassador to the United States. During the same period he served as Ambassador to the USSR and was High Commissioner to Canada from 1969 to 1971. He was Malta's representative at the Preparatory Commission of the Law of the Sea Conference in 1972, and led the Maltese delegation to the UN Seabed Committee from 1971 to 1973. On 1 November 1967 he called on the General Assembly to face the looming crisis that could devastate the seas. He closed his speech with a call for 'an effective international regime over the seabed and the ocean floor beyond a clearly defined national jurisdiction'. 'It is the only alternative,' he said, 'by which we can hope to avoid the escalating tension that will be inevitable if the present situation is allowed to continue'. Among his publications, see *The Common Heritage: Selected Papers on Oceans and World Order 1967–1974* (Malta, Malta University Press, 1975).

She built on Georges Scelle's ideas, without ever having read him. If you look at the manual Georges Scelle published in 1944,[33] the chapter on the sea is entitled 'The Public Maritime Domain' and considers the sea as belonging to the international community. For him, coastal States have privileges (access, view) which stem simply from their coastal locations, just like riparians on a public waterway in domestic law. Riparians cannot abuse their privileges and must always exercise them under the supervision of the public authority in order not to prejudice the public interest. Similarly, while coastal States have privileges regarding certain maritime spaces adjacent to their coasts, they must nonetheless exercise these privileges under the supervision of the international community. There is no discretionary power: it's a limited jurisdiction. This was the view of Scelle, of Elizabeth Mann-Borgese and Arvid Pardo. This idea of the delegated power has since made its way into international environmental law.

But how did Scelle's idea find its way to people like Pardo and Mann-Borgese? Via the Jesuit?

Father Breuverie played a very important role. I learned this through my friend Jean-Pierre Lévy, who is currently Director of the Law of the Sea in the Legal Department of the UN. When Lévy started out at the United Nations, he worked under Father Seguès de Breuverie and remains very devoted to his former boss, who was a very impressive man due to his powerful intellect and his global perspective of international problems.

III. The Role of the Jurist as Scholar and Practitioner

A. The international lawyer's role

Let's come back to this question, because it has to do with the jurist's role: must the jurist limit himself to applying the law, or should he seek to change it? In one of his last writings, the one on Grotius,[34] BVA Röling stated: 'In the nuclear age, the jurist's role is not to interpret the law, but to formulate the natural law of the nuclear age.' According to him, the jurist should now set aside the study of positive law and divert his attention instead to changing the law.

He must try to change it, to the extent that it is within his capacity. However, when you are representing a State, you have to push for whatever is in the interest of that State. That's when we apply whatever tools legal theory places at our disposal. Throughout my academic life, I tried to change the law,

[33] *Droit international public: manuel élémentaire avec les textes essentiels* (Paris, Domat-Montchrestien, 1944).

[34] 'Are the Ideas of Grotius Obsolete in an Expanded World?' in H Bull, B Kingsbury and A Roberts (eds), *Hugo Grotius and International Relations* (Oxford, Clarendon Press, 1992) 281.

especially at the Collège. In this vein, I always supported theories and sought changes in the law of the sea. I never defended the classical law of the sea. I justified attacks against unfettered freedom on the seas.

When you started looking at the new law of the sea, did you do so as a positivist ?

No. When I wrote the book *L'océan partagé*, in 1980,[35] I was fully reformist. In the little book I wrote about the seabed as well.[36] I always promoted the theory of the common heritage of mankind. I truly regret the fact that Part XI of the 1982 Convention was toned down to a less progressive spirit.

When you're acting as a technician during your functions as an international judge, or during your time as legal adviser to the French delegation, do you exert any special effort to change the law?

I didn't have too many problems in the French delegation because we were led by Guy de Lacharrière. He was a career diplomat (he was head of the Legal Department at the Ministry of Foreign Affairs), progressive in outlook and a man sensitive to the needs of developing countries, a *tiers-mondiste*. He managed to influence the French Government as best he could, until he was pushed aside. He was appointed to the Conseil d'État while waiting to be elected to the International Court of Justice.

Wasn't he the one to argue against jus cogens *at the Vienna Conference on the Law of Treaties?*

No. He wasn't Director of the Legal Department at the time.

France did nonetheless repeatedly insist on very positivist positions.

Do you know where I was at the time of the Vienna Conference on the Law of Treaties in 1968–69? I was the legal adviser—not to the French delegation for which Paul Reuter and Michel Virally worked—but to the Holy See delegation. I'm the one who spoke in favour of *jus cogens* on behalf of the Holy See delegation. A segment from my speech was included in a small book Paul Reuter published with Armand Colin on the Vienna Convention on the Law of Treaties.[37] My speech had of course been approved by the head of the delegation, Monsignor Opilio Rossi (who's now a Cardinal).[38]

[35] *L'océan partagé: analyse d'une négociation (troisième conférence des Nations Unies sur le droit de la mer)* (Paris, Pedone, 1979).

[36] 'Le fond des mers: héritage commun de l'humanité et le développement' in *Colloque SFDI d'Aix-en-Provence, Pays en voie de développement et transformation du droit international* (Paris, Pédone, 1974) 235.

[37] P Reuter, *La convention de Vienne du 29 mai 1969 sur le droit des traités* (Paris, Librairie Armand Colin, 1970).

[38] Cardinal Rossi (1904–2004). He was President Emeritus of the Pontifical Committee for International Eucharistic Congresses.

I had concluded the speech by saying that to stand for *jus cogens* is to stand for justice, since it is a principle which tends to exclude unequal treaties which create unequal situations between populations. We had cited human rights as the basis for *jus cogens*: if all men are equal, then by extension all peoples are equal. Under these conditions, treaties cannot systematically mistreat one people at the expense of another. I ended by saying that all those who act for justice apply the will of God even if they do not believe in him, because as Kierkegaard said: 'God is incognito in this world.' I could have just as well cited Proudhon's maxim: 'Justice is God's anonymity', another splendid formulation. The Kierkegaard quote actually really pleased the protestant Scandinavian delegations. I didn't harbour any Machievellian intention in citing it, it had just seemed so fitting in a global conference of the kind.

It's somewhat surprising that as someone who had such authority in France and elsewhere, you never officially attacked the French position on jus cogens.

Making this speech in favour of *jus cogens* while the French delegation sat a few benches away promoting a diametrically opposite position, drew some criticisms. I returned to the Quai d'Orsay again only when Lacharrière took up the position of Director of the Legal Department.

*Why not write against the French attitude, in order to highlight the differences between the French Government's anti-*jus cogens *stance, and that of the most reknowned French jurists? Americans, for example, openly criticise positions adopted by State Department officials on topics like US interventions abroad, use of force, etc. You frequently find very vocal articles by jurists who get politically involved. But in our countries, we have a tendency to be quiet. It's an unfortunate trait.*

I think it's an illustration of how French civil servants feel bound by the duty of discretion and reserve. We, professors of law, are appointed by the Minister. American professors aren't civil servants. However, since I wrote and publicly intervened in favour of *jus cogens*, it was clear that I didn't agree with the official French position. During my course in The Hague in 1979 notably, I upheld the principle of *jus cogens*, and I presented it as one of the great moments in the evolution of legal thought in the 1970s.

In your opinion, do we jurists put our tools at the disposal of our governments, or are we rather just an instrument in the hands of our governments?

It's the great dilemma of the academic who is often both a delegated practitioner, so an employee of the State who is not free to speak his mind, and a tenured academic who can adopt the 'prophetic' language, and by that I mean that he can testify as to truth and reality. But in doing so, he speaks only for himself and doesn't commit the State. So these are two distinct functions.

But when he's delegated by his government, he has to comply.

Not necessarily. He can still somewhat influence his government. There are some jurists who have enough moral authority to influence governments.

I have a somewhat dramatic example. Henri Rolin, who was always a leftist and a socialist senator, opposed Soviet proposals concerning the right to self-determination during the San Francisco Conference on the UN Charter. He was one of those who fought against the inclusion of a provision on the right to self-determination, a provision which was thankfully eventually included. Similarly, if you read the travaux préparatoires *of the European Convention on Human Rights, it's again Henri Rolin who stood against some fundamental provisions in the Convention, especially against the supervisory mechanism.*

That's the dilemma of the academic. I believe jurists can have an influence outside the legal world, but by getting involved politically, by participating in movements, by speaking on television, in the media. If called upon, they have the power to sway public opinion. But otherwise their opinions and influence are obviously confined to their technical field. Look at a jurist like Mario Bettati, who was my student for so long, and who affectionately says that he's my spiritual son. Mario Bettati is a friend of Bernard Kouchner, and he had a determining influence on Kouchner by showing him how a law of humanitarian assistance can be created. Kouchner is a doctor. He founded *Médecins sans Frontières*, then *Médecins du Monde* and then became Minister. From the day he became Minister, he was part of the machinery of power: he could go to the United Nations, he could present draft resolutions.

If I may, I would like to move on to a problem which greatly troubles jurists who are not strictly positivists. In your opinion, how can a jurist who does not wish to be restricted to commenting on positive law, apply the progressive values he believes in as a technician of the law?

You were telling me that, according to some people, I write philosophy books and don't spend much time on pure law. These are the reactions of purists, who consider doing something other than law as an act of betrayal. But contrary to them, being at the Collège de France, I felt it was my duty. The Collège de France is made for that. There, we all engage in a critical reflection about the world through our respective disciplines. And we precisely intend to cast a judgement on the world on the basis of the knowledge and learning that we have acquired as academics.

B. The legal practitioner and the scholar

Let's move on to another question. What influence did your activity as a legal practitioner have on your scientific method?

Attending the Law of the Sea Conference for 10 years greatly marked me. It showed me that there is a sociology of international organisations, because the Conference was an annex to the United Nations and an annex to the General Assembly. This sociological integration was a result of the periodicity of bi-annual meetings, since we would meet twice a year for six weeks, once in New York and once in Geneva.

The other conferences in which I participated, the Vienna Conference on the Law of Treaties and the Helsinki Conference of the Organization for Security and Cooperation in Europe (CSCE), although shorter than the Law of the Sea Conference, were also fruitful for me professionally.

C. Dupuy's contribution to international research

Let's discuss your contribution to positive law as a scholar. We started from Röling's idea that jurists in our nuclear age should not confine themselves to positive law. We spoke about jus cogens *and you told me what your position was. Have you contributed, in any other way, whether as a legal adviser or an international judge?*

It would be more as a writer. In my latest book (*L'humanité dans l'imaginaire des nations*)[39] and in *La clôture du système international: la cité terrestre*,[40] I insisted on the fact that Man can destroy the planet not only with nuclear weapons, but also as a result of pollution and of cataclysms aggravated by underdevelopment. Man can also destroy the planet through exponential demographic growth, which is a way of killing humanity through humanity, through uncontrolled and disorganised births. There is a myriad of ways for Man to destroy humanity today. In my opinion, international law—I have written about this from many angles—cannot remain a simple technical study of State relations. It has to include a certain number of norms: there is a *jus cogens* now which goes well beyond what was envisaged in 1968 during the Convention on the Law of the Treaties, and which embodies a compendium of norms which have to regulate the behaviour of States, in the global interest of Man and humanity as a whole.

In effect, for me, humanity is an entirely original transcendence, because it is implied in immanence. Humanity is first and foremost, immanence. It's the dispersal of men across the Earth. It not only consists of the horizontal mass of contemporaries, but also of those who have yet to arrive, because

[39] *L'humanité dans l'imaginaire des nations* (Paris, Julliard, 1991).

[40] *La clôture du système international: la cité terrestre* (Paris, Presses universitaires de France, 1989) (Grand Prix de Philosophie de l'Académie française).

humanity is the carrier of future generations. In these conditions, by this announcement of those who will arrive in the future, humanity is the carrier of a promise. It has a messianic value. Starting from a horizontal immanence, we see the emergence of a transcendence which conditions the behaviour of States. There are things they cannot do. For example, environmental pollution should be prohibited, even in the absence of a treaty. Otherwise, we will be the murderers of our grandchildren.

What do you consider your major contribution to the field?

I believe my major contribution is the idea that the international community is a conflictual community, one riddled with contradictions. My general course in The Hague in 1979 was founded on the double contradiction between power and law on the one hand, and power and justice on the other hand. In this latter contradiction, all the elements which coalesce to develop power collide with those elements which coalesce to develop justice. The Third World has to a large extent been the interpreter of the measure of justice. For me, it's an 'open dialectic', as I previously explained, meaning no one knows the ultimate outcome because men are free and are masters of their destinies. The ultimate outcome will only be known at the end of history, when history ends. *If* it ends. All this, of course, is a function of time. And time only exists for us. You're going to say that I'm philosophising again. Time and space are man-made notions. One day, Saint-Augustine was asked, 'What did God do before He created the world? How did He spend his time?' And Saint-Augustine replied: 'Before He created the world, God had not yet created time.' Because time was born with the world.

We jurists live in time. The jurist is born from the earth, works in the continuity and evolution of societies. He is in the City of Earth. That's why I gave my book on the closure of the international system the subtitle of *La cité terrestre*.[41]

Which of your books is your favourite?

Right now? The last one, *L'humanité dans l'imaginaire des nations*,[42] because I think it's the one in which my thinking is the most developed. It's a book on mythology, on international myths. So it's a book on how we conjure humanity. Everything is representation and language. When you examine a phenomenon, whether as a scientist in a field of hard sciences, or in the field of social sciences, you always make relativised observations which can vary based on the nature of the observatory, of the observer and of the observation itself.

[41] *Ibid.*
[42] Above n 39.

It depends on the observatory, meaning the place, the environment in which the observation is made; on the observer himself, his education, his culture, his social milieu and economic background; and on the observation, meaning the circumstances in which the observation is made. An African will observe the situation in Somalia differently from a Bosnian. Everything is steeped in relativity. That's very important to us international lawyers. In this book, I wanted to delve into how nations conceive their relationship to humanity. Do they consider humanity an external reality, or, on the contrary, do they feel, at least in some aspects, that they are members of it? The question has concrete implications because, today, humanity's survival is threatened by men.

Which of your purely legal books do you like most?

La communauté internationale entre le mythe et l'histoire,[43] which is derived from my general course at The Hague.

In that book, you talk about international law, institutional law, universal and situational law, declaratory law and programmatory law. You discuss resolutions of consecration, resolutions of incitement, the dialectic of power and law, and power and justice. They are very elegant concepts, expressed in elegant language, but they are not new concepts.

The formulae are new. They are didactic concepts. I'm a professor and I have always attributed a great deal of importance to them.

So the principal value of these concepts is their didactic nature.

These concepts are new formulations. First because law professors don't really use dialectical reasoning, which is interesting considering that the study of problems always yields more results when seen through the prism of the dialectic tensions created by opposing social forces.

What's more, I attach great importance to style. When I speak of 'savage custom', it's because I love writing. I find that it feeds the imagination. It's incredible that some people thought I was speaking of the custom of savages! I spoke about it because, evidently, a well-known phenomenon was occurring: accelerated custom. Other jurists had identified it. But I was the first one to formulate it and explain it.

I don't think my formulae are purely didactic. I think they are also analytical. With regard to savage custom for example, I explain that it's a custom whereby conviction, the *opinio juris sive necessitatis*, prevails over repeated conduct. Why? Because it's a custom of revolutionary scope, meaning it will not develop slowly over an extended period of time. Quite the contrary, it will catch people off guard because of its suddenness, like a wildcat strike. What's

[43] *La communauté internationale entre le mythe et l'histoire* (Paris, UNESCO,1986).

the element that makes it so sudden? It's the repetition of the formulae, it's their being verbalised.

Rather than the repetition of behaviour over time.

That's why the Americans at the General Assembly don't admit the existence of this type of custom, or they formulate reservations, like reservations are made to treaties, in order to resist the normative strategies of the Group of 77.

D. The creation of a school of thought in international law

Do you consider yourself to have founded a school of thought in international law?

Some of my students from Nice, Mario Bettati, Maurice Torrelli, Jean Touscoz, Joël Rideau and Claude Nigoul, have told me so. But they have each made their own way, brilliantly and entirely independently.

What are the essential characteristics of your School?

We perhaps all apply the methodology of the open dialectic, with the idea that new forms don't necessarily have to replace old ones. Accordingly, for me, institutions don't necessarily have to replace relations. There's a relational model and an institutional model. But in reality, both models are intertwined. One model is never expelled by the other. Society constantly integrates contradictory forces.

It could be said that there are two other elements which are perhaps common in all your pupils. On the one hand, they are not only positivists; they are all very interested in the political science side as well. On the other hand, there's a shared interest for human rights, for the humanitarian dimension.

That's interesting, because they all come from politically very different horizons.

E. Dupuy's contribution as a legal scholar

In your opinion, what is your major contribution to international law on a practical level, as a practitioner?

I'm not certain. But I attach great importance to my participation in the European Commission on Human Rights, and in the CSCE Conference where I was member of the Holy See delegation with Cardinal Silvestrini. Cardinal Silvestrini along with Casaroli[44] were the driving force behind the

[44] Cardinal Agostino Casaroli (1914–98) was Secretary of State for the Holy See (1979–90) and played an important role in Vatican diplomacy. He, among other things, headed the CSCE Conference in Helsinki from 30 July to 1 August 1975.

'Ostpolitik' diplomacy. During the CSCE Conference, we had contacts with many delegations and negotiated with the Soviet delegation. Some Eastern block countries which were unable to advance certain proposals on their own would approach us and ask us to pass such and such idea or amendment. We would do it. We were intermediaries in various settings and I think we did a very good job.

F. The Texaco *Case*

I'm going to ask you a question concerning what your detractors consider to be a negative point in your career: the famous arbitral award of 19 January 1977 in the Texaco *case.*[45] *They accuse you of having been biased in favour of multinational corporations to the detriment of Libya, a Third World country. But mostly, despite the beauty of your award (which Rigaux greatly admired for its elegance and what he called the 'intrepidity of its architecture'*[46]*), you are criticised for having discussed contracts between a private corporation and a State as a sort of international law treaty. On the basis of this legal theory, you ended by ruling in favour of the multinational corporations.*

This award was criticised by some commentators, but today it is no longer controversial. It is set law. At the time, it was the 1970s and doctrine was immersed in the ideology of the New International Economic Order which reached its peak with the 'Carta Echevarria', which has since fallen into oblivion.

I can make several observations. First of all, this award was not received well from a political point of view by a number of jurists who used to be known at the time as 'progressive' and *Tiers-mondiste.* The award surprised some of my friends because I had always been considered *Tiers-mondiste.* You can recall how my friend Prosper Weil, a great jurist from the opposing school, criticised the award. If you read his famous article in the 1982 *Revue générale de droit international public* on 'normative relativity',[47] he reproaches me precisely for having maintained in the *Texaco* award that General Assembly resolutions can be binding and have a normative value. In effect, an entire paragraph of the award affirms it. It's notably on this paragraph and on this reasoning that I based myself to state, along with the Third World countries, that States have the right to nationalise property owned by private foreign corporations. I based myself, in this part of the award, on relevant General Assembly resolutions.

Authors who, like Weil, lamented the trends in the General Assembly, thought I was adopting a far too accommodating stance towards what they

[45] Above n 2.

[46] Rigaux, above n 3, at 17.

[47] P Weil, 'Vers une normativité relative en droit international?' (1982) *Revue générale de droit international public* 5 (translated into English, 'Towards Relative Normativity in International Law' (1983) 77 *American Journal of International Law* 413).

called 'diluted binding force', that is, in their eyes, an intentional strategy of upgrading the status of acts having non-binding effects which was conceived and promoted by the Third World to further its own political and social interests. I was criticised like this from all sides really.

The best commentary on my award was by Dean Gérard Cohen-Jonathan, in the very important article he wrote for the *Annuaire français de droit international* in 1977.[48] He explained that my award was in reality a didactic and pedagogical one. Indeed, I had committed a grave error, and it lies in my not having contented myself by writing a concise ruling. I thought I needed to explain my reasoning with lengthy arguments. In a nearly identical case, Judge Lagergren ruled as a true judge: he gave his opinion, which was practically the same as mine had been, but he did so without expressing all the reasons and considerations I thought I needed to develop. In other words, I penned the award as a professor, not as a judge. In handing down a judge's ruling, one exposes oneself less to criticisms than when one issues a professorial ruling, which is more akin to an article than a judicial decision. I surrendered to my desire of issuing an award I wanted to be as explicit as possible because I had the chance, for once, of being sole arbitrator.

This award was didactic because I wanted to give some advice to developing States by telling them: you won't have any foreign investments unless you adopt a certain attitude. Because whether you like it or not, investors are nothing like the Red Cross. They act in function of their own interests. There is therefore a minimum of safeguards they need to receive. You cannot say, for example: 'I annul the contract, and by the same token, the arbitration clause is also annulled.'

I actually issued two rulings in the *Texaco* case. The first has never been cited even though I had issued it two months prior. It's the *Kompetenz-Kompetenz* ruling in which I declared myself to have jurisdiction to hear the case.[49] This, despite Libya's argument that the case couldn't be heard in arbitration since the arbitral clause was null and void due to the fact that Libya had declared the deed of concession null and void. I upheld the opposing view, which was based on the theory of the separability of the compromissory clause. Why separability? Because the arbitration clause is a separate and autonomous 'contract in a contract'. You are certainly familiar with this theory, which is one that the French Cour de Cassation confirmed in several decisions annotated by Lagarde, Oppetit and other French private international law specialists, and also notably in the *Gosset* case.[50] This solution is also a rule in many countries.

[48] 'L'arbitrage Texaco-Calasiatic contre le Gouvernment Libyen' 23 (1977) *Annuarie français de droit international* 452.

[49] Preliminary award of 27 November 1975, published in (1979) 53 *International Law Reports* 389.

[50] French Cour de Cassation, *Gosset* case, decision of 7 May 1963, published in (1963) *Recuiel Dalloz* 545, and in (1964) 91 *Journal de droit international* 82.

Moreover, I should stress that this award must be viewed in its juridico-historical context. It was issued at a time when frustration with the practice of having State contracts with aliens was still fresh. This era is now long gone. What I mean by that is that the *Texaco* award dealt with a completely archaic type of deed of concession. This kind of deed no longer exists. Today, participation contracts are concluded instead. I like to think that I contributed to this evolution, to some extent, with the *Texaco* award. I wanted to show that concessions had been the worst type of formula. But this was a concession which had been agreed to by the Libyan King, Idris, according to the old-fashioned concessions model. These concession deeds would contain clauses allowing the delocalisation of the contract, which by extension tends to give the investor a long-term protection. These clauses either provide for the application of the law of another jurisdiction, in lieu of the local law (and that's why it seemed to me to be international law), or they provide for the application of the local law but only after the contract is concluded. This means that the application of local law is suspended. In either case, it's by exercising its sovereignty, and on the basis of that sovereignty, that the State accepts to sign such contracts, as was recognised in the *Aramco* award.[51] These contracts were old-fashioned. Therefore, I had to base my ruling on the contract I had in front of me. That was my positivist side. My progressive side, on the other hand, led me to recognise the right to nationalise, and the value of General Assembly resolutions as bearers of new principles. In the case at hand, Libya had forbidden itself to nationalise for a certain period of time, and had accepted the stabilisation clauses in the deed on the basis of its sovereignty. In this context, Libya itself had been the one to set limits not on its sovereignty *per se*, but on the exercise thereof.

You are reproached for another problem. It is said that you insisted on the right of restitutio in integrum.

I discussed *restitutio in integrum* because the claimants did not seek to be indemnified. Few people realised this because the award was never published in its entirety, and so commentators were never able to read it. Texaco and Calasiatic simply sought declaratory relief; all that was sought from me was that I determine whether the nationalisation had been carried out invalidly or not. It was understood that if I declare the nationalisation to have been invalid, there would then be a second claim and a new arbitration to determine the quantum of the damages and compensation. Therefore I did not have to condemn Libya to pay any damages, since that was not a relief sought at that stage. I had to only make a determination on the validity of the nationalisation. I concluded that the nationalisation was not valid, and I discussed *restitutio in integrum* precisely because damages had not been sought by the petitioners.

[51] *Saudi Arabia v Arabian American Oil Company*, arbitral award of 23 August 1958, in (1963) 27 *International Law Reports* 117.

I had to put the legal principles back in perspective. In the end, there was no need for a second arbitration after my award was issued. The corporations didn't file a motion in damages because they negotiatied with Libya and an agreement was reached between the parties. The case was settled.

You could have perhaps said that the nationalisation could not be considered valid in international law so long as Libya refused to pay compensation.

The petitioners were not asking to be awarded damages.

You yourself have said that in international law, a State has the right to nationalise on condition that it pays compensation.

That's what the relevant resolutions say.

Then you could have said: 'Nationalisation without compensation isn't valid; as soon as the Libyan State indemnifies the two corporations, the nationalisation will be validated.'

There was a reason which, in my mind, nullified the nationalisation, drastically so. But unfortunately—and I have always regretted this—I didn't think it was necessary to mention it. Libya's default made me very uncomfortable. I would have preferred that Libya appears and cooperates with the Tribunal. I could have heard in-depth pleading on the merits, whereas I only had limited legal arguments from a written brief Libya had addressed to President Lachs, and in which they argued that there was no need to resort to arbitration. In the *BP* award,[52] which is factually identical, Mr Lagergren found the nationalisation invalid on the grounds that it had been politically motivated. As you know, in principle, nationalisation has to be founded on social and economic reasons. For my part, I didn't look at that aspect of the problem, because the Libyan Government's default did not allow me to rule on the merits of a sovereign State's policies because it had not been alleged at any point in the proceedings. If I had made any reference to political considerations and concluded that the Libyan nationalisations were meant to punish the United States for its support to Israel, several of those who criticised my award would have approved it instead.

On the other hand, Rigaux makes a criticism of your discussion of equitable compensation by the State, which I find very convincing. He says: 'The interest of foreign corporations is patrimonial in nature. Therefore a monetary indemnity must be deemed adequate.'[53] He argues that if you insist on restitutio in integrum, *you end up preventing a new government in a Third World country from changing its economic policy.*

[52] *BP Exploration Co (Libya) Ltd v The Government of the Libyan Arab Republic*, award of 10 October 1973, published in (1979) 53 *International Law Reports* 297.

[53] Rigaux, above n 3, at 441.

Whereas King Idris had friendly relations with the West, Qaddhafi thinks it's necessary to nationalise the means of exploitation of natural resources of his country, in order for it to take off economically. I think that's a prerogative of sovereignty. International law only requires the payment of an indemnity.Couldn't you have said simply that in this case Qaddhafi was wrong because he hadn't promised or committed to paying compensation?

Of course that crossed my mind. The Libyan Government had not committed itself to paying compensation. But I was only seized of a petition seeking the nullification of the nationalisation. This means it was an objective petition and not a litigated claim for damages, simply a petition seeking a declaratory judgment on the validity of the nationalisation. Therefore, if it wasn't valid, it would logically entail a *restitutio in integrum*, which didn't impede the Libyan Government in any way from changing its economy. It would merely induce it to adopt economic measures through an alternative route that wouldn't be considered illegal under international law.

But you tackled the core issue of the petitum *(the kind of reparation requested). If you had been asked to make a declaratory finding on the nullity or validity of the act, all you had to say was: the act was not valid because the nationalisation was not coupled with a compensation.*

No, for me the act was not valid because of the stabilisation clause. I was inspired by Prosper Weil's course in The Hague on the problems found in contracts between a State and an individual. I referred to stabilisation clauses which are agreed to by a fully sovereign State and which it can purposely violate in order to impose a premature end to the contract.

It's the reason for which, as I told you, Cohen-Jonathan found that my award was didactic, and that it sought to give a lesson to Third World countries, notably: never agree to a contract containing stabilisation clauses. The fact is, after this award, no one did, and participation contracts became the norm.

Don't you think you could have stopped yourself at saying: 'This nationalisation is null and void in international law.' You went well beyond that.

I explained to you already that this award has an archaic character now due to how the applicable body of law has evolved since. If I had issued the ruling in more recent times, I would have probably based my reasoning on transnational law instead of international law. I think it would have been possible to refer to transnational law, just as was done 10 years later in the *AMINOIL* case.[54] The result would have been the same.

[54] *State of Kuwait v American Independent Oil Company* (AMINOIL), award of 24 March 1982, published in (1982) 21 *International Legal Materials* 976.

Do you think that if you were called upon to rule on the same case today, you wouldn't hoist this deed of concession to the international level, and put it on the same level as an international treaty?

I was keen to apply positive law, and positive law at the time was the *Aramco* award which stated that it was within a State's sovereign powers to willingly put certain limits on its sovereignty. In fact, this award fulfilled its objective, as I previously noted, since it led to an agreement between the two parties. But I think it also had another effect: it undoubtedly encouraged States to change their practice, to resort to formulas which were more flexible than the old concession. Lastly, it paved the way for the *AMINOIL* award, which was issued by a bench composed notably of Paul Reuter and Sir Gerald Fitzmaurice. There is no doubt that *AMINOIL* was inspired by the *Texaco* award. It extracted its strongest points and yielded a similar solution.

G. Speaking and writing

Let's move on to the next segment of our interview. You are surely familiar with Plato's words to the effect that the written word is a lesser form of shared knowledge. Speech is the privileged form of communication and Plato is seen as having a certain disdain for writing, in a way.

I don't have any such disdain.

Nevertheless, for you, the spoken word is the principal or most effective form of communication.

Without a doubt. I take pleasure in speaking, but I am very partial to writing as well, and I take great care in my writing. If you read *L'humanité dans l'imaginaire des nations*[55] you'll notice it. It's a book driven by the writing. The same is equally true for *La clôture du système international*[56] and even for *L'Océan partagé*.[57] Speaking and writing are for me two very different art forms which I love in equal measure. Whenever I have to give a conference, or any talk, I always prepare a very detailed outline. In the French tradition, we always develop outlines with parts, subparts, transitions, etc. But also, writing is so wonderfully satisfying. I have always introduced literary formulae in purely technical legal articles. I always amused myself creating metaphors. I don't pretend that it's a better way of writing, but it's in my nature.

You come to my mind whenever I think about the distinction made by Roland Barthes between an 'écrivant' *(someone who writes) and an* 'écrivain' *(a writer). The* écrivant *uses language to transmit information, whereas the* écrivain *is the guardian*

[55] Above n 39.
[56] Above n 40.
[57] Above n 35.

*of common language. He goes beyond merely transmitting information. Language is the object of his research, language that is deprived of meaning (*non-signifiant*) or as disinformation. He is a craftsman who creates verbal objects by manipulating the materiality of words. Most of us jurists are people who write, we are* écrivants. *Whereas you, are a writer, an* écrivain. *You mould the language.*

I don't pretend to be a writer, but I would say that I nurse the ambition of wanting to become one. Also, the more I advance in life, the more I draw pleasure from writing. Perhaps precisely because I write books that are less legal and more philosophical. And obviously, the philosophical terrain lends itself to stylistic experimentation better than the legal terrain, notably in rhythm.

That's true. Indeed everyone immensely appreciates your books. But I think everyone is most struck by your words when you give conferences. Your style is magnificent and it reminds me of what Maréchal Leclerc said once: 'I will never be a great man because I know neither how to speak nor how to lie.' You don't lie, but you know how to speak very well.

I don't know, I think it's a gift. But in the end, I have worked a great deal on my speaking. Throughout the course of my life, I sought to improve it. I saw it as an art. This effort blossomed mostly after 1979, when I entered the Collège de France (I was the first jurist to enter). At the Collège, there are no law courses, just as mathematicians don't give maths courses and doctors don't give medicine courses. At the Collège, one reflects on one's science and one tries to engage in an epistemological and philosophical reflection on that subject. Therefore, we were led to abandon the purely descriptive discourse for a more critical reflection that lends itself so much better to stylistic experimentation.

What has been the legal community's response to your publications from your time at the Collège de France? I noticed that some jurists tended to say: 'This is philosophy.'

I was reviewed a lot in philosophical journals. But you know, I consider myself to have reached an age where I can have fun. I'm a playful man. One of your questions is: 'Do you regret anything in your life?' I can answer that right now. I regret not having written a treatise or a manual of international law. Twenty-five years ago, I had a contract with the Armand Colin publishing house to write one. I wrote about half of it, but I never had the time to finish.

Do you have any other regrets about your career?

You always have regrets, unless you're very silly or self-satisfied. I am nonetheless quite surprised to see all the things I have managed to accomplish at once.

IV. A Look at the International Community

A. The merits of traditional international law

We can move on to questions relating to the current tendencies of the international community. The first question is: in your opinion, which values of traditional international law should be preserved?

The traditional law wasn't so bad. It had qualities which have been a little forgotten. My friend Claude-Albert Colliard like to recall the creation of the first 'international public service groups' in the communications and railway industries during the 19th century. The status of the Danube before the Second World War was uniquely progressive. Classical law had a well-conceived system and minority regimes, because they had been created by realists, diplomats in the vein of Paul Rügger. We would do well, perhaps, to inspire ourselves from what had been done at the time when there was a sensitivity to the problems of minorities. No one spoke of human rights, there were no great messianic ideas, but there was a concrete practicality and experimentalism. Interesting projects could be developed.

I think therefore that classical international law had merits. Obviously, it was a body of law essentially dealing with relations, communication—it wasn't a very normative body of law.

It wasn't a law divided in subfields. Today, international law deals with societal problems. We see the Security Council appropriating Chapter VII and doing whatever it wants. It handles elections, democratic transitions, it manages, takes control, becomes a kind of world government. It's a fact that people at the time of the old law in the 19th century didn't envision the future this way. There were these coalitions that Georges Scelle called 'international *de facto* governments': international governments (because they were the ones who exerted the greatest power and the greatest force) but *de facto* (because no one had given them a democratic mandate to act as such). These people were able to convene a Berlin Conference on the conventional status of the Congo and put in place an entire colonialist and imperialist system; but at the same time, they could, in different contexts, find a perfectly good regime to govern the Danube, a good regime to govern the straits of Constantinople and deal with the problems of minorities. They were skilful. Today, progress in law lies in trying to respond to values. And the major value, in my opinion, is human rights, which have never been so talked about and yet so ignored.

B. Trends in the new international community

Do you consider human rights to be among the values which illustrate a positive evolution in international law?

Human rights and the right to self-determination.

More than the value of peace?

Yes. Peace is a fundamental value. But it is a substitute for human rights and self-determination. Men have a right to peace. Humanity carries within it a great peace project, and will continue to carry it until the end of time. But we will never have absolute peace. The value of international law is to present the following challenge to governments:

If you don't want to kill each other, if you want to build a peaceful solution, I, as a jurist, can provide you with the tools: mediation, conciliation, and arbitration. I can provide you with a way to set out a treaty, to make reservations to it, arrange it. I can provide you with all the means if you only consult me. Therefore, international law is a set of means which challenge the conscience of States. Obviously, a State won't accept this challenge if it is governed by a dictator, and it will manipulate international law to entirely different ends. But the true nature and function of international law is to challenge the conscience of good-willed heads of State. It puts at their disposal the means for establishing peace and saving face.

What are some of the values and factors which create a source of anxiety for the international community and have the potential of disrupting its actual structure?

Over the years, we have seen the emergence of the notion of international community. It has become a primary element in the language of the United Nations which, in its General Assembly resolutions, constantly refers to the international community as a whole. It's a development which was spurred by the Third World. These countries defended the global vision of the world and they forged this notion of the international community strategically, in order to demonstrate that all peoples are part of the same community, and that therefore, objectively, there is a solidarity between them. The rich countries which are members of the international community must assume the responsibility of helping the destitute. The rich countries must participate in development programs and projects. All the policies of the United Nations and all the overarching themes of the 1970s were precisely founded on the idea of an international community. This idea blossomed considerably in development law, and also in environmental law because the environment embodies the global vision and all of today's important problems are societal problems on a planetary scale.

The Africans, although they are a tribal people, had worked on the notion of an international community. The peoples of the East, and especially the

Far East, are less conscious of this. They fear the United Nations and don't gravitate towards it. The Third World countries on the other hand have always turned to the United Nations. It was their port of call, their rallying call and their forum for advancing their ideas. Since the Cold War, the Eastern bloc countries have been looking more to their immediate neighbours than to the world community. They are returning to a more localised version of international relations. All these bilateral conflicts create a very real breach within the international community. There is a sort of archipelago of despair, with islands of sovereignty which hoist their flags and create conflict with their neighbours. I am reminded of the title of a German book. It's a novel which has nothing to do with this topic but it has an evocative title: *Der Sumpf der Traurigkeit*, or *The Swamps of Sadness*. That's what the East is for me these days: its people, although they have great cultures, are pitted against each other in various conflicts. It's easy to see the difficulties the United Nations face in solving these conflicts.

There is another problem I wished to discuss with you. Aside from the problems which riddle the current international community, there is also a problem which has been in existence for the past 20 years. It concerns the gap between normative values and the effective reality of the international community. There is an inflation of norms, rules, jus cogens, *etc. There are all these rules in international law which are not applied, in human rights in particular but also in other domains which deal with the protection of developing countries' interests. Is there a way to reduce this gap between normative values and effective reality?*

It's a difficult question. The gap is created because of contradictions. It's a gap between two contrasting visions of the international community which I have labelled the 'historical community' and the 'mythical community'. The historical community is burdened with all the sin in the world and all its misery. The mythical community is what men conceive as an ideal of reconciliation, understanding and cooperation. This utopian vision shouldn't be dismissed, because it feeds a permanent critique of the historical community. It gets to the heart of the historical community by contesting its justice and its legitimacy. It therefore maintains an ongoing basis for contestation. Men have to have this critical vision. I'm speaking to you now as a moralist, not as a jurist.

But the new international law, the one that is not applied, it's a law that sanctions mostly the mythical community.

Yes, it marks the progress of the mythical community within the historical community. Various texts illustrate this evolution: the Universal Declaration, the Covenants, the progress of humanitarian law, etc.

Are all these texts manifestations of the mythical community?

Yes, of the mythical community manifesting itself in the historical community. Of course, the two run into various obstacles, but they are a given. People need Utopia. I have always distinguished utopic means from utopic ends. Utopia is bad when it is reduced to means. Such as, for example, the belief in a perfect constitution which would suit all countries in all epochs.

A utopic end, in contrast, is the aspiration towards an ultimate goal. Of course, it can't be achieved without the appropriate means. But these means can never be definitive, they can only be provisional: they are temporary, interim and can be corrected or discarded.

C. The role of international law in the present time

Can you comment on Baron d'Holbach's remark that 'the law of nations is the morality of madmen who put limits to their own insanity' ('Le droit des gens est la morale des furieux qui mettent des limites à leurs folies')?

I think that that expression applies well to current events, like those in Yugoslavia where we see what madmen are capable of doing, but where we also see how the law of nations has trouble regulating such violence, or even reducing its intensity. If men are furious and mad, would they accept any limitations? Only if they are forced to. And if they are forced to by authorities superior to their own.

But Baron d'Holbach's phrase also means that international law consists of a series of other limitations by the States. As soon as they accept auto-limitation, they cease being madmen. The reason for that is that the well-conceived consciousness of their interests trumps their instinctive impulses.

The phrase also presupposes a very negative assessment of the weaknesses of international law.

Absolutely. Of course, if today we look at international law, Baron d'Holbach's phrase is exceedingly negative. We have become so used to seeing the pathological violations suffered by international law that we increasingly ignore the fact that it is applied every day, at every moment. Many international treaties, conventions and institutions function very well and allow life to continue in front of our very eyes. The world exists, in large part, thanks to international cooperation in the scientific, technical and also political domains. Therefore, Baron d'Holbach's expression provides only a partial view of reality, one which only takes account of the unfettered violence and ignores international cooperation, which in our day and age is not altogether absent, to say the least.

D. The role jurists should fulfil currently

You believe that jurists should be positivists.

They should be revisionist positivists. They should be positivists in the sense that they can't discard the law in order to evade reality through theories, because this evasion would betray their vocation. The jurist must be a positivist in order to correctly measure the law, but he cannot bow down to the law. He always has to examine it with a critical eye. I think that's what great jurists have always done.

Before the Rio Conference on the Environment (3–14 June 1992), the French Government had asked Dean Vedel, my son Pierre-Marie and myself to conceive as elaborate a model as possible of an international organisation with supra-State powers to protect the atmosphere. A body which would have scientific power and the power to sound the alarm whenever atmospheric pollution occurred in a country, and to bring the perpetrator to justice in front of a competent tribunal. Furthermore, the international organisation would have to be aware of social development problems in its dealings with the environment, notably so as to predict financial compensation for developing countries which would be prohibited from engaging in certain income-generating activities. The other States found this project too avant-garde and regulatory. In any event, even with amendments to the project, that famous declaration of 3 April 1989, which was published in French newspapers like *Le Monde* and *Le Figaro*, remains. The declaration took up two entire pages and stated that all the States congregating in The Hague unanimously agreed to continue discussions in order to get an organisation with real powers on its feet. This is an area in which we came to exert an influence and get some of our ideas across.

In the case you just described, you were acting as a legislative assistant. Were there instances in your writings, during the interpretation of rules and international customs, where you made an effort as a technician of the law to inject some of your own interpretation of the existing law (such as peace, human rights, etc)?

Of course. First, with regard to *lege ferenda*, I wrote an article in the 1958 *Annuaire français de droit international* about the Antarctic[58] which, even before the Washington Conference on the Antarctic took place, surveyed possible solutions and contained the general thrust of the rules which would end up being adopted in 1959. I did it with the belief that the Antarctic should belong to humanity as a whole, and not be broken up in pieces like a big cake. This despite the fact that France, as you know, has always laid claim to Adélie Land (as have other States). I took the position that it should be at humanity's disposal. Even when a State has acquired a district through circumstance and

[58] 'Le Traité sur l'Antarctique' (1960) 6 *Annuaire français de droit international* 111.

through its expeditions, it is governed by the international rules which were established in the common interest of humanity.

Otherwise, I think I have advocated the idea of human rights and peace in all the articles I have written. In 1955, in the first issue of the *Annuaire*,[59] as in 1965 on the Dominican Republic affair,[60] I wrote articles which were very hostile towards American policy, a foreign policy which continued to be one of systematic intervention in the domestic affairs of Southern States. In that context, I wrote articles which were on legal technical issues, but all of which were nonetheless activist. In the first article I wrote about human rights; I looked at how the European Commission of Human Rights, despite its name, was in reality a full jurisdiction, even if it did not issue binding rulings on States. The findings it reaches on the conformity or non-conformity of a State's behaviour with the provisions of the Rome Convention of 1950, constitute precisely the exercise of a jurisdictional act. The first step taken by a judge is the determination of the conformity or non-conformity of the acts undertaken by subjects of the law in relation to a rule of objective law. I wanted to argue, in the interest of human rights, that the Commission was a jurisdiction and that it shouldn't be modest or timid to assert itself as such; it should forge ahead with the authority of a judge. When I finally did become a member of the Commission, I was pleased to see that it was truly, in practice, a jurisdiction.

V. The Jurist and Global Reality

A. The legal technician and the intellectual

I wanted to ask you a question about the relationship between being a technician of the law and an intellectual. It goes without saying that you are both, as Sartre envisioned. There is a beautiful definition by him: the intellectual is someone who meddles in what is not his business, who pretends to question all our received wisdom and the behaviour which it inspires, in the name of a global conception of man and society. Hence you are an intellectual. What is the relationship between being a technician of the law and an intellectual in your case? You have tried to be a technician of the law who uses the ideas of an intellectual, in the sense that you have transposed your general conceptions, your political and philosophical thoughts, etc into your legal analysis. At the same time, you still deal with law.

Your question creates a big problem for me because it reveals to me the fact that, deep down, I have always played a dual role. You have uncovered this by asking me your question. I have a played a dual role in the sense that when

[59] 'L'application du traité d'assistance mutuelle de Rio-de-Janeiro dans l'affaire Costa Rica-Nicaragua' (1955) 1 *Annuaire français de droit international* 99.

[60] 'Les États-Unis, l'Organisation des États Américains et l'Organisation des Nations Unies à Saint-Domingue' (1965) 11 *Annuaire français de droit international* 71.

I write a book like *L'humanité dans l'imaginaire des nations*,[61] I do so as a man from the Collège de France who reflects. But if I intervene in a case, to plead on behalf of Honduras as I did last year,[62] or when I am an arbitratror, at that moment I split my personality and become a legal technician.

B. The jurist and political activism

Have you also written in the print media, or participated in televised debates? Have you also been an activist on the day-to-day level?

I have often been on the radio.

Have you participated in political activities, at the national or international levels?

Never. My father was a politician and he made me promise never to enter politics. I have been offered political positions in my lifetime. I was offered a seat in the Senate at one point, of becoming mayor of Nice, but I refused, because of the promise I had made to my father who always felt I was too sensitive to be in politics. You have to have thick skin to be in politics, as he used to say.

Did you take a position on the Algerian war?

I was professor at the Law Faculty of Algiers from 1951 to 1956. So I left Algiers at the beginning of the Algerian War. But when I was there, I knew Algerian nationalists, moderates, people who were from Ferhat Abbas' party. I worked with Catholic groups on developing the idea of an Algerian community, an endeavour also shared by Albert Camus.

Did you take a position when Henri Alleg's book La question *(The Torture),*[63] *about the torture of Algerians by the French, was published? Did you sign the Manifesto of the 121 intellectuals?*

No, I didn't sign. I was very close to Albert Camus, and I also always abhorred terrorism. The Algerian War began with the FLN's (*Front de libération nationale*) terrorism, which in turn caused the French military reaction and the counter-terrorism of the OAS (*Organization de l'Armée Secrète*), since all terrorist acts dialectically provoke counter-terrorist acts. But I was no longer in Algeria at that point. I had been transferred to the Law Faculty of Aix-en-Provence. In December 1956, Albert Camus had come to Algiers (he

[61] Above n 39.

[62] Reference is made here to the *Case concerning the Land, Island and Maritime Frontier Dispute* (El Salvador v Honduras, Nicaragua intervening). Hearings were held in 1991.

[63] *La question* (Paris, Editions de minuit, 1958); translated into English by J Calder, *The Question* (Lincoln, University of Nebraska Press, 2006).

was a *pied-noir*[64]) and had given a lecture asking for a truce for the civilians, addressing himself both to the Algerians of the FLN and the French, in order to put an end to the killing of innocent people. He was rebuffed by both sides. Camus was for Man, so he was against terrorism. In his play *Les Justes*, his Russian character, Kalaiev, has to blow up a car carrying the Grand Duke, the Grand Duchess and their children. In the end, he refuses, because he cannot kill children. He cries out:

> If I am on this Earth, it is for men, it is for them that I suffer and accept to die, and I will not, in the name of a future just society, add to present injustice.

Therefore, a refusal of terrorism, a refusal of violence. That was his attitude. It was also mine.

You nonetheless did not consider it necessary to come out in public on the matter.

I didn't sign the Manifesto, but I did speak out on various occasions and my attitude was misjudged in the French colonial circles. I was in a position where I was misjudged by every one, in the sense that I would not admit that there was good violence and bad violence. I didn't want to have to choose between victims. One day I told my friend Bernard Kouchner,[65] who with Mario Bettati invented the idea of humanitarian intervention (the power to bring medical supplies and services, food to the victims, following a natural catastrophe or a civil war), that he reminded me of the Good Samaritan. For me, if, after two thousand years, we still talk about this character, it's not only because he is charitable; it's because when he sees a man in need, he offers him help without asking his identity. He was a man and that was enough.

C. The demon's commands

Max Weber states that any scholar must obey the demon who holds the reins of our life. My question is: Do you consider yourself to have listened and heeded to the commands of your demon? Do you consider to have answered the demands of your time? In your dealings with others, as well as in your calling?

In all modesty, I think I can answer positively. Last year, when the *Mélanges* in my honour was given to me, Evelyne Pisier, who is a professor of political science, told me something that has often been said to me by others:

> When you used to give lectures, they would always contain more than the mere description of phenomena. There would be attempts to explain and a quest for ideas. That's why we were attracted to your classes. It's because they would provoke discussion.

[64] A pied-noir (black-foot) was a French national or a settler of other European descent, born in Algeria, until Algeria's independence in 1962. That year more than one million pieds-noirs of French nationality migrated to mainland France.

[65] Bernard Kouchner (*b* 1939) is a French medical doctor who set up *Médecins sans frontières*. He was Health Minister 1992–93 and was French Foreign Minister 2007–10.

The fact that a professor voices ideas doesn't force students to adhere to them, but rather encourages in them a desire for discussion and deeper reflection. I think I have obeyed this demon and that I have sought to awaken it in those who listened to me. I think Max Weber's formula is remarkable.

D. Palliatives to make life bearable

Another question relates to something Freud once wrote: life is so unbearable because of suffering, disenchantment and misery. He speaks of three kinds of palliative measures to make life more bearable. The first kind, which attenuates the impact of life's misery—a very beautiful formulation—can be, for example, gardening or devoting oneself to scientific activity.

There is scientific activity, but there is above all teaching activity. Teaching has brought me extraordinary joy. I always went up to the lectern feeling an intense happiness. And I would be gripped by a deep internal joy when I would sit in front of students. I would feel all of a sudden that I loved these young people. I would have only one thought in my mind: to seduce them. That is perhaps why I sometimes gave in to easy manners, but I always included jokes and anecdotes in my lectures. I would nevertheless try to tie in these anecdotes to the issues I discussed. But I always had pleasure knowing that my students, from time to time, looked at me. I would tell them: 'My great ambition is to see your eyes, not the top of your heads.' Because students tend to take notes and write down everything, so that they can then learn everything by heart and regurgitate it on the day of the exam. I would tell them: 'If you look up, I would have earned my hour of teaching this class.' Teaching made me happy. I think that I would never have been able to only do research without this profound joy of interacting with an audience.

The second palliative, I see that it includes art.

Art, according to Freud, is not a palliative, it's a substitute gratification.

Yes, a substitute gratification. Art, for me, is fundamentally music. I have practised other arts. I have always done drawing, I studied it as a child. But music has had an enormous influence on me, whether by listening to it—notably lyrical music and opera, but also symphonic music, chamber music, old as well as modern—or by performing it. I have always played the piano, but I'm not a real pianist, although I have amused myself by composing. I have composed music for famous poems by French poets such as Guillaume Apollinaire, Aragon or Francis Carco. Sometimes humorous songs.

But I have most of all trained my voice classically, and seriously, with remarkable professors. When in my youth I was preparing my aggregation, I studied here in Paris with one of the greatest singers of the time, who sang *Lieder* and melodies by Debussy, Gabriel Fauré, Ravel, etc. His name was Charles Panzera. Panzera had distant Italian origins and was quite an exceptional man.

He was known world-wide and has made wonderful recordings, which at the time were on 78s[66] but which have since been reproduced as 33s and now on CDs. Roland Barthes, who was professor here at the Collège de France, also trained vocally with Charles Panzera. And he wrote about him. Even here, at the Collège, he would play Panzera's records during his seminars, he would comment upon them in his seminar on semiology, that is his seminar on signs, and he would show how there was a whole series of rich signs and evocations in Panzera's singing which would echo in the soul of the listener.

One thing which, strangely enough, Freud does not mention in his list of palliatives, is friendship.

I was about to tell you that. He speaks of drugs. I don't have drugs, but I think that in my life there are two things: love and friendship.

But there he was talking about physical things, wine, drugs, opium, etc, which desensitise us from our pain. I think friendship should perhaps be categorised as a gratification.

Friendship and love have to be included as gratification. I have had the great fortune in my life of having my wife and children's love.

And I have also had the privilege of friendship. I don't pretend to have had general, numerous and dispersed friendships, which in the end are quite superficial. But I have counted a number of real friends amongst my colleagues: Paul Rügger, Mustafa Kamil Yasseen, Eduardo Jiménez de Aréchaga, Roberto Ago; and also non-jurists: Georges Duby[67] and Pierre Tabatoni.[68]

Let me thank you for being so kind and answering all my questions with so much patience. I believe that this conversation, once transcribed and published, will prove very useful to young people, who will learn a lot. They will be grateful to you, as much as I am now.

[66] These of course are references to the sizes of vinyl records in the days before cassettes and CDs.

[67] Georges Duby (1919–96) was a great French historian specialising in the social and economic history of the Middle Ages. He was Professor of History of Medieval Society at the Collège de France (1970–91). He also was a member of the *Académie française* (1987–96).

[68] Pierre Tabatoni (1923–2006) was a member of the Académie des Sciences Morales et politiques (1995–2006). He had been Professor of Economics at the University of Paris (1960–79) and recteur of the Académie de Paris and Chancelier des Universités (1979–82).

Eduardo Jiménez de Aréchaga

EDUARDO JIMÉNEZ DE Aréchaga, even in his old age, impressed for his handsome face and the elegance of his bearing. Also, his sharp and inquisitive glance and his bushy eyebrows could not go unnoticed. In spite of his numerous professional successes, he remained affable, unassuming, ready to discuss legal matters freely. He was also keen to exchange ideas with colleagues and young persons. He adored his job as an international lawyer. And he was fully immersed in the theory and practice of international law. Even a few weeks before his sudden death, he was active at The Hague pleading before the International Court of Justice.

Eduardo Jiménez de Aréchaga (1918–94), born in Montevideo (Uruguay), took a Doctor of Law degree at the National University (*Universidad de la República*) in 1942. He was Professor of Public International Law at the same University from 1946 to 1969, and at the Law School of the Catholic University of Uruguay (*Universidad Católica del Uruguay*). His life was full of accomplishments. He worked in the UN in many capacities: as a staff member (serving for two years (1947–48) as a member of the UN Secretariat dealing with the Security Council), then as a member of the Uruguayan delegation to the General Assembly (1948 and 1950), subsequently as a member of the International Law Commission (from 1960 to 1969, serving as Chairman in 1963), and later as a founder-member and president of the Administrative Tribunal of the World Bank. He also served in his Government: in 1950 he was appointed Under-secretary of State for Foreign Affairs, acted as Secretary of the National Council of the Government from 1951 to 1954, and then was Minister of the Interior for Uruguay in 1968. In addition, he repeatedly acted as an international judge and arbitrator: he was a Judge of the International Court of Justice (ICJ) (1970–79), serving as President from 1976 to 1979, and earlier and later presided over many arbitral tribunals. He was involved in international adjudication too as a legal counsel for governments, acting in many cases as an advocate before the ICJ. He died in a car accident in Punta del Este (Uruguay) on 5 April 1994.

While coming from a developing country, Eduardo Jiménez de Aréchaga never acted as a representative of those States. He did not necessarily share their political and ideological leanings, let alone their most extremist views; neither was he attracted by their legal outlook, oscillating between an inclination towards natural law principles and a political science approach, all leading legal scholars to mix up the inquiry into existing law with proposals for changes in the law. From the outset he was instead a strict positivist and embraced the legal approach typical of Western European scholars. He was nevertheless open to the reasonable demands of the less advanced countries, as well as to the requirement for legal scholars also to promote the development of international rules. For instance, in his well-researched essay on 'Treaty Stipulations in Favor of Third States', published in the *American Journal* in 1956 (hence before the Vienna Diplomatic Conference on the Law of the Treaties), Jiménez de Aréchaga expressed his support for rules allowing treaty stipulations in favour of third parties.[1] After explaining the reasons for the need to have such rules,[2] he argued that these stipulations found their legal foundation in a 'general principle of law recognized by civilized nations'.[3] He then added:

> During the last century the international community has been trying to expand its contractual methods in order to find a way through which it could reach subjects which do not participate in the agreements, and give sanction to rules of law susceptible of general application. *The science of international law should assist this evolution* and admit the full effects of at least those enlargements of the contractual structure which have been already recognized by the municipal law of civilized nations . . .[4]

Jiménez de Aréchaga was not a prolific writer, although he enjoyed writing regularly on major problems of international law. His writings stand out for the acuity of his research and the originality of his contributions. Some themes attracted most of his attention: the handling of disputes by the UN Security Council, with the connected issue of the coordination between the UN and the Organisation of American States in the area of dispute settlement; the law of treaties; and the law of the United Nations. His masterpiece can nevertheless be held to be his Hague Academy General Course.[5] These lectures are without doubt among the best ever delivered at the Hague Academy. The author looks at international law from an historical perspective, constantly underlining the progress made by international rules and institutions in the last 30 years (1945–75). Also, the breadth of vision is unique: one feels that the author draws upon his huge experience as a diplomat, a negotiator, a counsel in international litigation and as a judge, and brings all this experi-

[1] (1956) 50 *American Journal of International Law* 338.

[2] *Ibid*, 355: 'In the international community there is no law making organ, and therefore in order to put into effect rules of international law it is necessary to make use of contractual agreements, which are very appropriate to establish rights and obligations between contracting parties, but not to create rules of law susceptible of general application. In view of this deficiency of international law, stipulations in favor of third states have become one of the most useful procedures to give a general scope to rules of international law which can only be put into effect through the agreement of a limited number of states, or to confer on those rules a sphere of application wider than the group of contracting parties which may concur in their establishment.'

[3] *Ibid*, 346–49.

[4] *Ibid*, 357 (emphasis added).

[5] E Jiménez de Aréchaga, 'International Law in the Past Third of a Century' (1978-I) 159 *Recueil des cours de l'Académie de Droit International de la Haye* ('*Recueil des cours*') 1.

ence to bear on his insight into the 'functioning' of international law. One cannot but admire the fine blend of a positivist approach and sensitivity to the new trends emerging in the world community towards less inequality and greater distributive justice. Although the choice (but not the sequence) of topics treated was classical (sources of law, general principles regulating the conduct of States, international subjects, the laws of the sea and of air and outer space, State responsibility), the discussion of the various issues is original and constantly based on a balanced and thoughtful intertwining of case law, treaty provisions or UN resolutions and the author's reasoning. The chapters on the interplay between treaties and customary law, as well as those on general principles of international law, State responsibility and the law of the sea, are probably the best ever scholarly contribution to these themes. They have become a 'must' for any international scholar.

The interview took place five months before Jiménez de Aréchaga's sudden and tragic death. There was no time for it to be revised and corrected by him. Jiménez de Aréchaga's own words have been edited only for clarity.

Interview with Eduardo Jiménez de Aréchaga

November 1993

I. The Role of Legal Scholarship at the Start of Judge de Aréchaga's Scholarly Activity

Who was the international lawyer who most influenced your thinking at the beginning of your scholarly activity?

You may be a bit disappointed, but the international lawyer who most influenced my thinking was Hans Kelsen.[6]

Why disappointed? I think he was a great international lawyer.

He was a great international lawyer, but of course that does not mean I am a Kelsenian in any respect. When I was about to finish my law studies, I was appointed to give lectures on international law to the young students who wanted to come into the law school in Montevideo. And I wrote a book, called *Introducción al derecho* (*Introduction to Law*),[7] which was Kelsenian. At that time I also got in touch with Kelsen. He came to visit South America, Argentina and then he came to Uruguay. He had a great intellectual influence in Mexico, in all of Latin America. He had been invited by an Argentinian philosopher of law, Carlos Cossio,[8] who thought he had invented something which went beyond Kelsen; he called it the 'ecological doctrine of law' (*Teoría Egológica del Derecho*). He wrote some books which were interesting, but he went a bit too far. So when Kelsen came to Montevideo, I asked him: 'What do you think of Cossio's philosophy of law, of Cossio's school?' And Kelsen, who was speaking in French, told me: 'Ce n'est pas de l'écologie, c'est de l'égolâtrie'.[9]

I then had contact with him through my first case, when I became a practising lawyer and I had to deal with topics of international law. It is curious, because at that time I was not specialising in international law, but the cases

[6] See 'Interview with René-Jean Dupuy', fn 23.

[7] Montevideo, Fundación de Cultura Universitaria, 1981.

[8] Carlos Cossio (Argentinian, 1903–87) was Professor of Jurisprudence at the Universidad Nacional de la Plata (1934–48), then Professor of Philosophy of Law at the Univerdidad de Buenos Aires (UBA). In 1956 the military government removed him from his chair on account of his alleged adherence to peronism

[9] 'This is not about ecology, it is about ego-worship.'

that came to me always had an international law aspect. One of them concerned the Italian Peace Treaty. In that Treaty there was a clause by which Italy renounced claims against States which had broken relations with Italy during the war. My country had declared war on Japan and Germany but not on Italy, but had broken diplomatic relations with the Fascist regime during the war. So Italian shipowners made a claim in our courts against the Uruguayan State for having requisitioned two ships which had been sunk by Axis submarines. I was at that time advising the national authorities who had taken over the ships (they were the respondent). When the Peace Treaty was published in the *American Journal of International Law*, I said: 'There is here a stipulation in favour of Uruguay, it's a third-party stipulation.' The claimants had obtained the support of a well-known Argentinian international lawyer, Podesta Costa, who was legal adviser to the League of Nations. This was 1948 or 1949. In order to strengthen my position, I asked Kelsen for an opinion on the subject, and he wrote a magnificent opinion on third-party stipulations in favour of sovereign States, saying that the renunciation applied in the case. The case was settled on the basis of that consultation. Kelsen was so modest that when I asked him how much he would charge for his opinion (of 20 pages) he asked for 1,000 dollars. Very little, even at that time. When I told one of my colleagues in the *Barcelona Traction* case[10] this story, he said: 'Mais ce Monsieur crée des difficultés pour notre gagne-pain.'[11]

Did Kelsen publish his opinion afterwards?

No, he did not publish it. But it is printed, because I wrote a booklet of 50 pages about that case, and in it I transcribed Kelsen's opinion fully (he wrote it in English and I translated it into Spanish). Of course when I read his book on the UN Charter[12] I became discouraged, because I recalled the comment Hersch Lauterpacht made about it in his review of the book. In Lauterpacht's view the book was a desperate effort to strike the maximum amount of fault from an admittedly imperfect instrument. You should not interpret the Charter of the United Nations as if it were an insurance contract.[13]

There was one other famous book review by an Australian, Julius Stone, who was also harshly critical of Kelsen's formalism. In his view Kelsen had taken a sort of bookish attitude to a political document.

Some people attribute Kelsen's attitude concerning the drafting of the Charter to the fact that he was not a friend of Pawlowski, who was the State Department's Legal Advisor in Dumbarton Oaks. Kelsen had not been con-

[10] *Barcelona Traction, Light and Power Company Limited, (Belgium v Spain)* 5 February 1970, [1970] ICJ Rep 3.

[11] 'But that gentleman is creating difficulties for our livelihood.'

[12] H Kelsen, *The Law of the United Nations: A Critical Analysis of Its Fundamental Problems* (London, Stevens and Sons, 1950).

[13] Book review published in (1950) 27 *British Yearbook of International Law* 498.

sulted. You know, he had written a book on the drafting of the League of Nations' Covenant. It has been said that he was not sufficiently consulted, he was not taken into consideration by Pawlowski, and that is why he was so critical of the drafting of the UN Charter.

You mean just for personal reasons? Was he so sensitive?

No, I don't think so.

In what respect were you influenced by Kelsen?

I had to explain to the younger students the definition of law, objective law, the subjective rights, and in this area I followed Kelsen's formulation.

Were you also influenced by him in your own writings on public international law?

At the beginning he was very influential. Then I took a more eclectic position as a result of studying all the courses in the *Recueil de Cours* by people like Verdross, Scelle and others.

Were you influenced by the great Latin American international lawyers? I am thinking of Álvarez.[14] *One would think that in Latin America, one would be closer to Latin American international lawyers. Álvarez, as a judge, was famous for his dissenting opinions. There, he tried to develop a new international law.*

Many of his opinions, which were *de lege ferenda* at the time, have become more and more acceptable. He had a very general experience, but he was not a man who influenced my scholarly activity at all. I think the Latin American writer who influenced my studies more at that time was Andrés Bello, from Venezuela. He worked in Chile, he was a great jurist. He wrote the Chilean Civil Code. He wrote a book on international law which was very avant-garde for his time.

Was he translated into French or English?

No. There is a bust of him at the International Court of Justice. He wrote in the early 1800s (1830, 1840). He was the first one to say that Grotius' theory

[14] Alejandro Álvarez (1868–1960), from Chile, was a member of the International Court of Justice (1946–55). He appended many Separate or Dissenting Opinions to the Court's judgments, where he propounded a 'new international law founded on social interdependence', on 'international solidarity' and 'international regionalism'; his was a vision sensitive to the demands of developing countries. He also set great store by the role of judicial bodies, in particular the ICJ, in developing international rules. On his views, see W Samore, 'The New International law of Álejandro Alvarez' (1958) 52 *American Journal of International Law* 41; L Obregón, 'Noted for Dissent: The International Life of Alejandro Álvarez' (2006) 19 *Leiden Journal of International Law* 983; K Zobel, 'Judge Alejandro Alvarez at the International Court of Justice (1946–1955): His Theory of a "New International Law" and Judicial Lawmaking', *ibid*, 1017. See also M Koskenniemi, *The Gentle Civilizer of Nations: The Rise and Fall of International Law 1870–1960* (Cambridge, Cambridge University Press, 2002) at 302-05, 308-09.

about fishing being free to all because the natural resources were accessible and could not be exhausted, was wrong, because the resources may become exhaustible. He was a contemporary of Bolívar.[15] He died in the 1920s.

Was he part of the cultural and legal scholarly heritage when you started?

He was still very influential not just because he was an international lawyer, but because he was a full jurist. He wrote the Civil Code of Chile, a Code that was then adopted with very few changes in other Latin American countries such as Uruguay and Venezuela. And it is very well written. He was a grammarian also. He was quite a figure in Latin America.

Among the international lawyers from Latin America, which one was more influential? Was there a Latin American school of international law when you trained as an international lawyer?

The Argentinean, Podesta Costa, the one I mentioned [in connection with the Italian Peace Treaty], had great authority. There were no distinguished scholars in my country. In my country there was a man who wrote a book with the title *Derecho naturál de gentes* (*Natural Law of Nations*) which was a good piece. Three professors of international law preceded me. I won't name them. One was a historian, the other was a poet, and the third, my immediate predecessor, was a diplomat. There was no school proper. They were teaching mostly the Spanish influence: Vitoria, Suárez, Grotius, also the school of Saint Thomas Aquinas, the theories of 'just war'. I learned from their teachings, but of course it had nothing to do with international law as it applies today.

So we can jump to the question about the influence in your country of foreign schools of thought. For instance, what about North America? There was an American school of thought. Did you go to the US to study?

No.

Was there any link between your training as an international lawyer and the North American school of international law?

The North American school of international law was not very influential in the countries of Latin America in general, nor in my formation. I owe much more to the European tradition, because in Latin America we suspected the North American lawyers of supporting the Roosevelt doctrine. So we preferred to follow the Europeans.

[15] Simón Bolívar (1783–1830) born in Caracas (Venezuela), was a military and political leader. He played a crucial role in the liberation of Latin American countries from the Spanish colonialism. He was President of Venezuela (1813–14), of Gran Colombia (Colombia, Venezuela, Ecuador, Panama; 1819–30), of Bolivia (1925) and Peru (1824–27).

You mean that you thought that the North American school of international law was somewhat ideologically biased?

It still is, even today. They write as the *legistas*, 'advisers of the King'. Their view of international law is hegemonic.

We started with the first international lawyer who influenced you, Kelsen. But later on you developed your own thinking.

No, I did not develop my own thinking, but under the influence of my studies, mostly of the European contribution, I became more eclectic. I think that you can reconcile the positivist approach (Kelsen) with a natural law approach. One of the ways to reconcile is to take a temporal view of the law. International law, and the law in general, as it exists in a single moment, is only the law which is positive, that is, positive law. But if you consider the law not statically, in a single moment, but in its evolution, you find that any legal system, in order to prevail and survive, has to incorporate elements of justice. It has to reform and adapt itself more and more not only to facts, but also to the demands of justice. One example contemporary to us is what happened with the exclusive economic zone. I remember that when President of Peru issued a proclamation about a 200-mile zone, Gros[16] said:

> How is it possible to have as president of the Court the man who signed that decree which is a complete violation of international law?

And yet, in the course of time, what initially appeared to be a violation of the law became the law. This came about on account of sociological requirements and of considerations of justice. You have to give control to the riparian State, which must control the fishing in its waters.

When you speak of 'elements of justice', do you mean principles of justice which are embodied in international law? By which means are they incorporated into international law? By political acts such as this declaration by President Bustamante?

I think that brings us to the theory of sources of law. I think international law particularly is in a state of permanent evolution. Take the example I gave you, it became law by consensus of States. I remember that in 1974, when we were debating in the Court the claims of the UK and Germany against Iceland,[17] there were people such as Gros, for instance, who said: 'Of course

[16] André Gros (1908–2003), Professor of International Law at the University of Nancy (1935) and Toulouse (1937), during the Second World War was legal adviser to the *Comité national français* in London. In 1943–48 he was the French representative on the United Nations War Crimes Commission. He became legal adviser of the French Foreign Ministry (1947–63), and then a member of the UN International Law Commission (1961–63) and its President in 1962. He also was a distinguished member of the *Institut de Droit international* (1959–79). In 1964 he was elected a judge of the ICJ and sat on the Court until 1982.

[17] Hearings of 25, 28 and 29 March 1974 before the ICJ in the *Fisheries Jurisdiction* case (*United Kingdom v Iceland*).

this is a violation of international law.' Yet the majority of the Court, including Waldock,[18] did not dare to go as far as to say: 'The law is that there is only a 12-mile territorial sea exclusive fishing zone.' I remember this judgment was criticised by the Law of the Sea Conference, but it is stated in that judgment that the judge cannot anticipate the legislator. The legislator was the Law of the Sea Conference acting by consensus. Some States, like the Latin Americans and the Africans, proclaimed the economic zone in order to protect their fisheries. And the long-distance fishery States could not deny the basis and the justice of that claim. So it became a rule of law through the mechanism of the Conference and through consensus.

To go back to your question about how natural law permeates the sources of law: you must have a more flexible approach to the sources of law. Prosper Weil[19] is too strict when he speaks of relative normativity.

I agree with you. But this penetration of natural justice into international law comes about always via the process of custom-making, not by treaty law, unless the treaty is part of the process of custom-making.

The codification conferences permit the formation of customary law. This happens in particular in codification conferences because all the States take part in them. It's not the big powers who dictate the law to the others. It's only States discussing and considering one point of view, on the basis of preparatory materials like those produced by the International Law Commission or the Law of the Sea Conference.

[18] Sir Humphrey Waldock (1904–81) was Chichele Professor of Public International Law at Oxford University and fellow of All Souls College (1947–72). In 1961–72 he was member and President of the UN International Law Commission. He was a member and President of the European Commission on Human Rights (1960–66) and then a member and President of the European Court of Human Rights (1966–74). He sat on the ICJ in 1973–81 and was its President in 1979–81. Waldock's major contribution to international law lies in his reports on the law of treaties to the International Law Commission, his masterly 6th edition of Brierly's *The Law of Nations: An Introduction to the International Law of Peace* (Oxford, Clarendon Press, 1963), and his two courses at the Hague Academy, on the use of force ('The Regulation of the Use of Force by Individual States in International Law' (1952-II) 81 *Recueil des cours* 451, and the 'General Course on Public International Law' (1962-II) 106 *Recueil des cours* 1). Waldock's writings are notable for the exceedingly concise, pithy and pellucid exposition of notions, rules and legal constructs. He had a strong personality and much charisma: it is no coincidence that whatever international body he joined, he soon became its chairman.

[19] Prosper Weil (*b* 1926) is Professor Emeritus of the University of Paris II: Panthéon-Assas Law School. He was a member (1980–99) and President (1989–93) of the administrative tribunal of the World Bank. Since 1999 he has been a member of the *Institut de France* (*Académie des sciences morales et politiques*). His celebrated article on 'Vers une normativité relative en droit international?' (1982) 86 *Revue générale de droit international public* 5 (translated into English 'Towards Relative Normativity in International Law' (1983) 77 *American Journal of International Law* 413) stirred up a spirited debate in the community of international lawyers and brought about a sound revisitation of the new trends of international law. See also his major writings collected in P Weil, *Écrits de droit international* (Paris, Presses Universitaires de France, 2000).

Now let's go back to our question about the other authors. You said that you became eclectic. Which other authors in Europe had some sort of impact on your thinking?

I should add that during my studies as a student of international law, one of the textbooks we used was the French edition of Anzilotti's textbook, translated by Gidel.[20] That was the main book which I used as a textbook to prepare for examinations.

Why in French and not in Italian? Isn't Italian more accessible to Spanish-speaking people?

For me at least, French is easier. Anzilotti was well known and well appreciated. We had a great admiration for Anzilotti; his opinions, his dissents are fundamental. There are two great judges from the old Court, Anzilotti and Max Huber, the Swiss, both outstanding. Huber wrote very concisely and very precisely. For instance, as President of the Court, he stated that preliminary measures must be adopted only when there is an immediate danger of irreparable damage.

Do you feel that Anzilotti still has some sort of influence in the Latin American countries?

Yes, very much so. There are many dualists still in Latin America who swear by Anzilotti. They still believe in the 'dogma' of dualism, which, I feel, goes too far in Italy. Anzilotti was very precise. He made a great contribution to the Permanent Court of International Justice from the beginning: if I remember correctly, he was first legal adviser to the League of Nations.

In 1968, I joined the International Law Commission. I was then very young compared to the other members. I had been called by the Commission because Alfaro[21] had gone to the ICJ. That was the start of my career. It was Scelle who promoted my candidature, because I had lectured a couple of years before at The Hague Academy. Scelle was the Academy's Secretary-General. He had prepared a draft on the arbitral procedure which had been circulated to States for comments. The Government of my country delegated the task to the Law School, and the Law School in turn asked me to prepare the comment. I made a comment which was very supportive of that draft, so Scelle proposed my name for co option by the Commission. So I got there and I sat next to people like Verdross.[22] I was also a great admirer of

[20] D Anzilotti, *Cours de droit international*, tr GC Gidel (Paris, Recueil Sirey, 1929).

[21] Ricardo J Alfaro (1882–1971), from Panama, between 1922–30 and 1930–36 was a diplomat. In 1931–32 he was President of Panama. From 1945 to 1948 he was a member of the UN Commission on Human Rights and took part in the drafting of the Universal Declaration of Human Rights. He was a member of the International Law Commission in 1949–53 and a judge of the ICJ in 1959–64.

[22] Alfred von Verdross (1890–1980) was one of the sharpest and brightest disciples of Hans Kelsen. Professor of International Law at the University of Vienna (1924–60), he was a member of the UN International Law Commission 1957–66 and a judge in the European Court of Human Rights in 1958–76. In 1961, Verdross presided over the Vienna Conference on Diplomatic Relations. From 1928 until his

Waldock, I think he had a great logical mind. He was able to build up the convention of the law of treaties on the basis of the work by his predecessors like Lauterpacht, who was the one who started to speak of the legal 'object' of treaties, and Fitzmaurice,[23] who tried to write a code. Fitzmaurice's code was very elaborate. Amado[24] once said that Fitzmaurice's draft was baroque, but at the same time was very good. On that basis Waldock was able to prepare this convention on the law of treaties with the support of the Commission. The Commission was an organ with a reduced membership, and there was a cross-fertilisation of ideas; everybody learned something.

death he was a member of, and in 1959–61 the President of, the *Institut de Droit international.* Verdross was a very prolific writer, dealing in dozens of papers with the theory of law, public law and international law. His major works in German relate to both international law and jurisprudence: *Die völkerrechtswidrige Kriegshandlung und der Strafanspruch der Staaten* (Berlin, Engelmann, 1920); *Die Einheit des rechtlichen Weltbildes auf der Grundlage der Völkerrechtsverfassung* (Tübingen, Mohr, 1923); *Die Verfassung der Völkerrechtsgemeinschaft* (Wien, Springer,1926). These works stand out not only for the profundity of their reflection on and conceptualisation of the major problems of international law seen in a broad theoretical context, but also for their clarity of exposition. Another major work, which has gone through many editions, is the manual of international law: *Völkerrech,* 1st edn (Berlin, Springer, 1937). The latest edition of this manual, edited by B Simma, is in my opinion a masterpiece: *Universelles Völkerrecht: Theorie und Praxis,* 3rd edn (Berlin, Duncker u Humblot, 1984). As I have repeatedly said in private to Bruno Simma, it really is a pity that this book has not been translated into English or French. Verdross published various articles in languages other than German, and gave two major courses at the Hague Academy: 'Le fondement de droit international' (1927-I) 16 *Recueil des cours* 247; 'Règles générales du droit international de la paix' (1929-V) 30 *Recueil des cours* 271. What is striking about Verdross is the discrepancy between his stature as an international lawyer and as a profound student of jurisprudence and the theory of international law, and his relatively scant achievements as an international figure. He should have deserved more prominent positions as a judge or as a leading international expert. It is said that this must be attributed to the initial acceptance by Verdross (clearly transpiring in the Preface to the first edition of his *Völkerrecht*) of some major tenets of National Socialism. He soon distanced himself from Nazism (after the German occupation of Austria in 1938, he was suspended from his teaching assignments; however, from mid-1939 onwards, he was allowed to resume the teaching of international law but not legal philosophy). Nevertheless, his initial attitude, and perhaps also his failure publicly to stigmatise his mentor Kelsen's persecution by the Nazis, brought about a critical or at least lukewarm attitude towards him in international circles after the Second World War. On Verdross's contribution to law, see the various important papers published in (1995) 6 *European Journal of International Law* 32–115.

[23] Sir Gerald Fitzmaurice (1901–82) was a distinguished legal adviser (1932–52), then, from 1953 until 1960, senior legal adviser to the Foreign Office. Later on, when Foreign Office documents were made public, it transpired that he had rightly advised the British Government, unheeded, to refrain from the 1956 Suez attack, which in his view was contrary to international law. Fitzmaurice was a member of the UN International Law Commission (1950–60) and a judge of the ICJ (1960–73). Upon stepping down from the ICJ he was elected a judge of the European Court of Human Rights (1974–80). Fitzmaurice is also well known for presiding over the arbitral court that dealt with Beagle Channel (Chile v Argentina) case in 1971 (see award in XXI *UN Reports of International Arbitral Awards* 53) and then the *Kuwait v American Indipendent Oil Co* (AMINOIL), award of 24 March 1982, published in (1982) 21 International Legal Materials 976. His general course at the Hague Academy is a superb contribution to international law ('The General Principles of International Law Considered from the Standpoint of the Rule of Law' (1957-II) 92 *Recueil des cours* 1).

[24] Gilberto Amado (Brazilian, 1887–1969) was Professor of Criminal Law (1911–30) and then Brazilian ambassador to various countries. In 1949 he was elected as a member of the UN International Law Commission (1949–69). Besides his legal and diplomatic activities, he also engaged extensively in politics and literature.

Therefore, through your contacts within the International Law Commission, you were able to absorb from the other international lawyers. I think Verdross was very close to your ideas because he also tried a synthesis of natural law and positive law, in a way.

I would say that I was close to his ideas. With Fitzmaurice we had a difficult relationship. He was a great jurist, but politically innocent. Naive.

Well, I would say that he was terribly conservative.

Yes, in the *Namibia* case[25] we had a serious fight. The proof of his lack of understanding of the evolution of the law was that he wrote in his dissenting opinion that there is no reason to move an irresistible force against any movable object, which was Namibia. On the other hand, I admit that he was a very good, indeed excellent, draftsman.

When I once asked a well-known British international lawyer, James Fawcett, what he thought about Fitzmaurice, he answered: 'Look, he reminds me of a school-teacher of mine who when I was a child corrected a paper of mine and wrote on it: "ingenious but idiotic".' And he said he could say the same of Fitzmaurice, namely that he is terribly intelligent, but far away from reality.

I remember the first time I met him, it was in the VIth Committee of the General Assembly, in 1950. The subject was reservations to multilateral treaties, and the subject was presented by the Secretary-General in connection to the Genocide Convention. Fitzmaurice advocated the system of the League of Nations: absolute unanimity for acceptance of reservations. You remember there was an alternative system, the Pan-American system. I was instructed to talk after him to explain the Pan-American system and defend it. And you know, when he realised what I was saying, he was sitting next to me (Uruguay, United States, United Kingdom); when he realised that I was advocating the Pan-American system, he took his earphones out and threw them with a big sound over the table—just to stress how heretical were the ideas propounded by this young man, namely me.

II. Meeting Other International Lawyers

Who of the international lawyers you have met in your career has impressed you most, and for what reasons?

In my country, when I started trying to specialise in international law, there were difficulties with getting access to books, to documents, to reading material. So the *Recueil des cours* played a great role. I am thinking in that respect of the general courses of Lauterpacht, Brierly, the Italians, Alfred Verdross,

[25] *Legal Consequences for States of the Continued Presence of South Africa in Namibia (South West Africa) Notwithstanding Security Council Resolution 276 (1970)*, 21 June 1971, [1971] ICJ Rep 16.

Charles de Visscher, Henri Rolin, and Maurice Bourquin.[26] Bourquin was the greatest counsel before the International Court. He was very effective. The only one who was almost as eloquent as him was Rolin,[27] although from a scientific point of view he was not up to Bourquin's standard. Rolin was more eloquent than scientifically sound. You remember how he won this case between Guatemala and Lichtenstein, the *Nottebohm* case.[28] He read in Court the letter of application for nationality in Lichtenstein that Nottebohm had signed, and he read the 'Heil Hitler' at the end of the letter, right before the signature, quite forcefully. It was a very effective means with judges, especially at that time near the end of the War.

So this was just to convey the idea that he was actually trying to avoid the application of German law.

He read it to produce an effect on judges.

Do you mean that, at that time, he was the best counsel before the ICJ?

In my opinion, judging from what I have read of the opinions, Bourquin was the best counsel.

[26] Maurice Bourquin (Belgian, 1884–1961), after being Law Professor at the University of Brussels (1920–30) and at the Belgian Ecole de Guerre (1920–30), was appointed in 1930 Professor of International Law at the Geneva Institut de Hautes Etudes Internationales (until 1960) and at the University of Geneva (until 1955). Bourquin had extensive experience of multilateral diplomacy, having served on Belgian delegations to numerous international conferences, such as those in Paris (1919), Genoa (1922) and London (1924), and to the Assembly of the League of Nations. Subsequently he was a delegate at the first session of the UN General Assembly. In 1949, he was head of the Belgian delegation to the Diplomatic Conference on the Red Cross Conventions. Bourquin was also a member of the *Institut de Droit International* (1923–60). See, among his writings, 'Grotius et les tendances actuelles du droit international' (1926) *Revue de droit international et de législation comparée* 86. See also his numerous lectures at the Hague Academy, in particular those on 'Règles générales du droit de la paix' (1931-I) 35 *Recueil des cours* 1; 'Stabilité et mouvement dans l'ordre juridique international' (1938-II) 64 *Recueil des cours* 347; 'Pouvoir scientifique et droit international' (1947-I) 70 *Recueil des cours* 331 and 'La Sainte-Alliance. Un essai d'organisation européenne' (1953-II) 83 *Recueil des cours* 377 are outstanding for the author's legal rigour, sensitivity to historical trends and clarity of exposition. Bourquin was also famous as a forceful orator, and an extremely articulate and effective advocate before the ICJ ('un plaideur exceptionnel' was how he was normally defined by those who had had a chance of listening to his speeches). He pleaded for Norway in the *Anglo-Norwegian Fisheries* case (1949–51) and in the *Norwegian Loans* case (1955–57), and for Portugal in the *Right of Passage in Indian Territory* case (1955–60). On his works, see G Kaeckenbeeck, 'Maurice Bourquin (1884–1961)' (1961) 49-II *Annuaire de l'Institut de Droit international* 499; J Salmon, 'Notice sur la vie et les travaux de Maurice Bourquin' in *Rapport sur l'année académique de l'Université de Bruxelles. 1960–1961* (Bruxelles, Editions de l'Université, 1970) 298.

[27] Henri Rolin (Belgian, 1891–1973), member of the Belgian Senate for the *Parti ouvrier belge* (1932–68) was Professor of Law at the Université libre de Bruxelles and member of the Belgian delegation to the San Francisco Conference on the United Nations (and President of the First Commission of the Conference). He was Minister of Justice in 1946 and president of the Belgian Senate (1947–49). He was member of the *Institut de Droit international* (1926–73). He wrote, among other things, 'Les principles de droit international public' (1950-II) 77 *Recueil des cours* 305. On his life and work, see R Devleeshouwer, *Henri Rolin 1891–1973: une voix singulière, une voix solitaire* (Bruxelles, Éditions de l'Université de Bruxelles, 1994).

[28] *Liechtenstein v Guatemala*, 6 April 1955, [1955] ICJ Rep 4.

Did you happen to meet Bourquin?

No.

And what about Rolin?

Rolin, yes. I was one of the counsel in that big circus that was the *Barcelona Traction* case.[29] Rolin was on the opposing side. After my intervention, Rolin said that my intervention was '*très méchante*' (very spiteful).

Was he nice?

He was very effective in the beginning, very nice, yes, of course. Counsel fight each other, but then they are cordial to each other. In his initial presentation of the case (you remember there was a withdrawal of a case, two stages concerning preliminary objections), he impressed the Court very much with his exaggerated description of what happened in Spain with the bankruptcy, and that influenced the judges to accept jurisdiction. But in the second phase, when there was a counter-attack by the Spanish lawyers describing the conduct of the Belgian shareholders, Rolin was no longer effective; he had to defend, not attack. There was another Belgian lawyer who was very, very good, his name was Grégoire, an excellent, very caustic counsel. Once, after the Spanish lawyers pointed out some discrepancy, he said about them: '*Il paraît qu'ils n'ont pas temperé leurs guitars*' (it would seem that they have not tuned their guitars). The Spanish lawyers answered two days later by saying that the Belgian counsel are making '*encaje de Bruselas*' (Brussels lacework). The Spanish answer was not as good as the Belgian quip.

Are there other international lawyers who impressed you?

I first met Röling[30] at the General Assembly in 1950, in Paris, where he was a delegate for his country, The Netherlands. I recall that the Committee was discussing the definition of aggression, and Röling said: 'Aggression is like a beautiful girl, very difficult to define in advance but everyone recognises her as soon as they see her.' We had a great laugh.

Did you see Röling on other occasions?

Yes, I visited him when I was in The Hague during my years at the Court. I visited him in Groningen. He had already retired, but we had some friends in common who took me to his house and I had the opportunity to talk to him. He was a great man, a great personality.

[29] Above n 10.

[30] See 'Interview with René-Jean Dupuy', fn 31.

What in particular struck you in Röling?

His idealism.

Actually, he was not a positivist lawyer.

No, he was not, but he was a great human being.

Another international lawyer who impressed me with his capacity and his modesty was Sørensen,[31] a great man. Excellent in his Hague General Course. He was also the editor of this manual which we prepared.[32] He took a subject which was of no interest. Nobody wanted it, and he took it. He was a great man.

So did you like him not only because he was a great international lawyer, but also as a person?

Yes.

I think his general course is one of the best at The Hague Academy. But I was told by some people who had attended his General Course that it was terribly tedious.

Maybe the delivery was poor; it probably was part of his modesty.

He was probably a shy man. Also, his book on sources of international law[33] is one of the best.

Did you happen to meet Morelli?[34]

Yes, I met Morelli at the *Institut de Droit International.* He was a warm and very nice personality, a courteous gentleman. I think his great speciality was

[31] Max Sørensen (Danish, 1913–81) was Professor of Constitutional and International Law at the University of Aarhus from 1947. Legal Adviser to the Danish Ministry of Foreign Affairs from 1956, he headed the Danish delegation to the Diplomatic Conferences on the Law of the Sea of 1958 and 1960. He was member and President of the European Commission on Human Rights (1980–81) and sat as a judge in the European Court of Justice (1973–79). His major works are the book on *Les sources de droit international* (Copenaghen, Einar Munksgaard, 1946) and the General Course at The Hague Academy, 'Principes du droit international public: cours général' (1960-III) 101 *Recueil des cours* 1, a set of lectures that offers a masterly presentation, from a positivist viewpoint, of traditional international law and the new trends emerging in the world community.

[32] M Sørensen (ed), *Manual of Public International Law* (London, Macmillan, 1968).

[33] *Les sources du droit international*, above n 31.

[34] Gaetano Morelli (Italian, 1900–89) was Professor of International Law at Naples University (1935–51) and then at Rome University (from 1951). He was a judge at the ICJ (1961–70) and author of many publications. His writings, based on a strict normativism, were admirable for their logical and theoretical rigour. He excelled in procedural law, as also shown by some Separate Opinions he appended to judgments of the ICJ. His textbook on public international law (*Nozioni di diritto internazionale*, 7th edn (Padova, Cedam, 1967)), although notable for its theoretical foundations and logical stringency, is a far cry from the social and political reality of the world community. In a way Morelli formalised, rendered abstract and brought to its extreme consequences Anzilotti's positivism, which was much closer to reality. His qualities and flaws are manifest in his general course at the Hague Academy, 'Cours général de droit international public' (1956-I) 89 *Recueil des cours* 437.

procedure, but he went a bit too far in developing arguments based on legal procedure. For instance, I do not agree with his position in the *South West Africa* cases[35] in which I think the six to six decision was clearly a revocation of the 1962 decision,[36] an unprecedented revocation, a contradiction in the jurisprudence already established. So he became too theoretical.

And did you ever meet Perassi,[37] who was a bit older?

I read some of his contributions, but I never met him. I understand he was very much admired by Roberto Ago.

Yes. Although they are very different. Perassi was a good international lawyer, like Ago, but a bit formalistic, very theoretical, very abstract. He became a member of the Italian Constitutional Court, Vice-President of the Court. I met him when I was still a student, at the suggestion of my professor, Giuseppe Sperduti, who was Perassi's disciple. Perassi was a very shy man, he never spoke. So it was terribly embarrassing to stay with him because he kept silent and you did not know what to say. Did you ever meet other Italians?

Yes, I met Quadri,[38] a very nice person, a warm personality. His ideas are interesting; he was a monist, which was heretical then in Italy. I liked him and we became good friends. I also met Sereni, as an adversary in the *Barcelona Traction* case, and I have seen his books; they are good.

[35] *Ethiopia v South Africa; Liberia v South Africa*, 18 July 1966, [1966] ICJ Rep 6.

[36] *South West Africa* cases (Preliminary Objections), 21 December 1962,[1962] ICJ Rep 319.

[37] Tomaso Perassi (Italian, 1886–1960) was Professor of International Law at various Italian Universities and then, from 1937 until 1955, at Rome University. He acted as a legal adviser to the Italian Ministry of Foreign Affairs from 1931 until 1943. In 1946–47 he was a prominent member of the Constituent Assembly, the elected body charged with drafting a new Constitution. In 1955–60 he sat as a judge in the Italian Constitutional Court.

[38] Rolando Quadri (Italian, 1907–76) was Professor of International Law at Naples University (1953–70) and then at Rome University (from 1971). He also taught in Egypt (at Alexandria and Cairo Universities) between 1950 and 1967. He authored many books and articles on public and private international law. His major work in public international law is his manual (*Diritto internazionale pubblico*, 5th edn (Napoli, Liguori, 1968)). His Hague lectures include: 'Le fondement du caractère obligatoire du droit international public' (1952-I) 80 *Recueil des cours* 579; 'Droit international cosmique' (1959-III) 98 *Recueil des cours* 508; and 'Cours general de droit international public' (1964-III) 113 *Recueil des cours* 237. Quadri was notable among Italian positivists of the period 1930–80 because he was attentive to the social reality of the international community, without confining himself to investigating legal institutions and legal rules. He reacted to the positivist and 'contractual' vision of the international community advocated by previous writers such as Anzilotti, as well as to the normative approach taken by such scholars as Kelsen (to a large extent followed in Italy by Gaetano Morelli, above n 34). He argued for a realistic approach to international law by, among other things, outlining a theory of the 'inherent authority of the collectivity' (*'autorità del corpo sociale'*) (in *Diritto internazionale pubblico*, 25 ff). In his view States as members of the international community act both *uti singuli* (in their individual dimension, to pursue private interests) and *uti universi* (as entities operating on behalf of the whole community). The limits of this view were rightly underscored by B Conforti ('L'opera di Rolando Quadri' (1978) 61 *Rivista di diritto internazionale* 5, 14–18). In the end Quadri overemphasised the role of force and authority as opposed to law, by attaching excessive importance to the Great Powers and their de facto authority, thereby unwittingly legitimising their possible abuses. Quadri was a great teacher and had many distinguished disciples, among whom Benedetto Conforti and Georges Abi-Saab are indubitably the best known.

Who are, at present, the Italians who are fairly well known in Latin America?

Ago is very well known and very appreciated. I think his contribution to the Vienna Convention was masterful. I once said that he managed to put in precise terms the ideas advanced by Waldock, whose drafting was a bit complicated and cumbersome. Ago put it very well, he contributed to the drafting of the Convention to a great degree. I once said he reminded me of what Charles Péguy said: '*La pitié pour l'ouvrage bien fait*' ('taking pity on a well done job').

Yes, you are right. He has this sense of finishing, he likes polishing up things. In this respect, he was totally different from Quadri, who was rather impressionistic. What about other European scholars who have some sort of influence in Latin America today. What about French or English authors?

Well, French authors have a great influence. Charles Rousseau,[39] for instance, has been translated into Spanish. The recent book by Alain Pellet and others[40] is very useful as an instrument.

III. Jiménez de Aréchaga's Academic and Political Career

A. The jurist as a scholar and politician

Now we can move on. By and large, what was the status of legal scholarship when you initiated your scholarly activity? In a way you have already answered this question when you were talking about Uruguay and natural law. But I am interested in knowing whether in your country, there was a positivist approach or rather a natural law approach?

A natural law approach. You remember I mentioned the doctrine of the just war [section I. above], the Spanish writers. The first lecture in international law given by my predecessor was the life and work of Grotius. The historical approach prevailed, not the systematic approach. Of course, it was a difficult period, because the League of Nations had been bankrupt. There was nothing for the time.

You know how I had to overcome the difficulty of access to materials? When the professor of international law resigned and the chair became open, there was a competition. The system in our law school was the Spanish system, whereby the candidates for a chair, the assistant professors who want to compete for a chair, had to make a presentation and criticise each other.

[39] Charles Rousseau (1902–93) was Professor of International Law at Paris University and author of a multi-volume book on international law (*Droit international public*, 5 vols (Paris, Sirey, 1970–83)). He was member of the *Institut de Droit international* (1948–93).

[40] Reference is made here to the book by NQ Dihn, P Dailler and A Pellet, *Droit international public*, 2nd edn (Paris, Librairie génerale de droit et de jurisprudence, 1980).

The Spaniards call it '*la trinca*'. We have no system of open competition before a jury. There were two other candidates, and I said to myself: 'How am I am going to prepare?' It was 1946. There was no material in Uruguay. The United Nations had been set up, and through some friends I got a job at the UN Secretariat and became a member of the Security Council division, which was composed of two parts: the part which serviced the Council was directed by Prosit (Yugoslav), and the other took an intellectual approach, the people who studied disputes and examined the problems on the whole. The director of that was García Robles, who won a Nobel Prize, from Mexico. I joined that group under García Robles, and there I was assigned the task of studying the voting and the question of veto in the Security Council. I wrote a book,[41] because after that work I became an expert . . .

How long did you stay in New York?

Two years: 1947 and 1948. I remember in 1948 I resigned, because I was appointed assistant delegate of my country to the General Assembly in Paris. I was crossing the Atlantic from New York to Paris, when we stopped at Terra Nova and learned that Count Bernadotte[42] had been killed in Israel that day. That period was very important for me, because I specialised in the Law of the Charter, not only the veto but everything, and I wrote a book on *Derecho constitucional de las Naciones Unidas*,[43] which is not article by article but section by section, but it has not been translated.

That is really a pity.

It is a pity. But you know, sometimes I think about bringing it up to date and publishing it in English, but I am discouraged by it. I would have to do it by hand, a terribly difficult job. I don't type.

I have a different question: what philosophical or ideological schools influenced your intellectual development? Or did you endeavour to stay aloof from any non-legal schools of thought? Was there a sort of political, ideological or philosophical school which in a way influenced you outside the legal arena?

Well, the answer is no, I have not been influenced by schools like Marxism. I am teaching now again at the Catholic University in my country, and I have now directed my teaching a bit more towards human rights, *jus cogens*, humanitarian law—like you.

[41] *Voting and the Handling of Disputes in the Security Council* (New York, Carnegie Endowment for International Peace, 1950).

[42] Count Folke Bernadotte (1895–1948), a Swedish diplomat, was appointed by the United Nations Security Council mediator in the Arab–Israeli conflict of 1947–48. He was assassinated in 1948 in Jerusalem by the militant Zionist group Lehi (commonly known as the Stern Group), while pursuing his official duties.

[43] *Derecho constitucional de las Naciones Unidas: comentario teórico-práctico de la Carta* (Madrid, Escuela de Funcionarios Internacionales, 1958).

In a way, you are influenced by the Catholic approach to life and to social problems to some extent.

Yes. Although I am not a practising Catholic, my general approach is Christian. They say that you belong to the religion to which you have stopped attending. I am a member of a political party. I was some time in government.

You were Minister of the Interior.

It created a lot of problems for me. I was Minister for one year. In 1968, the students' revolution became affected by the Castrist influence. The Tupamaros were starting to gain force. I had to control that situation. The university was controlled by extremist groups so I was suspended from the university. That was 1968. In 1969, I was elected to the ICJ. At that time, I was what we call *sumarius, summariano*: by an administration decision, a member of the university is suspended and a commission inspects his activities. I was elected to the Court, so I resigned. I said the two [positions] were incompatible. The University rejected the resignation and said the person who is *summariano* cannot resign.

But you were not investigated in your capacity as Minister of the Interior but as a professor.

The university decided that all the professors who had been in government had to be suspended and were subject to investigation.

This was only because of your political action. Did you belong to a political party?

I belonged to the political party that was in power, and that is now in opposition. It is called *Partido Colorado*. It's a centre party.

But previously you had been Under-Secretary for Foreign Affairs.

I had been Under-Secretary for Foreign Affairs. The Minister had been my predecessor in the university. He was a diplomat.

Was this political experience enriching for you, was it important for your intellectual thought and development?

Well, it was important in the sense that I gave up politics entirely as a result of that experience and the consequences I have suffered, because of the attitude of the people who gained control of the university. I decided I was not made for politics. I did not want to be a politician. So I support the party, but I am not active.

Do you have good memories of your political experience?

Well, I have good memories. I think it enriches your experience to have been in those positions. Also, I was Secretary of the Council of Government for three years.

What does that mean? I saw in your biography that you were Secretary of the Council of Government.

It was a proposal made by a leader of our party who wanted to replace the President of the Republic by a Council of Government. This new approach was tried from 1951 to 1962, but it was a complete failure, because this body gradually turned into a debating society.

How many people made up this body?

Nine people: six from the majority party, three from the minority.

And the function of this body was to act as President of the State, a collegiate presidency in a way?

Yes, on the Swiss model. The only difference was that in the Swiss model each of the members of the collegiate body is responsible for a ministry. In the Uruguayan experience, which was a failure, we did not have enough people to fulfil those roles. It was a source of delays, the minority objected, created difficulties. It was impossible, it could not work.

Did this political experience of yours have an influence on your legal thought, on your legal approach to international law, or were these two separate things?

No, they were completely separate.

So there was no sort of spill-over effect, a ripple effect?

No, the two experiences remained completely separate. The only thing I learned was to keep away from politics. But of course, it was useful for the development of my career as a practising lawyer, because you know that, in our country, as in most countries in Latin America, a professor has no choice but to work as a practising lawyer on the side because the salary is very low, it's insufficient. It doesn't even allow you to buy the books you need.

You were saying that it was good for your private practice. Did you get to know many people?

Yes, you get in touch with foreign ambassadors, for instance, who asked for your help with their problems, and after you left office they would recommend your legal services to their acquaintances. For instance, after I left the

Council of Government I was asked to advise on the building of a transfer station in our country, an important investment which continues today.

So for a time, I had to practise law. There is a professor in our country who said that law professors and the crocodile are alike, in that they have to eat while they swim. The idea is that you have to work while you teach. On the other hand, some of these cases I had to handle when I left the Council of Government were useful for international law, because they had international law aspects.

So what precisely was the prime motivation behind your non-academic career as a practitioner? Did you perceive this activity mainly as a calling, or did you undertake it just because you were interested, or because it was good to get money? I am not thinking only of a practitioner as a private practitioner but also as a judge of the ICJ, as a member of the International Law Commission.

Well, I think one has to combine academic activity with some real-world activity.

So your motivation was also to enrich your academic activity.

Yes. I think that the two support each other: you are a better professor if you practise law; you are a better practitioner if you have an academic background. I would say that of the two activities, the one which has really attracted me most is to act as counsel, even more than to be a judge. I like fighting.

And try to outwit the adversary probably. To be more clever.

Well, that you cannot be because you can win and lose your cases, and I can be losing . . .

Yes, but you try to be more clever.

No, I think maybe it's a question of family tradition, because my father, my uncle, my grandfather were practitioners, though not in international law: my father was in commercial law, my grandfather in constitutional law.

Why do you enjoy being a counsel so much?

I like answering arguments, I like attacking what I think are the weak points of the adversary. Attacking 'at the jugular', as they say.

Do you enjoy pleading?

Not so much, because I have problems with my English pronunciation. I prefer to write briefs.

So the written part of the proceedings. Going back to your political experience, for how long did you act as a politician?

My political career was very short. It began in 1950 and ended in 1954. I was Under-Secretary for Foreign Affairs. Then in 1951, the Council of Government was established and I became Secretary in that body until 1954. In 1954, a new election took place; the opposition won, so I could not continue.

But then you resumed later on when you became Minister of the Interior.

That's a different history. I was at the Vienna Conference on the Law of Treaties, attending the Conference as a delegate of my country. I was general rapporteur of the 'Committee of the Whole', and I received a phone call from a friend of mine who was then Acting President of Uruguay (the President had died and he had taken over because he was Vice-President). He asked me to take up the job as Minister of the Interior, because he couldn't find anyone ready and willing to do it. I could not refuse. One of the reasons I could not refuse was because he had promised to support my candidacy to the International Court of Justice. He said Brazil wanted to nominate one of their own as a candidate. He went to Brazil and asked that they give up, which Brazil did.

So you were Minister of the Interior for about one year?

A little less, from March to early December.

But I understand you didn't enjoy your job as Minister very much, particularly because of the Tupamaros. Was it a tough job?

It was a very tough job.

Have you ever written in national or international newspapers, or have you been frequently on radio or television? Are you a public figure in your country?

Well, yes, an ex-public figure. I can say, for instance, that the current President of the Republic, the Minister of the Interior, the Minister of Foreign Relations and the Judges of the Supreme Court of my country, were all pupils of mine; so when they shake hands with me, they call me 'Professor'.

Was there ever a time when you were frequently on television, or took up a public role in the mass media?

No. I get interviewed sometimes, but in fields other than law. In the case of the Falklands War, the newspapers and the radio wanted to have my opinion, but I refused because I had to criticise Argentina, I would have had to take a critical position with respect to what they did.

So you preferred to stay aloof from this kind of political discourse?

On the other hand, now I am assisting the Foreign Minister in the plans for integrating my country into the Southern Cone of Latin America, which is called the Mercosur. I am trying to advise about how we can create institutions following the European example. And for that I am attending meetings in the Foreign Office, consulting with the Under-Secretary, who is a former pupil of mine, and a former assistant professor. I have been appointed honorary President of that group.

So now you are active in this project. Yet you try to avoid appearing in mass media. But did you used to comment on issues of international affairs at any point in time in the past?

No. It's not that I tried to avoid it. I work in various activities now, mainly as a practitioner in international cases and arbitrations.

And you are also President of the World Bank Administrative Tribunal.

I was. I was not re-elected because they considered that I had reached a certain age and was too old. Because you know, the people in the World Bank have compulsory retirement, and they thought that at 75 I should also retire.

Did you enjoy that job?

I enjoyed it. It was not very attractive from the point of view of international law; it was administrative law. But you know, it was very interesting because it was a very congenial group with Prosper Weil, Eli Lauterpacht, myself, and an American lawyer who is very, very good and a specialist in labour law. He drafted most of the judgments. He was Dean of the Law School in Philadelphia.

And for how long did you chair this tribunal?

Ten years. We met twice a year, once in Washington and the other time in London.

Who replaced you?

A young Latin American lawyer who is very, very good: Orrego Vicuña.

Do you consider that an international lawyer should get involved in social activities useful to the national or local communities, or do you feel instead that he should exclusively concentrate on his activity as an expert? To put it differently, do you think that as an international lawyer one should also be committed to some sort of social or political goal, or take part in a political party or in a trade union movement?

Well, I think it should be desirable. The only problem is that I am not doing that. I have never done so.

But you had a political experience which was part of your social commitment.

I was more active, I think. What happened is that when I was in the Court from 1972 to 1979, I could not participate in social and political life. Afterwards, I was terribly busy with my private practice in international law, and arbitrations. I was President of the arbitral court in a French-Canadian arbitration.[44]

I was told that you drafted most of the judgments yourself, is that true?

Yes. I was with Arangio-Ruíz[45] then. We held the hearings in the American Bar Association in New York. There was air conditioning and he hated air conditioning. He used to wear a pullover. And then one day, one of the counsel was speaking from Canada and I heard a noise to my left. I thought 'what is happening?' It was Arangio-Ruíz protecting his arms against the draught with newspaper. He is a character.

You said that you have always been a member of the Partido Colorado. Was there a period when you were very active as a member, when you were in power?

Only when I was serving in public office.

Before you joined the Cabinet, you were not very active in the party, I assume.

No. I was appointed Under-Secretary by my predecessor, who was a former professor of international law, and in that capacity, I had to work closely with the President of the country who was promoting the 'council' government. He gave up his three years of power in order to have the Council, and I cooperated with him. So he offered me the post of Secretary of the Council of Government.

When you were Under-Secretary for Foreign Affairs, were you instrumental in achieving something useful to international law?

Very much so, because it was a very difficult time for Uruguay in its relations with Argentina. The President of Argentina was Juan Domingo Perón [1946–55 and 1973–74], but he had not been elected yet. And there were people against him who were exiled in Montevideo, and who wrote against Perón and criticised him. They not only wrote, but also spoke on the radio, and those radios broadcasts and newspapers reached Argentina. So Perón was furious with the Uruguayans for allowing these criticisms, to the point that he forbade the Argentineans from going to Punta de l'Este, where many had residences. So it was a very difficult time with Argentina. We had to

[44] Reference is made here to the *Case Concerning the Delimitation of Maritime Areas Between Canada and the French Republic (St Pierre and Miquelon)*, 10 June 1992 (see award in (1992) 31 *International Legal Materials* 1149).

[45] See 'Interview with René-Jean Dupuy', fn 14.

answer the complaints and diplomatic notes Argentina was sending, in which it argued that our penal code forbade criticism of a foreign government. The Argentineans sent a note saying: 'Why don't you apply your penal code?' And I had to answer that our obligation was not to apply our penal code; our international obligation (the only one they could claim from us) was to prevent insults without penalising the expression of opinions under the Constitution.

The Argentineans also sent another note because there had been a attempt by the air force against Perón. They said that it was not possible to start a revolution from the air, so after their trial, the pilots went into exile in Uruguay and I had to deliver their planes to the Argentinean Government. At the same time, I had to declare the pilots political refugees. And that was criticised by Argentina. That was part of my job.

Did you pursue some foreign policy lines? Did you have a strategy as Under-Secretary of Foreign Affairs, or was the foreign policy of your country decided upon collectively, with other politicians and statesmen?

There was a Treaty with the United States, on military assistance, which was opposed by the minority party. I had to defend it, even on the radio, on public radio. I remember another problem of international law for which I had to go on the radio. There was a Pan-American Conference in Venezuela, and a very distinguished lawyer from my country, the leader of the party, proposed that we should not send delegates to this conference because it was under the dictatorship of Marcos Pérez-Jiménez [1952–58]. But I had to oppose that, stressing the inconveniences of not attending a Pan-American Conference; in the end the delegation was sent.

So I think it's desirable that one should participate in the political activity in one's country. The main thing I did for my country when I was Minister of the Interior concerned strike laws. We had a lot of strikes, a terrible amount of strikes, and all the professors of labour law were at that time difficult to be found. So I consulted a Brazilian, a very distinguished man who had worked in the International Labour Office in Geneva. He advised me: 'The remedy is a declaration concerning public services. If a service is essential, the government must say so and the strike may be declared illegal.' That law had a difficult passage through Parliament, but in the end was passed. It is the only provision in our country which gives some control to the Government against strikes. It is still in force. It was adopted in 1968 when I was Minister of the Interior. I presented it and defended it; there was much difficulty but in the end they approved it.

Do you perceive yourself mainly as a technician, or rather a fully-fledged intellectual operating in the cultural context of your country?

Well, maybe it was the experience of being a judge for nine years, but I cannot really describe myself as a full-fledged intellectual operating in the cultural context of my country. It is only, as I told you, at the time when I was invited to lecture at a meeting of Supreme Court Judges of Latin America describing the constitutional reforms which are necessary in order to implement the Mercosur. Maybe that's still the work of a technician.

Well, maybe half-way between being a technician and a socially and politically committed personality. So you would think of yourself more as a technician than an expert?

Yes, I think so, I am afraid so.

B. The writings of Jiménez de Aréchaga

How have you integrated your activities as an academic into your activities as a practitioner when you were a judge, or a member of the International Law Commission? Do you see a link between your activity as a practitioner and your activity as a scholar? Do you think there has been a sort of cross-fertilisation?

Yes, very much so. For instance, if I recall the books I have published, they have come out of some experience or other I had as a practitioner. The first book I wrote, on recognition of government,[46] in Spanish, was the one which gave me the most problems. I was very unlucky because it was published the same year as Lauterpacht's book on the same topic.[47] That book came out of my experience as a practitioner fresh out of university, when I was working for a Committee which existed in Montevideo and was an organ of the OAS (Organization for American States); it was a Committee for Political Defence, working during the war. Its function was to supervise the laws or regulations adopted by Latin American countries in order to control subversive activities, particularly by the Axis: espionage, sabotage, that kind of thing. There was a revolution at the time in Bolivia. The new government was established by a military man, and there was a suspicion that he was pro-Nazi, pro-Axis. So, this Committee met and decided to recommend to the Latin American States that they consult with each other before granting recognition to a State, and to refuse recognition if they suspected subversive activities. So it was a new theory about recognition. I became immersed in that work of the Committee, and that gave me the idea of writing on the topic. So, this book grew out of my practical activities. Also, my experience with the secretariat of the Security Council led me to write that book on the *Handling of Disputes* by that body.[48]

Was your book on the constitutional law of the UN[49] also the result of your experience in the UN Security Council?

Yes.

[46] *Reconocimiento de gobiernos* (Montevideo, Biblioteca de publicaciones oficiales de la Facultad de derecho y ciencias sociales de la Universidad de Montevideo, 1947).
[47] *Recognition in International Law* (Cambridge, Cambridge University Press, 1947).
[48] Above n 41.
[49] Above n 43.

What about your article on the nationalisation of foreign property?[50] *There, you developed a very original theory which you took up again in your Hague General Course.*[51]

That came out as the result of my work with the ILC. At that time we were studying the question of State Responsibility. You remember that García-Amador was the Rapporteur, he had joined forces with Harvard University. And he took the approach whereby responsibility had to do with indemnity. Tunkin[52] was very much against that. Ago found the solution: the idea of secondary rules. That was a brilliant idea. I then developed this theory about nationalisation, first in a paper on compensation of foreign property and undue enrichment submitted to the ILC, which was printed in one of the *Yearbooks* of the ILC in 1960 or 1961. So I claim priority, because these ideas have become general. This is documented in the *Yearbook*, I don't remember which one, of the International Law Commission. It was drafted in connection with García-Amador's approach, before we took the other approach proposed by Ago.

Did you ever have the opportunity to apply these views of yours in cases of nationalisation?

I applied these views in an arbitration case by ICSID. It was a case concerning *Klöckner v Republic of Cameroon.*[53] Klöckner was a German company which had promised Cameroon a fertilisation plant. Klöckner had recommended or established the feasibility process and then had become the investor. The factory was a complete failure, materials brought from Poland were second-rate and failed completely, there was no market. It was a terrible loss. Cameroon had to stop paying. The company claimed compensation. So there was a tribunal composed of an American, William Rodgers, and a French law professor, Dominique Smit, professor of commercial law in Strasbourg I think; I was the President. On the basis of the *exceptio non adimpleti contractus*, we decided that Cameroon owed nothing to Klöckner.

But unfortunately, that was not the end of the story, because you know that ICSID arbitration awards are subject to appeal. There was an appeal to a panel of lawyers[54] who took a European approach to the subject: Pierre

[50] 'State Responsibility for the Nationalization of Foreign Owned Properties' (1978) 11 *New York University Journal of International Law and Politics* 179.

[51] Above n 5.

[52] Grigory Tunkin (Russian, 1906–94) was Professor of International Law at the University of Moscow (1965–94). He was a member (1957–66) and President (1961) of the UN International Law Commission. Among his publications, see *Theory of International Law*, 1st edn (tr WE Butler) (Cambridge, MA, Harvard University Press, 1974); 'Co-existence and International Law' (1958-III) 95 *Recueil des cours* 1; 'The Legal Nature of the United Nations' (1966-III) 119 *Recueil des cours* 1; 'International Law in the International System' (1975-IV) 145 *Recueil des cours* 1; 'Politics, Law and Force in the Interstate System' (1989-VII) 219 *Recueil des cours* 227.

[53] *Klöckner Industrie-Anlagen GmbH and others v United Republic of Cameroon and Société Camerounaise des Engrais* (ICSID case n ARB/81/2), 21 October 1983 (published in [1994] 2 ICSID Rep 9).

[54] Ad hoc *Committee Decision on Annulment*, 3 May 1985 (published in [1994] 2 ICSID Rep 95).

Lalive, from Switzerland, an Egyptian, El Kosheri, and Seidl-Hohenveldern, an Austrian. They rejected the award. They criticised it, and I understand that some amount has since been paid by Cameroon. So, I had an opportunity to apply my views, but I failed. But the mistake I made in that case was to put forward an argument which had been developed by Rodgers, by saying that in the case of developing countries, you have to take a more lenient attitude. That was the ground upon which the award was quashed.

By the way, would you regard yourself as what the French call 'Tiers-Mondiste'? In the sense that, if possible, you try to side with developing countries.

That is a good question. I don't think so.

Or would you regard yourself as rather Western-oriented?

I would regard myself as Western-oriented, not systematically *Tiers-Mondiste.*

Actually I am wondering whether there are many international lawyers in Latin America who are really Tiers-Mondiste.

Not many.

Castañeda[55] *probably; he wrote a few things in favour of developing countries.*

Yes, he was very active on the Economic Charter; actually he was a protagonist. Lately, he has not been so active. He was member of the panel that took part in the final decision on the *Klöckner* case,[56] and I was surprised he did not write it himself. He dissented but he did not express the dissent in writing.

Would you regard yourself as more Tiers-Mondiste than Gros Espiell?[57]

Less. Gros Espiell is very much in favour of self determination, human rights, the right to development. I do not believe that you can speak of such a right.

[55] Jorge Castañeda (1921–97) was a Mexican diplomat. He served as Secretary of Foreign Affairs from 1979 to 1982. Later he was ambassador to France, Egypt and the United Nations, and member (1967–86) of the UN International Law Commission. In the United Nations he was a vocal advocate of the sovereignty of developing countries, and laid much emphasis on the need to restructure international economic relations, so as to take into account the needs of developing countries.

[56] Award rendered on 26 January 1988 (unpublished).

[57] Héctor Gros Espiell (Uruguayan, 1926–2009) was Professor of Constitutional and International Law at the University of Montevideo (Universidad de la República). He was a member and President of the Inter-American Court of Human Rights (1987–90) In 1990–93 he was Uruguyan Minister for Foreign Affairs. He gave two lectures at The Hague Academy: 'Le système interaméricain comme régime régional de protection internationale des droits de l'homme' (1975 II) 145 *Recueil des cours* 1, and 'La Convention américaine et la Convention européenne des droits de l'Homme: analyse comparative' (1989-IV) 218 *Recueil des cours* 167.

I agree with you. The right to development is essentially a political slogan. So how would you place yourself ideally vis-à-vis Gros Espiel, because I think you are more of an international lawyer? Gros Espiel is a specialist in human rights.

He comes from constitutional law and human rights.

So he is more oriented towards human rights. I think he is a very courageous man and a man of great heart. Let us go back to your own position. If you have two solutions to legal problems, one which is favourable to developing countries, the other which is more favourable to industrialised States, do you think that you would tend to choose the one which is better for developing countries?

Not necessarily.

So you don't operate on ideological values.

Reference is made to the invasion of Grenada in 1983 by US forces. The attack was triggered by a military coup which had ousted a revolutionary government.

I can tell you this. I had another arbitration, where I was successful; it was the *Pyramids* case.[58] Sadat of Egypt had given a concession to some investors from Canada to build a development area close to the pyramids. And then, when the Egyptians realised it was too close to the pyramids, they cancelled it. So there was a claim regarding the expenses involved, and we arbitrators granted the indemnity: Egypt was to pay the investor for the initial expenses. This is a case that has a long history, because at first it was decided favourably by the International Chamber of Commerce. It was annulled by the French Court of Cassation, so they came to ICSID, and it was decided by ICSID.

In this case you sided with the investor. So, your choice was not made on ideological decisions. But in many international law cases you have some leeway, some sort of discretionary power between two parties.

Montaigne said that in doubtful cases one decides '*pour les amis*'.

'Les amis' could be the developing countries, which you seem not to accept.

I don't believe in '*les amis*'. No '*parti pris*'. Let me add that it is not in the interest of the developing countries to take a position against foreign investment.

But you tend to take very wise and balanced positions. I quoted in one of my books[59] what you wrote so well in the Vienna Conference on the Law of Treaties about

[58] *Southern Pacific Properties (Middle East) Limited v Arab Republic of Egypt* (ICSID case n ARB/84/3), 20 May 1992 (published in [1995] 3 ICSID Rep 189).

[59] A Cassese, *International Law in a Divided World* (Oxford, Clarendon Press, 1986) 178.

jus cogens. *You said: 'Let us not be scared by jus cogens because it is not such a revolutionary concept.' Actually, what you said is true, because so far* jus cogens *has never been applied. There was a sort of ideological fight. I remember Ghana and other countries said: 'This is a new weapon for attacking imperialism.' And then there were the French and the Americans who were terribly scared. You said: 'Well let us not be scared because this, in any case, is not really a weapon.'*

States are unlikely openly to make a treaty which would be in violation of *jus cogens*. The only example I could find is the *Krupp* case,[60] in which a party was accused of having made an agreement permitting prisoners of war to work in favour of the State which held them. But there was no evidence, so it's hypothetical in that case.

C. Jiménez de Aréchaga's main contributions to international law

Now we come to a very important part: what would you consider as your major scholarly contribution to international law?

Well, the book on the *Constitutional Law of the United Nations*,[61] at the time it appeared, was a good contribution. Now it has become outdated because all international law books need substantial revisions.

It's out of date, but the main ideas are there.

Also, the book based on my *cours général* of The Hague,[62] *El derecho internacional contemporáneo*,[63] needs revision. I think these two are the main pieces of work that I have contributed.

Which ideas in these two books of yours do you regard as the most original ones, where in a way you have broken new ground?

Well it is very difficult to say that you break new ground.

But you did break new ground. One area, for instance, related to what you said before about your very original view of compensation, is the idea of unjust enrichment.

Perhaps one thing that has received attention from other sources is the tripartite characterisation of the relations between customary law and treaty law: the declaratory effect of treaty law, the crystallising effect and the generating effect.

[60] *United States v Alfred Krupp et al*, Case n 10, published in *Trials of War Criminals Before the Nuremberg Military Tribunals under Control Council Law No 10*, vol 9 (Washington, United States Government Printing Office, 1950).
[61] Above n 43.
[62] Above n 5.
[63] Madrid, Tecnos, 1980.

Do you regard this tripartite division as an original piece of work?

I don't know how original, because I based myself on the case law of the ICJ.

But you theorised this distinction?

I would say—without being impertinent—that I not only theorised, but I also contributed a little bit within the Court to a more flexible conception of customary law: for instance, in the *Namibia* case,[64] the idea of resolutions of the General Assembly becoming customary law like Resolution 1514; in *Western Sahara*,[65] the idea that a diplomatic conference itself can be a mechanism for developing international law. In these cases, the Court stated that the articles of the Vienna Convention on the Law of Treaties on interpretation, the articles on breach, had become rules of customary law on the basis of a treaty which had not been ratified.

So this was a contribution of yours.

It is very difficult to say. The Court's deliberations are secret. I cannot claim authorship for that.

But Ruda is very proud of that famous sentence on good faith which he put in the Nuclear Tests *case.*[66] *And Judge Lachs always told everybody—adding 'Please don't tell other people'— that he was behind that famous dictum on obligations* erga omnes, *in the* Barcelona Traction *case.*[67] *Since other judges have disclosed their contribution, you could also do so. Were you behind this new approach to customary process?*

I think so. I drafted the Advisory Opinion on *Namibia* together with Lachs, but mostly it was my work.

I see that you enjoy drafting judgments and briefs as a counsel, although you were drafting in a language which is not yours.

Yes.

[64] Above n 25.

[65] 16 October 1975, [1975] ICJ Rep 12.

[66] 'One of the basic principles governing the creation and performance of legal obligations, whatever their source, is the principle of good faith. Trust and confidence are inherent in international co-operation, in particular in an age when this co-operation in many fields is becoming increasingly essential. Just as the very rule of *pacta sunt servanda* in the law of treaties is based on good faith, so also is the binding character of an international obligation assumed by unilateral declaration. Thus interested States may take cognizance of unilateral declarations and place confidence in them, and are entitled to require that the obligation thus created be respected.' See *Nuclear Tests (New Zealand v France)*, 20 December 1974, [1974] ICJ Rep 457 at 473, § 49.

[67] Above n 10, at 32, § 33.

Were there other cases in which you were instrumental in changing things, either at the ICJ or the International Law Commission?

At the ICJ, the period of my presidency was a very empty one from the point of view of cases. We had only the *Aegean Sea Continental Shelf* case.[68] That gave me the idea of the chambers, which from an organisational point of view was considered my major contribution.

Was this an idea of yours?

Well, the idea had been put forward in an article by Jessup,[69] so I cannot claim to be the inventor, but I was the one who put it into practice, brought it into the rules. Also, I was instrumental in getting it accepted in the *Gulf of Maine* case.[70] You know I was then Judge *ad hoc*, so I was in the building. Ruda had just lost his wife and was in Buenos Aires. I was told there was no majority for accepting the chamber. It would have been a very close vote. So I called Ruda and said: 'You have to come, because if you don't and the Court doesn't accept the setting up of a chamber in this case, that's the end of the Court.' So Ruda flew from Buenos Aires, voted in favour and created a majority for the setting up of a chamber. Because the vote was divided, there was a tie. Do you know what Judge Padillo Nervo called the seven judges who voted in the majority in the *South West Africa* case?[71] He called them the 'seven up judges'.

So you are proud of these chambers?

This chamber system is doubtful from the point of view of legality, as demonstrated by Judge Shahabuddeen.[72] But really, it was an injection for the Court, at the time when it was moribund.

At the level of new ideas injected into judgments, do you think that your major contribution was at the level of sources?

At the level of sources, the adoption of a more flexible approach and the taking into account of certain resolutions of the General Assembly in the

[68] *Greece v Turkey*, 19 December 1978, [1978] ICJ Rep 3.

[69] Philip Caryl Jessup (1897–1986) was Hamilton Fish Professor of International Law and Diplomacy at Columbia Law (1946–61). He served as the Assistant Secretary-General of the UNRRA (UN Relief and Rehabilitation Administration) Conference in 1943. He was a technical adviser to the American delegation to the San Francisco UN Charter Conference in 1945. In the 1950s Jessup became a target of Senator Joseph McCarthy, who accused him of being a security risk for he had 'an unusual affinity . . . for communist causes'. Jessup served as a judge in the ICJ (1961–70). He published, among other things, *A Modern Law of Nations: An Introduction* (New York, Macmillan, 1948); *Transnational Law* (New Haven, Yale University Press, 1956); *The Birth of Nations* (New York, Columbia University Press, 1974).

[70] *Delimitation of the Maritime Boundary in the Gulf of Maine Area (Canada v United States of America)*, 12 October 1984, [1984] ICJ Rep 246.

[71] Above n 35.

[72] Mohamed Shahabbudeen (*b* 1931), from Guyana, was Minister of Legal Affairs in 1978–87, and First Deputy Prime Minister and Vice-President (1983–87). He was a judge in the ICJ (1988–97) and then on the International Criminal Tribunal for the Former Yugoslavia (1997–2009).

process of codification, the production of consensus on rules of law including resolutions which failed to get adopted at a conference (as we said in the *Icelandic* case[73], referring to the proposal for a zone of exclusive fisheries jurisdiction extending to 50 nautical miles from the baselines around the coast of Iceland).

And what about your contribution to the International Law Commission?

I am proud of my contribution to the Convention on the Law of Treaties with respect to the articles on third-party stipulations, the articles on treaties in favour of third States. With the support of Waldock, we defeated the idea of the collateral agreement, the idea that there were two successive agreements, one between the parties and the other between the parties and the third-party State. This idea was defeated in the Commission and finally in the Vienna Conference. For the benefit of the right, you don't need to show a collateral agreement.

Was there an ideological underpinning to these two positions, the idea behind the collateral agreement and your own idea? Was it ideologically motivated?

No, I don't think so. It was just a legal conception. Yasseen[74] was very keen on the collateral idea, and I was able to convince Waldock that the right is created in favour of another State, which has the power to use it or not, but the right is established. And the proof that it is established is what happens when they want to withdraw the benefit.

You know the case of the *Great Belt*,[75] which was ended by agreement? I was able to invoke the clause on third parties in this case, because Finland was not a party to the Treaty of Copenhagen which established the right of passage through the Straits. It was not a party, because at that time Finland did not exist. So it was a third-party beneficiary, and it accepted to be a third-party beneficiary in the pleadings after I called attention to that. What is interesting is that Denmark had consulted all the embassies in Copenhagen. All of them, including all the parties, agreed—except Finland (or it did not raise objections). So I claimed before the Court that there had been an agreement between the parties, and according to the Vienna Convention, the third party had to respect the condition for the exercise of the right agreed to by the parties. Unfortunately, the case was settled out of Court very cheaply.

[73] *Fisheries Jurisdiction (United Kingdom v Iceland)*, 25 July 1974, [1974] ICJ Rep 3; *Fisheries Jurisdiction (Federal Republic of Germany v Iceland)*, 25 July 1974, [1974] ICJ Rep 175.

[74] Mustafa Kamil Yasseen (Iraq, 1920–81) was a member (1960–81) and President (1966) of the UN International Law Commission. His lectures at the Hague Academy of International Law include: 'Problèmes relatives à l'application du droit étranger' (1962-II) 106 *Recueil des cours* 499; 'Principes généraux de droit international privé' (1965-III) 116 *Recueil des cours* 383; 'L'interprétation des traités d'après la convention de Vienne sur le droit des traités' (1976-III) 151 *Recueil des cours* 1.

[75] *Passage through the Great Belt (Finland v Denmark)*, 29 July 1991, [1991] ICJ Rep 12.

In a way your solution is more favourable to the making of treaties, because it makes it easier for a third party to draw benefits from the treaty. So in a way, it's less conservative. I would say that it is more progressive, more international community-oriented, less oriented to State sovereignty.

I think so. Think of treaties for freedom of navigation in rivers, canals. If you need a collateral agreement, the party interested in denying the right could say: 'Where is the collateral agreement?'

Of course, logically speaking, both your solution and the one supported by Yasseen are valid.

From the point of view of the practical effects, the other one was much worse. That was the reason the Conference failed to adopt an amendment by Castrén.[76] He wanted to go back to the collateral agreement. The Russians and India supported it. We said: 'What would happen to the treaties for freedom of navigation?' Think of the treaties which exist for the River Plate. I had had problems with Argentina for the navigation of the Paraná in the part which crosses Argentina (80 per cent). They had treaties with France and the United Kingdom for freedom of navigation. But what about third parties?

When you proposed your solution, were you thinking of the possible impact on Latin America, on these problems of freedom of navigation? Were you also somewhat influenced by national interests to some extent? You were thinking of Latin America?

To some extent. At the same time, I think that legally the correct approach has been established in private law.

Yes, but this view was also more conducive to a good solution in Latin America. Usually when you took a stand, say in the International Law Commission or as a delegate of your country, did you tend to take a sort of nationalist attitude, namely to help the national interests of your country, or were you more oriented towards world community values?

Well, a delegate of Uruguay is in a very comfortable position. Our interest is the rule of law. We are a small country with two powerful neighbours, and for us the rule of law is essential. Fortunately, we have treaties providing for the jurisdiction of the Court both with Brazil and Argentina. With Brazil we have the Pact of Bogotá; with Argentina we have the Treaty of the River Plate, which includes a compromisory clause.

So it is in your interest to stick to international law, to the rule of law. Do you think that the rule of law is more favourable to small countries? Some people argue that the present international law is still shaped by the interests of the big powers.

To a great extent, it is true. Think of the interpretation of self-defence, of pre-emptive self-defence, of what happened in Nicaragua.

[76] Erik Castrén (Finnish, 1904–85) was a member of the UN International Law Commission (1962–71).

Have there been cases during your time as a delegate or a member of the International Law Commission when you have made an effort to speak on behalf of developing countries, as a sort of advocate of small countries?

Not that I recall.

So you rather tended to favour a sort of neutral, middle-of-ground position. In any case, you were never acting on behalf of big powers.

No, of course.

But you were not explicitly advocating the interests of small countries. Now leaving aside developing countries.

I had a very short activity as a delegate. Only in 1948 and in 1950, and mostly in connection with legal matters.

And as a member of the International Law Commission?

Well, at my time in the ILC the interests of States appeared very remote. I think I had the luck of serving on the ILC when the Commission was composed mostly of scholars, who were guided by the goal of having a good draft.

We have gone a bit astray. We were talking about your contribution on an academic level. You spoke of your two books on the UN and The Hague General Course, and then in particular of your tripartite distinction. What else in your scholarly works stands out in your view? Don't you feel that your Hague lectures have had a great impact on international legal scholarship?

Yes, I noticed that, I would not say big impact, but I noticed that they are being quoted, and this surprises me.

Well, you know, when we talk among friends and we ask ourselves: 'Who are the best international lawyers from the third world' (a category which probably does not make much sense any longer), well normally the conclusion is that you are number one and then maybe a younger scholar, Abi-Saab,[77] who is also first-rate. This is a view shared by many people.

I would not place myself above Abi-Saab, who is excellent. He is younger, of course.

[77] Georges Abi-Saab (Egyptian, *b* 1933) has been Professor of International Law at the Geneva *Institut de Hautes Etudes Internationales*. He was a member of the International Criminal Tribunal for the Former Yugoslavia (1993–95), member of the WTO Appellate Body, member (since 1981) and Vice-president of the *Institut de Droit international*. Among his numerous writings, his Hague lectures stand out: 'Wars of National Liveration in the Geneva Conventions and Protocols' (1979-IV) 165 *Recueil des cours* 353; 'Cours général de droit international public' (1987-VII) 207 *Recueil des cours* 9.

We have already discussed your contribution to the International Law Commission. Can we focus now on other activities of yours which are likely to have a lasting effect on the international community?

It is very difficult to believe that in a field like international law, which is subject to great changes and modifications, one can make a lasting contribution. I think that one of the features of international law which probably attracts the interest of young specialists is the fact that it is not a finished product. It is always in the process of being developed, changed, improved. That's the great attraction, because it gives a lot of room for invention and imagination.

I think that one of the contributions that may last is what I spoke about yesterday: my involvement in the review of the Rules of Procedure of the ICJ and the establishment of the chambers composed in consideration of the wishes of the parties. As R-J Dupuy pointed out, that injects something of the spirit of arbitration into the judicial institution. It has been criticised as not being legally correct, but I think it has proved a success and is going to last.

Actually, I remember that you wrote an article on the new rules of procedure of the ICJ in the American Journal of International Law.[78]

Yes, that article was the result of the work I did with Lachs and other members of the Court in the first review, the one which was adopted in 1973 and which was maintained in the final revision, in 1978. We introduced the chambers system and also tried to resolve the problem that had arisen in the *Barcelona Traction* case,[79] where the question of jurisdiction was discussed twice before the Court, first in the preliminary stage, where the Court joined the exceptions to the merits, and then in the final stage. In the end, the final decision of the Court was based on the preliminary objections. So we tried to avoid that duplication by having all questions related to jurisdiction or admissibility decided in the initial stage, even if it would touch upon the merit (in the event that some of the objections relate to the merit).

During this process of revision of the Rules of Procedure, did you also contribute to other issues, in addition to the setting up of chambers?

Yes. The Court was not busy at that time, so I was able to devote a lot of time to studying the various proposals which had been made earlier for a revision of the Rules. So we did deal with other subjects. For instance, giving more control to the Court over the proceedings, such as avoiding repetition of arguments between the written proceedings and the oral ones. The Court now has the power to control and ask questions, and to indicate to counsel those matters which it prefers counsel to address.

[78] 'The Amendments to the Rules of Procedure of the International Court of Justice' (1973) 67 *American Journal of International Law* 1.

[79] Above n 10.

Can you think of other areas where you contributed to international law, say as president of arbitration courts or in ICSID, or when you were a judge in international tribunals?

I wrote a separate opinion in the two cases in which I was involved as judge *ad hoc*,[80] and I think that some of the views expressed in these separate opinions have had some influence on subsequent studies and commentaries concerning, for instance, the concept of national prolongation in delimitation cases, the role of equity in those cases, the role of proportionality, these kinds of subjects which have become the main source of cases for the Court, the disputes which arose as a consequence of the extension of the economic zone and the continental shelf. So I consider those separate opinions to be of some interest.

D. Jiménez de Aréchaga's disciples

Do you feel that you have been able to create a school, by training disciples?

Well, it is a fact. I would not say a school in the sense of a new approach, but it is a fact that I have set up a group of people who have been my assistants and continue teaching or are active in this field. One of them is the Ambassador in Rome, Julio César Lupinacci. He was active in the area of law of the sea. He has just published a book on the economic zone and the continental shelf.[81] Paolillo[82] was also my assistant, and he is now in Geneva. There is a young man in the International Law Commission's secretariat, Rama-Montaldo, who is very good, and the Under-Secretary for Foreign Affairs, Gamio.[83] They are former assistants, who have become professors and continue my thinking in a way. I created an institute in the Law School of Montevideo, and an association.

Do you think they have been influenced by your thinking?

I think so.

Can one say that your school has some special characteristics which distinguish it from other groups of scholars in Latin America?

Well, it would be presumptuous to say that I have a school of my own. But I can say that the present-day professors who were my assistants and who continued their careers close to me, followed the same methods and the same

[80] *Continental Shelf (Tunisia v Libyan Arab Jamahiriya)*, 24 February 1982 [1982] ICJ Rep 18 at 100; and *Continental Shelf (Libyan Arab Jamahiriya v Malta)*, Application to Intervene, 21 March 1984, [1984] ICJ Rep 3 at 55.

[81] *La plataforma continental como instituto del derecho del mar* (Santiago, Universidad de Chile, 1984).

[82] Felipe H Paolillo (Uruguayan, *b* 1931) was legal adviser to the Uruguyan Foreign Ministry and ambassador, member of the *Institut de Droit International* (from 1989). He was Judge ad hoc of the Chamber of the International Court of Justice (*El Salvador v Honduras*, request for revision, 2002–03).

[83] José María Gamio is Professor of International Law at the Catholic University of Montevideo. In 1993–95 he was Subsecretario del Ministerio de Relaciones Exteriores.

approach to international law matters, to the point that now we are in the process of publishing a five-volume treatise on international law,[84] written by myself, by my former pupil Heber Arbouet, who is now a full professor, by Puceiro[85] and other young professors who wrote specific chapters; for instance, a chapter on transboundary ecological damage has been written by another of my former assistants, Mrs Lujan Flores,[86] who is now presiding over the VIth Committee of the General Assembly. Now there are four volumes already out, volumes 1, 3, 4 and 5. We are in the preparatory stage for volume 2 concerning general principles. But the plan has been discussed by us, and established by me and Arbouet. I am the director of the whole project. In that respect I could say there is a school, but not in the sense that I have invented new international law.

No, but I understand that all of them take the same approach to international law.

A similar approach.

So they are not strictly positivist, but they try to understand international law within its general context.

Yes, as I told you yesterday, the general approach is to try to reconcile the positivist approach with the natural law approach, on the assumption that positive law is the only law that exists today, but that law needs to be corrected, reformed under the dictates of justice.

Have you had a chance or the opportunity to rely on Latin American practice as far as the State practice is concerned, or did you have to rely only on, say, the American Digest *or the* British Yearbook of International Law, *that is European or North American practice?*

Well there is a communication problem between Latin American countries in that respect. We try to get hold as much as possible of experiences and publications in other Latin American countries, but there is a weakness in that respect, to the point that now there is a movement intended to publish under the auspices of the OAS a Latin American Yearbook on International Law. It is still in the preparatory stage, but we are working on that with Orrego Vicuña[87] and some other Latin Americans.

[84] Jiménez de Aréchaga *et al*, *Curso de derecho internacional público* (Montevideo, Fundación de Cultura Universitaria, 1979).

[85] Elias Roberto Puceiro Ripoll (*b* 1939) is Professor of International Law at the University of Montevideo.

[86] María del Lujan Flores has been Permanent Representative of Uruguay to the OAS since July 2006. She was President of the Permanent Council of the OAS in 2007. Previously, she was a Professor of International Public Law at the University of Uruguay. She also was legal adviser to many government departments, including the Uruguay Ministry of Foreign Affairs.

[87] Francisco Orrego Vicuña (Chilean, *b* 1942) is Professor of Public International Law at the University of Chile. He was Member of the Advisory Committee on Foreign Policy, Chilean Ministry of Foreign

This will come out in English, or Spanish?

In Spanish.

It will be a Latin American Yearbook and will also include a part on State practice?

We expect to include State practice, yes.

Because there is a big gap in Latin American scholarly activities; you don't have any digest or repertoire, except Brazil where there is the one by Cançado Trindade.[88]

That's very useful, but there are no similar publications in our Latin American countries.

Do your pupils also follow your line of thought, or do they maybe enhance one of the two elements, either positive law or natural law?

Of course, they write independently. Although I am the director of that project, I do not try to control their approaches. But there are approaches similar to mine that try to reconcile the positivist approach with the natural law approach.

E. Ad hoc judges

What is your feeling about this strange figure or institution of ad hoc judges? Is it true that the ad hoc judge plays a minor role because everybody knows that he, in principle, should side with the country that has appointed him?

Although the usefulness of the office has been discussed, the judge ad hoc is imperative as a consequence of the fact that the big powers, normally represented in the Court, will not accept that the judge of their nationality should step down when these countries are involved in a case. So it was necessary to establish the office of judge ad hoc as a compromise. Also, I think that it's always a guarantee for a State that its point of view, its legal approach in the case, is being taken into account at the deliberation stage. My experience as a judge ad hoc was to develop very good relations with the judge ad hoc appointed by the other party; in general, the 'normal' judges attribute some importance to this approach between ad hoc judges, not as a sort of compromise but as a sort of way of trying to find a solution which would be acceptable to both parties in accordance with international law. In the cases in

Affairs (1978–82; 1998–); Ambassador to the United Kingdom in 1983–85. He has taken part in and often presided over many arbitral courts. Since 1991 he has been a member of the *Institut de Droit international*, of which he was President in 2005–07.

[88] Antônio Cançado Trindade (Brazilian, *b* 1947), since 1978 has been Professor of International Relations and International Law at the University of Brasilia and legal adviser to the Brazilian Ministry of Foreign Affairs. Member (1995–2008) and President (1999–2004) of the Inter-American Court of Human Rights, since 2009 he has been sitting as a judge in the ICJ.

which I have been involved, I had as counterparts two excellent international lawyers. One was Evensen,[89] who was appointed by Tunisia and became a judge afterwards, the other was Valticos,[90] who was appointed by Malta, and you know I have excellent relations with him. My experience as a judge ad hoc is that this is a useful institution.

Do you see it mainly as a protection for small powers vis-à-vis great powers, ie the permanent members of the Security Council?

It is a protection against permanent members having judges of their own nationality in the Court, which is not a requirement of the Charter but is an established practice.

It's striking to me that you suggested that an ad hoc judge should try to get on well with the other ad hoc judge. Is this for the purpose of together devising views or solutions then to be offered to the plenary Court?

Well, not necessarily, because in the *Tunisia/Libya* case,[91] for instance, Judge Evensen dissented, so we could not reach an agreement. The problem in that case was that Evensen was for equidistance, but none of the parties had asked for equidistance. And that created a problem for the Court, which had to invent equidistance without having the support of pleadings from the parties on the subject. In the other case, in *Malta*,[92] both Valticos and myself joined in the decision; we only put forward some expressions of whether we would have preferred something else. And we were able to join in the decision.

Was this thanks to this good rapport with Valticos, namely your exchange of views?

Yes, I think it was very useful.

I had the feeling that normally the judges ad hoc tend in a way to distance themselves from the other party and to take a stand in favour of 'their' country.

It was not my experience. I can tell you this. After that experience with Valticos as ad hoc judge, I recommended twice as counsel that he be asked to sit as a judge ad hoc in another case in which I was involved, for Bahrain and Salvador. I have a very high regard for him and his approach to the office of

89 Jens Ingebret Evensen (Norwegian, 1917–2004). In 1961–73 he led the Legal Department of the Foreign Ministry. In 1972–73 he was Norwegian Minister of Trade and Shipping. In 1979–84 he was a member of the UN International Law Commission; in 1985 he joined the ICJ until 1994.

90 Nicolas Valticos (Greek, 1918–2003) was a prominent figure in the International Labour Organisation, being Assistant Director-General and Chief of the Standards Department. He was a member and Secretary-General (1981–91) of the *Institut de Droit international* and President of the Curatorium of The Hague Academy of International Law. He sat as a judge at the European Court of Human Rights (1986–98).

91 Above n 80.

92 *Continental Shelf (Libyan Arab Jamahiriya v Malta)*, 3 June 1985, [1985] ICJ Rep 13.

judge ad hoc, which is not that of an advocate of 'his' country; he acts above all as a judge.

Recently, a very important former member of the ICJ told me: 'When I was a member of the ICJ, I pitied the ad hoc judge because, of course, everybody knew that he would put forward views on behalf of "his" country.' You feel, on the contrary, that an ad hoc judge can be unbiased.

I think so, and I can give you an example. The judge ad hoc appointed by Morocco in the *Western Sahara* case[93] (a judge from the Ivory Coast, his name was Boni) voted against the position which had been taken by the country who nominated him.

I think there is also the case of Mme Bastid.

I don't know if she sat in the Salle de Justice, but she sat in the deliberations as judge ad hoc for Tunisia in the *Interpretation* case[94] and she voted against Tunisia.

I think she voted against Tunisia.

Yes, she did.

So it's the second case of an ad hoc judge who votes against their country.

The famous case of a 'normal' judge who voted against [his country] was McNair in the *Anglo-Iranian Oil Company* case.[95] On the issue of jurisdiction, he voted against the UK. Of course he was not re-elected.

And there was a case when Anzilotti voted against Italy. And he even wrote a dissenting opinion against Italy; but again, he was an old man, independent of Fascism, and he knew he would not be re-elected.

Allow me this commentary which is not intended to be pejorative. Clive Parry, the English international lawyer who contributed to Sørensen's *Manual of International Law*,[96] once told me that as a bachelor he was lonely; he had a pet cat and he gave it the name Anzilotti.

[93] Above n 65.

[94] *Application for Revision and Interpretation of the Judgment of 24 February 1982 in the Case Concerning the Continental Shelf (Tunisia v Libyan Arab Jamahiriya)*, [1985] ICJ Rep 192, 10 December 1985.

[95] *(United Kingdom v Iran)*, 22 July 1952, [1952] ICJ Rep 93.

[96] Sørensen, above n 31.

IV. Thoughts About the International Community

A. Merits of its present configuration

The next question is about your views of the international community. How do you perceive the current trends emerging in the international community? In particular, what are the positive and meritorious values of traditional international law? What, in your view, should be kept in the present international community and what should be changed? It's a very big question. What do you think, in particular, of the recent 'revival' of the Security Council?

The initial reaction to Iraq's invasion of Kuwait led to the revival—the resurrection—of Chapter VII of the Charter and the application of sanctions against aggressors. In that respect we, especially in Latin America, were satisfied, especially as small countries interested in the maintenance of the rule of law and the fight against aggression. There was great support for the UN action, even if it involved the use of force; the action was authorised by the Security Council in the presence of a flagrant aggression, so there was a trend emerging in the international community which was satisfactory.

I think that interpretations of what happened in Kuwait were advanced that tried to say that it was self-defence. This was said by [Oscar] Schachter, for instance, who argued that it was an Article 51 action. I think that's very dangerous, because if you say that this action was authorised by the Security Council then you have the control of the Charter. If instead you try to base it on collective self-defence then you run the risk of a wide interpretation of self-defence such as the one adopted by the United States. Even in case of an attempt to attack a former President, the reaction (bombing a country) is an act of self-defence. There are no more limits, it becomes a unilateral decision not controlled by the UN organs.

I think there is a further great danger in the *Lockerbie* case. I think Libya, whatever its actions have been, is in the right, because even though it is not prepared to extradite the suspects, it is willing and prepared to try them. The obligation under the Montreal Convention is to extradite or try. I don't know how the Court is going to come out in this case,[97] but I think the refusal of

[97] By an Order of 14 April 1992 the ICJ had declined to order the interim measures requested by Libya. Subsequently, in the case on *Questions of Interpretation and Application of the 1971 Montreal Convention Arising from the Aerial Incident at Lockerbie (Libyan Arab Jamahiriya v United Kingdom and Libyan Arab Jamahiriya v United States of America)*, judgments of 27 February 1998, the Court found that it had jurisdiction to deal with the merits of the case brought by Libya against the UK and the US concerning the aerial incident at Lockerbie (see [1998] ICJ Rep 9 and [1998] ICJ Rep 115). It also found that the Libyan claims were admissible. This judgment had no follow-up because Libya took responsibility for the bombing (on 15 August 2003, Libya's ambassador to the UN submitted a letter to the UN Security Council formally accepting 'responsibility for the actions of its officials' in relation to the Lockerbie bombing), and in addition accepted both to pay compensation to the victims of the bombing and to transfer the two Libyans accused of the act to The Netherlands, to face trial before a Scottish Court there. On 3 May 2000, the trial of the two Libyans, Abdelbaset Ali Mohmed Al Megrahi and Lamin

the preliminary measures and the submissive position taken by the Court vis-à-vis the Security Council gives rise to concern. I think the article by Graefrath[98] is excellent. And I think there is an answer in the Charter. It is a difficult point, but I think it was Bustamante who said that Article 25 of the Charter renders actions by the Security Council binding on all States, provided they have been taken in accordance with the Charter.[99] Article 25 is a bit ambiguous but it says 'in accordance with the Charter'. So, in order to be binding [the actions of the Security Council] have to be in accordance with the Charter. But who is to judge that? It is the Court. The Court already judged that. In the *Namibia* case,[100] we said:

> We have to pronounce on the validity of Security Council resolutions; we find that the General Assembly resolution, which is the basis, is in accordance with the Charter. We find therefore that the Security Council resolutions are in accordance with the Charter.

Now if you assume that power to say 'They are in accordance', you have also the power to say 'They are not in accordance'. The power to condemn implies the power to acquit, and vice versa.

But if the Court states that the action taken by the Security Council is not in accordance with the Charter, then what happens? It could be dangerous.

Of course it would be dangerous. It happened in Nicaragua. After all, what is the danger? The danger is that the Security Council becomes an instrument for the implementation of American power. The veto has had the function of counteracting the attempts of a State to exceed its powers. The Americans may discover that through the Security Council, they can do anything and protect it under the banner of the UN.

Khalifah Fhimah, began. Al Megrahi was convicted of murder on 31 January 2001 and was sentenced to life imprisonment in Scotland. His co-accused, Fhimah, was found not guilty. The defendant appealed the conviction, but the Appeals Court rejected his appeal. In 2009 Mr Al Megrahi was released on compassionate grounds and returned to Libya.

[98] B Graefrath, 'Leave to the Court what Belongs to the Court: The Libyan Case' (1993) 4 *European Journal of International Law* 184.

[99] Reference is made here to the Dissenting Opinion appended by Judge Bustamante y Rivero to the ICJ Advisory Opinion of 20 July 1962 on *Certain Expenses of the United Nations (Article 17, Paragraph 2 of the Charter)*. Judge Bustamente stated that 'the real reason for the obedience of States Members to the authorities of the Organization is the conformity of the mandates of its competent organs with the text of the Charter. This principle of the conditional link between the duty to accept institutional decisions and the conformity of those decisions with the Charter is enshrined in Article 25, which, although referring explicitly to the Security Council, in my opinion lays down a fundamental basic rule which is generally applicable to the whole system of the Charter. Article 2, paragraph 2, confirms this interpretation.' ([1962] ICJ Rep 151, at 304)

[100] Above n 25.

In a way, the ICJ could act as a sort of countervailing factor to the excessive power of the Security Council.

What has to be exercised is control over the constitutionality of the actions of the Security Council. Of course it has to be exercised in a very wise and limited form. For instance, I think the Court will have a chance to do so in the *Lockerbie* case, to say: 'We are refusing interim measures because the Security Council has the primary responsibility for the maintenance of peace. The Security Council having taken action, we cannot.' But now that we are in the merit stage, I find that Libya's position is justified. And I found that Nicaragua's position was justified. Of course, I don't think that the UK and the US will apply sanctions against Libya if it conforms to a pronouncement by the Court.

It would be difficult if the Security Council and the ICJ were to head towards a clash, and the Court were to say that what was decided by the Security Council was not in accordance with the Charter.

It would not need to say that in so many words. It could say instead: 'Libya's position is justified under the Montreal Convention, to which the two States are parties, and you do not need to challenge the Security Council.' There are certain limits, because otherwise the US could do anything through the Security Council by taking advantage of Article 25.

On the other hand, what the Americans and British claim is that the trial in Libya would not be a fair trial.

But I think Libya announced at some point that it was prepared to send them before an international court.

Not international, to Switzerland, or to Egypt or to a Nordic country. But the British and the Americans don't accept this.

There's clearly a pre-judgment in the position taken by the US. They consider these people as more than suspect, so there's no fair procedure.

Let's go back to the question. We were discussing the issue of what, in your view, is to be kept in the present international system and what should be changed. You said Chapter VII of the UN Charter is good, as a safeguard for small countries.

Chapter VII is good as a safeguard for small countries and control of aggression.

On the other hand you have Article 51, which is not for small countries but could be used for small countries.

I think that Henkin's demonstration that Article 51 must be interpreted as applying after an armed attack occurs, is conclusive.[101] Pre-emptive

[101] L Henkin, 'The Reports of the Death of Article 2(4) are Greatly Exaggerated' (1971) 65 *American Journal of International Law* 544.

self-defence is an abuse of the Charter. This theory that there was a right to use of force in self-defence under the international law which existed prior to the Charter (think of Waldock or Bowett[102]) is clearly wrong, because before the Kellogg-Briand Pact, there was no control on the use of force. So if you have no control on the use of force, it means the concept of self-defence has not arisen yet.

What else would you keep in the present international community?

Well, Chapter VII and particularly Article 51 should be respected. They have not been respected up till now, to a certain extent. But the action of the UN under the conventions of human rights is an essential aspect. Self-determination has been exhausted in this application to end the colonial situation.

Do you think there is still some role for self-determination in the present international community?

Now that colonialism is over, self-determination has taken on dangerous aspects in the sense that it can destroy the unity of existing States. Think of the Basques in Spain.

In my view the current legal regulation of self-determination does not go so far as to also give a right of secession to minorities. Therefore, in my view, the Basques have no rights, the Kurds have no rights under international law. They have a political claim, but not a right. Do you think that self-determination could be disruptive of the present legal system?

The legal content of self-determination is not disruptive because, as you say, it doesn't extend the right to minorities.

I think the concept of self-determination ought to be maintained, but when applied to situations which don't have a history of colonialism, it should be implemented by paying regard to the traditional international law pertaining to the position of minorities within a State. It should not to be a disruptive factor for existing States, as is happening with the Basques in Spain, the Québec minority in Canada, or in Yugoslavia, where self-determination is invoked by everybody and where they really have a terrible conflict right now.

[102] Sir Derek Bowett (1927–2009) spent two years in the UN Codification Division in New York, and in 1960 he went to Cambridge as a University Lecturer, becoming a fellow of Queens' College. In 1966–68 Bowett was in Beirut as Legal Adviser to the United Nations Relief and Works Agency for Palestinian Refugees (UNRWA). When Sir Arthur Armitage left for Manchester in 1970, Bowett was elected to succeed him as President of Queens' College. In 1980 he was elected to the Whewell Chair. He held this Chair until taking early retirement in 1991. He served a term on the UN International Law Commission from 1992–96. Bowett gained a great reputation not only as a distinguished academic, but also as a forceful advocate. He appeared many times before international tribunals, in particular before the ICJ. As has been rightly written, he had the ability to simplify without distorting, and to reduce cases to carefully chosen essentials. His major work is *Self-Defence in International Law* (Manchester, Manchester University Press, 1958).

Do you think that the notion of State sovereignty should be, in a way, adjusted to new developments in international law?

Yes, it should be adjusted according to the Charter: sovereignty under international law and limited by international law—only international law. In other words, the correct interpretation of equal sovereignty of States implies that they are all equal legally; and above the sovereignty of each State there is international law, which establishes this equilibrium or this equality under the law.

And are there other legal institutions which, in your view, are designed to protect small powers against the excessive use of force or power by big States?

The possibility of having access to the International Court is important. As I told you yesterday, our country is very keen on that. For instance, we are bound to have problems with Brazil, because of Brazil's important territorial expansion due to its population increase. Fortunately for us, Brazil has ratified the Bogotá Pact, which the Court has already declared establishes its jurisdiction as binding. But the Bogotá Pact binds only 10 Latin American countries, including Mexico, Brazil, Uruguay, but not Argentina, nor Colombia or Venezuela (you know Colombia has a claim against Venezuela concerning the maritime delimitation in the Gulf).

Your point is that it is very important for States to have access to the Court.

It is important to have the right to institute proceedings unilaterally against another party.

But that means that other small countries or big countries should have accepted the compulsory jurisdiction of the court.

Or they may have ratified a treaty like the Pact of Bogotá or a compromissory clause. I don't like the idea of the optional clause so much, because that clause has become too flexible (it allows reservations, allows withdrawals), while a pact, like the Pact of Bogotá or the Act of Geneva, establishes the jurisdiction without reservations, unless you make a reservation to the treaty. And also it does not provide for unilateral withdrawal at any moment: you have to give notice, and you are released only after three years. So it's a different regime, and the Court has accepted this distinction. As you may remember, the *Nicaragua v Honduras* decision[103] said there are two ways of seizing the Court, but I think this possibility (which is not the optional clause), is Article XXXI, para 1 of the Pact of Bogotá, a treaty which establishes the jurisdiction of the Court 'as compulsory *ipso facto*' and 'in relation to any other American State'.

103 *Border and Transborder Activities (Nicaragua v Honduras)*, Jurisdiction and Admissibility, 20 December 1988, [1988] ICJ Rep 69.

Your point seems to be that it is better to have a system like the one of Bogotá. Let me sum up: you would keep some parts of the Charter system concerning the use of force and human rights; you would protect the right to self-determination, but wouldn't interpret that as including the right of minorities to secede; and then this issue of access to the ICJ. What about the Law of the Sea, do you think that the present regulation is fair?

I think so. But you know what is happening? This claim of 200 miles which seemed so exaggerated in the beginning, but which was eventually imposed by consensus, may have become insufficient in certain parts of the world. What is happening is that a great number of vessels are coming to fish right outside the 200-mile zone of countries other than their own, and in a way which depletes, diminishes the resources within the 200 miles of the coastal State. The provision in the Law of the Sea Convention is very weak in this respect; it only gives the border States the right to call for coordination with the fishing powers whose ships fish outside the 200 miles. So there is great dissatisfaction in Latin America about what is happening beyond their 200-mile [zones], namely the concentration of these fishing fleets from Poland, Korea, China, from the whole of the Soviet Union and Japan too.

And what sort of system would you envisage?

Well, you can't extend the 200 miles, that is for sure. What is needed is an obligation to negotiate, which does not exist now, and to impose restrictions based on the need to maintain the fishing resources. I think that's needed. Up to now there is [only] a very weak provision, Article 66 of the Law of the Sea Convention, which provides for consultations and coordination of activities. There must be an obligation to negotiate and to apply the principles concerning shared resources.

What do you think of the whole machinery which has been envisaged in the Law of the Sea Convention?

Well, of course, that part is the part which is not binding as customary law. It creates new organs and new provisions. Although, after the Law of the Sea Convention, and even after the General Assembly Resolutions declaring the resources of the seabed 'common heritage of mankind',[104] I think that there is now a basic international law rule forbidding any individual State from exploiting common resources without the agreement of the international community. I believe that the mechanism which has been established is too complicated and it is difficult to implement. The problem now is that the countries which have ratified the Convention do not have the means to set

[104] A/RES/2340 (XXII) 18 December 1967; A/RES/2467 (XXIII) 21 December 1968; A/RES/2574 (XXIV) 15 December 1969; A/RES/2749 (XXV) 17 December 1970.

up all those organs such as the Law of the Sea Tribunal, the Commission on delimitation between the economic zone and the seabed and the 'Area'. This part has to be revised.

Is this the only area where you think that some revision is needed?

Well, I mentioned also the problem which has arisen for many coastal States who have problems with fisheries immediately outside their 200-mile [zones]. That part will perhaps need to be completed by establishing some stronger duties [on] distant water fishing States concerning the exploitation of resources immediately neighbouring the 200-mile zones.

What about the whole body of international law on treaty-making, and customary law? Do you think this is a part which can be kept as such?

I think the Vienna Convention on the Law of Treaties and the other convention concerning relations between States and international organisations[105] are satisfactory. I would not touch them. And it is very difficult for customary law to change treaties; it is a spontaneous process, as Ago said.

There is another area, ie the few principles or rules on economic relations, in particular economic development. I understand that the new international economic order was a flop. It has been forgotten. Ten years ago it was 'à la mode'*, but now it has been completely forgotten.*

I think that still there are parts of the Charter on Economic Rights and Duties[106] which are useful, if you consider the changes which have been experienced in that field. When I first began to study international law, one of the big issues was the nationalisation of the agrarian industry in Mexico. And of course it was assumed by everybody that that had been an unlawful act, and that therefore compensation was to be 'just, fair and prompt compensation', according to the standards established by the Permanent Court. Today, nobody questions the permanent sovereignty over natural resources, which gives a country the right to nationalise natural resources or to exploit them the way it wants.

Do you know who first proposed these resolutions, this concept of natural sovereignty over natural resources? It was my country. In 1952. Once I had a talk with Bedjaoui,[107] and I explained to him: 'It's very interesting. It came out as a result of the nationalisation of the tin industry in Bolivia.' I was then in

[105] Reference is made here to the 1986 Vienna Convention on the Law of Treaties between States and International Organisations or between International Organisations of 21 March 1986 (reproduced in (1986) 25 *International Legal Materials* 543).

[106] A/Res/3281(XXIX) 12 December 1974

[107] Mohammed Bedjaoui (Algerian, *b* 1928) has been Minister of Justice then of Foreign Affairs of Algeria, and member (1982–2001) and President (1994–97) of the ICJ.

the Secretariat-General of the Council of Government. We appointed a senator from the opposition to complete the delegation, his name was Cusano. He was appointed in order to balance the delegation. He went to New York, he sat in the economic committee of the General Assembly. He was pro-Bolivia, like his party, which was always in favour of Bolivia having access to the sea, etc. Without instructions, without consulting his government, he presented a resolution on natural resources, proclaiming sovereignty over natural resources. There was a great opposition by the United States, but India got the idea.

First there was a resolution by Uruguay which was not adopted, and gave rise to discussion, debate. Then there was a joint resolution, by Uruguay and India, and there was a further resolution of the General Assembly in 1952. It's interesting how it came out.

So this man was acting on his own.

Because of sympathy with Bolivia. Nobody realised that it was considered unlawful to nationalise.

Actually, people claimed it was regarded as unlawful if there was no compensation.

Yes, that's true. But if you recall the debates with Mexico, not only compensation but 'just, prompt and fair compensation' was required under Cordell Hull's formula. Otherwise it was unlawful. Under the *Chorzow Factory* case,[108] you had to 'restore' the previous situation (*restitutio in pristinum*) because it was forbidden to nationalise.

Are you happy with the present legal regulation of international economic relations, with particular regard to poor countries?

The negative position of earlier times (to the effect that international investments, capital investments, are wrong, are bad for developing countries) is being overcome now. People realise that to have jobs and to develop you need investment, and you need to provide a guarantee for investment. For instance, traditionally in Latin America it was bad to have treaties for the guarantee of investment. It was considered pro-imperialist. Also, from the legal point of view, it was felt that to have an arbitration of the kind provided by the World Bank would be detrimental to national courts. Now this sort of nationalistic feeling is changing. I think you will find that several Latin American countries have ratified the ICSID text.

I can tell you what has happened in our country, which used to be dead set against arbitration on guarantees for investment as being detrimental to the

[108] *Case concerning the Factory at Chorzów (Germany v Poland)*, 18 September 1928, Publications of the Permanent Court of International Justice, Series A–No 17.

authority of the local courts. Now we have treaties of guarantee with certain European countries, with France and Germany, in which a system has been established. If a dispute arises concerning investment, the matter has to go to a national appeal court in Uruguay; but if in 60 days it is not decided then it becomes open for arbitration. Or an appeal can be lodged with an international arbitral court.

What is the law to be applied by the Uruguayan court of appeal?

The law is provided in the investment contract. The treaty gives the general framework. This system has not been accepted by the United States. They have refused to sign a treaty along the same lines. The European countries have accepted.

Why did the Americans refuse?

Because they want to go immediately to arbitration; they don't want to go to national courts. They are probably concerned that if they accept this system, it would complicate their negotiations with other countries.

So, you think that this system you follow in Uruguay takes care of the interests of both categories of States, the investing and the developing countries, in a balanced way?

I think so.

Do you know of the actual implementation of these treaties?

No, not yet. Because the guarantees are provided, they operate, have a preventive effect. The fact that you can go to this court, and if you fail you can go to an international organ, constitutes a guarantee which avoids discretionary or arbitrary action.

Are these only between Uruguay and European countries, or is it a widespread practice in Latin America?

I would not say that it is widespread.

In sum: what, in the existing international law, should be kept in your view? If I understand you correctly, this idea of going before international arbitration is crucial.

Yes, but provided there has been a prior exhaustion of local remedies. That's why this mechanism [regarding disputes on investment] provides for a local remedy and a time limit.

I wonder whether in your view, in the present legal system, there are elements which can, in a way, be instrumental to overcoming the problems of economic development.

I think that, for instance, the GATT negotiations, which end in a month's time, have shown that the position of developing countries, especially of those depending on exports of agricultural goods and natural resources, has become worse, because there are no guarantees of protection, particularly in the European Community which is protectionist for its own products. So the great preoccupation in governmental circles in Latin America concerns these GATT negotiations, what is called the Uruguay Round. I think that is the biggest problem we confront. The economic system is not organised in a way that protects the interests of developing countries. There is therefore large room for improvement in that respect. At present the proceedings of GATT do not provide guarantees.

Also UNCTAD, I understand, has, in a way, been changed completely.

UNCTAD is no longer so influential. I have not followed this matter closely. I agree with you that the new economic order has been a flop.

B. Areas of international law which need change and improvement

This is related, in a way, to those areas of international relations which in your view can be maintained. Now we can move on to a new part, about the areas where in your view there is a need for improvement, a change in international law. Is the area of the use of force in need of improvement?

The problem is that any revision of the Charter would create enormous difficulties. One cannot be certain that, if a reform of the Charter is attempted, we will end with a better instrument than the one existing now. There will be great difficulty. That is why it is said that attempting to reform the Charter is to open a Pandora's Box. This was said with respect to recent attempts by Germany and Japan to become permanent or quasi-permanent members of the Security Council. It is very difficult, in realistic terms, to embark on a revision of the provisions of the Charter. Of course, it would be better to have resolutions of the General Assembly interpreting the terms of the Charter; like, for instance, Resolution 2625 (XX), which has been given a prominent position by the International Court in the *Nicaragua* case,[109] stating that it represents the law of the Charter, which has also become customary law. That judgment, I think, is a very important judgment of the Court, defining self-defence and in particular collective self-defence (which has to be requested by the State benefiting from it and has to be reported to the Security Council).

[109] *Military and Paramilitary Activities (Nicaragua v United States)*, 27 June 1986, [1986] ICJ Rep 14 at 101, § 191.

Between these resolutions and the judicial interpretation of the resolutions by the Court, the system has been reinforced, and I think it is possible to find, for instance, a definition of humanitarian intervention in terms which provide guarantees that there are no attempts to violate this territorial right and the territory of the other States; or the definition of the ban laid down in Article 2(4), because this provision was drafted in such a way that it gives rise to the imperialistic interpretations advocated by Waldock and Bowett, according to whom, if you use force against a State and do not intend to occupy a territory permanently, you are not violating Article 2(4).

Because you are not endangering the territorial integrity or the political independence of the State.

That was the position taken by the United Kingdom in the *Corfu Channel* case[110] with relation to 'Operation Retail', and there the Court gave a complete answer: 'This is a violation, an act of intervention not justified by international law.'

In your view, the only way of revising the present system is via General Assembly resolutions. But do you think it is feasible, because the General Assembly is a body consisting of 184 States?

Well, it is possible following the same procedure that was followed for Resolution 2625. You set up a special committee with a limited membership, giving it several years to negotiate, and then a resolution can be adopted by consensus.

What about the International Law Commission?

The International Law Commission has embarked on very precise legal subjects such as offences against peace and humanity, the question of State responsibility, control of trans-boundary harm. I don't think the International Law Commission is embarking on that type of work now.

Do you then feel that the International Law Commission would not be the appropriate body for drafting a new sort of Declaration on Friendly Relations?

I don't think so, because the political element would be very important there. For instance, if you want to define the right of humanitarian intervention as a limit to Article 2(4), if you want to establish strict enough conditions for that to occur, it has to be drafted by a committee with political representation. States should be represented there, as they were for Resolution 2625.

[110] *United Kingdom v Albania*, 9 April 1949, [1949] ICJ Rep 4.

Actually, there are three ways. One is the amendment of the UN Charter, and you are right that this is a blind alley, because in a way it is a Pandora's Box. Then there is the setting up of a special committee such as the one on the Declaration on Friendly Relations. The third way could be a customary process of revision. But it is very dangerous, because customary law (in this area of use of force) is made primarily by the big powers.

Yes, but take for instance the judgment of the Court in the *Nicaragua* case.[111] They said that even if there have been infringements of a principle, the law still remains. And the fact that a State tries to justify its actions constitutes a demonstration of the existence of the rule forbidding the use of force. Of course, you can have exceptions. If I may insert a story here: once I discussed the right of intervention by the United States with an American who had been a merchant ship captain. He told me: 'I have studied international law in the Merchant Maritime School and I know that intervention is forbidden, except if it is carried out by the marines; then it is justified.'

Let us move on to other areas, say relations between North and South. Do you think that some sort of new regulation could be introduced in this area?

It would be very convenient to introduce new regulations in this area, but the recent experience we have had concerning the trade relations between North and South and between developing countries and the European Community, gives us little hope that an improvement can be achieved in trade relations between States. It seems that the protectionist ideas are gaining ground. That will cause very bad consequences for all countries, not only those in the South but also in the North, because that could lead to a trade war in a couple of years.

If somebody wished to introduce new regulations, do you think it should be done via a treaty or by General Assembly resolutions?

It would be preferable, I think, to try to work that out through General Assembly resolutions, because that would give the countries representing the South more forceful representation. I mean, not only General Assembly resolutions, but also committees like the one in the Law of the Sea Conference.

We had the bad experience of the resolutions on the new international economic order, which do not bode well for any future action in this area, because the two famous resolutions on the new international economic order ended up in failure.

I agree with you. The idea of the new economic order was a complete failure. On the other hand, some of the features of the Charter of Economic Rights and Duties of States are worth preserving.

[111] Above n 109.

Are you thinking in particular of some provisions of the Charter?

Yes. I think the Charter could be analysed from the perspective of sources of international law in order to find some provisions which are declaratory of international law, other provisions which crystallise norms, others which are clearly *de lege ferenda* and may in due course generate rights and duties of States. I don't think you can dismiss the new economic order entirely.

Do you think that some improvements should be introduced in the area of human rights as well?

I think that progress has been made in that field recently, among the American States, with the ratification of the San José de Costa Rica Convention on Human Rights.[112] The Commission and the Court have considerably improved the situation of human rights in Latin America. Of course we have the problem of the United States' failure to ratify, because it has taken the position that the rights and duties included in the Convention are not self-executing; they have to be implemented by national laws. Of course, that's contrary to the jurisprudence established by the Court of Human Rights in San José in Costa Rica, which has concluded that provisions granting rights, except when they explicitly require to be completed by law, are all self-executing. So the United States wants to place itself in a privileged position, to become a party but not be obliged to apply it within its territory.

Leaving aside this Convention, do you think that the UN Covenants are sufficient as a means of protecting human rights, or is it necessary to introduce improvements to the implementation of human rights?

I think that, at least in the Inter-American field, it is difficult to improve on a Court and Commission. The Commission has great authority, it has even referred to the Court violations by a country like Uruguay, which has accepted the Convention with some restrictions. The Commission has referred to the Court a law approved and confirmed by plebiscite in our country, providing for what is called 'Ley de caducidad', which establishes an amnesty for both those who violate human rights as criminals and also those in the military who participated in the violations.

The terrorists and the military.

Both of them. An amnesty law was adopted; it was criticised by the extreme left, but approved by plebiscite. Yet the Inter-American Commission of Human Rights has denounced Uruguay and also Chile for that amnesty law. So the mechanism of control is operating and in order. The problem which

112 Reference is made here to the *American Convention on Human Rights*, OAS Treaty Series No 36, 1144 UNTS 123, entered into force on 18 July 1978, reprinted in *Basic Documents Pertaining to Human Rights in the Inter-American System*, OEA/Ser.L.V/II.82 doc. 6 rev. 1 at 25 (1992).

I find in other parts of Latin America is the disappearances, which are very difficult to handle or correct because they have a permanent consequence. Compensation is not enough.

You had a wonderful chapter in your Hague lectures on the general principles of international law. You deal mostly with the seven principles enshrined in the Declaration of Friendly Relations. Do you think that those principles are sufficient as guidelines for future action, or do you think again that some revision should be introduced?

The principles themselves are ok. One of them is about the use of force and the limits of self-defence as an exception to the use of force. The principles are clear, but their interpretation by the big powers, especially when it comes to the use of force and self-defence, pre-emptive self-defence, [is] subject to criticism. I think I've already told you that in the field covered by Article 2(4), ie the provision on the use of force, one interpretation allows the use of force provided you do not intend to remain permanently in the territory or attack the political integrity of other States. I think the Court gave the right interpretation to this principle in the *Nicaragua* case,[113] and also in the *Corfu Channel* case.[114] But of course these ideas have to be more generally accepted, especially in the legal literature on international law, which still insists on retaining some use of force by the big powers.

Also on the interpretation of self-defence, individual or collective self-defence, which the Charter authorises only as a response to an armed attack. This rule is not widely accepted. We have seen recent examples of the loose interpretation of this rule which detracts from the effect of Article 2(4) of the Charter. Also, to interpret the recent action of the Security Council as a case of self-defence, as Schachter does,[115] for instance, is again to open the door to unilateral interpretations by dominating States.

Don't you think that the ICJ, in this area of defining principles, of specifying principles, could probably step in and exercise an important role?

I agree with you. I think it is the role of the Court, and I think the Court has to a great extent fulfilled that role in the *Nicaragua* case,[116] where it interpreted the provision on the use of force and the limits of collective self-defence in a progressive and solid way, by requiring that the State attacked request it in order for collective self-defence to be exercised, by interpreting the use of force as a restriction on the freedom of States; also in the *Corfu Channel* case,[117] by limiting the right of unilateral intervention. You remember 'Operation Retail', in which the UK carried out the mine-sweeping operation. The Court

[113] Above n 109.
[114] Above n 110.
[115] See above, section IV.A.
[116] Above n 109.
[117] Above n 110.

condemned this, saying that it was an intervention entailing the use of force. I think there is still room not only for judgments of the Court in particular cases, but also for the General Assembly in specific cases. For instance, there is much discussion now about the limits of humanitarian intervention. That could be a field where the General Assembly could set up limits and restrictions: when to allow, when to condemn unilateral or multilateral humanitarian intervention.

You are right. This is a new area where probably some sort of intervention by the international community is needed. In my view, humanitarian intervention, so far, is prohibited.

It is not allowed. It has a legal status which is not very defined. For instance, the typical humanitarian intervention which everybody found justified was the Entebbe operation.[118] It was lawful. To a certain extent, if Uganda had taken measures to repress terrorists, it would not have left that possibility open to Israel.

I see that you regard this operation as an instance of humanitarian intervention. One could also probably think of that operation as an instance of protection of nationals abroad, because actually the Israelis went there mainly to protect the Israeli citizens. Most of the hostages had Israeli nationality. Do you think the General Assembly is well equipped to pass a resolution on humanitarian intervention? The General Assembly is a political body, and you can have a lot of loopholes. The International Law Commission could embark upon such a task instead of dealing with diplomatic bags or similar problems.

Yes, it would be possible, but I think there is a political element there. Latin American countries condemn the idea of 'protection of nationals abroad' because it has been invoked as the basis for intervention, as recently as in Grenada.[119] On the other hand, it is a highly political issue. I think it would involve the International Law Commission in certain difficulties because they do not represent States, they act as independent lawyers, or presume to act as independent lawyers, while a Special Committee could try to settle the matter. After all, even more difficult questions concerning friendly relations were examined, and settled after many years of discussion, by a Special Committee composed of representatives of States. So I do not see an objection to a Special Committee. It would be preferable to the ILC.

[118] Reference is made here to the operation carried out by Israeli armed forces at Entebbe airport (near Kampala in Uganda) on 4 July 1976, to rescue 248 passengers of an Air France plane originating from Tel Aviv and hijacked by Palestinians from the Popular Front for the Liberation of Palestine. Shortly after landing, all non-Jewish passengers had been separated from the Jewish ones. Some hostages were released, but 105 remained captive. The hijackers threatened to kill them if Israel did not comply with their demands. The Israeli forces rescued most of the passengers.

[119] Reference is made to the invasion of Grenada in 1983 by US forces. The attack was triggered by a military coup which had ousted a revolutionary government.

Moving to sources of international law, do you think that in the area of jus cogens *something could be done to improve the present situation? Because in a way, everybody is dissatisfied with this huge progress at the normative level which has never become reality.*

Jus cogens has never been applied because of the nature of *jus cogens*. The way it is mentioned in the Vienna Convention means that a treaty by which two countries agree on a programme of aggression is null and void. But the existence of that kind of treaty will be a rare occurrence. It means that two or more States band together to openly agree to perform a violation of international law. I think that is the reason why the notion of *jus cogens* has more importance or more significance in the field of academic international law than the real one.

But don't you feel that there is also another drawback, namely the fact that only one of the contracting parties to this treaty can then invoke jus cogens *before the International Court of Justice if compulsory jurisdiction is provided for? Don't you think that an improvement could be introduced by establishing that even third States can claim that a treaty between two or more other States is null and void, because of its inconsistency with* jus cogens*?*

Well, the way I interpret the Vienna Convention, the nullity of *jus cogens* is an absolute one. So I think that, under the system of the Convention, any State could raise an objection that the treaty concluded between two *other* States is null and void because it is contrary to *jus cogens*.

In short, you think that in the area of the law of treaties there is no need for any major improvements.

I think so. I think the Vienna Convention by itself is an excellent piece of work which was the result of 10 years' work or more by the ILC and the Vienna Conference. I think Ago distributed strategically the members of the Commission to govern the Conference. He himself was President, Waldock was sitting as a special expert to the right of the President, Yasseen was President of the Drafting Committee, I was General Rapporteur, at the right of the President of the Committee of the Whole, and Elias[120] was President of the Committee of the Whole.

[120] Taslim Olawale Elias (Nigerian, 1914–91) was judge (1972–85) and President (1982–85) of the ICJ. He had left Nigeria for the United Kingdom in 1944 and had been admitted to University College London. He graduated with a BA the year he entered University College London, and two years later received the LLB. In 1947 he was called to the bar at Inner Temple. He continued his graduate education at the University of London and in 1949 earned a PhD in law. In 1954 he became the Oppenheimer Research Fellow at the Institute of Commonwealth Studies, Nuffield College, Oxford, and Queen Elizabeth House. He was instrumental in organising courses in government, law and social anthropology, and in establishing the African Studies Department. As the constitutional and legal adviser to the National Council of Nigeria and the Cameroons (which later became the National Convention of Nigerian Citizens), he participated in the 1958 Nigerian Constitutional Conference in London. He was one of the architects of Nigeria's independence constitution. In 1960 Elias became Nigeria's Attorney-General and Minister of Justice. He served in this capacity through the whole of the first republic. Although later dismissed

So you were all members of the ILC. You were a sort of ILC mafia. It was very ingenious of Ago. I believe that, leaving aside the area of international treaties, there is an area where probably there is need for improvement, namely the area of settlement of disputes.

I agree. At the time there was a proposal in the Commission to have judicial settlement as a binding obligation; it was opposed by States; Tunkin was very forcefully against it. So, a compromise was found at the Vienna Conference for compulsory negotiation and compulsory conciliation. But judicial settlement became compulsory in relation to *jus cogens* only. That was the success of Elias, who performed an important role in bringing together the African States at the very end of the Conference, otherwise it seemed that the Conference would fail because of that problem. The compromise he obtained (compulsory jurisdiction on *jus cogens*) has never been acted upon by States, but it is important.

It's a safeguard.

Do you know that at San Francisco all the Latin American States proposed the compulsory jurisdiction, but they were told by both the US and the UK, and [by] the USSR that under that condition they would not ratify the Charter, so they had to drop the position.

By the way, do you think that the Latin American countries have a joint policy in international law, a sort of common stand on various issues of international law?

There are disagreements. For instance, Venezuela will never agree to favour compulsory jurisdiction nowadays, because of its ongoing dispute with Colombia.

There are therefore national interests which in a way condition their behaviour.

I am afraid so.

Can you think of other issues where you are able to identify a common stand taken by all Latin American countries on some crucial points?

Not on judicial settlement. In other areas: exhaustion of local remedies, for instance, subversive activities, the Calvo clause.[121] Those are Latin American

after the coup d'état in January 1966, he was reinstated in November of that year. In 1966 Elias was appointed Professor and Dean of the Faculty of Law at Lagos University. In 1967, he was appointed Nigeria's Commissioner for Justice, and five years later, in 1972, became Chief Justice of the Supreme Court of Nigeria. He was a member of the United Nations International Law Commission from 1961 to 1975, and was its Chairman in 1970.

[121] Named after the Argentinean jurist Carlos Calvo, the Calvo doctrine holds that jurisdiction in international investment disputes lies with the country in which the investment is located. It was intended to ban diplomatic protection or (armed) intervention before local resources were exhausted. An investor, under this doctrine, had to use the local courts, rather than those of its home country or international courts. See A Cassese, *International Law*, 2nd edn (Oxford, Oxford University Press, 2005) at 32–33.

dogmas. Their stand on human rights depends on their internal political situation. A lot of Latin American countries have now ratified the San José de Costa Rica Convention. But you have countries which have dissociated themselves from the protection of human rights, like Peru has in order to suppress rebellion, the 'Sendero Luminoso' movement.

May I ask you a question which is very big, relating more to futurology than to legal scholarship: how do you envisage the future of the international community? Do you think that we are moving towards a world government, or do you think that the nation-State is still a vital pillar of the international community, or (this is the third option) do you think that we should move towards a sort of gradual decrease of the power of nation-States and the spread of power? How do you envisage the evolution of the international community?

I think that the evolution towards a world government is very far off; I do not think it would even be useful.

You think that neither the UN nor the US will ever have enough power to become the 'world government'?

I think that they would need some control on the way the provisions of the Charter are utilised. I don't think we will find a way for a single State to be able to exercise authority over the rest of the world.

Now what about this second option, whereby the nation-State is still viable?

Very much so. Very valid.

In your view, the international community will continue to have its current structure and configuration.

Single sovereign States under international law.

What about increased integration in international supranational bodies, regional organisations, a sort of European Community spreading everywhere?

I think that in Latin America at least, we are very far from an integration of the type [that] has occurred in Europe. Governments continue to retain control [of] the movement towards integration, and they resist incorporation of the features [that] allowed the emergence of the European Community: the institution of supranational organs and supranational authority. In Europe there have been amendments to the Constitutions in order to allow this process to develop, but in Latin America this has not occurred. And the States, for instance, in the southern corner of South America, the Mercosur, continue to believe that they can develop an integration through meetings of Foreign Ministers, where political considerations prevail and there is no common organ such as the Commission or the Court of Luxembourg.

C. Values and elements of the present international community which may give rise to disquiet

My next question is about the values and characteristics of the present international community: which values, in your mind, might give rise to anxiety and disquiet, and possibly disrupt the fabric of the current world community?

The interpretation of Article 2(4); the interpretation of Article 51; the interpretation of Article 25; the fact that control by the five Permanent Members through this veto has disappeared; the temptation to use Chapter VII of the Charter; and the compulsory effect of Security Council resolutions as an instrument for exercising power over the international community. These are disquieting factors. Another factor relates, for instance, to the *Lockerbie* case.

When you said interpretation of Article 2(4), did you mean interpretation of Article 2(4) by the US and the great powers?

By the US, by Waldock and Bowett.

D. Towards a better international community

What ideological and political values, as well as legal values, are instead indicative of a dynamic and positive evolution toward a better world community?

The international concern for human rights, which has improved of late; the trend towards compulsory methods for the settlement of disputes.

I do not think that the notion of international crimes of States is a value; I think there is a risk in that notion. I was struck by the fact that in explaining the concept of international crime, the reports by Ago and by the International law Commission showed many instances of declarations by statesmen from prominent countries like the US and the UK, which showed that they are attempting to become a sort of policemen of the world, or of a continent. This could happen, unless the exercise of the repression of international crimes is entrusted to an international organ. But it is a fact that one or two permanent members can now control that international organ and use it for their political ends.

Would you be unhappy about a system whereby, if one claims that a State is responsible for a crime of State, one could not act against that State unilaterally but only multilaterally through the UN, and even if it were accepted to be subject to the ICJ's scrutiny, ie to procedures for the peaceful settlement of disputes?

But take the example of what happened in Argentina. I am not condoning what Argentina did in The Falklands. On the contrary, I think it was an act of aggression. But the European Community met and sanctioned Argentina on the basis that it had perpetrated an international crime of aggression.

Now this is dangerous, because in this instance a powerful entity such as the European Community exercised its power properly; but it may exercise its power of sanction improperly, or for political ends.

Therefore, this system is unacceptable even if accompanied by judicial safeguards?

Well, if it is accompanied by judicial safeguards, no. Then I would accept it. Because you have to rely on the International Court or an ad hoc court of arbitration acting in accordance with international law. But I would not rely on an organ such as the Security Council, where, for political reasons, the power of certain States has increased lately to an abnormal degree.

What about the repression of crimes against humanity?

That also is a value which is much needed in the present world community. We have seen what happened in Yugoslavia—it's terrible. Fortunately, the Security Council there has acted. You see you have another example of the strange function of the Security Council: establishing a tribunal. Normally tribunals are set up by a treaty between States. Here you have the Security Council setting up a tribunal, appointing the members. I think it's a new development which, in this case, is good, progressive, very much needed. On the other hand, it shows to an extreme how the powers of the Security Council can be exercised.

At the beginning I was enthusiastic. Chapter VII at last has been applied, has been resurrected, the plans for the repression of aggression are accomplished. Then I became concerned, because the biggest States, particularly the United States, realise the amount of power they have at present. They can go their individual way, or they can use the UN in order to obtain the approval of the Security Council.

The next question is whether in your view there is a means of bridging the present gap between the normative values and the actual reality of international relations, namely between such values as peace and human rights, and the reality of nationalist, sovereignty-oriented tendencies.

One should take a longer view and think not only of what happened in our lifetime. I was impressed by a statement by the Vice-Chancellor of Cambridge University, a historian of the conduct of States. He said he had learned more from the writings of international law about the evolution in the conduct of States, than from any other source. He referred to Kant's idea that the time would come when States will forbid war, will cease to consider war as a legitimate means. We are not at that stage, he said, but the progress which has been made in recent years is greater than in any other period of time. He added: 'I tell you, as a historian, that you are too modest about the achievements of international law.'

Therefore you think that there is some hope in the long run?

As somebody said, in the long run, we will all be dead.

I agree with you: we will stick to the present structure of the world community consisting of sovereign States, a State-oriented community. You think that regional integration is not the real way of achieving progress. Do you suggest that one ought to promote more international organisations, a sort of network of international organisations which would mitigate State sovereignty?

I am not ruling out the possibility of regional integration. I see the present difficulties. Of course the European model is so important and so effective that it may, at a certain stage, be copied in other parts of the world: think of the treaty between Canada, Mexico and the United States, the treaties of the southern part of South America, the treaties between Latin American countries; these treaties may become a reality, let us say in half a century's time, provided the States follow the European example, which is to organise institutional organs capable of supranational measures. The governments of these countries still jealously guard their powers, which they don't want to give up, or they want to control the process of integration. And then what happens? They control the process of integration, but they decide on the development of integration on political grounds. For instance, if you take a particular measure, two factories in my country will close. You take that other measure then workers in the agricultural area will strike. When you have that, you cannot develop your integration. You need what you have in Europe, a Commission of independent people who are devoted to integration, and also a Court which implements and ensures a uniform interpretation of the rules adopted by the Community.

V. The Jurist and Global Reality

A. The commands of one's demon

We come to the last section, which deals more with your personality. Here I quoted Max Weber, who wrote that each scholar should find and obey the demon who holds the fibre of his very life. Do you feel that you have heeded the commands of your demon? Do you feel that you have met the demands of the day in human relations as well as in your vocation? Do you feel that you have fulfilled your vocation as a scholar, or have you got regrets about things which you have not accomplished?

I can say that I have realised my aims in life, in the sense that from the beginning of my legal studies I became interested in, and caught by, international law. At the beginning, as I told you yesterday, I was teaching 'Introduction to Law' and I thought that I could become a civil lawyer, specialising in civil law. But then I got this appointment to that Inter-American body. I became attracted by international law, by the very limits of international law which gave room to imagination, to invention. There are no finished products like the Civil Code.

I remember the first time I was studying international law; it was as a student in the third year of Law School, in 1939. When I was studying in my house, the *Graf Spee* incident occurred. You remember, it was during the War. The *Graf Spee*, a German battleship, entered the River Plate and was attacked by three British cruisers. The *Graf Spee* took refuge in the Port of Montevideo, and then the legal fight commenced (Uruguay was a neutral country). The British ships remained at the entrance, they did not enter the port, waiting for the *Graf Spee*. The German Ambassador in Uruguay asked, under the 1907 Hague Convention XIII (concerning the Rights and Duties of Neutral Powers in Naval War), for the stay-rule [to be applied] in order to provide time for repairs to the ship. The British Ambassador, under instructions from Churchill, asked for the application of a strict 24-hour stay-rule under the Hague Convention. So, there was a conflict there. Our Foreign Minister, who had a lot of experience (he had been President of the Assembly of the League of Nations), appointed a Maritime Commission to study the requirements for repair. This Commission reported that the Germans needed 48 hours for repairing their navigation capabilities. But they needed several days to repair their fighting capacities. So the Foreign Minister decided to grant only the hours needed for repair to the navigational capability: 48 hours. In view of this, the men on the *Graf Spee* disembarked, the crew was sent to Argentina, which was then more pro-Nazi, the captain scuttled the ship and killed himself. This was in 1939, it was the first victory of the Allied forces 'in the dark waters of the River Plate', as Churchill said. I followed that with great interest because I was studying the subject.

Then, as I told you, I became appointed to this Committee as Under-Secretary, and I realised how much more attractive international law was than the civil law I wanted to study. So I became addicted.

As I finished my studies, I joined as assistant to the professor who was a friend of mine, who then became a Foreign Minister and appointed me as Under-Secretary. Then I had this problem, as I told you, the competition for a chair, when he resigned. In view of the difficulty of access to materials in 1945–46, I decided to get a position in the UN Secretariat. I got that position in the Security Council Department. First, I finished my thesis on the recognition of governments,[122] which was published in 1946 or 1947, the same year as Lauterpacht's, so I was unlucky in that respect. And then I went to the UN. I worked there for two years. I came back. As a result of my going to the UN, my competitors for the professorship had withdrawn their candidacies. So I ran unopposed.

[122] Above n 46.

This is how you carried out your career. Do you feel that you in a way have fulfilled your personal objectives?

Yes. For instance, when I studied international law and the proceedings of the Court, I was interested in reading the pleadings, and I became interested in the pleadings by Bourquin, by Rolin, by Waldock. I said to myself '*Anch'io sono pittore*' ('I too am a painter').[123]

Do you have any regrets, anything you think you have missed in your career, in your studies, in your scholarly activity?

You'll be surprised by my answer, which is not for printing. This is the only regret I have: I had to make a choice, when I was a young sportsman, between football and basketball. Football was professional in my country at that time, basketball was amateur. I made the mistake of choosing basketball, not having enough faith that I would be good enough to become a professional footballer. Otherwise I could have become a football player.

B. How to make life less unbearable

The next question starts with a citation from Freud, who wrote in Civilization and its Discontent[124] *that life is very tough, very hard; and he said it's unbearable because there is too much pain, disillusions, tasks that cannot be fulfilled. So he said that you need palliatives. There exist three sorts of palliatives: either powerful diversions, such as scholarly activity or gardening; or substitute gratifications, such as wine, or art or 'chemical' drugs. Wine, to induce forgetfulness, because life is so painful.*

Yes, life is painful. I have serious family problems. My eldest daughter, who has children, suffered brain damage in a terrible car accident. My youngest son has a disturbed personality. So we have serious problems in the family. My powerful diversion is scholarly activity, which also includes drafting briefs as a counsel before international courts. What worries me is when this scholarly activity ends; it may end shortly, because I am already 75. I have difficulty recollecting names, as you may have noticed.

No, not at all.

It may end at any moment. Then I will have to start gardening. My wife is very keen on gardening. I am interested in that, but at present do not actually work in the garden.

You don't need drugs, not even wine. You don't drink a lot of wine.

Well, no, I drink several bottles . . .

[123] Statement attributed to the Italian painter Correggio. It would seem that he uttered that exclamation in face of the painting 'Santa Cecilia' by Raphael, in Bologna.
[124] S Freud, *Civilization and its Discontent* (ed and tr J Strachey) (New York, Norton, 1961).

But this is nothing. It is not a way of forgetting.

No, no.

In a way, what is really important to you is your writing and reading international law.

When I had to work as a private lawyer my refuge was international law. My '*gagne-pain*' was commercial law, corporation law. At the weekends I enjoyed working in international law. International law was my '*maîtresse*'.

I agree. Working hard on something one relishes doing is the best way of forgetting everything around us. Well, we have come to the end of our long conversation. Thank you, Eduardo. Perhaps it has been somewhat tiresome for you, but I believe it was worth doing. Our readers will enjoy your comments and your answers.

Sir Robert Jennings

THE CHARACTER TRAIT I never expected to see in a man like Robert Jennings was also the first one to be noticed about him: his modesty. Physically unassuming, if a little plump, his gentle and often ironical smile quickly revealed how affable and urbane he was. Within minutes he would ask you simply to call him Robbie. This would inevitably create much embarrassment in all those who, like me, were full of awe and keenly aware of the enormous difference in knowledge and authority between them and this highly-respected Cambridge scholar and eminent judge. As Rosalyn Higgins noted:

> Sir Robert felt no need to impress, never sought to impose his ideas: he was content quietly to be as he was. . . . More than most, his life was 'all of a piece'. The Robbie Jennings who allowed himself to be button-holed by a thrilled student was the same Robbie Jennings who dines with the Queen of the Netherlands. A young colleague in the Registry of the Court would be listened to with the same courteous attention as Robbie naturally showed to the Emperor of Japan when received as the President of the International Court of Justice.[1]

This quality defined his greatness: to be the same gentle and simple person with everybody, regardless of the status and position of the other. His human style was not separate from his approach as a scholar: 'the simplicity and directness of his written and oral style' has rightly been emphasised.[2]

Robert Yewdall Jennings (1913–2004) had a long and distinguished academic career. In 1955, at the young age of 42, he 'inherited' Sir Hersch Lauterpacht's chair and was appointed Whewell Professor of International Law at Cambridge, where he taught until 1982. He was elected later that year to the bench of the International Court of Justice to replace Sir Humphrey Waldock. He sat in the Court until 1995, being elected President for a three-year term in 1991.

Jennings was a typical representative of the British school, a school which prizes quality over quantity. He was not a prolific writer. His publications before joining the Court primarily consisted of a booklet in 1963, entitled

[1] R Higgins, 'Sir Robert Yewdall Jennings 1913–2004' (2005) 75 *British Yearbook of International Law* 1, at 1.

[2] V Lowe, 'Sir Robert Yewdall Jennings' in V Lowe and M Fitzmaurice (eds), *Fifty Years at the International Court of Justice: Essays in Honour of Sir Robert Jennings* (Cambridge, Cambridge University Press, 1996) at xxiii.

The Acquisition of Territory in International Law,[3] and two courses at the Hague Academy: one in 1949 ('Some Aspects of the International Law of the Air'[4]) and a general course in international law in 1967 ('General Course on Principles of International Law'[5]). These works do not stand out as much for their innovative approach to international law problems as they do for the remarkably pellucid analysis undertaken, for the balanced views, the pragmatism, the structured logic that inspires the legal inquiry and for the clarity of the exposition. These qualities are also shown brilliantly in *The Acquisition of Territory*, where an extraordinary *esprit de finesse* shines through. Jennings' Hague 'General Course' is an astute classical exposition of international law.

Readers looking for easy answers might get frustrated with Jennings' tendency, like that of many British jurists, meticulously to lay out the various possible interpretations that might be given to a rule, or the different constructs that might be advanced, without necessarily betraying his preference.[6] It is as if the author's mission is to provide guidance about existing issues rather than offering solutions, leaving it to the reader to adopt that which may seem more convincing.

Another feature of Jennings' writing was the recurring underlying suggestion that solutions to a problem often rest with the policy-makers rather than the legal interpreters.[7]

Perhaps Jennings gave his best in short articles. This is consistent with the old British tradition of asking young scholars to write few papers but of high quality. (Jennings recalls that his mentor, McNair, when discouraging students from attempting a PhD, insisted 'that a good short article published in a reputable journal would stand him in better stead than a research degree'.[8]) His first paper, published after a year at Harvard, is a small masterpiece: 'The *Caroline* and *McLeod* cases'.[9] There, Jennings, uses all the natural legal acumen of his 25 years to set a string of historical documents in their proper legal perspective, and succeeds in writing a short essay that remains today a 'must' for any student of international law. He also published many articles during the period when he was an international judge, and indeed probably his best scholarly works date from that period.

Jennings' legal outlook was positivist in essence. He insisted on the difference between *lex lata* and *lex ferenda*. Normally, at least in the tradition of

[3] R Jennings, *The Acquisition of Territory in International Law* (Manchester, Manchester University Press, 1963).

[4] (1949-II) 75 *Recueil des Cours de l'Académie de Droit International de La Haye* ('*Recueil des cours*') 509.

[5] (1967-II) 121 *Recueil des cours* 323 ('General Course').

[6] As examples of this approach to and style of scholarly investigation, see, *inter alia*, Jennings, 'What is international law and how do we tell it when we see it?' (1981) 37 *Annuaire suisse de droit international* 59, at 67–71, 75–77.

[7] For instance, see what Jennings wrote on the use of force and Art 51 of the UN Charter on self-defence: 'General Course', above n 5, at 584–85.

[8] R Jennings, 'Arnold McNair' (1975) 34 *The Cambridge Law Journal* 177, at 180.

[9] See (1938) 32 *American Journal of International Law* 82.

Continental Europe (particularly in Germany, Italy, France and Spain), those who set great store by this dichotomy draw two consequences. First, once the distinction between the two levels is established, they remain at the level of *lex lata*, expressly or implicitly leaving the task of proposing changes in the existing law to politicians, diplomats, political scientists and so on. In other words, they carve out for themselves the role of interpreters of the existing legal reality, refusing to look beyond that and suggest improvements. Secondly, they deal only with specific rules and legal institutions, and shy away from any overall appraisal of general problems of the world community, lest they should then discover the pitfalls of the world community's legal structure and consequently have to express their dissatisfaction with those pitfalls. Implicit in this attitude is the notion that legal scholarship must be '*wertfrei*' (to borrow one of Max Weber's expressions), that is, free from values, being based not on 'value judgments' but on 'scientific judgments', ie evaluations and conceptual constructs that reflect and interpret the existing reality (in our case, the legal reality) without pronouncing on whether or not it is congruous with social needs and the demands of the relevant constituencies.

Jennings did not fit into this scheme. True, substantially he was a positivist and prioritised the careful examinations of traditional or new institutions such as the legal status of territory, sources and sovereignty. In this, he was intellectually very close to Lord McNair.[10] Also, in dealing with these issues he normally concentrated on interpretation of existing law, without venturing into proposals for changes in the law. In addition, his writings, while impeccable from a legal viewpoint, belie a conservative streak: it is notable that he was never particularly alert to the demands of developing countries.[11] In particular, Jennings was not especially supportive of the principle of self-determination of peoples, adopting a somewhat hostile attitude towards it instead. Without asking himself whether that powerful if ambiguous and polyvalent political concept had been translated into law, and, if so, what meaning it could hold, he simply discarded its legal impact out of hand. In 1967 he defined self-determination as 'a political catchword totally without certainly ascertainable content'.[12] Many of his writings betray almost a sense

[10] See, eg, Jennings, above n 6, at 67; R Jennings, 'An International Lawyer Takes Stock' (1990) 39 *ICLQ* 513. Jennings wrote that in his approach to international law he was 'more a McNair man than a Lauterpacht man': R Jennings, 'Hersch Lauterpacht. A Personal Recollection' (1997) 2 *European Journal of International Law* 301, at 302.

[11] Eg, see R Jennings, 'The Progress of International Law' (1958) 34 *British Yearbook of International Law* 334.

[12] See 'General Course', above n 5, at 564. See also Jennings, above n 3, at 3. In his last paper, 'The Imbalance of the International Law System' (2004) 8 *International Law Forum* 126, at 127–28, Jennings wrote: 'International lawyers have tended not to look for better ways of making policy territorial decisions but have instead tried to extend the legal "modes"; as for example by the transformation of "self-determination" from being a useful political notion, into a "right" of "self-determination", apparently enjoyed by "peoples". This circular and question-begging "right" still calls for a political decision about what is a "people" for this purpose, as indeed also what status they self-determine on a scale varying between independence and dependence.'

of regret for the disappearance of traditional international and domestic institutions, the sort of nostalgia typical of a *laudator temporis acti*.[13]

Jennings was nonetheless keenly aware of those areas of international dealings where the lawyer is needed less than the policy-maker. In some of his papers he pointed to areas where the lawyers should stop inquiring into law if they sense that it would be more appropriate for policy-makers to step in.

In addition, particularly in some writings undertaken in his old age, in a remarkable evolution of his legal thinking he insisted on the need for international lawyers also to propose ways of changing the law and filling its gaps, or of remedying its inconsistencies. In 1990, he wrote:

> It is undeniably important that scholars with imagination and vision should publish ideas for a better international law. Good ideas, if they are timely and blessed by good fortune, possibly accomplish as much as, or more than, the diplomatic conferences, with their compromising drafts of articles, so beloved by those who seek to further 'progressive development' of international law.[14]

In his last paper he not only repeated this argument, but even went so far as to take the blame for not having contributed to this undertaking himself.[15]

It is also notable that, unlike most pure positivists, Jennings did not refrain from general appraisals of the legal mechanics of the international community, and was always rather critical of the present state of affairs.[16] His appraisals would be steeped in historical context, and would trace the evolution of the law since Grotius.

In sum, anybody wishing to enjoy a fine and sophisticated analysis of legal rules and institutions, and to appreciate interpretations that are balanced, supported by much common sense and experience and written in a clear and plain style, will have to read or re-read papers by Jennings. He will find such reading fully rewarding. For those who had the chance to meet him, that reading will conjure up images of his gentle and affable smile, as well as of the witty irony which sprinkled his conversation—all qualities that emerge from the interview, to which Robbie devoted much time, first in preparing for the questions (he had asked for the questionnaire in advance) and then in carefully revising the typescript (I still have and treasure the text, with his many handwritten notes and additions).

[13] Eg, referring to the teaching at Cambridge in the 1930s, Jennings speaks of 'those enlightened days' ('Hersch Lauterpacht: A Personal Recollection', above n 10, at 301) and also recollects with regret 'the "Third Programme" of the BBC—that former glory of English civilization, alas no more' (*ibid*, at 304).

[14] 'An International Lawyer Takes Stock', above n 10, at 527–28.

[15] 'The Imbalance of the International Law System', above n 12, at 130: 'May I finally say that in thus pointing out what seems to me to be a failure on the part of us international lawyers to think and talk more about these big policy-making problems of international law and order of the present time, I must, writing near the end of a long career, humbly include myself among the short-sighted ones. There are distinguished international lawyers who have long worked hard and effectively at these crucial problems. I put forward my worries fully aware that I can only speak as one of the host of guilty parties at last waking up to the present crisis of international law.'

[16] See in particular 'The Progress of International Law', above n 11; 'An International Lawyer Takes Stock', above n 10, at 513–29; 'The Imbalance of the International Law System', above n 12, at 126–30.

Interview with Sir Robert Jennings

October 1994

I. The Beginning as a Scholar

Who was the international lawyer who most influenced your thinking at the beginning of your scholarly activity?

I am quite clear who it was, and I'll tell you in a minute. But first, I am a little unsure what university activity counts as 'scholarly' activity. There was for me a large grey area. Furthermore, I must recall that my generation—this is now often forgotten—had six years of war, just at the age when one would normally begin writing. Immediately after Cambridge I had gone to Harvard for a year, and then in 1939 started scholarly activity during my first job, which was as assistant lecturer at the London School of Economics. In 1939 I was elected to a fellowship at Jesus College in Cambridge. But in 1940 I went into the army, and eventually found myself in India and Sri Lanka. I was very lucky in having a relatively comfortable war, if war can ever be comfortable. I was never a very good soldier, but I enjoyed the army all the same. I greatly liked all my commanding officers, and they seemed to tolerate me as a sort of comic turn. So I survived the war. But it did take away many of the formative years when normally one would have been occupied with academic matters.

For, six of those years is a long time, and I am not sure that one ever quite makes up the loss. When I came back from the war, I went back to Jesus College because they had paid my fellowship 'dividends' throughout the war—not a great sum but it was very generous treatment—and therefore I was under some obligation to go back; and I was glad to do so. But then I quite soon found myself Senior Tutor of the College, which in those days was to be a principal administrative officer of the College, in charge of all subjects and not just law: the organisation of them and the College teaching, and undergraduate welfare. Perhaps I should explain that the traditional system at Cambridge—as also at Oxford—is in effect a federal one. The University is the federal authority and the Colleges are the equivalent of member States. The Colleges were indeed sovereign in many respects. For example, they alone were in charge of the admission of undergraduates. The University simply had to accept those admitted by the separate Colleges. Thus, as Senior Tutor I decided on all admissions to membership of the College in all subjects. Of course I was much guided by the Fellows teaching those subjects. But in the end the decision was mine. There was an entrance examination. (I should explain that in Oxford a 'tutor' is a College teacher, but in Cambridge the term is much nearer to the original Latin: a tutor is a guardian and administrator; the College teacher is called the 'supervisor'.) College teaching was tuition within the college of small groups—reading essays, discussing questions, arguing, sometimes about things in general. It was the University that put on formal lectures and administered examinations for degrees. So the College and University teaching complemented each other. The idea of the College system was that, both at the senior level and at undergraduate level, one lived and worked and talked and ate and played mainly with people in subjects other than one's own. So I knew some teachers of classics, or English, or natural sciences at least as well as the lawyers, and probably, in the College, talked with them more. For I was, at that time, the only lawyer in my College.

I also, as almost in duty bound as a Senior Tutor, went onto the central bodies of the University and their committees. That meant that I spent those years after the war in College law teaching—not just international law, but law in general, contract and so on—and also a great deal of time over university politics and administration, as well as College administration. After some few years of this combination of teaching and administration, I was greatly tempted and under great pressure to take on the office of Secretary-General of the Faculties, which was and still is one of the main administrative offices of the University. I remember Hersch Lauterpacht, then the Whewell Professor of International Law, was at first horrified; but he was persuaded not to oppose. He told me that he'd been told by the Vice-Chancellor that I was the man they wanted and that I would do the job well. I think I would have enjoyed it greatly, and it was an office carrying great power and influence in all faculties. But in the end I decided to refuse and went on as Senior Tutor, looking after subjects in general but law in particular, and already specialising somewhat in international law, very much under the influence of McNair[17] and Hersch Lauterpacht. In 1955, when Lauterpacht was elected to the ICJ, I was elected to the Whewell Chair, which meant a switch from teaching generally and from administration to specialisation in international law.

The personal history I have described was by no means an untypical career at Oxford or Cambridge in my young days: the main administrative responsibility was always taken by Dons, both in Colleges and the University. In my opinion this was vastly superior to the modern tendency of having 'professional' administrators, who seldom wholly understand academic needs.

You will now understand why I am not able to say that there is any particular date for the beginning of what you could call 'serious scholarly activity'.

[17] Arnold McNair (British, 1885–1975) in 1935 was appointed Whewell Professor of International Law at Cambridge. He left this chair in 1937 to become Vice-Chancellor of Liverpool University. In 1945 he returned to Cambridge to take up the position of Professor of Comparative Law. In 1946 McNair was elected a judge of the ICJ, a post he held until 1955 (in 1952–55 he was President of the Court). He later served as the first President of the European Court of Human Rights at Strasbourg from 1959 to 1965.

Another thing I have to say is that when I began in Cambridge, and I am sure that it was true of Oxford as well, 'scholarly activity' was not necessarily number one in priorities. And again I think this was a superior system to what we have now. The main thing was teaching; and many of the best teachers in those days hardly got around to writing their books and felt that if they'd imparted their ideas to pupils, they were doing their job. We then regarded teaching of undergraduates as the most important activity of a Don. If you were given to writing and scholarship, splendid, you were allowed to do that; but it was given to relatively few people to excel in that sort of way. Now of course there's enormous pressure, as you know, on people to write, and write all the time, and I don't think that's an improvement. I think there is far too much writing anyway; but the new type of administrators demands it in their ignorance.

Now for the last part of your question, Nino, about the man who influenced me more than anybody: there's only one possible answer to that. It was Arnold McNair. When I was an undergraduate reading international law in the second year, he was not Whewell Professor; Pearce Higgins was Whewell Professor and Arnold McNair was 'Dr McNair', who did some of the lectures for the Tripos (the Law Tripos being of course the honours examinations; the name refers to the three-legged stool of the time of the Middle Ages, on which candidates sat when it was an oral examination). McNair was a superb lecturer; very clear, interesting because interested, and with a wry sense of humour sometimes almost mischievous. I got to know him a little and greatly admired him. I think my wish to pay particular attention, from a pretty early stage, to international law was not at first because of the subject but rather because of McNair. I felt then, as an undergraduate, that if I could become a little like McNair I would be on the right lines. I have no second thoughts on that, I still regard him as my ideal of an international lawyer.

There is I think, or was, an English school of international law, and the great examples are, for me, Arnold McNair and James Brierly.[18] Of course McNair was a Scot, but he went to school and university in England, and he began by teaching Common Law. He was one of the most persuasive speakers I have ever heard. He not only got people to agree with him on committees;

[18] James Brierly (British, 1881–1955) was Chichele Professor of International Law at Oxford University and a member of the UN International Law Commission in 1949–51. He was Rapporteur on the law of treaties in 1949–50 and was elected Chairman in 1951. He was a member of the *Institut de Droit international* from 1929. His works include the splendid booklet, *The Law of Nations: An Introduction to the International Law of Peace* (Oxford, Oxford University Press, 1928, 6th edn, ed Sir Humphrey Waldock (Oxford, Clarendon Press, 1963)), unequaled for conciseness and conceptual density, as well its balanced assessment of legal reality (as noted by Waldock in their obituary of Brierly, 'This book has a strong claim to be considered the most masterly introduction to the study of the law of peace in any language', in 'James-Leslie Brierly (1881–1955)' (1956) 46 *Annuaire de l'Institut de Droit international* 460, at 462). Also important are the short writings, all of high legal quality, included in *The Basis of Obligation in International Law and other Papers*, selected and edited by H Lauterpacht and H Waldock (Oxford, Clarendon Press, 1958). I believe that another short book, written during the war, *The Prospect for International Law* (Oxford, Oxford University Press, 1944), is still worth reading.

they enjoyed agreeing with him. I owed an enormous debt to him. He was very cautious in his approach to legal problems. I remember when—in 1936 I suppose it was, at the time of Mussolini's adventure in Abyssinia[19]—the big question was whether it was possible as a sanction to close the Suez Canal to Mussolini's supplies. Everybody was writing to newspapers, to *The Times* especially, on one side or the other about this problem. A little bunch of us who were in McNair's seminar thought we'd get the truth of this matter. So at the end of one seminar we asked McNair what the position was about the Suez Canal. And there was a long pause and then he said, 'Well, that is a matter which requires more thought than I've yet been able to give it.' I've always admired that answer, because he was right, you see. And you might say that he ought to have given it more thought already, but he hadn't and this was the truth of the matter; so that was what he said to his pupils. He was not going to give an opinion to anybody off the cuff without looking at all the documents again and considering it very carefully. I hesitate to contemplate what he would have thought of the off-the-cuff soundbites that 'experts' now daily provide on television and radio.

How would you comment on Sir Hersch Lauterpacht?[20]

My association with Lauterpacht came much later. The first big influence was McNair. And of course this was before I knew anything about Lauterpacht, because Lauterpacht then was a lecturer at the London School of Economics [LSE]. And he had just left the LSE to go to Cambridge when I took up my first job which was [as] an assistant lecturer at the LSE. So it was after the

[19] In 1935, Mussolini, Prime Minister of Italy, decided to attack Ethiopia (also called Abyssinia). Italian troops move there from Eritrea (an Italian colony) on 3 October 1935; the war went on until 5 May 1936. At the end of the conflict Italy annexed Ethiopia.

[20] Hersch Lauterpacht (1897–1960) was born in Austrian Galicia, then belonging to Austria-Hungary, into a middle-class Jewish family. After completing his secondary schooling and studying law at the University in Lemberg, he moved to Vienna in 1919 for further university studies. There he worked under Hans Kelsen and obtained qualifications first as a Doctor of Laws and then as a Doctor of Political Science. In late 1923 he settled in England. He entered the LSE as a research student, spending the years 1923–37 at LSE teaching, researching and writing. Lord McNair became his mentor, and with his encouragement and support, Lauterpacht completed his London doctoral thesis, which was published as *Private Law Sources and Analogies of International Law (with Special Reference to International Arbitration)* (London, Longmans, Green and Co, 1927). Together with McNair, in 1929 he initiated the *Annual Digest of International Law* (later renamed the *International Law Reports*). Lauterpacht completed another major work, *The Function of Law in the International Community* (Oxford, Clarendon Press, 1933) and edited Oppenheim's *International Law: A Treatise* from 1937 onwards (5th edn, London, Longmans, 1937). In 1937 he was elected to the Whewell Chair of International Law at Cambridge in succession to McNair. He taught there until 1955. Lauterpacht was a member of the UN International Law Commission from 1952 to 1954, and a judge of the International Court of Justice (ICJ) from 1955 to 1960. A prolific writer, he published *An International Bill of the Rights of Man* (New York, Columbia University Press, 1945), *Recognition in International Law* (Cambridge, Cambridge University Press, 1947), *International Law and Human Rights* (London, Stevens, 1950), as well as *The Development of International Law by the International Court* (London, Stevens, 1958). He was also editor of the *British Yearbook of International Law*. On Lauterpacht, see the important considerations of M Koskenniemi, *The Gentle Civilizer of Nations: The Rise and Fall of International Law, 1870–1960* (Cambridge, Cambridge University Press, 2002) at 353–412.

war, when I returned to Cambridge in 1946, that I got to know Professor Lauterpacht, as he then was. He became a very dear and close friend, who helped me in every possible way. McNair I admired somewhat from a distance; but Lauterpacht I spent a lot of time with, and was very frequently at his home. It was he who started me writing articles for the *British Year Book*, proposed me for the *Institut de Droit international*, and was constantly a kind, generous and close friend.

II. Encounters with Other Scholars

Who of the international lawyers you have met in your career has impressed you most, and for what reasons?

I am not sure that my answer to that is a very straight answer to 'who impressed me most'. I always accept McNair with comfort as number one, because Hersch Lauterpacht felt exactly the same about McNair. He also was greatly helped by McNair: even financially in the days when they were very poor and McNair got to know him when he and Rachel were first in London. Hersch Lauterpacht was quite clear; for him, that number one was McNair. You will recollect that Lauterpacht's *Function of Law in the International Community*[21] was dedicated to McNair.

I got to know Hersch Lauterpacht of course when I went back to Cambridge after the war. He made the greatest impression on me in a way that is not quite, I think, what you are asking for in your question. Of course, his work and his industry, and his great learning and his utter devotion to international law, [were] impressive to me and to anybody else. He also was a very fine lecturer, quite different from McNair, utterly different, but a very fine lecturer.

But Lauterpacht had a tremendous influence on me simply because we were such friends; I think he was in many ways the closest friend I've ever had. He was a wonderfully generous man, and I used to spend a lot of time with him and he used to spend a lot of time furthering my career in one way or another. I owe a tremendous amount to him and to Rachel: for sheer generosity and kindness and friendship.

Were you also influenced by his ideas?

Yes, inevitably. I was influenced by his ideas, always with a feeling, however, that he was not part of the English school of international law. He was Continental in many of his ways. I think he never wholly understood the University and Colleges, and how the system worked, though he was of course a very popular figure: everybody loved him because he was such a lovable man. It was typical of him that, when it was his turn to do three years as

[21] Above n 20.

chairman of the Faculty Board of Law—a job he found most uncongenial—he put all he had into it nevertheless, and was a very good chairman indeed.

Outside the circle of British lawyers, did you meet non-British international lawyers who impressed you?

Not a lot, because of my life then as Senior Tutor of a College, and cultivating Head Masters of schools with promising pupils was more important to me than cultivating international lawyers. I had to spend most of my time in Cambridge or back in Yorkshire, or [in] the Lake District on holiday sometimes. Moreover, I didn't travel abroad very much. I came from a class of people in Yorkshire who would never have thought of going abroad. When I went to Harvard in 1936, that was my first venture outside my own country; and in the war I found myself in the army in India and Ceylon before I had ever ventured to the European Continent. So I didn't meet a lot of other international lawyers, except occasionally when Lauterpacht had a guest, and he would invite me to dine with them. I remember, for example, meeting Baron von Asbeck,[22] who'd come to Cambridge. He was very kind and pleasant. Sometimes, Hersch used to use me a little. I remember that Verdross,[23] fairly soon after the war, came to Cambridge. Lauterpacht asked me to give him lunch, which I did. And Verdross was charming and delightful, but rather teasing and pulling my leg all the time. He'd say, 'Why is Professor Lauterpacht so busy at lunchtime today, do you know?' And he knew perfectly well it was because of the experiences of the war: after all, Lauterpacht had lost practically all his family in the holocaust. He could not bring himself to meet Verdross, whose excellent company, however, I enjoyed.

I was told that Verdross had somewhat ambiguous relations with the Nazis.

Yes he had, I suppose, though I don't know the details or the evidence. He was certainly a fine international lawyer. But I began to meet international lawyers from other countries when I got into the *Institut de Droit international* at the Amsterdam session in 1959. I was impressed by a lot of people. I met Guggenheim[24] quite a lot, because he used to come to Hersch Lauterpacht's

[22] Baron Frederik H van Asbeck (Dutch, 1889–1968), was Professor of International Law at the University of Leiden. He gave two lectures at the Hague Academy: 'Le régime des étrangers dans les colonies' (1937-III) 61 *Recueil des cours* 1; 'Le statut actuel des pays non autonomes d'outre-mer' (1947-II) 71 *Recueil des cours* 345.

[23] See 'Interview with Eduardo Jiménez de Aréchaga', fn 22.

[24] Paul Guggenheim (Swiss, 1899–1977) was appointed Assistant Professor of International Law at the *Institut de Hautes Etudes Internationales* (Geneva), in 1930, subsequently lecturer, then Professor of International Public Law until 1969. He also held the same chair at the University of Geneva from 1955 to 1965. He was a follower of H Kelsen. Member of *the Institut de Droit international* (1948–77). Author of a two-volume book *Lehrbuch des Volkerrechts: unter Berucksichtigung der internationalen und schweizerischen Basel: Verlag fur Recht und Gesellschaft* (Basel, Verlag fur Recht und Gesellschaft, 1948–51); translated into French: *Traité de droit international public: avec mention de la pratique internationale et suisse* (Geneva, Georg, 1953–54).

house, and I remember meeting him there and got to know him quite well. At one meeting of the *Institut de droit international*, the one at Neuchatel, I even met Max Huber.[25] We were both staying in the hotel up the mountain, and I went for a little walk after breakfast one morning before going down to the meeting which he was not attending (he was quite old then). And up on this little seat looking at the view was Max Huber, and he beckoned to me, and he talked to me and was very pleasant. I was very impressed, of course, by Suzanne Bastid[26] and by Charles de Visscher.[27] And Verzijl.[28]

[25] Max Huber (Swiss, 1874–1960) was Professor of International, Constitutional and Canon Law at the University of Zurich (1902–14), and retained this title until 1921, but could not teach due to World War I. During the War, he was legal adviser to the Swiss Defence and Foreign Affairs Ministries. In 1922–39 he was a judge of the PCIJ (Court's President in 1925–27). In 1928–44 he was President of the International Committee of the Red Cross. He also acted as the arbitrator in the famous *Island of Palmas* case between the United States and The Netherlands in 1928 at the Permanent Court of Arbitration (text in 2 *UN Reports of International Arbitral Awards* 829). He was not a prolific writer. He wrote, among other things, *Die soziologischen Grundlagen des Völkerrechts* (*The sociological foundation of international law*) (Berlin, Grunevald, 1928). His main contribution to international law lies in his celebrated award cited above, plus his opinions appended to some judgments of the PCIJ. On Max Huber, see the various papers published in (2007) 18 *European Journal of International Law* 69–133.

[26] Suzanne Bastid (French, 1906–95) obtained her *agrégation de droit public* (academic admission to university lecturing) in 1932. In 1936, in the first Léon Blum cabinet, she acted as *chef de cabinet* of her husband, Paul Bastid, then Trade Minister. She was Professor of Law in Lyon in 1933–45; she obtained a chair at Paris University in 1946. From 1950 she was a member of the UN Administrative Tribunal (President in 1953–63). Member of the *Institut de Droit international* from 1956, she also became in 1971 a member of the *Académie des sciences morales et politiques*, of which she was elected Vice-president in 1981 and President in 1982. In 1985 she acted as judge ad hoc for Tunisia in *Application for Revision and Interpretation of the Judgment of 24 February 1982 in the Case Concerning the Continental Shelf (Tunisia v Libya)*, 10 December 1985, [1985] ICJ Rep 192, and voted against the request for revision of the previous judgment, made by Tunisia, also appending a Separate Opinion (*ibid*, at 249–52) explaining why she had taken this position—a unique instance of an ad hoc judge voting against the country that had designated him or her.

[27] Charles de Visscher (Belgian, 1884–1973) was Professor of International Law at Ghent University and later at the Katholieke Universiteit Leuven; he was Secretary General, President and Honorary President of the *Institut de Droit international*; judge at the PCIJ (1937–45) and the ICJ (1946–52). Among his important scholarly contributions to international law some stand out: *Théories et réalités en droit international public* (Paris, Pedone, 1953), translated into English by PE Corbett as *Theories and Realities in Public International Law* (Princeton, Princeton University Press, 1957); *Problèmes d'interprétation judiciaire en droit international public* (Pedone, Paris, 1963); *Aspects récents du droit procédural de la Cour internationale de Justice* (Pedone, Paris, 1966); *Les effectivités en droit international public* (Pedone, Paris, 1967). On de Visscher, see the various papers published in (2000) 11 *European Journal of International Law* 871–938.

[28] Jan Hendrik Willem Verzijl (Dutch, 1888–1987) was appointed Professor of International Law and Diplomacy in 1920 at Utrecht University. In 1927–29 he was President of the Franco-Mexican Mixed Claims Commission, where he among other things delivered the famous award in the *Georges Pinson* case of 19 October 1928 (see (2006) 5 *UN Reports of International Arbitral Awards* 327). In 1938 he became Professor of International Law and Administrative Law of the Dutch Overseas Territory at the University of Amsterdam, a post from which he was fired by the German occupant in 1940 (in 1938, in his inaugural lecture, he had publicly condemned the Third Reich). He was incarcerated in Buchenwald but released in 1941. After World War II he returned to the University of Utrecht. In 1945–52 he was member and Vice-President of the Dutch Special Court of Cassation (*Bijzondere Raad van Cassatie*) dealing with war crimes. His major work is *International Law in Historical Perspective* (11 vols, Leiden, Sijthoff and Noordhoff, 1968–98). On Verzijl, see in particular M Bos, 'Professor JHW Verzijl, 31 August 1888 21 May 1987' (1987) 34 *Netherlands International Law Review* 285, as well as CG Roelofsen, 'Verzjil' in WP Heere and TPS Offerhaus (eds), *International Law in Historical Perspective*, vol XI, at xv–xxxi.

Did you meet Hans Kelsen?

Yes, I met Kelsen.[29] Again I have an impression mainly of very kind, nice gentleman.

But his thinking was a bit far away from your approach to international law.

It was very far away from my approach to international law. On the other hand, I used to have to teach it when I taught jurisprudence at the London School of Economics. There I met a man called Charles Wilson, who later became Vice-Chancellor of Glasgow University. He had written an article, I've forgotten where it is now, trying to describe Hans Kelsen's system.[30] I read this and that helped quite a bit. Yes, I tried to understand Kelsen's system, but I can't say that I admired it. I must say that I still cannot see the purpose and use of Kelsen's theories about law. So I couldn't say that he influenced me. I had to absorb him to some extent for my teaching. I could not think of him as being in the same league as either McNair or Brierly, both of whom I still regard as much more profound thinkers than Kelsen. But as a human being he was delightful.

Don't you think that Kelsen's book on Principles of International Law *is really a major contribution? Is it too abstract?*

You are asking me for personal opinions. I'm saying it's not a major contribution for me, but I'm quite willing to recognise that that probably is a shortcoming in myself. In the Cambridge Law School I was brought up to be very suspicious of 'doctrines'. As McNair would have put it, the first thing you have to learn is to see clearly the difference between *lex ferenda* and *lex lata*.

The positivist approach.

Even that one regards with a little suspicion, because it gets mixed up with the Austinian ideas[31] that international law is not really law but a kind of positive morality. This McNair would not have accepted, nor anybody who's teaching international law. So that I hesitate even to call it positivism. But I prefer simply to call it the English approach, or the approach of the English school of international law. James Brierly, for a doctrinal or philosophical approach, is my ideal still. He was a very wise man. He was very underrated in his time—compared with Hersch Lauterpacht and Kelsen and so on—I

[29] See interview with René-Jean Dupuy', fn 23.

[30] Jennings was referring to C Wilson, 'The Basis of Kelsen's Theory of Law' (1934) 1 *Politica* 54.

[31] Reference is of course made here to John Austin (1790–1859), the British initiator of the school of analytical jurisprudence and of the approach to law known as 'legal positivism'. One of the basic postulates of Austin's doctrine was: 'The existence of law is one thing; its merit or demerit is another. Whether it be or be not is one enquiry; whether it be or be not conformable to an assumed standard, is a different enquiry. A law, which actually exists, is a law, though we happen to dislike it, or though it vary from the text, by which we regulate our approbation and disapprobation.' J Austin, *The Province of Jurisprudence Determined*, ed W Rumble (Cambridge, Cambridge University Press, first published in 1832, reprinted in 1995) at 157.

would have thought wrongly, because if you look at Brierly's writings now, you'll find that he had foreseen problems and developments in international law much more accurately than they did.

Why was he underrated?

I think he was underrated because he hadn't written a great deal, and his best-known book was one for students. That little book on the 'Law of Nations'[32] is a lovely book—very short, of course. I found that when I began, as you put it Nino, my 'scholarly' career, I would go back to Brierly's *Law of Nations* over and over again when I felt I wasn't seeing the wood for the trees. (Am I talking too much? To an Englishman it's almost disgraceful, baring one's soul is terrible, just what my mother said I should never do.)

McNair also had this facility of illuminating a problem by going back to the elements. Clive Parry[33] and I once compared notes and found we had had much the same experience. When Clive and I were both reasonably well-known international lawyers and had found ourselves puzzled by some question of international law, we would seek an opportunity to ask McNair about it. He would look very thoughtful and then, after quite a while, he would begin expounding the various elements of the law involved. And we both had the same first reaction, saying to ourselves: 'Oh, silly old man, why did I ask him, of course we know all that, it's this difficult problem we are concerned about!' But he would persist, and then gradually you'd realise that he had shed light on that 'difficult' problem by seeing it in the perspective of the elements of the law. Thus a great light would dawn, and then one went away grateful. Instead of getting confused by trying to concentrate only on this particular problem, being made to see it in the context of the elements of that whole branch of international law was really illuminating.

Hersch Lauterpacht used to do it in his own way when teaching. I remember him taking the graduate seminar in my rooms in Jesus College, and he would begin a seminar by asking an extremely elementary question. And you could see all the students from many countries looking puzzled at him: Why did he ask that? Surely we all knew the answer? Then some bright spark would confidently give the textbook answer and look rather smug. But there'd be a long silence, and Hersch Lauterpacht would frown and look puzzled, and then he'd say in his accent (because he never lost his strong accent), 'Is that so? Is that so?' and still look puzzled. And then the thought would dawn on everybody: was it indeed so; the book said so, but really, if you think about it, was this answer adequate? And he'd get a real discussion going in that way, simply by going right back to the elements and insisting on asking 'Is this so?' To that extent McNair and Hersch Lauterpacht were

[32] JL Brierly, *The Law of Nations: An Introduction to the International Law of Peace*, 1st edn (Oxford, Clarendon Press, 1928).

[33] Clive Parry (British, 1917–81) taught international law at Cambridge University.

parallel in their methods of teaching, which is not surprising because they spent a great deal of time together.

At that stage or later, did the French school of international law to some extent influence your scholarship? Did you meet any outstanding French international lawyers?

Yes, I did indeed. I met Georges Scelle,[34] and again my main impression was straight away: well, one of the nicest people I've ever come across. It was here in the Hague Academy; I came to give some lectures, and he was here as a member of the Curatorium and couldn't have been kinder or more welcoming.

But I think you're probing me really to see what the great influences were on my kind of international law. To be honest, I have to say that I'm going to disappoint you. You see those were rather confident days in England and I was content with McNair, Hersch Lauterpacht and of course Brierly; and I can't say that I read widely. Indeed it was hardly possible, because for a Senior Tutor of a College there were other things to do, and we spent a lot of time with the undergraduates in College. Then I myself lived in the College. Also I think it's important to remember the almost enclosed life of a Fellow of the College in those days; a life, though, to which I was totally devoted. It was a very different life. From a specialist scholarly point of view, perhaps inadequate, Nino. Moreover, I've always been a late developer and you have to look to much later on, I think, for a full appreciation on my part of the varied contributions to international scholarship. But of course I was absorbing it gradually, attending meetings at the *Institut de Droit international*, the International Law Association, and so on.

If you press me on the French school, another man who greatly influenced me, very much later, was Michel Virally.[35] He was one of my heroes because, though I felt differently about things in many respects, we did quite a lot of practice together (the *Tunisia v Libya* case[36] and so on). I think that though approaching things from very different starting points, we both were very struck by the fact that we nearly always arrived at the same conclusion. And indeed I remember one day, when we were meeting with the team for this case (*Tunisia v Libya*) before the Court, saying to him: 'Michel, we really must attempt to differ one day, just for decency's sake, it's getting really

[34] See 'Interview with René-Jean Dupuy', fn 4.

[35] Michel Virally (French, 1922–89) was Professor of International Law at Strasbourg University (1957–61) then at Geneva University (1962–87). In 1985–89 he was a member of the Iran–US Claims Tribunal. From 1971 he was a member of the *Institut de Droit international*. He authored many books, among which the following stand out: *L'ONU: d'hier à demain* (Paris, Editions du Seuil, 1961); *Le nouveau droit international de la mer* (Paris, Pedone, 1983); *Le droit international en devenir: essais écrits au fil des ans* (Paris, Presses Universitaires de France, 1990); *Le droit international au service de la paix, de la justice et du développement: mélanges Michel Virally* (Paris, Pedone, 1991). He gave a general course on public international law at the Hague Academy: 'Panorama du droit international contemporain: cours général de droit international public' (1983-V) 183 *Recueil des cours* 9.

[36] *Continental Shelf (Tunisia v Libyan Arab Jamahiriya)*, 24 February 1982, [1982] ICJ Rep 18.

absurd.' He said: 'We will try but I'm not sure we'll succeed.' And of course he was the other kind of Frenchman, if one may put it that way: he had an ice-cold mind, warm personality; a kind and lovely man, but always dry (in the good sense); no rhetoric—ice-cold, sheer intellect. I greatly admired Michel and valued his friendship, and read a really good deal of his work and found it extremely valuable.

I assume the way he approached international law was closer to your thinking than, say, the approach taken by René-Jean Dupuy, who is more philosophical.

Yes, you've caught the thought from my mind. In a way I was contrasting Virally with René-Jean Dupuy who had a very different approach. The differences of approach and way of thinking were fascinating. René-Jean is a wonderful speaker. As an Englishman I was a little wary of that, you know. In a way it was a relief to me to meet Michel, because I then realised that there was this cold intellectual approach to be found in the French school, as well as tremendous oratory. I first felt the force of René-Jean Dupuy's oratory in peculiar circumstances. He was Secretary-General in the Academy here when I gave a course of lectures, and his speech of thanks was tremendously highly set up—I hadn't expected anybody to be quite so fervent in thanks and tributes, and so on, because McNair would never have done that you know, or indeed Hersch—but as a piece of composition and oratory lasting four or five minutes, it was a gem. I had met him earlier than that. We were both members of the Committee, chaired by Wolfgang Friedmann,[37] which recommended important reforms of the Academy. The other members were Oda,[38] Panhuys[39] and Boutros Boutros-Ghali.[40] It was to institute those

[37] See 'Interview with René-Jean Dupuy', fn 10.

[38] Shigeru Oda (Japanese, *b* 1924) has been a member of the ICJ (1976–2003). He is the author of numerous Separate or Dissenting Opinions, now published in E McWhinney and M Kavani (eds), *Opinions on the International Court of Justice 1993–2003* (Leiden, Sijthoff, 2006). See also his 2 vol book *The Law of the Sea in Our Time* (Leiden, Sjithoff, 1977).

[39] Haro Frederik van Panhuys (Dutch, 1916–76) was Deputy Legal Adviser to the Dutch Ministry of Foreign Affairs (1950–59), then Professor of International Law at the University of Leyden (1959–76). His writings include the book on *The Role of Nationality in International Law: An Outline* (Leiden, Sijthoff, 1959). See M Bos, 'In memoriam Professor H F van Panhuys' (1976) 23 *Netherlands International Law Review* 3.

[40] Boutros Boutros-Ghali (Egyptian, *b* 1922), a Coptic Christian, was born into a prominent Egyptian family. His grandfather had been Prime Minister, and his uncle, Wassif Ghali, was Foreign Minister. He got a PhD in international law in 1949, at the Paris *Institut d'Études Politiques*. He was Professor of International Law at Cairo University (1949–77). He was a member of Parliament, and Minister of State for Foreign Affairs (1977–91). In September 1978, he attended the Camp David Summit Conference and had a role in negotiating the Camp David Accords between Egypt and Israel, which were signed in 1979. He led many delegations of his country to meetings of the Organisation of African Unity (OAU) and the Movement of Non-Aligned Countries, as well as to the Summit Conference of the French and African Heads of State. He also headed Egypt's delegation to the General Assembly sessions in 1979, 1982 and 1990. He was a member of the UN International Law Commission from 1979 until 1991. Boutros-Ghali was UN Secretary-General from 1992 to 1996. He is currently President of the Curatorium of the Hague Academy of International Law. In 2003 Boutros-Ghali was appointed as Director of the Egyptian National Council of Human Rights, a position he still holds.

important changes that René-Jean became a first-class Secretary-General of the Academy. It has always been a matter of regret to me that, owing to perfectly good reasons, I was never myself a member of the Curatorium, as indeed all the survivors of that Friedmann Committee were—excepting that is Panhuys, who died tragically young, and Friedmann, who was murdered in New York.

This was when you gave the general course at The Hague Academy?

Yes, I suppose it could have been. Or it could have been earlier. Michel and René-Jean, though close friends and colleagues, represented two different schools of thought. I was much influenced by France in any case; what Englishman is not? This curious relationship—I mean the English suspicion of France, and yet the English go to France on holiday every year. There used to be with the Cambridge Law Faculty a strong connection with the Faculty in what is now Paris II in the Panthéon, and we used to exchange visiting lecturers to give just one lecture about every two years. It was not an international law connection; it was a general law connection made by a property lawyer, Professor Holland, who was very fond of Paris, and indeed of the French language.

I went once to lecture there and met quite a lot of people. Shall I tell you about that, because it's a comical story. I can't remember when it was, but it was long before I was a Professor. It was—I suppose—about 1950 or a little later. I was invited to go and lecture in Paris. But there was a curious man there who was then the 'doyen'; I've forgotten his name. When I had first been in Paris with a group from the Cambridge Law Faculty, it was my first ever visit to the European Continent, apart from a call for breakfast at Gibraltar when on the way in a seaplane to my army posting in India. And then we had a delightful time with the Panthéon people,[41] including that great French lawyer René David,[42] who had studied in Cambridge with Gutteridge.[43] But when I went later to lecture, there was this 'doyen' whose name I've forgotten, a curious man. On this occasion I arrived in Paris and went to see the doyen, who was very busy with a lot of reference books, and obviously he'd been looking up who this Jennings was. Now of course there were two Jenningses in Cambridge. The other one, a constitutional lawyer, was Ivor Jennings, who was much better known than I was, a great scholar and long-standing friend of mine; we'd been together at the LSE (I was quite a bit younger), and then I'd met him again when I was in Sri Lanka in the army and he was Vice-Chancellor of the University of Ceylon. I think the 'doyen' had got things mixed up, because he then took me to a wonderful lunch at the

[41] Reference is clearly made here to the Law Professors of the University of Paris-I Panthéon.

[42] René David (French, 1906–90) was Professor of Comparative Law at Paris University.

[43] Harold Cook Gutteridge (British, 1876–1953) was Professor of Comparative Law at Cambridge University (1930–41).

Restaurant Lapérrouse. And I didn't know anybody at the lunch: they were all constitutional lawyers, and they were very pleasant and obviously having a splendid time, having this wonderful lunch at the expense of the doyen, I imagine. And then after this lunch, I was taken back to the Panthéon and faced with all the people I knew, the international lawyers, Suzanne Bastid leading them of course, and they were dead sober, had had no special lunch; and how it went I don't know, they were very kind about it. And of course the constitutional lawyers, very French, had their lunch and then went home. They didn't come to listen to me. So it was a very odd situation.

The French constitutional lawyers who had lunch with you, did they discover that actually you were not a constitutional lawyer?

Oh, I think they knew perfectly well. They were all very happy when I got to the luncheon, enjoying the situation enormously. They didn't talk about the law, they talked about French cheeses and that kind of thing. There was a nice sequel to it. I went around Paris and then found myself on a bus somewhere near the Luxembourg Gardens, and there was Suzanne Bastid next to me. And she said: 'Would you like to come to lunch tomorrow?' I don't think many people have been inside the Bastid flat, and I went and had lunch with the whole family.

Her father was Basdevant.

Yes, in fact the famous Basdevant.[44] Her husband, Mr Bastid, was the French judge, not an international lawyer, and the girls were there, the daughters. I have always been grateful to the Bastids for being so kind, especially after this dreadful lecture and no lunch. However, you talked about French influences. I was almost beginning by denying that they had any influence, but when you get me talking and thinking about it, enormous influence, yes. And of course I greatly admire the Panthéon and the wonderful mess they have with unorganised lectures and so on, but they do manage to produce some wonderful scholars.

Would you single out one particular book in French legal scholarship which has most impressed you?

No, I couldn't do that really. I remember being made by McNair to read one little book, in French, *Les Nouvelles Tendances du Droit International*, by Politis.[45] It came out about that time when I was an undergraduate, was it in the thirties? Yes, I read that and that was a sort of corrective to my too-English sources. Again, McNair's idea.

[44] See 'Interview with 'René-Jean Dupuy', section I.B.
[45] NS Politis, *Les Nouvelles Tendances du Droit International* (Paris, Hachette, 1927).

Actually Politis was Greek.

Oh, yes, but he wrote in French and it was published in Paris; and his 'Introduction' was written in Paris. But your question about French legal scholarship, and not just books in French, reminds me of a French lawyer of great distinction who influenced me a great deal. I mean Paul Reuter.[46] I got to know him well when we were together in the *Tunisia v Libya* case[47] before the Court. He was an admirable colleague and a good companion. I have found many of his writings important for me; and especially for the readability and their clarity. I have always especially enjoyed his *Introduction au droit des traités*.[48] It is not a big book, but I have always found it not just helpful but truly illuminating of problems in the law of treaties. He had a great gift for showing one, in a spare but elegant way of writing, what one might call the architecture of a branch of the law.

We were talking about Georges Scelle, who wrote various excellent books on public international law.

I know him only really from articles describing his theories. You see my French then was very inadequate. It still is, because at my school in Bradford the French taught was simply for written examination purposes, and the man who taught us French would never have thought of actually speaking the language. It never occurred to his mind that one might even do that. We had a very splendid master teaching English, and once the French master was away, and this man came and took the French lesson and started talking in French. And we little Bradford boys, we liked this man, we blushed for him: it seemed so embarrassing for an Englishman in England actually to speak French; moreover, you see, with a rather good French accent. We thought, 'Oh, poor man, somebody ought to have told him, one doesn't do that sort of thing!' At a fairly early stage at that school one could change to German, and I did, because the German teaching was much better. I am not a great linguist; I've learnt quite a bit of legal French here in the Court, a late starter again. You know I do on the whole now follow the French rather than the simultaneous translation.

What about Anzilotti?[49] Did you ever read his famous book on Public International Law?[50] I am afraid it was never translated into English, but it came out in French.

I knew about Anzilotti, of course, because Hersch Lauterpacht used to talk about him. But, no, I'm afraid that many of these foreign influences passed me by, because at the beginning I was busy doing many other things. It is indeed a weakness, and I recognise that.

46 See 'Interview with René-Jean Dupuy', fn 18.
47 Above n 36.
48 P Reuter, *Introduction au droit des traités* (Paris, Colin, 1972).
49 See 'Interview with René-Jean Dupuy', fn 15.
50 D Anzilotti, *Cours de droit international*, tr by GC Gidel (Paris, Recueil Sirey, 1929).

To go back to jurisprudence, you told me that you were primarily influenced by the British approach.

What happened in Cambridge when I was an undergraduate, between 1932 and 1935, was that jurisprudence was taught by a man who simply taught Austinian jurisprudence. (There was a younger man coming on, Brian King, who changed that teaching radically shortly afterwards, and taught general jurisprudence and his own little brand as well. A curious man in many ways, one of his great hates was Hart,[51] and he rather expected me to disagree with Hart whatever else one did!) But when I was attending jurisprudence lectures, jurisprudence for the purposes of the Tripos examination was simply Jethro Brown's textbook on Austinian jurisprudence.[52] And of course one result was that inevitably we got some antidotes from the international lawyers, who all felt they had to spend the first two lectures or so trying to persuade us that this was really law and not Austin's 'positive morality'. This was a mistake on their part. Even McNair did it, but it was a great mistake because, quite honestly, as an undergraduate going to the lectures of the Cambridge University Law Faculty, it never occurred to our minds that there was something taught here which was not really law. We would have accepted it straight away, but of course apologising for it at some length did tend to make us rather suspicious about the standing of international law.

The other thing I wanted to say was (it comes in one of your questions) that although jurisprudence was this rather wooden retailing of what Austin had said, or rather what Jethro Brown said he said, I respect Austin. There was also lots of good legal history, and in the first year one even prepared for international law by doing a sort of international relations-diplomatic history paper. There was also legal history of the common law. This was in my opinion superior to what happened since, because in those days one had to read the history where one could find it. So we dipped into the first of Holdsworth's 16 volumes of [the] history of English law,[53] we read quite a bit of Maitland, and I even read Maine's *Ancient Law*[54] as an undergraduate. This was splendid; but later it was ruined because eventually people produced student textbooks summarising all these things, which made things easier but not so interesting as reading the original sources. There was also an awful lot of Roman law taught at that time, including the history.

[51] Herbert Lionel Adolphus Hart (1907–92) was Professor of Jurisprudence at Oxford University and the Principal of Brasenose College, Oxford. He authored *The Concept of Law* (Oxford, Clarendon Press 1961).

[52] W Jethro Brown, *The Austinian Theory of Law: Being an Edition of Lectures I, V, and VI of Austin's "Essay on the Uses of the Study of Jurisprudence" with Critical Notes and Excursus* (London, Murray, 1906).

[53] W Holdsworth, *A History of English Law in Sixteen Volumes* (eds AL Goodhart and HG Hanbury) (London, Methuen, 1952).

[54] H Maine, *Ancient Law: Its Connection With the Early History of Society, and Its Relation to Modern Ideas* (London, Murray, 1861).

So there was no textbook on public international law?

Oh yes, several, both English and American (the lack was just in some aspects of legal history and jurisprudence). There was Oppenheim of course,[55] and there was Lawrence[56] and there was Hall,[57] the last still the best written. McNair used to say 'you just look and see which suits your temperament'. But McNair himself produced a considerable printed syllabus full of headings, references, the odd sentence giving a clue to a legal principle. The first thing he said in his lectures was 'You have this syllabus before you, will you please prepare your lecture and write your notes on these subjects that I am going to talk about next week before you come to the lecture'; and then he said with a friendly smile, 'You might be able to sit there with a reasonably intelligent look on your face.' Of course that was an ideal one didn't always attain, but that was his method of teaching: a good one. Write your lecture notes with the help of the fairly elaborate syllabus, and before going to the lecture.

III. The Role of the Jurist as Scholar and Practitioner

A. Participation in Public Life

Let us move on to the next question: have you ever contributed to newspapers, in an effort to popularise, as it were, international law?

I think the answer is that I have written one or two articles in newspapers or periodicals, like the old *Listener* we used to have in England, now defunct. I did one or two talks on international law on the old, magnificent radio Third Programme we used to rejoice in, in England, now long defunct in these less civilised times. You see in the Third Programme, then, you could actually give a talk on a chosen subject, and talk for 20 minutes without interruption. It was before this modern technique of interviewers whose main endeavour is not to reveal the person being interviewed but to show how clever they themselves are. It's very noticeable, especially on English television I regret

[55] Lassa Francis Lawrence Oppenheim (1858–1919), born in Germany and educated at the Universities of Berlin, Göttingen, Heidelberg and Leipzig, obtained in 1881 his PhD of Law at the University of Göttingen. He completed his Habilitation at Freiburg (Breisgau). He moved to the UK in 1895, acquiring citizenship in 1900, and lived there until his death. He first lectured at the LSE. In 1908 he became the Whewell Professor of International Law in the University of Cambridge. He is the author of *International Law: A Treatise*, 1st edn (London, Longmans, Green, 1905–06).

[56] Thomas Joseph Lawrence (1849–1919) was a professor of international law.

[57] William Edward Hall (1835–94) was called to the Bar in 1861 at Lincoln's Inn. He was elected to the *Institut de Droit international* as *associe* in 1875, and as *membre* in 1882. He became famous for *A Treatise on International Law* (2nd edn, Oxford, Clarendon Press, 1884), which, according to the *Encyclopedia Britannica* (*ad vocem*), is 'unquestionably the best book upon the subject in the English language. It is well planned, free from the rhetorical vagueness which has been the besetting vice of older books of a similar character, full of information, and everywhere bearing traces of the sound judgment and statesmanlike views of its author.'

to say, that as soon as the interviewee looks like saying something interesting, he or she is interrupted. I remember quite recently with enormous pleasure listening to an interview which had been arranged (I've forgotten the subject now); but they'd got two people apparently at opposite poles, Enoch Powell and Tony Benn, very much left and right, and obviously this was going to be great fireworks. And to the interviewer's manifest total dismay, they agreed on almost everything: 'Oh, Tony's absolutely right, I agree entirely with what he says. I've only just one little thing to add . . .' That sort of thing all the way. And you could hear the interviewer was getting more and more upset and frustrated because they would not fight. And they did genuinely agree; things come full circle so often.

Later I did do a little in the way of interviews on news and TV and so on, and commenting on the news. I soon gave up because I found I felt I wasn't good at that, because you need a quick mind and it's so easy to say things that you regret later on. And you find that if you have recorded interviews, the editor can take liberties without telling you. I've certainly given one interview here at The Hague, where half of my closing sentence was taken and not the qualification that followed. This is so dangerous.

Did you give the interview when you were President of the ICJ?

Yes, that's right. It didn't matter very much, but I gave it up. Some people can do it much better and are good at that sort of thing, and I thought it was wiser to leave it to them. You need the sort of mind that gets a good, sound answer on the spot, and not the following morning as you are having breakfast.

And what about the contributions to newspapers, did you give up there as well?

Yes, I did give that up. I still think it is very important that somebody should do it because I think it comes in one of your later questions, in a way, but perhaps I could say it now. It is one of the things that dismays me, in England anyhow (I can't speak for other countries). The media there, the newspapers and even the BBC, they are so ignorant about international law, and it's very difficult to get them to take it seriously. I mean they have no idea that it is a real system of law; it is a working law that Foreign Office legal advisers are dealing with across their desks every day, settling questions and discussing things with their opposite numbers in other countries, and so on. They have no idea that it's a working system, and this I find very dangerous, because awareness of the existence of a system of law is much more important in my view than any sanctions. If you haven't awareness of the existence of the law, you are nowhere. *The Times*—at the moment, it's under curious ownership of course—produced one example. The *Chad/Libya* judgment,[58] which is a remarkable judgment in many ways: 16:1, it decided that the disputed

[58] *Territorial Dispute (Chad v Libyan Arab Jamahiriya)*, 3 February 1994, [1994] ICJ Rep 6.

territory, then under occupation by Libyan troops, really belonged to Chad. And what happens? The Libyan troops are withdrawn under UN supervision. I think Ghadafi has been very wise and statesmanlike, and we have to be grateful to him. But you know *The Times* the other day had an article by an African correspondent about Colonel Ghadafi in which they mentioned the withdrawal of the forces from the Aouzou Strip and never mentioned the Court or the judgment; it gave the impression that this was an accomplishment of the Organisation of African Unity, which certainly had a part to play in the early stages. *The Times* used to report our judgments in the legal section, but they no longer do. Why not, I don't know. Steve Schwebel[59] and I have protested but we've had no acknowledgement of our letter.

But they do report the judgments of the European Court of Justice, and of the Luxembourg Court.

Yes, they do, but not the International Court judgments. They did do so for a time. Fitzmaurice[60] tried very hard to get them to do so, but in vain. And Steve Schwebel and I tried again with a former editor, and he said 'Yes, of course, this omission is stupid, we will report them', and they did for a time; but with a change of editor it stopped again.

Yes, probably this is because most ICJ cases do not have a direct impact on British public opinion.

But how can they, if they are not thought newsworthy? Yes, it is extremely dangerous. It's not only international law that suffers, because they do select the news. And they're so powerful in a way that what they don't select might as well not have happened.

So you do see a need for international lawyers to try to inform the public opinion?

I do. This comes under some of your later questions, but I do see an enormous task for international lawyers to popularise and to get our message across. And I get a bit impatient (this is a rather touchy subject), but I get impatient with the *Institut de Droit international* and such organisations. You know, we spend such a lot of time talking to each other but we don't go out and talk to people in other walks of life, or even in related subjects. The *Institut de Droit international* in many ways is a very bad example because they make reports on questions such as maritime boundaries; but they don't think of consulting or associating with their work other experts, such as hydrographers and geographers. I think this is wrong. It is high time the *Institut* realised that there

[59] Stephen Schwebel (*b* 1929) in 1967–81 was Edward B Burling Professor of International Law and Organization at the School of Advanced International Studies (SAIS), Johns Hopkins University in Washington DC. In 1961–81 he was Deputy Legal Adviser to the State Department, then judge (1981–2000) and President (1997–2000) at the ICJ.

[60] See 'Interview with Eduardo Jiménez de Aréchaga', fn 23.

is such a thing as inter-disciplinary study. The way forward is not to be found by confining the *Institut* to an elitist group just of international lawyers. I am all for elites, they are at the core of civilisation; but when one contemplates the *Institut*, one begins to see that those who condemn 'elitism' may sometimes have a point.

I gather that Rosalyn Higgins[61] *was very often on TV.*

Yes, that's partly why I gave up trying to do it, because I heard Rosalyn once or twice and I heard Chris Greenwood.[62] Both of them I thought were admirable, and it was pointless for me to attempt it because I really wasn't very good at it, and felt uncomfortable, whereas they speak clearly and with confidence. I like speaking to an audience, and answering their questions, but I dislike speaking to a microphone.

Both spoke about the Falklands war.

Yes, I vaguely remember. But that's a subject on which I would hesitate to speak anyway, because I spent such a lot of time as a Counsel advising Argentina. They never consulted me about the Malvinas, of course. But I think the British Government likewise would never have consulted me about The Falklands. And also there is some passage, I've never been quite sure which it is, in my book on *Acquisition of Territory*,[63] which makes me a sort of juristic hero in Buenos Aires. I think it's taken a little out of context perhaps. Still, I'm not discontented with that position, but I would not talk about The Falklands publicly for that reason. There are people better able to do it.

Can we move on to the other question about whether in your view an international lawyer, or any lawyer for that matter, should get involved in social activities, say, politics or any political activity at international level?

Yes, I think it could well be. Some people have to do the things in a democracy.

You, yourself, have you ever been involved in politics?

I really don't see how, short of being a hermit, one can avoid being 'involved'. One does vote at elections. I haven't been involved in party politics. McNair was a bit; he was a great Liberal and spoke once or twice in the House of Lords on Liberal matters, and his son was a great Liberal. He once tried to persuade me to stand for Cambridge as a Liberal candidate, but I resisted

[61] Rosalyn Higgins (*b* 1937) was Professor of International Law at the University of Kent at Canterbury, 1978–81, then at University of London (LSE), 1981–95. She was elected a judge (1995–2009) and then President (2006–09) of the ICJ. Member of the *Institut de Droit international* since 1987.

[62] Christopher John Greenwood (*b* 1955) was a barrister and Professor of International Law at the LSE until his election, in 2008, to the ICJ.

[63] Above n 3.

that, even from McNair. I didn't want to. No, I've never been a member of any party. I have voted for all three one time or another.

But in answer to your question, I would say that really all lawyers, even international lawyers, are citizens of their country, and in that capacity they may or may not feel that they ought to take part in politics. There's no particular reason why international lawyers should be different from anybody else in this respect. It is important that good and important people are concerned with politics. I'm concerned of course with the government of my country. One has to be. But I have no great stomach for party politics of any hue.

Does the decision not to get involved in politics stem from your own temperament? Or is it the result of a sort of decision to remain neutral, as it were?

It depends what you're doing of course. As a professor I would have never felt any need to be neutral in the matter of party politics, except insofar as it might interfere with teaching. It could even help. But as a judge I think one ought to be very careful about party politics.

Such a question may arise in connection with the giving of legal advice to a Foreign Minister. You have been consulted on many issues of international law, and I wonder whether you were aware of the political implications of your own legal advice.

Oh, yes, I think one must be aware of the political and social implications all the time. So should a judge for that matter.

Did you ever refrain from giving legal advice just because you were aware that this would lead to politically 'dangerous' consequences?

I think not, because of the tradition of the English Bar whereby if you are offered a brief and you can do it, you ought to take it on. And if you don't like the client, or don't like what he is doing, you're probably the best man to take it on as an advocate. The feeling is that everybody is entitled to their day in court, and the barrister's job is to see that they get a fair hearing and to pick up any brief he is asked to undertake. There might be limits. It depends what you are asked to do. A former colleague of mine, whom I admired, and who used to be very much in favour of apartheid (and this impressed me, because he was a very good, gentle person), tried to persuade me to come to the Court and help South Africa during the *South Africa* case.[64] I said 'No', I didn't want to do that. That was beyond my limit. Anyhow I said 'No', at that point I didn't want to. I think another colleague of mine did accept the invitation. But I was clear that I didn't want to. It was the right decision, I am sure.

[64] *South West Africa cases (Ethiopia v South Africa; Liberia v South Africa)*, 18 July 1966, [1966] ICJ Rep 6.

Because you would have been requested to support apartheid.

I would have been very uncomfortable to be sitting there with them, at that time anyway. Of course I would be very comfortable with South Africa at present.

Assuming that you were not a judge but a professor of international law, and your Foreign Office asked you to give legal reasons to justify the use of force by the British authority somewhere; if you felt that this use of force would not be in keeping with the UN Charter, would you be prepared still, as a sort of neutral adviser, to give your advice to try to justify legally that use of force?

It would be very difficult. Fortunately, I've never been in that position. I've said about the rule of the English Bar that you pick up any brief you are asked to do. In any event, one would first have to find out the factual position from a study of the documents, etc. One could hardly rush to judge on the basis of what one only knew from the media. But there must be limits, and you reminded me of course of that extraordinary situation of Fitzmaurice and the Suez Canal business when he was the Legal Adviser to the Foreign Office. He had extraordinary courage; he not only insisted on saying that the adventure was unlawful, but I believe in the minutes (the material is in the Public Record Office and can now be consulted) there is a memo he wrote, and he and every legal adviser signed, saying that this was done contrary to their advice. Well, I am a tremendous admirer of Fitzmaurice of course, and I think his rule there would guide me in a question which involves not merely a difference of legal opinion but of fundamental morality. If Fitzmaurice could do that as the Legal Adviser of the Government, splendid. I think it has to be said that it's a great tribute to a lingering tradition in the British Government and in governmental circles that he was able to do that without very serious repercussions for him, or for the other legal advisers. They all survived, which I think is magnificent. I'm very proud of that.

Later on he became a Judge at the ICJ.

Yes, yes indeed; he was nominated by the national group, and then elected to succeed Hersch Lauterpacht.

Was it the same government which nominated Fitzmaurice as a judge, the same government or a new government?

Well, the Government doesn't nominate anybody in the UK. The national group is truly independent. I am a member of it now; we consult with the Foreign Office Legal Adviser and we consult the Lord Chancellor's Department[63] and we consult the Law Officers. But it is only consultation.

[63] Currently in the UK the Lord Chancellor's Department, as such, no longer exists, having been merged into the Ministry of Justice.

We're entirely independent, and at least once—not for a British nomination, but for a foreign one—we decided differently from the Foreign Office. They accepted our choice immediately, of course. This question arose, as you know, in the United States, and there was a great revolt of the academics. When Dick Baxter[66] came here [to The Hague, at the ICJ], the President of the United States, as I understand it, had assumed that it was his nomination, and he was going to nominate Foster Dulles.[67] And there was a revolt of the academics, who pointed out that, according to the Statute, they should be consulted; and they were successful because Webster,[68] who was a great man and a powerful one, and one of the national group, stood out with them. The result was that the national group decided on that wonderful man, Dick Baxter, who was sent here. And I think that boosted morale generally. So there are at any rate two countries, but I hope more, where the nomination procedure accords with the provisions of the Court's Statute.

Therefore the national group in England might even decide to nominate somebody who would not be acceptable to the Foreign Office?

They might. It would be difficult to this extent, Nino, that one's always conscious that it's the Foreign and Commonwealth Office people in New York who have to sell the candidate and get the votes; but it could be done. And I am quite certain that the Foreign and Commonwealth Office would, in that event, do their duty by the nominated candidate, even if they had hoped for a different one.

Normally it would come to a sort of agreement with them.

We agree upon one name and put it forward; and in my experience anyhow, it's always been accepted by the Foreign and Commonwealth Office.

For instance, if the Foreign Office suggests that a former legal adviser should be nominated, a member of the British national group might say no, we prefer an academic.

Yes, they might, but not because he or she was an academic. We don't think in those terms. The national group, in my experience anyhow, would say 'Well, we look entirely at the merits'; nothing against legal advisers, some of them are very, very good, or against professors, some of them are very

[66] Richard Baxter (1921–80) was Professor of International Law at Harvard University (1955–80). He sat as a judge in the ICJ in 1978–80.

[67] John Foster Dulles (1888–1959) was US Secretary of State (1953–59) under President Dwight Eisenhower.

[68] Judge William H Webster, a former federal judge, served in the US Court of Appeals for the Eighth Circuit (1973–78) and in the US District Court for the Eastern District of Missouri (1970–73). He served as Director of the Federal Bureau of Investigation from 1978 to 1987 and as Director of the Central Intelligence Agency from 1987 to 1991, during which time he led some of the most prominent and sensitive legal commissions.

good too. And we simply look at the merits and see who would be the better person in the present circumstances to take that job on. It ought surely to be a question about suitability for the job at a particular time. It is not a prize for any particular kind of virtue. No, I think it must be one of the few countries, but we [British] really are independent; and Steve Schwebel assures me that they are too, in the United States. Because, after all, the purpose of the national group is to insulate the nomination from the government itself. On the other hand, it has to be said that the national group is itself appointed by the government; in effect the legal adviser chooses, and they've tended always to have a couple of academics, and a couple of retired Foreign and Commonwealth Office people. I must add that (again I can only speak from my experience on the group for my time on it) I have never felt that the ex-Foreign Office people were pushing one of their people at the expense of the academics, or vice versa.

In the UK you have a wonderful tradition of both academics and legal advisers.

Yes, looking back historically, there has been a tendency to use both sources. Of course, I suppose Fitzmaurice is recently the only one who has professionally been pure Foreign Office; on the other hand, he wasn't really, was he? He was made by God to be an academic. He would have been a wonderful professor, because he was so widely read and educated in things other than law. Also I am sure he would have been an excellent teacher. I still have several pages of letters in his own hand, carefully discussing some question I had put to him. He was also very encouraging: the secret of good teaching. Again we're getting off your syllabus, but I remember asking him to give a Lauterpacht Memorial Lecture; and my idea of those lectures was not a graduate lecture. I used to give the Lauterpacht visiting lecturer my Tripos class of some 200 people, mainly undergraduates. I was a little worried because Fitz, in his writings, can go on and on finding more and more distinctions, but I told him when he ought to finish. And bless him, he gave a perfect lecture for that audience and finished it right on time. Wonderful performance.

B. Technician versus Intellectual

Let us move on to another question. Do you perceive yourself merely as a technician?

I have no doubt about the answer to that question. I hope that I'm not just a technician. If so, I would feel that I'd failed in what I'd tried to do. Again I go back to McNair, I would have been troubled to think I might be what he called 'a mere lawyer'. And this would be contrary to the whole tradition of Cambridge and Oxford University, and the College system. It's very difficult to be a 'mere lawyer' when you are living and eating and talking the whole time with people in quite other subjects, including the sciences. Also I think you would fail the undergraduates, because many of them, the most important, are not going to be technicians. They are going to be educated people. After all, my main career was as a University Don, and in that respect I would have thought that I'd failed completely if I was a mere technician.

We should agree upon the distinction between a mere lawyer or a technician. One of the elements to be taken into account, in my view, for somebody to be an intellectual and not a mere lawyer, is also that he or she attaches great importance to ethical values and tries in a way to use them.

Yes, I would accept that.

In addition to your writing and your acting as a judge, what in your view could be regarded as making you not a mere technician?

How do you define what is being a good intellectual: it's very difficult, isn't it? I think the intellectuals in any country are a distinct class of people. My own origins were very humble, but at Cambridge I gradually learned new mental attitudes. I think being an intellectual should denote a different sort of attitude to discussion for one thing. In the University, well in my experience of the University anyhow, one learned to discuss everything as far as possible with an open mind and to look at every argument as a possibility. I would say today you could almost define (this is a little mischievous, Nino) a true intellectual as one who refused to be 'politically correct'. There's always something to be looked at. I said that I refused to join the South African team in any capacity; nevertheless, I do recognise that there was a sort of curious, misguided idealism behind it, because I'm thinking of this man from South Africa, Manning[69] I think it was, at the London School of Economics, who was a gentle idealist, and somehow he thought apartheid was an ethically correct solution of their undoubted problems. It's an extreme case that—something to be said for apartheid—but even that, I think, as an intellectual one ought to be willing to discuss with Manning, his point of view, and to listen to it even though one might reject it, as I did.

I should add that all this about intellectuals should not be understood as being dismissive of the need to be a good technician as well, because it is very easy—and I've seen it happen in various people—to be a good intellectual and to indulge oneself in this kind of life, and to persuade oneself it doesn't matter too much if one doesn't actually know the black-letter law. That won't do.

[69] Charles Anthony Woodward Manning (1894–1978), born and educated in South Africa, was a Rhodes Scholar at Brasenose College, Oxford. In 1922, he became a barrister, and served as Personal Assistant to the Secretary-General of the League of Nations. He was then at Oxford as Fellow of New College and Lecturer in Law, specialising in Jurisprudence. He subsequently taught at the LSE, first as Cassel Professor of International Relations, and later as Montague Burton Professor. On Manning, see H Suganami, 'C A W Manning and the Study of International Relations' (2001) 27 *Review of International Studies* 91.

C. Lawyers' Contribution to Changing the Law

Would you agree that for a lawyer to be not a mere technician, but also somebody who has a broader mind, it would also be important to try to contribute to changing the law in addition to interpreting the existing law?

Yes, certainly. Law reform is a very, very important subject intellectually, and not just for lawyers either. I was thinking in my own mind as you put this question, Nino, that in a way I am almost contradicting what I said at the beginning about the McNair feeling that you have to be able to distinguish between proposals and what is really law and so on, almost stick to the law because that's your particular job. Well, life is full of contradictions and ambivalence. A great friend of mine who taught English at Jesus College, AP Rossiter, was very devoted to the idea that ambivalence leads to the truth. Given two contradictory ideas you may then find that neither represents the truth, but that something that involves both of them and is part of both of them is at any rate a nearer approximation to the truth.

Probably, as a judge you have realised this is true.

Yes, as a judge you realise it, and dramatically too, because, you know, most people who speak here are pretty persuasive. And when you've heard one side, you feel very sympathetic; when you've heard the other side you feel very sympathetic; and then comes what Roberto Ago[70] once called very wisely, 'your agony'. He told me, he said 'unless you are in agony, you are not a good judge'.

We were talking about law reform. Did you have any opportunity to contribute to changing international law?

I don't know that I've had much, except perhaps just a little as a judge. I'm very concerned about the future of international law. Do you know the work of Philip Allott, *Eunomia*?[71] A beautifully written book, and I am quite a bit influenced by Philip in feeling that we need a new vision of international law and relations. I am a bit disappointed in Philip that he hasn't been able so far to take it a bit further and say what we should do next week. That's what we want to know. But I'm afraid I've rather taken refuge in the old man's privilege of drawing attention to problems and asking the younger people to

[70] See 'Interview with René Jean Dupuy', fn 20.

[71] P Allott, *Eunomia: New Order for a New World* (Oxford, Oxford University Press, 1990). Philip Allott (British, *b* 1939) is Professor Emeritus of International Public Law, Cambridge University. He was at one time a legal adviser in the British Foreign and Commonwealth Office. Among his publications, see also *The Health of Nations: Society and Law Beyond the State* (Cambridge, Cambridge University Press, 2002); and *Towards the International Rule of Law: Essays in Integrated Constitutional Theory* (London, Cameron May, 2005). He is a Fellow of the British Academy. On his contribution to jurisprudence and international law, see the various comments and papers published in (2005) 16 *European Journal of International Law* 255–313.

do the work. I do feel the need very strongly for a new vision of international law. I mean, there is this nonsense talked about sovereignty still; countries are fragmenting and talk about sovereignty and independence seems to be very fashionable. At the same time the necessary interdependence and lack of independence is demonstrated daily in Foreign Offices especially, in any matters of detail. I remember Ian Sinclair, to mention one Legal Adviser whom I know very well, telling me one day, 'You know, Robbie, you've no idea how I spend my time. I spend so much of my time saying "Minister, that is a very good idea but I'm afraid you can't do it"'. This is the reality of things. I'm not sure we've done as much as we ought to bring it home to people.

I came across it again in trying to write an Introduction to Philippe Sands's new book, an enormous textbook, on environmental law.[72] It's rather frightening, because all these problems are essentially international and need an international solution, and yet the international solution has to be carried out very often in the municipal law and not merely in international law. The old idea, in England anyhow, that you're either a private international lawyer or a public international lawyer, is really nonsense now. We have to bring it all together, and what frightens me when I read Sand's work (which is very good I think, it gives you a conspectus of the whole thing) is that one point that shines out clearly, is that specialisation is no good.

Narrow specialisation is one of the tendencies of modern international law I greatly regret: specialisation in human rights or environment for instance; trendy, modish subjects that seem to attract people who want to specialise without bothering about the rest of international law. Let me stress the dangers in specialisation because, for example, one really needs to know the Law of Treaties. One can't get far on environmental law unless one also knows the Law of Treaties. But it's true the other way round too, Nino, to an extent I hadn't quite realised: the extent to which environmental considerations now infiltrate all the rest of international law, so that you can't do these other subjects without knowing something about the law of the environment.

One example, that I've mentioned in my Introduction to Sand's book, impressed me: I was a bit involved at one time in this great debate we used to have, in the 1960s, about sovereignty over natural resources, on the one hand, and *pacta sunt servanda* and concessions and investments, on the other, and the famous Resolution of the General Assembly.[73] Now of course you can't look at that problem without looking also at environment. The Brazilian rain forests are a very good example, because there you have a natural resource subject to the local sovereignty, undoubtedly, but which is also a resource of major international concern so that one needs to look at the whole of international law.

[72] P Sands, R Tarasofsky and M Weiss (eds), *Principles of International Environmental Law*, 2nd edn (Cambridge, Cambridge University Press, 2003).

[73] Reference is made here to the UN General Assembly Resolution 1803 (XVII) of 14 December 1962.

The other thing that bothers me a little is the appalling amount of environmental law we have already; I mean the present tendency in international law, as well as municipal law, to try [to] solve everything by regulations and bureaucratic offices and inspectors of various kinds, and feel that you've done something. This is where I think we do need a new broad vision of international law and international relations. Of course I am influenced a bit by this wretched, stupid debate we have in England now about the European Community and sovereignty, and it's so ignorant on both sides in a way, especially in the idea that we have any choice about belonging. You know there isn't a choice ultimately.

To go back just one second to the book by Philip Allott,[74] why do you find it is an important contribution?

Because of the new vision of international law. I enjoyed reading it partly because I know and like Philip very much, but I think partly also because he is an international lawyer who (a) does know his international law—he's a very good technician, and (b) he's prepared to criticise strongly the fundamentals of the subject; that I found refreshing.

I think that his book has not had any major impact on international lawyers.

No, it hasn't, no; it's too difficult for most people to read, and at the same time it's not really a programme, it is mainly a criticism of what happens now.

One also has the impression sometimes it is a bit dogmatic; it is a catalogue of hard and fast propositions.

I'm not sure that he's produced an idea that's going to have significant power. It's also rather negative—effective in attacking the present system; but what do we do about it? This business of environment, for example, what do we do now? We have this enormous problem; the law we have is frightening in the sheer amount of it, and yet at the same time it's totally inadequate to the problem.

Have you had a chance of reading other general, theoretical books, such as those by Koskenniemi[75] or David Kennedy?[76] Are you familiar with this new school of international law?

[74] Allott, above n 71.

[75] Martti Koskenniemi (Finnish, *b* 1953) is Professor of International Law at the University of Helsinki. Member of the UN International Law Commission (2002–06). Author of numerous publications, among which *From Apology to Utopia: The Structure of the International Legal Argument* (Helsinki, Lakimiesliiton Kustannus, 1989) and *The Gentle Civilizer of Nations: The Rise and Fall of International Law, 1870–1960* (Cambridge, Cambridge University Press, 2002) stand out.

[76] David Kennedy (*b* 1954) has since 1981 been successively Assistant Professor, Professor and Faculty Director at Harvard Law School. He teaches international law, international economic policy, legal theory, law and development, and European law. He has authored, among other things, *International Legal Structures* (Baden-Baden, Nomos, 1987).

Yes, I have looked at them. Koskennieni I've looked at because I like him very much, he's a nice man, very able, really top-class mind, a very good technician—yes. When he gets into the more sort of jurisprudential and abstract field, I get the same reaction that I think you do from Philip [Allott]. It may be laziness of mind on my part, but I don't really follow it easily, and I don't easily understand quite what he's saying. It's partly a matter of language, certainly also with Kennedy. It leaves me cold. Ideas can be very powerful, but I sometimes wonder whether high-flown ideas are not a kind of escapism from the urgent problems in the field.

Arguably, it is difficult to find there a link between what they say at the theoretical level and the innate problems that practising lawyers have to face. One has the feeling that their theoretical constructs are not of great help to the international lawyer.

I agree entirely. That's right, and that's what one longs for of course. What we badly need is a great vision or imaginative idea which helps us next week in the particular problems we have to solve. I'm afraid I can't offer it, but it's what we badly need—a sort of new look at international law, at its fundamentals. It should perhaps be said that we now have a quite splendid statement of the present problem of international law, in the statement of Ambassador Owada, at the UN Congress on 13 March 1995, and entitled 'Justice and Stability in International Law'.

Do you remember the various books by Richard Falk?[77] *He has an original vision of international law.*

He has a vision, and again a great intellect and mind. Again, it may be laziness on my part, but I don't find it easy reading at all. Well I was thinking of Falk's book[78] about the relationship between international law and municipal law. One has this problem all the time in practical situations. I don't find I run to Richard Falk for a solution to my problems. I might run to him for general ideas, but it doesn't quite come down to the practical I think; though he can, of course, when he wants to. As a legal adviser I am quite sure he'd be very good indeed.

D. Scholar versus Practitioner

The next question is about how you have integrated your activity as a scholar into that as practitioner.

Of course becoming a judge didn't arise in any difficult form with me, because I only became a judge after I had retired from the Chair and from academic life, so that made it much easier.

[77] Richard Falk (*b* 1930) until his retirement in 2001 had been Albert G Milbank Professor of International Law and Practice at Princeton University.

[78] Reference is made here to RA Falk, *The Role of Domestic Courts in the International Legal Order* (Syracuse, NY, Syracuse University Press, 1964).

I would cavil a little at the implied distinction between scholarly activity and what a practitioner has to do, as I am sure you would. Your addresses to the Court in the *Chad v Libya* case[79] were very scholarly, and I don't find a contradiction there.

Practice came to me very late. I did some private consultancy as well; a legal adviser at Shell used to use me quite a lot, and I found that very interesting. He was called John Blair—the name sounded as if he was a Scotsman—he was Viennese actually; a very good legal adviser, I think, and far-seeing and very sympathetic to the ideas of developing States, and this of course was also very wise. I found working with him rewarding, I was lucky. But I valued practice, let's not beat about the bush, because it brought in money. The academic salaries in England have gone right down. And so even in my day, with a growing family, I was glad of the extra money, and that was one of the reasons for being glad to practise. But I also was glad of it because I felt it did help teaching. You had concrete examples. One had a much better idea of the sort of situations that arise; also your pupils knew you were doing a certain amount of practice and that gave you a certain authority. I remember Humphrey Waldock saying that when a pupil was saying 'Is there such a thing as international law anyway?', he was tempted (perhaps even succumbed to the temptation once) to say, 'Well, the so-and-so government is offering to pay me for advice on international law, so I think they must think there is something.' And this was very valuable to an international lawyer, because there's a sort of background of scepticism when international law is mentioned, in England anyway; and I think that's probably not confined to England, and even in the profession, which saddens me. I was hearing the other day, from one of my colleagues in Cambridge, of a man who is doing quite well in chambers on the international law side, and some of the seniors were saying, you know, 'Why do you waste your time? You ought to be doing good common law or whatever.' This is the sort of feeling; and of course the general English Bar seems to be quite ignorant of the fees you can earn in this place—the ICJ—by pleading, so it's left to the professors, which is nice for professors but I'm not sure it's the ideal situation. Occasionally an Attorney-General will turn up, for example in an important case involving the United Kingdom; but everybody knows that it's a set formal speech written by somebody else, one of the other people sitting there. And after this ceremonial he will check out of the more expensive hotel he alone was staying in, and go back home, leaving the rest of the team to do the real arguing.

So, your activity as a practitioner has had a major impact on your scholarly activity?

Yes, I think it has done, Nino. I have said that I was always a late developer. The practice made me feel that I had something to say. Perhaps it gave me more confidence, and that was something I much needed for writing. I felt

[79] See above n 58.

that if governments wanted my ideas, they might be worth putting into articles. So the practice was important to me. It may be a matter of individual temperament. There are people after all, dons and scholars, who could retire as a hermit and work and produce. Kelsen must have been one, I think. But I could never have done that. I need to be stimulated, I need to have a deadline by which it has to be done. And I like working with a team. Then I enjoy it. I can do it and I like doing it, but I do need the help of colleagues discussing—and for that practice was ideal. The other part of practice which I did enjoy was being part of a team that had to work together under constraints of time; and getting the thing done on time gave great satisfaction.

This also applies to your activity as a judge?

It does. You're quite right.

IV. A Look at the International Community

A. Jennings' major contributions to international law

What would you consider as your major contribution to international law as a scholar?

I think I would be tempted to put at the top, on the scholarly side, my contribution to teaching. It's the thing of which I am most proud. I used to enjoy enormously teaching this large class of 200 or more international law undergraduates (a few graduates came as well); a very mixed body of people. As a rule there was the dreadful nervous first lecture in a new year, when one wondered whether one would be able to make a rapport with a new class. Once that nervous time was over, I enjoyed my lecturing, and I think they were fairly successful lectures. People kept on coming; and lectures are not compulsory in Cambridge, and you soon know if your lectures are not very successful. I lectured to many generations of undergraduates, lawyers and some in other walks of life. I would like to think of that as a major contribution.

Did you also give seminars?

Oh, yes, I gave seminars to graduates studying for the LLM. On the whole I enjoyed the lecture more: a larger class, and one didn't have to stop and ask questions and so on.

One of the questions we've rather missed was about the great personalities in Cambridge Law School when I was myself a young Don. One of them was the great Roman lawyer, WW Buckland.[80] I went to his lectures on the part of

[80] William Warwick Buckland (1859–1946) was Regius Professor of Civil Law at the University of Cambridge from 1914 to 1945. His works on Roman Law include *A Textbook of Roman Law from Augustus to Justinian*, 2nd edn (Cambridge, Cambridge University Press, 1932).

the *Digest* in the second year. He lectured very fast, very fast. He had heard of the method of asking questions and the American casebooks, no doubt. Once he was moved to stop lecturing for a moment and said with a great smile, 'Can any gentleman [there were no ladies then] tell me the answer to this . . .', and he propounded a simple problem no doubt—dead silence. A frown came on his face immediately: 'Haven't time to wait, haven't time to wait'; and on he went with his lecture with the feeling that we've got to get through this stuff, and if you can't answer straight away I'm not waiting for you.

Now that's not seminar stuff. I enjoyed the seminar very often. I enjoyed especially, I think, being present at Hersch Lauterpacht's graduate seminar, when he was professor. I always attended as one of the students really, though present as a member of the faculty. But it was giving lectures that I particularly enjoyed, because I could teach a large number of people.

Did you use to cover all the various topics of international law?

It was supposed to be a complete course on international law. We didn't do very much in the way of what you might call 'Volume 2 of Oppenheim' in those days, but certainly in the Law of Peace: one covered pretty well every major subject. I used to change it every year. I think I was one of the very first to mention the pollution problem at a very early stage. But then I found myself in company with these awful one-cause people and dropped it a little. Human rights and the rest of it—I brought it all in as it developed. Every year there would be interesting changes, perhaps because of a case, or one or two subjects would appear as more important than the others and I'd spend more time on those, on the topical things. It was interesting how the topics seemed to come and go in importance.

Which of your writings would you consider as your major contribution?

I think that's for other people to judge, not for me.

Is there one particular article or book of yours that you regard as more significant?

Well, *Acquisition of Territory*[81] has been, rather surprisingly in a way, quite influential. And I'd like to think also that the General Course[82] that I gave at the Academy had quite an influence. Otherwise there were some useful articles in the *British Yearbook*. That on Germany after the war ('Government in Commission')[83] had some influence, I think. And there was one that was not so much noticed but which I still think is one of my better articles: 'The Progressive Development of International Law and its Codification',[84] and

81 Above n 3.
82 Above n 5.
83 (1946) 23 *British Yearbook of International Law* 112.
84 (1947) 24 *British Yearbook of International Law* 301.

'Extraterritorial Jurisdiction and the United States Antitrust Laws',[85] and of course the article on 'State Contracts in International Law'.[86] Incidentally, that long interval between 1947 and 1957 is pretty exactly the time when I was primarily a College and University tutor and administrator.

One of your first articles, that on the Caroline *case,*[87] *was published in the* American Journal.

Yes, the one about the *Caroline* and *McLeod* cases in 1938. That takes me back to McNair, who was such an unselfish man. Before I went to Harvard, when I was still doing the LLB (a post-graduate degree in Cambridge) and I was McNair's pupil, he put me onto the Public Record Office in London and how one could find Foreign Office papers; and he gave me the reference numbers for those papers on the *Caroline*. I went and spent a day or two looking through them, and at Harvard used them as a basis for that article. I've often thought, what a splendid thing for McNair to do. He'd discovered the value of these papers from the Foreign Office, and he immediately passed it on to a pupil and said 'You know, these are very interesting, have a look at them, you could use them'. Isn't that marvellous? I was at Harvard and Hudson[88] was there, of course. I took the article to him. He was very laconic in his office (not in lectures!); he wasn't very encouraging in a way, and yet I took along this article and said 'What do you think of that?' He said, 'Well, send it to the *American Journal*.' And I said 'Are you sure?' 'Yes', he said, 'send it now to the *American Journal*', and no further comment. And I did and they accepted it, and there it was.

Can I just tell you about Harvard for a minute. It's very personal. I can't tell you how green I was then; I don't mean 'green' in the modern sense, I mean 'green' as in that famous book about Oxford about Mr Verdant Green,[89] as they called him, the new undergraduate who makes all the mistakes possible. When I went to Harvard it was the first time I'd ever been away from England; I'd never been abroad, even on the Continent. It was 1936/37. I got to Harvard and I was terribly homesick; I can't tell you how homesick I was, really almost a disease. I was waiting and waiting to get home, and yet I made wonderful friends there, and I loved Harvard. It's curious (you mentioned Freud—he might have been interested in this): I wanted to get away from this place and back home to Yorkshire. When I did get back home to Yorkshire,

[85] (1957) 33 *British Yearbook of International Law* 146.

[86] (1961) 37 *British Yearbook of International Law* 156.

[87] Above n 9.

[88] Manley Ottmer Hudson (1886–1960) became professor at Harvard in 1919, heading the department of international law from 1923 to 1954. A member of the Permanent Court of Arbitration since 1933, he sat as a judge on the PCIJ (1936–46). From 1936 he was an associate and then member of the *Institut de Droit international.*

[89] Reference is made here to *The Adventures of Mr Verdant Green* (London, Nathaniel Cooke, 1854), a novel by Cuthbert M Bede, a pseudonym of Edward Bradley (1827–89).

for years I used to have wonderful dreams, sometimes, in which I was back in Harvard. How contradictory humankind is.

I did enjoy Harvard in that peculiar way, through the homesickness; I did enjoy it very much, and not only the Law School. The Law School was a shock to me because it was so ruthlessly competitive; they had a lot of nervous breakdowns. There was one lecturer, I've forgotten his name, who used to begin his first lecture by saying 'Look to your right, look to your left, one of you three won't be here next year'. And yet at the same time these were the golden days of the Harvard Law School. Pound[90] was lecturing on jurisprudence; and Williston[91] on contracts; and Felix Frankfurter[92] on the constitution. [Frankfurter] gave me a lot of good advice. I put myself down for the LLM at Harvard, and he said to me, 'Well, you've got two degrees at Cambridge, what do you want another for?' He said, 'Browse, go to the lectures you enjoy, read books, and enjoy Harvard and America.' And so I did as he told me, and that was good advice from Felix Frankfurter. I spent one year on my Choate Fellowship and I didn't spend all my time in the Law School, because Whitehead[93] was lecturing on philosophy in the College and I went to his lectures in the College. I didn't understand everything, but he was such a personality and so charming and delightful, it was just a joy to be there with him. And one got some inkling of a mathematical approach to thinking.

Who was the professor of international law at Harvard?

Hudson was the professor. I didn't see a lot of him because he was already a judge at The Hague. But I got to know him a bit later; and then, to my astonishment, last year I got the Hudson Medal. I told the audience in my little speech that I was staggered at this award, but was able to say 'nothing like as staggered as Hudson would have been'.

[90] Nathan Roscoe Pound (1870-–1964) in 1903 became Dean of the University of Nebraska College of Law. In 1910, he began teaching at Harvard and in 1916 became Dean of Harvard Law School. He authored, among other books, *Outlines of Lectures on Jurisprudence*, 5th edn (Cambridge, MA, Harvard University Press, 1943), *The Spirit of the Common Law* (Boston, MA, Marshall Jones, 1921), *Law and Morals* (Chapel Hill, NC, University of North Carolina Press, 1924), and *Criminal Justice in America* (New York, Henry Holt and Company, 1930).

[91] Samuel Williston (1861–1963) from 1895 to 1938 was a law professor at Harvard Law School.

[92] Felix Frankfurter (1882–1965) was born in Vienna, Austria, in 1882. His family emigrated to the United States in 1894. Frankfurter worked for three years as an Assistant United States Attorney in New York under Henry Stimson, later a Secretary of War under three Presidents. When Stimson was appointed Secretary of War by President Taft, Frankfurter moved to Washington, DC and joined the War Department as a legal counsel. In 1914, Frankfurter joined the faculty of the Harvard Law School. He would remain at Harvard until his appointment to the Supreme Court in 1939. He served on the US Supreme Court from 1939 to 1962. He wrote 247 opinions for the Court, 132 concurring opinions, and 251 dissents.

[93] Alfred North Whitehead (1861–1947) was a British mathematician, logician and philosopher. Elected a fellow of Trinity College, Cambridge, in 1884, he taught mathematics until 1910. There he wrote with his former pupil, Bertrand Russell, the first edition of *Principia Mathematica*. From 1924 to 1937 he taught philosophy at Harvard University.

In Harvard did you absorb some of the American legal approach?

I absorbed more in a different way. As a Choate Fellow I had a very beautiful room in Winthrop House, so that I lived right in the middle of the Harvard system. And there I found the company and my neighbours so very interesting. There was the now famous but then rather shy young economist, JK Galbraith.[94] I got to know him quite well. And there were other Englishmen in John Winthrop House. I did, in my curious way, love the place, the beautiful buildings and the sights. I also did see quite a lot of New England. I made a great friend of a man called Sam Hill. We became very great friends. He took me up to Concord to see the monuments to the 'Minute war' and so on. One evening I said, 'I'd like to go there again to look around.' And he said, 'Well, borrow my car and go.' I didn't dare to, actually. To an Englishman, to say 'borrow my car' was then, 1936, if you had a car indeed, astonishing. One of my favourite occupations when at Harvard was to go to the Boston Symphony Orchestra concerts under Koussevitzky in Symphony Hall in Boston. Of course they also played in Cambridge to a mainly Harvard audience. But it was one of my idiosyncrasies that I thought one should go to Boston for the Boston orchestra. So I always did, to the amazement of my Harvard friends.

Is this the only time in your life when you have spent such a long period abroad?

Away from home? Yes, in peace time. In wartime I was quite a long time in India and Ceylon, but that was rather different because by that time—I was still a bit homesick of course, who wasn't—but I had really begun to grow up. I think I owe a lot to the army, Nino. I started in Aldershot in an infantry officers' training unit. That was shock treatment, and pretty tough. And that is when I began to grow up. I was an only child, you see. I'd forgotten that, but I should have told you, and it's not easy to grow up if you're an only child. But the army did it for me. The discipline I quite liked, in a way, because you don't have to think very much, you just do as you're told. And there were plenty of people with a good sense of humour. I was not a very good soldier but I did quite enjoy it. I remember once I was given the job of leading a platoon in a drill, and I got it all wrong and I was disappearing into the middle distance, not having learnt the drill properly. And you would think in the army, especially in wartime, you'd be in terrible trouble. But I looked round and I was rescued: there was the Regimental Sergeant Major and the Adjutant just doubled up in laughter, and nobody said a word—they were all very humane I think. Another experience surprised me in a way: our commanding officer in that unit was Lt Col Bingham, of the Coldstream Guards, quite something, and he had written to *The Times* complaining that

[94] John Kenneth Galbraith (1908–2006) was a Canadian-American economist. From 1939 to 1940, he taught at Princeton University. From 1943 until 1948, he served as editor of *Fortune* magazine. In 1949 he was appointed Professor of Economics at Harvard University.

they were not getting the right material in the officers' training unit; and how right he was. But he was a nice old boy and he gave us his one lecture, which was only repeating time after time in all kinds of situations what he called 'keep buggering on', and that was his lecture. But he was the old-time regular officer, and once I found myself on guard duty outside the officers' mess when he came in. So I presented arms. I got a message in the evening from my platoon commander, who again was doubled up in laughter, saying, 'The Commanding Officer says that in future if he passes you when you are on guard duty, he will be very content if you just attempt to stand at attention.' Again, nothing more. I was with a very humane lot, they just regarded me as a sort of comic turn.

To go back to your writing, you also gave other lectures at the Hague Academy.

Yes, I did something on air law at one time. It was typical of me why I wrote those books. The first, *The Acquisition of Territory*,[95] was because Ben Wortley,[96] who was a great friend of mine, another Yorkshireman, asked me to go and give the Schill Lectures at Manchester University. Otherwise I might never have written that little book, Nino. The General Course on international law[97]—I suppose it was Fitzmaurice who engineered the invitation through the Curatorium. He gave me some hints, 'you know how important it is' and so on, and I just had to do it. And I did it. I've always been a bit like that. If I'd had somebody with a big stick behind me, I would have written more, Nino. Laziness, that's what you must bring out.

Now let us move to international adjudication. Of course I know that it's very difficult to talk of your contribution to adjudication, an area where one cannot disclose confidential matters. Probably you could simply hint at very general ideas.

Well, in general, I can only say that I have for one reason or another greatly enjoyed it. I would like to think that my major contribution was being President for three years at the time when the Court was so extremely busy, and surviving. We did become a very good club, and towards the end we had that decision of 16:1.[98] I enjoyed the work partly because I think it was almost a reversion to my first period as a Don when I was in university politics, and was chairman of one or two important committees. It's not the done thing to pretend to like committees, but I did like committees, and being President at the ICJ was a bit the same sort of thing; I found it wasn't altogether strange, though there was a different set-up, with different nationalities and different people and so on. But I found I could manage it and I enjoyed it very much.

[95] Above n 3.

[96] B Wortley (1907–89) was Professor of Jurisprudence and International Law at the University of Manchester, author of *Expropriation in Public International Law* (Cambridge, Cambridge University Press, 1959).

[97] Above n 5.

[98] See text to n 58 above.

I like to think of that as a major contribution; and of course I've done a lot of drafting one way or another.

Do you attribute this busyness of the Court to the importance of the Court resulting from a change in international relations because of the end of the Cold War?

I have no clear answer to that question, because I think we are still a bit too near to it to see very clearly. To get a good historical assessment one needs to be some distance in time away. But I suppose that the end of the Cold War must have helped. I think what helped more, perhaps, was some of the decisions. The Third World, as we used to call it—the developing States—seem to have overcome their suspicion of one time that the Court was a European, or at any rate western, institution, western-dominated. We have been rather careful to avoid giving that impression, and it is certainly no longer true; you have only to look around the Court to realise that some of the powerful voices come from elsewhere other than the West. I think that that must have helped a great deal because after all, our customers, if one can use the trendy term, have recently tended to come from developing States. Who would have thought at one time that the most persistent customers would be Libya? And Nicaragua? This is a change. I think our image now is of a World Court; that's what I tried to foster very hard during my Presidency, and I think we achieved it—thanks, of course, to my predecessors who began this good work some time ago. Again I think I was lucky in being President at a sort of culmination period when the work of my predecessors was beginning to bear fruit. Once States are seen using the Court then the example is followed.

Did you try to inject ideas into the various judgments?

Yes, certainly; but one does not need to be President to do that. Anyone who serves as the drafting committee can do that; or indeed judges who are not on the drafting committee. All judges, even at the Notes stage, can and do inject ideas.

Do you find that at the ICJ you can do that? I remember that Judge Lachs[99] *was so proud of his contribution concerning* erga omnes *obligations.*

Actually I think his major contribution was the excellent dissent in the *North Sea Continental Shelf* cases.[100] It is one of those dissents that should still be read.

[99] Manfred Lachs (1914–93) was a Polish jurist and diplomat. He was director of the Department of Treaties and Legal Jurisdiction of Poland's Foreign Affairs (1947–60). In 1960 he became legal adviser to Foreign Minister Adam Rapacki (until 1967) and played a central role in the development of the 'Rapacki Plan' for making central Europe a nuclear-free zone. During the Paris Peace Conference he acted as the Polish delegate. He became a professor of international law at the University of Warsaw (1952–93) and served as a member of the Polish delegation to UN General Assembly. He was elected judge of the ICJ (1967–93) and presided over the Court in 1973–76. He was a very influential judge and President.

[100] *Federal Republic of Germany v Denmark; Federal Republic of Germany v Netherlands*, 20 February 1969, [1969] ICJ Rep 3.

Was it difficult to coordinate so many different people and try to run the show?

As President? No, I didn't find it too difficult. I think I've been very fortunate in my colleagues. Once I got into the swing of it, I found they were very helpful and cooperative.

When problems arise between two or more judges, is it necessary ever to go there and to try to negotiate privately?

Yes, a lot of work is done at lunchtime or in each other's offices, trying to get really clear what people want. What they say they want isn't always what they ultimately want.

I do not remember whether you have appended dissenting opinions.

Yes. Three come to mind. One was my dissent in the case where Italy was refused permission to intervene in the continental shelf boundaries case between Libya and Malta.[101] I may say that in dissenting in that case I was in very good company. Another was in what became known as the *Yakimetz* case (concerning an Administrative Tribunal decision in the case of one who was dismissed from employment by the UN).[102]

A third dissent was recent, in the *Nauru* case on jurisdiction; a very short dissent.[103] In the end that didn't matter much because the parties settled. With regard to this trend towards out-of-court settlements, I think we were getting more like a municipal court. In a municipal court at a preliminary stage, you get a feel for the other side and you might think that perhaps it would be sensible to settle. So I think that is a good development.

Another dissent was indeed the case of the *United States v Nicaragua.*[104] But there the Court decided 16 issues, and as I agreed with the Court on seven of them, I was in some doubt whether to call the opinion 'dissenting' or 'separate'.

B. Adjudication versus political machinery for change

I sometimes feel that academics, professors of international law, are a bit too much in love with litigation. It stems from Hersch Lauterpacht's time, when I was under his influence very much: it was very important indeed if any case came to the PCIJ or the ICJ. And then of course one was very concerned that it should help develop international law, because so much of

[101] *Continental Shelf (Libyan Arab Jamahiria v Malta)*, Application to Intervene, 21 March 1984, [1984] ICJ Rep 3 at 148.

[102] *Application for Review of Judgment No 333 of the United Nations Administrative Tribunal*, 21 May 1987, [1987] ICJ Rep 18 at 184.

[103] *Certain Phosphate Lands in Nauru (Nauru v Australia)*, 26 June 1992, [1992] ICJ Rep 240 at 301.

[104] *Military and Paramilitary Activities in and against Nicaragua (Nicaragua v United States of America)*, 27 June 1986, [1986] ICJ Rep 14 at 528.

it needed development and elaboration; it got this piecemeal development depending upon a case arising in one particular corner. I am reminded again of something McNair once said, that he was very impressed with the way sometimes you read a passage in a book, or even in a case, which seems to be the essence of legal wisdom, and then you get an actual concrete case on the matter and you find it doesn't help you very much because it just doesn't address at all the particular case. I think that has long been a weakness of international law: there's a bit too much of the essence of wisdom, but not enough experience. For that reason litigation was in the early days obviously very important indeed, especially before the World Court.

At the same time I think one must recognise that international law is singularly lacking in developed, adult, grown-up machinery for international political decision. You get international conferences and so on, and diplomatic conferences, you have the Secretary-General and the Security Council with its limits, you have General Assembly resolutions. But it's inadequate compared with the machinery you would find in any State for executive and administrative political decision, legislation and so on. I feel that this has an impact on the International Court of Justice. A municipal court would find life difficult in that sort of context. The Court survives partly, I feel, because essentially jurisdiction is consensual. Therefore I have hesitations about the sort of monocular drive for compulsory jurisdiction that academics have always backed, with its objections to reservations to declarations under Article 32 and so on. The difficulties that arise from this drive were to some extent faced in the inter-war period under the heading of 'the need for peaceful machinery for change in the law'. I remember some essay of Lauterpacht's, given I think when he was at the London School of Economics, saying that unless we are very careful, an international tribunal under the present system will be administering injustice, because there is no proper machinery for changing the law other than war (which was still legal, and was the normal method, after all, of changing the law radically). After a peace treaty, things could change completely.

We've now made war and the use of force illegal, but again we haven't quite put adequate machinery in place for making changes by other means. This is not an easy climate for a world court. I feel there is a whole area here that needs investigation. There's an interesting article of Brownlie's[105] pointing out that the 'waste of time', as some people have called it, over questions of jurisdiction before the ICJ, is not without justification. Sometimes in the past the ICJ seemed to be spending much of its time finding it had no jurisdiction. It's not quite as simple as that, because if you look at domestic jurisdic-

[105] Ian Brownlie (1932–2010) was Chichele Professor of International Law at Oxford University, member of the *Institut de Droit international* (since 1977), member of the UN International Law Commission. His numerous publications include *International Law and the Use of Force by States* (Oxford, Clarendon Press, 1963) and *Principles of Public International Law* (London, Oxford University Press, 1966).

tion, courts spend quite a lot of their time deciding they have no jurisdiction (think of the typical sort of cases involving universities where some person doesn't like the examiner's result).

Again I'm using the old man's privilege of pointing out a problem somebody had better get down to and work on. But I think there's a large area there of how much you can do by simply having a court with compulsory jurisdiction without a corresponding growing-up of the political decision organs: administrative decisions, executive decisions, legislative decisions. Of course we've got nearer to legislation than we sometimes recognise. The Law of the Sea Conference and the 1982 Convention is the impressive example. But this whole area raises great problems which need detailed investigation and a lot of imagination to provide answers to the problems the various clauses raise. At the same time the law is being changed and developed as never before; and we have here a machinery growing up one way or another for, in effect, legislating. I think we haven't recognised it to the extent we ought to do because we've all been looking for the wrong thing; we've been looking for something like a parliament to legislate, which internationally is a horrifying idea. It is almost impossible. But we are getting, through sheer necessity, something which serves much the same purpose. And I do think practical necessity is a very important factor in the development of law: space law, for example, and so-called 'instant custom', which is important but, whatever else it may be, it is not custom, nor even the least bit like custom. It is a weakness of international lawyers that any new thing we have to try to fit into the 1920s categories.

You don't think the Security Council could play an important role.

It could and does, and of course the Security Council is at last actually doing its job to a large extent. That has been one of the greatest dividends from the ending of the Cold War. Nevertheless, this action by the Security Council is after all very new, and a lot more experience is needed. Again I think there ought to be a lot of careful study and commentaries on what the Security Council has been doing. But the fact that it is now able to act is very promising—a great relief. But it does raise the other problems, such as we have in the Lockerbie case,[106] of how far the International Court should become a constitutional court also, and deal in matters of *ultra vires*. My own feeling about that is that this should be developed gradually on the common law basis, case by case. One should not attempt too much to lay down general principles, but to be content to let it grow gradually, because I think you have to be very cautious. As somebody reminded me in New York once: do remember that the Security Council sometimes has to decide things overnight, and that's

[106] *Questions of Interpretation and Application of the 1971 Montreal Convention Arising from the Aerial Incident at Lockerbie (Libyan Arab Jamahiriya v United Kingdom and Libyan Arab Jamahiriya v United States of America)*, judgments of 27 February 1998, [1998] ICJ Rep 9 and [1998] ICJ Rep 115.

very different from a court; judges sometimes forget it's very different from spending some months deciding after elaborate and formal argument and pleadings.

Still, do you feel that the Court can undertake a judicial review of Security Council decisions?

I do not rule it out. I want to be very cautious, and I want the Court—for heaven's sake—to be imaginative about the problems and difficulties of the Security Council. At the same time I do think there is a role for the Court to play in judicial review to some extent. I said a long time ago at the Heidelberg Seminar on the Court, many years ago now, that there is an anomaly in the international system (Article 34 of the ICJ Statute) that no government can bring an international organisation before the court on a charge of acting *ultra vires*. It's an extraordinary lacuna which you wouldn't have in any decent international constitution or national constitution. Therefore I do think that judicial review is an important question, a possible development that needs to be looked at cautiously; and I would hope that the Court would adopt a carefully and cautiously defined role in that respect, because I think we do need some sort of control of international organisations generally and not just the Security Council. I think it's a big gap in the international system.

I wonder whether the five Permanent Members of the Security Council would be prepared to accept judicial review. In a way, they have an unfettered power to make political decisions.

That's why I want a cautious case-by-case method. I think their acceptance of it would depend very much on circumstances in a particular case, even the membership of the Security Council. I hope the Court would look at everything before taking a bold line there, and look at the desirability too, whether a bold line is appropriate and helpful. One should always remember that even judges are not immune from a sort of self-righteous ambition, when it is a question of expanding jurisdiction.

Also because if the Court were to take a very bold line and decide that a particular resolution by the Security Council is illegal, the Security Council might then decide not to comply.

I think that it would be very damaging for both bodies if either allowed a clash to arise.

Therefore the Court should be so wise as to adopt decisions which would be acceptable to the other body.

Well, I'm not sure that I would quite put it that way; but I think the Court would have to be cautious and wise and imaginative, partly because I do think the Court does have a lot of political clout, especially in the United Nations, and we have to be careful how we use it. But I do think we have it.

Do you feel that in the UN system the Court can play an important role in this area of international organisations?

I think there is a need there, because one has had many instances of international organisations generally being a little too imaginative sometimes, and spending money rather wildly; there's surely room for some sort of judicial review control there. Of course you do get it to a small extent through the compulsory advisory opinion procedure which Roberto Ago doesn't like, but I think it has its uses as a sensible way of getting certain matters involving international organisations before the Court.

C. Judicial versus political decisions

Do you think the Court should also deal with questions which have political overtones?

I think the Court has to cover whatever is brought to it, and it's very unlikely that any case will come to the Court that is purely technical. They all have some political importance, otherwise they would almost certainly be solved in a different way. I think the Court should deal with them, but I believe that to deal with a legal question which has big political implications is an exceedingly delicate task. One should be aware of the political implications and the political importance, and one will be told about it by counsel, of course, very often from different points of view. At the same time one has to stay within the permissible legal framework, because otherwise one will lose one's authority. After all, looking at us sitting up there, nobody in his senses would bring a purely political question to be decided politically by that body of persons; we wouldn't be any good at it. We are trained to follow adjudication procedures. I think it is important to realise that adjudication in all its forms is a very specific method: it's quite peculiar; it's very different from other ways of settling disputes, and it has its virtues and it has its limitations. But you have to deal with cases in that particular way, given that one ought to be, as I said, very aware of the political importance and implications not only of the dispute but [also] of your proposed solution. But it's an exceedingly difficult task to get it right, so that whilst doing something one hopes is politically sensible and workable, one is nevertheless fairly strictly applying one of the possible legal solutions and not inventing law for the purpose, because that I think would make governments rightly suspicious. That would make for the kind of 'unpredictability' that is not acceptable. So there are great dangers for the Court, as we can see from the past history in certain highly political cases; even the PCIJ in the Austrian case.[107] There are great dangers, but we have

[107] *Customs Regime between Germany and Austria (Protocol of March 19th, 1931)*, 20 July 1931, Publications of the Permanent Court of International Justice, Series A/B, No 41.

to tackle the problem. All important courts are faced with this; the Supreme Court of the United States is highly political in many instances. You have to face it and you have to acquire the skill to do it. And you acquire the skill to do it by having the cases.

Would you agree that it is wrong to say that there are non-justiciable disputes?

To that particular question, which is partly technical, I have a relatively complicated answer. I do not have a great deal of sympathy with the point of view that Hersch Lauterpacht used to be rather a proponent of, that anything is capable of a legal answer and therefore general compulsory jurisdiction should be conceded by governments tomorrow. I don't think that is right. Though it's true that some sort of legal answer can be given to virtually any dispute by this very specific method (and I'll say a little bit more about it in a minute), nevertheless I think one has to recognise—as I mentioned last time we met—that you do need adequate working and wise machinery for essentially political decisions as well.

After all, this is what happens in a State: very often you'll get a highly delicate, very political matter and you don't go to the court to have the law applied, you go to parliament and change the law, and concede to the most powerful side. And if that's necessary in a State, it must be desirable at least in the international sphere. So that I would tend to be, to put it no higher, a little understanding even of some reservations to the declarations under the optional clause[108] because, after all, those governments which have accepted the optional clause with reservations have done a lot more than those who stand on the sidelines, as Waldock pointed out years ago. I am quite happy to see what we've got recently: a development of the compulsory jurisdiction under the optional clause, but just a little cautious, though much encouraged that the Security Council, as we mentioned last time, has begun making the necessary complementary political decisions now that the Cold War is over. But their experience of sometimes urgent political decision is quite new, and you would expect that gradually a technique and tradition would develop, and the practice would get stronger. Then I think there will be a better prospect for compulsory jurisdiction.

Generally I think one needs also a well-developed machinery for the alternative methods of doing things, by law-making, by administrative decisions and by political decisions as well as by adjudication. After all, the Law of the Sea Conference is a very remarkable example of actual law-making; though there are problems about what the limits are, about the large grey areas where there are differences of opinion about what is law and what is not law for non-parties; nevertheless, to have got a grey area is something, it's an advance.

[108] Reference is made here to Art 36(2) of the ICJ Statute, whereby States may at any time declare that they recognise the jurisdiction of the Court as compulsory *ipso facto* and without special agreement, in relation to any other State accepting the same obligation.

To go back to the ICJ, I wonder whether you have developed any system whereby you supervise the extent to which States comply with decisions handed down by the Court.

I think that's an interesting question that ought to be asked more often: what is the result of decisions, and how far are they followed? We do have a mechanism here: we do get reports, anything that comes in, and even newspaper clippings and so on, we do follow up; the Registry staff does follow up cases. There have been some studies recently. Gilbert Guillaume has written an article on this very subject, examining the jurisprudence to see the degree of compliance, which he finds good and which compares almost favourably with some State situations. So often, I think, there is a tendency (perhaps the very system of law reports creates this idea) that especially litigating lawyers, practitioners, barristers and so on tend to have, that once the papers have gone out, wrapped in red tape, that's no longer our business. So often in the law reports one wants to know what happened afterwards, not least in international law, and it's not easy to find out. More attention should be given to this.

But that means that you have not developed, within the Court, a special mechanism designed just to watch over the attitude of States after the delivery of judgments or advising opinions. This mechanism could also help apply Article 94 of the UN Charter.

If we had to develop anything new, of course, the immediate question would be: can we get the budget for it? And the answer would certainly be 'No'. But after all, the ultimate courts of appeal in a State system don't usually do that follow-up themselves; they regard that as other people's business—that the disappointed parties in a case of non-compliance should themselves do something about it by drawing it to the attention of the court. After all, some sort of machinery was created, and is now documented. In the *Libya/Chad* case,[109] as you well know, it was Chad that expressed, by correspondence with the other party and with the United Nations, anxiety at one point; and some sort of machinery was put in place. But I am not sure it is the Court's business to administer the law in that sense, unless there is the question of appeal, or we are asked by a party or by the Security Council or whatever to express a view on the matter.

There might be a very easy way out that would not involve any financial burden. For instance, as soon as the judgment is handed down, the Registrar could simply request the parties to report within, say, six months or 12 months on the follow-up, just as a matter of information.

I think there is machinery in place which doesn't perhaps quite do it in that way. The Registry staff collect information and send it round to all the

[109] Above n 58.

judges; this includes correspondence or reports they see anywhere. So we do have this information after the judgment for a period, but of course then it tends a bit to get lost. It is up to a scholar to go through past cases and find out what has happened. An interesting case with a delayed subsequent history is the *Corfu Channel* case.[110] The most important aspect of that judgment was immediately complied with because it altered or reconfirmed and clarified the law about international straits, and nobody has questioned that. It became part of the accepted law that was codified in the 1982 Convention. But the actual damages awarded to the United Kingdom have only just been realised by an agreement between the two governments and the other two interested parties, France and the United States.

So in your view, it is for either scholars or one of the parties to inform the Court about the follow-up to any judgment. There is no need for a sort of special machinery based on routine reports by States.

Yes, we haven't thought of having a sort of rule of thumb about it. At present it's simply collecting relevant information and making it available to the judges, and if the Court or the judges wanted to do anything about it then there would be a meeting of the Court. But it hasn't gone further than that. But I was thinking of the problem of the follow-up of the past cases, for example the Permanent Court of International Justice, exactly what happened subsequently in those cases; it's not easily available at all. And that's a work for scholars, I think.

D. About disciples

Let us now move to the question whether you have been able to create a school of international law.

No, I hope not. I hope I've created a school in the sense of the many undergraduates, and graduates, to whom I have lectured, putting various opinions before them without ever attempting to create a school. I am suspicious of a 'school' because it usually in practice means using pupils for the professor's personal aggrandissement and probably making certain aspersions about somebody else's school. This I don't think is quite a teacher's job. I'd like to think I'd created a school of those devoted to international law among the members of the legal profession. But in no wider sense than that; and anyway I don't think I'm capable of creating a school, Nino.

But you do have disciples.

Oh, yes, disciples. Yes, but I wouldn't say that my disciples necessarily agree with me, and I certainly don't expect them to.

[110] *Corfu Channel (United Kingdom v Albania)*, 9 April 1949, [1949] ICJ Rep 4.

They have been already trained by you.

Oh, yes, certainly. All over the place. Not only Cambridge, but also from when I used to lecture to the many many foreign students we used to get, especially from the Commonwealth, at the Inns of Court where I used to give regular courses of lectures. So many of them I meet now are Lord Chief Justices or Attorney-Generals, or Ministers of Justice, or even Prime Ministers, who say, 'Do you remember that I came to your lectures at the Inn's of of Court School of Law years ago?'

They were influenced by your teachings; in a way this could be lato sensu regarded as a sort of school.

Well, it's a school in a certain sense perhaps. I think governments—certainly I can only speak for the British Government now—but I do think governments generally grossly underestimate the power of teachers. I am constantly pleased and surprised by the loyalty of one's former pupils; even those who perhaps greatly disagreed with one's message, or disagree now, nevertheless they are loyal in the sense [that] they will always be friendly, and always attempt to help you in some way. I hope I never ask that they agree with my opinions; that seems to me inconsistent with the idea of a university.

Are there any disciples of yours who are now teaching in the UK?

One of them is of course Rosalyn Higgins, she was a pupil of mine. John Greig, now in Australia, was a pupil of mine at Jesus College. And John Dugard,[111] South African—you know what a wonderful job he's done there in very difficult times—he was one of my students. And Georges Abi-Saab;[112] Ted Meron.[113] These are just names that occur to my mind at the moment. But there are scores of them. Hans Blix[114] was another. And Ian Sinclair,[115] indeed. And I must surely also mention Ambassador Hitashi Owada.[116]

[111] John Dugard (*b* 1936) has been Professor of International Law at the University of Witwatersrand (Johannesburg) and then at Leiden University (since 1998). He is currently a member of the UN International Law Commission (elected in 1997). Member of the *Institut de Droit international* since 1995.

[112] Georges Abi-Saab (Egyptian, *b* 1933) has been Professor of International Law at the Geneva *Institut de Hautes Etudes Internationales*. Member of the International Criminal Tribunal for the Former Yugoslavia (1993–95), has also been a member of the WTO Appellate Body (2000–08). Member of the *Institut de Droit international* since 1981. Author of numerous important publications.

[113] Theodor Meron (*b*1930) currently US national, has been Ambassador of Israel to Switzerland and Canada, then Professor of International Law at New York University and judge at the International Criminal Tribunal for the Former Yugoslavia since 2001 (President in 2003–05).

[114] Hans Blix (Swedish, *b* 1928) has been Legal Adviser to the Swedish Foreign Ministry (1963–76), Minister of Foreign Affairs (1978), and Director General of the International Atomic Energy Agency (IAEA). Member of the *Institut de Droit international* since 1975.

[115] Ian Sinclair (1926–2005) was Legal Adviser, Foreign and Commonwealth Office (1976–84) and a member of the UN International Law Commission in 1981–86.

[116] Hisashi Owada (*b* 1932) has been Legal Adviser to the Japanese Foreign Ministry, Ambassador of Japan to the UN, and has been a judge in the ICJ since 2003 (President of the Court since 2009). Member of the *Institut de Droit international* since 1995.

E. British versus US approach to international law

Rosalyn Higgins in a way has been strongly influenced by the American School, especially at Yale.

Oh, very much by Yale. McDougal[117] inspired her tremendously. He is a very great teacher. I was a bit bothered by the way McDougal in his writings posited questions and then nearly always came round to what was the American Government's point of view; and perhaps he got a bit of a shock when his own pupil, Richard Falk, got different answers by the same method. But for the importance of policy, I do think it is tremendously important, not least in a judge.

I always think of the *Lotus* case[118] as an example of the danger of ignoring policy. Its famous solution, pleasing to the lawyer, elegant, goes in all the books—and yet it managed to unite both the employers and the employees of the maritime world against it. They were not willing to accept that on a dark night, in a storm, a sailor might find himself subject to a criminal law he's never even heard of, and for a reason he cannot begin to understand. I think that was where the policy school had great strength, because you would try and make yourself aware of that and say: 'This is going to look very nice in the textbooks, but is it going to produce a result or will they have to have a treaty to change it?' And there I've come round to the policy school to that extent. I think, as a judge, you have to stick within the permitted framework of legal choices, but I think you ought to be aware of policy considerations.

Another illustration is anti-trust. As you know, I did a lot of work on the extraterritorial aspects of that at one time. I'm not sure that I would write the same way again, because the 'effects' doctrine and the 'impact' doctrine, and all that sort of thing, are all very elegant legal inventions but what about the economic and financial results for [the] companies and countries involved? I think a weakness of universities generally is the difficulty of establishing inter-faculty studies. I remember trying once to [arrange] a graduate seminar which would involve economists who were studying anti-trust from the economics point of view. I couldn't get them to come. They pretended to be interested but there wasn't time in the end. But really you do need both sides. I was taught this by RM Jackson,[119] even when I was an undergraduate: he was a great teacher, and there was a decision, in a common law case, which was regarded as a great victory against bureaucracy, standing up for the liberty of the subject and so on; it looked very exciting and noble. But RM Jackson said quietly:

[117] See 'Interview with René-Jean Dupuy', fn 22.

[118] [1927] Publications of the Permanent Court of International Justice, Series A , No 10.

[119] Richard Meredith Jackson (1904–86) was Solicitor of the Supreme Court, Fellow of St John's College, Cambridge, Downing Professor of the Laws of England in the University of Cambridge. Author of *The Machinery of Justice in England* (Cambridge, Cambridge University Press, 1940).

> Of course there's another thing you ought to know about this case, it isn't in the reports, but the fact is that it destroyed a scheme of slum clearance, stopped it in its tracks, and nothing could be done for a very long time to improve the housing.

Well, it's a point, and therefore I've a great deal of sympathy with the Yale School in that. So, if you like, I've grown up a bit and no longer pretend to be a black-letter lawyer entirely.

I think you are right in saying that the major flaw in Yale is that McDougal projected his own values.

Yes, he got the value answer a bit too pat. But in almost all cases that come before a court there are choices to be made, even in terms of applying the law. One might try to become aware of the social and political consequences of the choice you are proposing to adopt.

You would not start from, say, predetermined values?

Well as a citizen you might, but no, I would rather do it experimentally. On a smaller scale you get the problem even in such highly technical matters as maritime boundaries, Nino. Do you remember the *English Channel* case[120] and the half-effect for an island, there's a splendid article by Peter Beasley, the hydrographer, not in a legal journal, it's *The Hydrographer's Journal*, in which he goes into this matter very carefully with the help of charts, and derives I think six possible meanings from the interpretation of half-effect to an island. Well, you know, judges ought to be aware of that. And it's only a question of asking people who do understand charts and maritime surveying. But so often we don't even stop to ask. This goes back to what I say about the *Institut de Droit international*, you know, and the hothouse atmosphere of international lawyers talking to each other, and not talking as much as we ought to other technicians, to economists, to financiers and politicians.

Do you feel that the resolutions of the Institut de Droit international *have an impact on diplomats and politicians?*

No, I don't think anybody looks at them, except for some international lawyers searching for materials for some article they find they have to write. Whereas if the *Institut de Droit international* had involved other people, other technicians, the resolutions might have acquired more significance. The International Law Association (ILA) is better at this; much broader. They haven't this exclusive class business, you know, and the preoccupation with who gets in and who does not.

[120] Reference is made here to the *Minquiers and Ecrehos case (France v United Kingdom)*, 17 November 1953, [1953] ICJ Rep 47. In a unanimous decision, the Court found that sovereignty over the islets and rocks of the Ecrehos and the Minquiers groups, in so far as these islets and rocks were capable of appropriation, belonged to the United Kingdom.

F. Any regrets?

We'll move on to your views about the current trends emerging in the international community. But first of all let me ask you whether you have any regrets about something that you might or should have done as a scholar or practitioner.

I think so many regrets that it's impossible to trace them. Life consists of making choices, and about almost every choice there is some pleasure and some regret. And of course how far the regret should extend one never knows, because 'ifs are history' is a dangerous and inexact subject. Supposing I had accepted appointment many many years ago as Secretary-General of the Faculties at the University of Cambridge, my life would have been very different. I can't say that I have many regrets about it, but who can tell; if I had decided otherwise life would have been very different, but whether better, more useful to society, I don't know. So it's all regrets, but nothing too great to bear. I have no great regrets, but maybe that's just from not thinking enough about it. I think one regret as a scholar is that I tended to be idle and procrastinate, and rather regret that I didn't write more when I was younger. And yet I wonder if I had anything much to say then—I don't know. But of course I was very much taken up with the administration at that time, and with my teaching and with the normal university activities, college activities. But here I am making excuses already; I'd better shut up about it.

G. On current trends in present international law

What are, in your view, the positive and meritorious values of traditional international law? And what parts should instead be discarded?

That's a very difficult question. As I said before, what I rather fear and regret is the tendency nowadays for many people to become devoted to modish parts of international law. I think human rights is an example. At the meeting of the *Institut de Droit international* in Milan, I went as far as to mention, perhaps exaggerating somewhat, what I called the tragedy of human rights; and that dear man, Professor Schermers,[121] was upset about that and asked me where was the 'tragedy', especially in the European system. Well, of course, he was quite right. But what I was complaining about was people becoming human rights specialists without being good general international lawyers: a sort of one-cause devotion.

Of course, we need specialists on human rights, a very important subject, but there are quite a lot of people, I suspect (I may be wrong) involved deeply

[121] Henry Schermers (Dutch, 1928–2006) in 1953–63 worked in the Legal Department of the Dutch Foreign Ministry. In 1963 he was Professor of International Organisation at Amsterdam University, from where he went to the Law Faculty of Leiden University in 1973 until his retirement in 1993. In 1981–96 he was a member of the European Commission of Human Rights. He became a member of the *Institut de Droit international* in 1989. See on him the notice by AVM Struycken in 'Henry Schermers (1928–2006)' (2007) 72 *Annuarie de l'Institut de Droit international* 435.

in human rights who haven't had the opportunity or taken the time to learn about the rest of international law. And one of the lessons you learn—you were asking last time about how practice helps in scholarship—one of the things you learn very very quickly, as you know, Nino, very well, in practice, is that often your first case which is supposed to be about your speciality, you find to involve lots of other questions, some of which you hadn't thought of and which are not your speciality. To take the simple and obvious example, one from domestic law: you have specialists in taxation at the Bar, a very lucrative speciality, and if as a young man or woman you think that you'll become a specialist in taxation, you might find that your very first brief has not very much about financial legislation but involves some difficult questions of the law of contract, and then you jolly well have to know the law of contract. And the same, I think, with international law. Practice makes you realise that you have to know pretty well everything about the traditional system.

I wouldn't want to discard any part of the traditional system, because so often you find that the quarries that you thought were worked out suddenly become really rather important again after all. I don't see how you can discard law anyway. There's no machinery for discarding, for one thing; this is a limitation on codification which I think should be mentioned rather more by the people who write about codification, and that is that you can by treaty law (a much-modified treaty law now) create new and better law with luck, but can you be sure of discarding the old or does it remain alongside it as a complication, either as general customary law or as the law binding non-parties and so on? We don't have this clear machinery as you would in a codification statute in a domestic system. You would simply pass a new code-statute and you would repeal all the previous law; but we can't do that, we have no repeal machinery.

Yes, you are right. But my question was an abstract question.

I know perfectly well that I have evaded your question.

Let us assume that you are a sort of international legislator and you are asked about the segments of international law which are worth being kept. For instance, what would you say about State sovereignty and non-interference in domestic affairs? Would you retain those parts?

I think I would. I would seek to modify the existing system and would not easily discard. The sort of example that just comes to one's mind is the *Western Sahara* case,[122] where for historical reasons you had to go back even further than territorial sovereignty; you had to consider a quite different culture and tradition of nomadic tribes, and what is the relevance of that in questions of

[122] 16 October 1975, [1975] ICJ Rep 12.

territorial sovereignty. Again I have this feeling that whatever you've decided could be discarded as not important is quite likely to be in your next brief. You never know what reality will turn up, except that it's going to be quite different from whatever anybody anticipated.

On the other hand, which values or parts of international law in your view should absolutely not be discarded?

Again you might think this is an evasion of the question: my feeling is that international law is changing and developing all the time. Sovereignty is a very difficult and dangerous question at the moment; we have all this nonsense about sovereignty in my own country—a sort of reactionary wing that is always going on about the need not to surrender British sovereignty. What they really mean of course is parliamentary sovereignty, and in the end they mean what they regard as their own sovereignty as MPs, not having noticed that even in the constitutional law they have very little indeed. I think it's much the same in international law. State sovereignty has a meaning and it's important legally, but it is qualified and restricted and elaborated upon in quite remarkable ways, and I would have thought the primary problem with it is to educate public opinion a bit about the ways in which it has been changed. I am always struck by an example I use perhaps too often. You know the number of people you see at Schiphol Airport, all expecting confidently, without any question whatever, to be taken through several different territorial air sovereignties and to land in another sovereignty without any specific permission and without forms to be filled in; which of course is a quite remarkable achievement, but it's the achievement of an extremely complicated law of the air which has been developing for six or seven decades at least. Like a lot of international law it works so extremely well and smoothly, and is so generally observed, that it never occurs to people's minds that it is there. This I think is very important for international law; that much of it works so well that people don't even notice. It is possible for intelligent, observant people with great general interests in international relations to travel all up and down the world as a result of this air law, without being aware at all of its existence; if you ask them about international law they would shrug their shoulders and say 'Well, is there any?' And if it comes to discarding things, I wish first we could explain to people what we have got: we were talking about popularisation the other day, and here is an example. Explaining international law to people seems to me to be the primary problem.

Perhaps I should have thought more about it. I can't think of anything that I would want to discard because I think of international law as developing out of its own history, which you can't discard anyway, and I want to see lots of developments and modifications, codifications, growth, new law; but I wouldn't easily discard the old, even supposing it could be possible.

I probably did not put the question in the right way. I was thinking of areas which in your view are bound gradually to evaporate or die because they are no longer congruous with the new demands of the world community. I am thinking in particular of State sovereignty. Do you think that the international community could survive without State sovereignty?

I see the point of your question. It is a exceedingly difficult problem because, as I said, sovereignty and independence in reality [are] extremely qualified today. Every government finds it; every party when it gets into power finds that there are so many things it can't do because it just does not enjoy sovereignty in the sense of real choices in that particular department for various reasons. Some of them sometimes relate to international law, sometimes financial, sometimes economic, sometimes political, sometimes all of those things.

At the same time (this comes back again to something I said before) I do think more attention should be given, especially by scholars, to what alternative arrangements are available. It is really a question about who decides things. One is bound to have some sympathy with the sovereignty people, if one can put it that way, because they are bound to say, 'Well, who else decides then?' In the European situation you have at any rate an answer: the EU decides certain matters. But in international law we haven't really any clear answer there at all.

Sovereignty is still a strong idea because it is surrounded by all this mystique, and dangerous because it seems to give a simple answer to many questions. But when you look at it, it's very far from being simple. But I do think there is this problem of the question of what is to be the alternative: what other political decision machinery are we going to get instead? In international law, have we got a satisfactory answer to the layman who says, 'All right, you say I discard or should discard the sovereignty of my country or my parliament, but who else decides these matters?' We haven't really got an answer there. It's time we did. I'd like to see much more attention from young imaginative scholars on this question of what sort of political machinery internationally should be established. Of course there are lots of classic answers, idealist solutions, abstract concepts and so on; but one has to concede that any idea of a vast international bureaucracy is an appalling idea, frightening in the extreme. And what you do instead is obviously going to be a much more complex machinery, with different degrees of power and so on in different matters. But can we say more than that. Perhaps I ought to have read harder, but I haven't seen much in the way of answers to this classical dilemma

H. The future of the world community

You know that generally speaking there are three options which have been propounded as to the future development of the world community. First of all the idea of a world government. It goes back to Hans Kelsen and has been developed

by the Americans in the 1950s. We should gradually reach a stage where a world government, a world bureaucracy in a sense, would prevail and there would no longer be State sovereignty. Then a second option would be to enhance the role of the UN; then we would still have a system of inter-State relations with a larger degree of cooperation through the Security Council and General Assembly. A third option which is very often advocated as a sort of alternative would be just to set up a network of regional organisations modelled on the European model, the European Union. It might gradually lead to some sort of network of regional bodies. Which of these three options is, in your view, the most realistic?

I'm not sure I've given enough thought to this question to be confident to give an adequate answer. From my basis of ignorance, if I may put it that way, I am attracted by the regional development idea. I think it's promising. But there's one thing I'd like to say about the question in general, and that is that we international lawyers as a class, we have in the past anyhow been a little misguided in tackling this kind of question always on the basis of settling disputes. The emphasis has traditionally been on this and preferably adjudication, but other methods too, of settling disputes. I well remember when I was an undergraduate in the 1930s this total myth, as it seems to me, this extraordinarily narrow, blind view of many international lawyers, that wars are caused by what international lawyers understand by 'disputes'. There are usually some disputes involved, but that's only one factor, as one very well knows, and the whole thing is much more complicated. We spend such a lot of time on the dispute settlement business that we've forgotten that any living system of law is not just about settling disputes. In fact, insofar as it's working very well—like, say, air law again, for example—you have disputes, yes, but they are not dominant. There is a system of law which is really working all the time.

This is the view of international law that we need scholars to examine much more closely. I think, if I may put it that way, you asked about the growth of the jurisdiction of the Court and the cases coming to it and so on. Well, from the point of view of Foreign Office legal counsellors (I've no actual experience, but one knows a little about what happens) it seems to me that they, especially legal counsellors in a busy Foreign Office of an important country, are seeing international law across their desks everyday. It's only occasionally that there's a 'dispute'. Sometimes there is a mainly technical dispute with, say, the Quai d'Orsay: What do they do? They get on the telephone and say 'What do you think Charles?' and it'll be settled in that way. A major dispute, yes, they might think of the Court as a specific and useful way of settling the dispute. That's excellent and I think it's going to grow, and my feeling is that the more attention is given to work on real international law and not just on settling disputes, the more the major disputes will in fact come to the Court. I am much devoted to the idea in Perez de Cuellar's last statement to the General Assembly of the use of the Court and similar methods of adjudication in dealing with specific legal factors or 'components' of a much larger political situation. I know that idea was very much connected with the proposal that the Secretary General should have the power to ask the Court for Advisory Opinions; but it is a valuable idea quite apart from that scheme.

Going back to the three options I set out before, I see that you favour the 'regional' option. Of course you are aware that one of the drawbacks on that option is that you can end up with a fragmentation of the world community. You very much believe in international law as a universal system, whereas under that option you might eventually have an African 'international' system, a European one, and so on.

Yes, it'll have to be watched, but I think you could develop a regional system along the right lines if it's ordered wisely because, after all, one of the most interesting aspects of the European Community is its having 'foreign relations'. I think there has to be room, even in the other two of your three possibilities, for regional variations. After all, traditional international law itself is no stranger to that. The *uti possidetis juris* principle means that territorial questions in South America and Central America are approached quite differently from those in other parts of the world; so we are already used to that idea of regional variations. This makes regional developments more palatable, and the bureaucracies won't be quite so enormous. I mean, the idea of a sort of World Commission instead of European Commission is a bit frightening; but one needs to give much more attention to this problem than I have done. Nevertheless, I can see the possibility of regional development coming about whether academics like it or not. One can surely see the beginnings in South-East Asia and the Antipodes. I am told that the second language in Australian schools is now Japanese. That sort of development has, I suspect, and indeed hope, more influence than the writings of Hans Kelsen.

I. Once again on disruptive factors in the world community

I have a question which is closely related to what I have just asked you: what values or factors in the present international community may give rise to anxiety or disquiet as possibly disruptive of the present fabric of the world community?

I think in a way I have answered that question, because we agreed pretty well that sovereignty is one of the things that is not only very important and full of problems to be resolved, but is also very frightening if it goes the wrong way, and one is a little dismayed by the tendency to fragment into separate little sovereignties nowadays.

There's one thought I might add, if I may Nino, about this general question. I've said that I think international lawyers in the past perhaps concentrated too much on disputes, as if that's going to bring heaven on earth—a sort of idea that heaven must be litigation all the time, you know: a great Court with compulsory jurisdiction, and everybody in heaven is litigating all this to settle their disputes in a Court, which is nice for lawyers in heaven;

no doubt very much a practising lawyer's idea of heaven!—but I sometimes also wonder about the tendency to feel that everything has to be governed by law. I have grave doubts now about Hersch Lauterpacht's idea of recognition governed by law, that he managed to sell to both the British and American Governments. It seems to me that that was in fact almost a self-deception, a pretence that there were not big political questions involved that must be decided politically. I think I see the same tendency again in some lawyers' treatment of self-determination. Self-determination seems to me to be at least half political; for what constitutes a 'self' calls for political, not legal, determination. I have always thought that the pretence that this could be made a purely legal doctrine is nonsense. These big political questions need a wise statesman – like political decisions. The present situation in Yugoslavia shows both how very important recognition is, and how political a matter it is. So that here again, international lawyers have to be rather more aware of the danger of making the wrong turn on certain routes and of pretending that the whole thing has to be solved by lawyers applying the law.

Do you think that there are some areas of international law which in a way 'have a future', as it were, say jus cogens *or repression of crimes against humanity, the notion of international crimes of State and these new areas of obligations* erga omnes*?*

I'm not really sure of the answer, Nino, on that. I think there are interesting questions about humanitarian law and so on, or about the whole question of international criminal law. And again what is to be *jus cogens* I think needs a political decision by some competent body about what should be *jus cogens*. After all, there has inevitably been a tendency to put into that box things that are important to oneself or one's own country, or [to] one's own particular endeavour at the moment. I find some difficulty about an international criminal law because, in the case of common crimes like murder, it raises questions about the relationship to municipal law and courts that need a lot more thinking about. Moreover, practice in Nuremberg and Tokyo and so on has always been to bring it down to the individual. And yet, in spite of what was said at Nuremberg, it is a fact that criminal acts are sanctioned, if not committed, by what Nuremberg called 'abstract entities'. It is all very well bringing it down to the individual, but I am loath to let off some of the 'abstract entities' all the same. Many breaches of human rights are committed by faceless bureaucracies, ie 'abstract entities'.

Well in the case of aggression, if you say that it is not only an 'ordinary' breach of international law, ie a 'delict', but a very serious breach, namely a 'crime', you may take special sanctions against the delinquent State.

I think something of this sort must be the ultimate aim if we are to have a proper international community because, after all, the '*temperamenta*' rules in a developed international society would simply decay presumably, because how can you have a law which says that certain things you must not do, but if you do them you should try to do them humanely? It's like saying in a State system that you should not murder, but if you must, then you should do it decently and having all possible regard in the circumstances to the feelings of the victim.

I think the rationale behind the distinction between delicts and crimes is that 'crimes' such as aggression, gross and systematic breaches of human rights, forcible denial of self-determination and so on, are to be equated to what is 'murder' in national systems.

My thought is rather different. The only point I'm trying to make is that if and when we do achieve that position where aggression is really under control, and war in one disguise or another is no longer a dominant feature of international relations as it still is alas today, then the purely '*temperamenta*' rules will decay because then people will not be doing that sort of thing anyhow. After all, the traditional rules on the war crimes were developed to deal with the situation that war was lawful and that governments could indulge in it at their discretion. If they can no longer do that, and indeed will have to be dealt with in some sort of criminal context for aggression or even for starting that kind of unlawful armed hostilities, then '*temperamenta*' will become a part of history, that's all I am saying.

Of course, even within the context of an 'unlawful' war, resulting from aggression, one should apply the laws of warfare, the 'temperamenta belli'.

At present, absolutely. They are of tremendous importance.

They might gradually decay.

Logically, yes. But this is looking very much to the future. We began with what would I like to discard; this is not something I want to discard at the moment.

Do you think that in the future development of the world community individuals should have a greater role, say by having standing before international courts similar to the European Court of Human Rights? Do you think that this would be a healthy development?

I doubt whether it would be a healthy development. There are just too many of us. Again, the difficulty one has to bear in mind to some extent is not so much theoretical as practical: the sheer impossibility of having recourses available to that extent for persons generally. Again, it's a point that I was making in regard to the environment. There are many kinds of pollution, some more dangerous than others; but certainly one kind of pollution is having too much law, too many regulations and too many complicated different kinds of law applying to the same situation. So that you get disputes inevitably, because the law is not clear. This is one of the things where again I wish more attention were paid. I was very pleased with Philippe Sands's book[123] on the environment. It is an attempt to set out all the existing laws about the environment. This is a first step to understanding where we are, instead of just coming across bits of environmental law here and there. But it's this same problem of international organisation in the end. Again I speak modestly, because it may be that what I am saying is either that I haven't read deeply enough, or far enough or broadly enough; but it does seem to me that, on the whole, books about international organisations are descriptive, they tell you what is happening now, but we don't have these great imaginative works telling us what we need instead. Not only developing things as additions, but perhaps instead of what we've got. But you see it's a different kind of task, isn't it Nino? Immediately one thinks, well, what about the McNair's insistence that the first duty of a lawyer is to know the difference between proposed law and what is in fact law. That is surely the first step towards law reform. Moreover, it's interdisciplinary studies we need. It's such a tragedy for international law, I think, that the big thinkers about international relations and diplomatic history don't look much at international law, because it's not in the syllabus, so to speak. In England few such scholars seem to look at international law papers from the Foreign Office files, and available in the Public Record Office under the '30 year rule'. McNair did, and HA Smith[124] did, but diplomatic historians do not much use the legal sources. Clive Parry of course was producing his splendid *Digest*[125] exactly on these historical lines, and he gave up partly—as he told me he got fed up—because he said that 'nobody reads it'—a few international lawyers, yes, but politicians, diplomats, historians even, don't read it. We have this compartmentalised thing which is a sin of universities and we need a new Maitland.[126] It never occurred to his mind to ask himself whether he was an historian or a lawyer. He was a Professor of Law who also became one of the best historians ever.

To go back again to this question of individuals, I see that, although you have reservations about the multiplication of international bureaucracy, you would favour their having a greater role.

I think in a really developed system of international law and relations, obviously there is a strong tendency for individuals to become what they now call 'actors' in international law. This will now develop inevitably, whether international lawyers 'favour it' or not.

[123] Above n 72.

[124] Herbert A Smith was Professor of International Law at London University. He authored *Great Britain and the Law of Nations: A Selection of Documents Illustrating the Views of the Government in the United Kingdom upon Matters of International Law*, 2 vols (London, King, 1932–35).

[125] Clive Parry (ed), *A British Digest of International Law: Compiled Principally from the Archives of the Foreign Office* (London, Stevens and Sons, 1965).

[126] Frederic William Maitland (1850–1906) in 1884 was appointed reader in English law at Cambridge University, and in 1888 became Downing Professor of the Laws of England. He is generally regarded as the modern father of English legal history.

However, this development, I guess, will never supplant the present composition and structure of the world community.

Yes. Well, you see the modification again in the European system, don't you? Your individuals go to the Court of Appeal, say in London, and the judge says this is a matter of European law and I refer it to Luxembourg for their answer before I can decide the case. Well, then, you have an individual approaching a kind of international law (European law whatever they say, is international law, it's a treaty-made law)—in an English court. This is the right sort of development, it seems to me. This question of the relationship of international law and municipal law is now much bigger and more complicated and more important than the classical books indicated. And again, more scholarly work needs to be done.

Within this general context of new areas of international law, do you think the ICJ or, for that matter, other inter-State courts or tribunals may have a role in gradually contributing to the building up of a better international law, by not simply applying existing international law but by promoting, in a way, the further development of international rules?

Well, I don't much like suggesting that further development is in contradiction with applying existing international law. I have no hesitation in accepting that judges make law and indeed, within limits, have to. I don't see how anybody trained in common law can hold otherwise. At the same time you have to keep this framework of developing the law within limits, which involves essentially a legal decision, but also political awareness. That's why I want judges to be aware of the political implications and the possible political results of what they decide, so that they don't do something which is unwise.

You know, all good judges have tackled this problem: in my own country, our own Lord Mansfield[127] or Lord Atkin[128] and others. I always think of the right technique being illustrated by a famous case, *Donoghue v Stevenson*[129]: you must have heard of the great snail in the bottle case of 1932. It was a

[127] William Murray (1705–93) was a King's Scholar at Westminster School, and Christ Church, Oxford, and was called to the Bar at Lincoln's Inn in 1730. In 1737 his eloquent speech to the House of Commons in support of a merchants' petition to stop Spanish assaults on their ships brought him renown in his profession. In 1742 he became Solicitor General. In 1754 he was appointed Attorney-General and was leader of the House of Commons. In 1756 he was appointed Chief Justice of the King's Bench where he served with the utmost distinction, making many important contributions to the development of English commercial law. He retired in 1788. He was made Baron Mansfield, becoming Earl of Mansfield in 1776.

[128] James Richard Atkin, Baron Atkin (1867–1944) was a lawyer and judge of Australian–Welsh origin. He became a judge of the King's Bench Division of the High Court in 1913, then a Lord Justice of Appeal in 1919. From 1928 until his death he was a Lord of Appeal in Ordinary under the title Baron Atkin of Aberdovey in the County of Merioneth. In 1932, as a member of the House of Lords, he delivered the leading judgment in the landmark case of *Donoghue v Stevenson* concerning the alleged adverse effects from a decomposed snail in a bottle of ginger beer served in a cafe in Paisley. The case established the modern law of negligence in the UK and, indirectly, in most of the rest of the common law world (with the exception of the US).

[129] [1932] AC 562.

development of the law of tort, in a Scottish appeal to the House of Lords. A girl [X] bought a bottle of ginger beer in a dark glass bottle which, unknown to anybody, also contained the decomposed remains of a snail. X bought the bottle from a retailer and treated the appellant to the contents, the snail's remains not appearing until X replenished the appellant's glass. The appellant was said to have become ill in consequence of what she then saw. There was no contract between X and the suppliers, in whose factory the snail presumably entered the bottle (there was a contract with the shop, yes, but they were hardly worth suing, and anyhow they could not have discovered about the snail in the bottle). Was there nevertheless a relationship between the girl and the manufacturer, which made the manufacturer liable? Lord Atkin, though, asks 'Who then in law is my neighbour?' (I remember Percy Winfield,[130] a great lecturer, actually began his lecture on this case by taking out his *New Testament* and reading the parable of the good Samaritan.) Now to hold the manufacturer liable was to make a notable change in the English law of tort. To accomplish this Lord Atkin carefully examined earlier cases in English, Scots and United States law. None of them covered the 'snail in the bottle' kind of situation. But looking at all the cases as a whole, he felt justified in discerning a tendency towards a general principle in favour of liability towards

> persons who are so closely and directly affected by my act that I ought reasonably to have them in contemplation as being so affected when I am directing my mind to the act or omissions which are called in question.[131]

Thus was he able to present an epoch-making decision as one firmly based on the precedent cases, and very far from mere innovation. This seems to me to be the true art of the judge. He may change the law but he does it without moving out of the legal framework within which the law requires him to work. For to do so is to forfeit his authority, which derives not from himself but from the law. I cannot forbear to quote Atkins's clinching final phrase, when he says that, if this proposition is accepted as representing English and Scots law, it is also one 'that I venture to say no one in Scotland or England who was not a lawyer would for one moment doubt'.[132]

In a way, you take the law a small step further.

Yes, that's right. A judge has to be highly skilled at the job, and I think it's a question of combination of learning, historical sense of the development of the law and the past law, and sensitivity to the situation of the present litiga-

[130] Sir Percy Henry Winfield (1878–1953) was Professor of English Law, St John's College, Cambridge, and the Inner Temple, Barrister-at-Law; as well as Lecturer in Law at St John's and Trinity Colleges, Cambridge. He was also the Editor of the *Cambridge Law Journal*. He authored numerous books on law.

[131] [1932] AC 562, at 580.

[132] *Ibid*, at 599.

tion. But Atkin was not taking a small step; he was taking a giant final leap, but was able to do so by showing that it was what all the earlier steps were leading up to, even if their designers had not always appreciated where they were heading.

V. The Jurist and Global Reality

A. Obeying one's demon

Let me move on to the question—I cite Max Weber—whether you feel that you have obeyed the demon who holds the fibre of your own life. This question actually revolves around the issue whether one believes that he has fulfilled his mission as a scholar or a practitioner, or as a citizen.

I am quite clear about the answer to that: no, I don't have this demon for scholarship. You know, Nino, I recognise it when I see it and I greatly admire it, but I've never had that. Well it leads on to your next question about palliatives and comforts. I have many, but I don't regard them as such. I mean I completely reject the nonsense from Freud about life being a misery and so on. I expect his life was; served him right I say! I regard life's activities much more as a whole, and that seems to me to be in the proper university tradition. Some people have this demon for scholarship, and that's splendid, and this was recognised when I was young in Cambridge. Most people, it was recognised, did not have it but were every bit as important to the University in other ways, and would do quite a bit of pure scholarship work as well while doing many other things. Let them get on with it and hope that they would be socially acceptable as well, and occasionally appear, so to speak, and talk to one and not just go on reading and writing in their own little corner. But no, I don't really have that demon. I've already made it clear in a way; if I had decided at that early stage to be Secretary-General of the Faculties, I think I would have lived my life completely differently, or had a different demon if you like. The other way of putting it would be to say 'I have many demons'.

B. Things that make life more bearable

So you don't agree with Freud that life is unbearable . . .

No, I think he was a silly old fool when he said that. I don't think life is unbearable at all. I think it's marvellous and much to be enjoyed by sensible people, and being miserable about it is no help at all. I don't regard my many activities other than being an international lawyer as a catalogue of palliatives or comforts. I regard them as important aspects of living a full life. Music, for example, I would regard in many ways as vastly superior to international law as an intellectual discipline and an imaginative discipline. I can't do more than respectfully enjoy it from a distance, because I haven't got that demon, if you like, I haven't got the gift. Well, didn't somebody say—who was it now?—who had a life of great scholarship, that if he could have written one first-class sonnet, he would have given up all his books in exchange for that. It's just a respect for other ways of doing things, other gifts of other individuals, and thank God we have variously gifted people.

What are the other activities you enjoy?

Well, I'd put music very, very high; that's grown with me rather. Again I have no great accomplishment: well, I'm rather like Christine [Jennings' wife], we have a piano and we both play it if there's nobody else within a hundred yards, and quite enjoy making the attempt. We don't seek to inflict it on others. So that it's mainly going to concerts or listening to the 'gramophone'—I still like to call it that. But I also have an enthusiastic attachment to 'hi-fi' and take all the magazines, realising that much of what I read in them is absolute rubbish, intended for gullible people; nevertheless I quite enjoy it. Christine knows (I am getting too near Freud for my comfort) that when I am tired or a bit depressed I find some reason to talk to my friends in the local hi-fi shop, and probably get them to talk about some apparatus which they know that I probably will not buy, but they are very kind, and I do buy from time to time. And that is a sort of palliative perhaps; though I would rather think of it as just refreshing. Well, it is interesting because it's *more* than a palliative—it does enable you to listen to records with a very high quality of reproduction; and it does also satisfy a side of me which was rather damaged at school.

I went to a school, a good school I think, very humble but I think it was good; but good on the arts side. And the arts (humanities) people who taught me were slightly intellectual snobs, and I caught from them the idea that science was inferior and that no really civilised person indulges in science, with its messy test tubes and things. I even abandoned mathematics, which I used to enjoy and was pretty good at up to about Form IV but then decided to become bad at because, you know, it seemed right for an arts man; and if you really try you can become very bad at a subject, quite quickly. I was shaken out of that when I was an undergraduate at Cambridge. I made great friends, through a religious connection—membership of the Methodist Society—with a man from Newcastle Grammar School, a similar school but on a rather higher level, who was a mathematician. He became a Wrangler (ie in the First Class of the Maths Tripos) and then had a very distinguished career as a civil servant. He'd been to a school where science was on top, with excellent science teachers; and there it was the humanities that were rather looked down upon. Comparing notes we discovered one day that we had each been cured gradually at the University of our respective monocular views, instilled into us, probably, because of good teachers who wanted to enthuse us about their own subject and to pull us away from the others.

The hi-fi satisfies, I suppose, the remains of feelings at Cambridge that I wished I knew more about physics and about electricity and sound, and science generally.

Other things, Nino: I did make a list. Well, very important to me all along (I can no longer do it as I would like) is walking, and especially walking in *our* Tuscany, the English Lake District, where we now own an old farmhouse, as you do in Tuscany. Walking the fells, a bit of mountaineering: I used to enjoy it enormously as a young man, when I liked especially walking alone. I rather resented company, and I'd spend the whole day walking the mountains quite alone. The little of it I can now manage I still enjoy; and fortunately, so does Christine. And now I am grateful for the company.

Reading, of course. I was saying to Christine this morning, one tends not to mention reading novels, classics, poetry, biographies and history; one tends not to mention it because, having been to university, my generation rather assumes that *everybody who has been to a university* does it, though I'm afraid that's no longer true, is it, so it has to be mentioned specially.

And apart from that, well, I think one of my great joys is the college scene in Cambridge, where you have this intellectual companionship of people from different disciplines living in the college, each teaching and talking about his or her own thing. There was a great tradition which has rather died, I think. We used to have many more bachelors living in college as a sort of backbone of an almost monastic college life, and there was a tradition of the whole College dining together, several times a week in term time; and by the whole College I mean undergraduates as well as the Dons. After dinner the Dons 'combined' in the 'Combination Room', that is to say you would sit there, perhaps with a glass of wine, often not, and talk for perhaps half an hour before going home or retiring to one's own room in College. In the Combination Room in the earlier times you had a cup of coffee unless somebody brought in a guest; then you would have port. It was a very good rule, because whenever you brought in a guest in those days, they would all smile and say 'Oh, there's a guest', and they'd all pay attention to your guest and make him or her feel happy and at home. It was a good discipline, you know, an automatic pleasure at seeing a guest come in. In any event, dining and combining were important. Conversation has largely gone out, except in universities, which remain oases of civilisation I feel. It has been preserved to a considerable extent in ancient universities, and I think and hope to a large extent in the others too. This intellectual society I've always found a tremendous joy, not a palliative but a great stimulus. I should explain that I am still a Fellow of two Colleges, so I can still enjoy this society, not as a guest but a member. For this stimulating and delightful company there is no retirement age. (And, one should not forget to mention, one finds this sort of refreshment in the International Court of Justice too.)

Did you talk in College about your own research, or were you not allowed?

You were not supposed to talk 'shop'; but in my early days as a Fellow, the society was so relatively small that quite a lot of serious decisions were in fact made in Combination Room. The sort of lobbying conversation we have here in the Court over lunch works in the same way. It wasn't regarded as shop to talk about one's own pupils' difficulties and ask advice. Otherwise, no, we'd talk about the news, or indeed about your neighbour's subject. If you had a guest you had to talk about his activity anyway, you asked him what he did and took an interest in it, and asked him questions about it. I think the shop rule was very sensitively interpreted. When I was first a Fellow there was a chemist, a crystallographer called WH Mills, a very senior Fellow, and he would preside a good deal at high table in Combination Room. He was a delightful man. I a little feared him in one way: he used to ask the most penetrating questions about legal problems that had occurred to his mind—not the questions in the books, that was the difficult thing, but very good questions indeed, probably about something in the newspapers. He would say, 'What do you think, what about so-and-so?' And you would think, 'I never thought of that, they don't ask that at law school'. But very penetrating questions, and this kind of discussion could be stimulating and useful.

Would you also discuss politics?

Yes, within rather strict limits, and avoiding that vulgar business of *party* politics. To get into an uncivilised argument would probably mean losing your fellowship in those days, it would be regarded as simply not done; but gentle disagreement yes, or teasing, that would be splendid. You know, everybody would join in and tease somebody about his politics. But, like all these social rules, not talking shop and so on much depended on personality. A charmer, a respected authority, or perhaps an accepted eccentric, could probably get away with anything.

And tell me, when you were an undergraduate, was Wittgenstein[133] in Cambridge?

Yes, he was, I suppose, when I was first a Fellow. Yes indeed. I was not aware of him then at all. Many of the people who are now my friends and colleagues were, but of course he was not easy to approach; and he was a Fellow of a

[133] Ludwig Josef Johann Wittgenstein (1889–1951), the famous Austrian philosopher, worked primarily in the areas of logic, philosophy of mathematics, philosophy of mind, and philosophy of language. He wanted to study with the German mathematician and logician Gottlob Frege (1848–1925) in Jena, but Frege suggested that he should attend the University of Cambridge to study under Bertrand Russell. In October 1911 Wittgenstein thus arrived unannounced at Russell's rooms in Trinity College and spent a few years there studying philosophy. In 1929, on returning to Cambridge, Wittgenstein was appointed a lecturer and made a fellow of Trinity College. He held the position of Professor of Philosophy at the University of Cambridge from 1939 until 1947.

different College. There was one man who tried to go to his lecture, but Wittgenstein recognised a stranger and he said 'What are you here for?' and then told him to go. He was a funny chap, very eccentric. His lectures, one gathered, were not really prepared: he just began talking about something, and sometimes would get excited and develop something very important; sometimes would not get excited and look bored, and say 'Well, that's the end of the lecture'. But it was just a small group of people who were interested in philosophy, and also were for some reason acceptable to Wittgenstein as members of his lecture class.

Were you aware that there was at Cambridge a most distinguished philosopher?

No, I was not aware of Wittgenstein. But I knew there must be several philosophers; as indeed there were.

So he was not very well known?

Well, I imagine he probably was well known to many people who mattered. The fact that I, as an undergraduate, had never heard of him is neither here nor there. But it's very certain he had never heard of me!

I was aware of some scholars in other subjects. I knew, for example, about AE Housman,[134] who was a very great classical scholar and of course a poet. And I knew about all those world-class physicists in the Cavendish Laboratory. But Wittgenstein was a rather specialised taste, after all. Of course you were asking whether I knew Wittgenstein when I was an undergraduate. Later, as a Don, I got to know other Cambridge philosophers, like Wisdom,[135] Broad,[136]

[134] Alfred Edward Housman (British, 1859–1936) was a classical scholar and poet best known for his cycle of poems *A Shropshire Lad* (London, Kegan, Paul, Trench, Trubner & Co Ltd, 1896). He was appointed Professor of Latin at University College at London, and in 1911 took the Kennedy Professorship of Latin at Trinity College, Cambridge, where he remained for the rest of his life.

[135] John Wisdom (British, 1904–93) was a philosopher influenced by GE Moore, Ludwig Wittgenstein and Sigmund Freud. He was for most of his career at Trinity College, Cambridge, and became Professor of Philosophy at Cambridge University. His books included: *Philosophy & Psycho Analysis* (Oxford, Basil Blackwell, 1953); *Paradox and Discovery* (Oxford, Basil Blackwell, 1965); *Proof and Explanation* (Lanham MD, University Press of America, 1991).

[136] Charlie Dunbar Broad (British, 1887–1971) was an English epistemologist, historian of philosophy, philosopher of science, moral philosopher, and writer on the philosophical aspects of psychical research. He was appointed professor at Bristol University in 1920, and worked there until 1923, when he returned to Trinity College as a College lecturer. He was a lecturer in 'moral science' in the Faculty of Philosophy at Cambridge University from 1926 until 1931. In 1931, he was appointed 'Sidgwick Lecturer' at Cambridge University. He kept this role until 1933, when he was appointed Knightbridge Professor of Moral Philosophy at Cambridge University, a position he held for 20 years, until 1953. Broad was President of the Aristotelian Society from 1927–28, and again from 1954–55. He was also President of the Society for Psychical Research in 1935 and 1958. He was known for his thorough and dispassionate examinations of arguments in such works as *The Mind and Its Place in Nature* (New York, The MacMillan Company, 1925), *Scientific Thought* (New York, Harcourt, Brace and Co, 1923), and *Examination of McTaggart's Philosophy*, 2 vols (Cambridge, Cambridge University Press, 1933–38).

Lewy[137] and Braithwaite.[138] Indeed, at one time I sat on the General Board of the Faculties as a member of the Faculty Board of Moral Sciences, as philosophy was called in Cambridge.

I think we've done everything, even my palliatives disguised. Well, thank you.

Thank you so much, Robbie! I have learned a lot. And thank you for so many delightful reminiscences.

[137] Casimir Lewy (1919–91) was a Polish-born British philosopher. He taught at the Faculty of Moral Science in Cambridge in the years 1943–45. He was a Fellow of Trinity College, Cambridge from 1958. He became a Fellow of the British Academy in 1980.

[138] Richard Bevan Braithwaite (British, 1900–90) was a lecturer in moral science at the University of Cambridge from 1934 to 1953, then Knightbridge Professor of Moral Philosophy there from 1953 to 1967. He was president of the Aristotelian Society from 1946 to 1947, and was elected a Fellow of the British Academy in 1957. It has been noted that Braithwaite's work was important for his theories on the nature of scientific inductive reasoning and the use of models, as well as on the use of probabilistic laws. He also applied his scientific background to his studies of moral and religious philosophy, particularly in the application of mathematical game theory. In his book *Theory of Games as a Tool for the Moral Philosopher* (Cambridge, Cambridge University Press, 1955), he demonstrated the ways in which game theory could be used to arrive at moral choices and ethical decisions. His major work was *Scientific Explanation: A Study of Theory, Probability and Law in Science* (Cambridge, Cambridge University Press, 1953). It is reported that it was Braithwaite's poker that, on 25 October 1946, during the famous heated debate between Ludwig Wittgenstein and Karl Popper, the former brandished at the latter during their confrontation at a Moral Sciences Club meeting in Braithwaite's rooms in King's College. It would seem that, in the presence of Bertrand Russell (then Professor of Philosophy at Cambridge), during Popper's presentation of a philosophical paper, Wittgenstein became infuriated and started waving a hot poker at him, demanding that Popper give him an example of moral rule. Popper offered one ('Not to threaten visiting speakers with pokers'), at which point Russell told Wittgenstein to put the poker down; Wittgenstein stormed out.

Louis Henkin

THE INTERVIEW WITH Louis Henkin took place in New York, in his small office at the Columbia Law School, in 1995. Although he was a ripe 78 years of age, his mind was still youthful, sharp and vivacious; so sharp, indeed, that the interview did not last very long, since all his answers shot out rapidly and confidently, without a hint of hesitation.

Louis Henkin was born in 1917 (he died in 2010). His father was a rabbi. After studying mathematics at Yeshiva University, Henkin forged a law career by graduating from Harvard Law School and clerking at the US Supreme Court for Justice Felix Frankfurter. He spent all his life in academia, teaching first at the University of Pennsylvania, then at Columbia after 1962. He did not confine his work to scholarly pursuits, however. He acted as a consultant to the UN (1947–48) and the US State Department (1945–46 and 1948–57). Subsequently he was a member of the UN Human Rights Committee. He had a great impact on generations of law students in the US, and on scholars both there and abroad, not to mention the American judiciary, which has cited Henkin in some 250 Federal Court of Appeals decisions and at least 20 Supreme Court rulings. In addition, he was instrumental in compiling and editing the *Third Restatement of Foreign Relations Law of the United States*,[1] where his imprint is most visible in the sections dealing with human rights.

Henkin's greatest legal contribution is to the field of human rights.[2] More than a mere topic for academic specialisation, for Henkin human rights represented a set of moral standards which deserved a committed struggle. It was a natural consequence of his profound belief in human dignity that he never refrained from criticising US policy on human rights. Indeed, he is said to have lamented that

> in the cathedral of human rights, the United States is more like a flying buttress than a pillar—choosing to stand outside the international structure supporting the international human rights system, but without being willing to subject its own conduct to the scrutiny of that system.[3]

[1] *Restatement of the Law (Third): The Foreign Relations Law of the United States*, 2 vols (St Paul, Minn, American Law Institute, 1986).

[2] L Henkin, *The Rights of Man Today* (Boulder, Col, Westview Press, 1978); L Henkin (ed), *The International Bill of Rights: The Covenant on Civil and Political Rights* (New York, Columbia University Press, 1981); L Henkin, *The Age of Rights* (New York, Columbia University Press, 1990).

[3] Cited by HH Koh, 'The Future of Lou Henkin's Human Rights Movement' (2007) 38 *Columbia Human Rights Law Review* 487, at 490.

A portrait of this brevity can hardly do justice to Henkin's significant contributions to international law. I will nonetheless endeavour to highlight three works which in my eyes are remarkable. The first of these is a brief but penetrating article from 1971, brilliant not only for its intrinsic merits but also from a methodological viewpoint. 'The Reports of the Death of Article 2(4) are Greatly Exaggerated'[4] was written as a rebuttal to a famous paper by another leading US scholar, Thomas Franck, entitled 'Who Killed Article 2(4)? Or Changing Norms Governing the Use of Force by States'.[5] Franck's diagnosis of the ills plaguing the Charter, and in particular its crucial article banning the use or threat of force in international relations, had been exhaustive and severe. He had concluded that the ban was dead. Henkin's retort was that 'Article 2(4) lives and, while its condition is grave indeed, its maladies are not necessarily terminal.'[6] Henkin outlined his basic approach by pointing to what he considered the flaws of Franck's approach: '[I]t judges the vitality of the law by looking only at its failures.' He pointed out that even if one were to admit that changing political realities, such as the existence of nuclear weapons and shifts in the balance of power, had reduced the temptation to resort to force and reduced the number of international wars,

> Article 2(4) would not be the less a norm: law often reflects dispositions to behaviour as much as it shapes them. . . . What has become obsolete is the notion that nations are free to indulge it [war] as ever, and the death of that notion is accepted in the Charter.[7]

Henkin went on to stress that 'no government, no responsible official of government, has been prepared or has wished to pronounce it [Article 2(4)] dead.'[8] He also emphasised that major powers, including the US, were constrained by that rule not only in inter-State relations, but also with regard to intervention in internal armed conflict or other strife in other States' territory.[9]

The approach Henkin adopted in this paper towards fundamental rules of international law reminds me of the reproach I once received from another illustrious international lawyer, Bert Röling. At a roundtable on humanitarian law in 1977, I had presented a paper assessing the observance of general

[4] (1971) 65 *American Journal of International Law* 544.

[5] (1970) 64 *American Journal of International Law* 809.

[6] Henkin, above n 4, at 544.

[7] *Ibid*, at 545.

[8] *Ibid*, at 547.

[9] 'Assuming—as many do—that Article 2(4) intended to forbid these interventions [in internal wars and affairs], clearly it has not prevented, deterred, or terminated a number of them although, again, one cannot say confidently that it has not deterred many others. To me, if Article 2(4) signaled the effective end of conventional war though not of intervention, even, indeed, if it induced this alternative form of organized violence, it would signify a substantial advance in international order: the temptation to military intervention in internal affairs is largely an affliction of the few big Powers and even for them military intervention to promote or maintain internal wars is not always and everywhere possible; intervention by invitation on one side is not so great an aggression against sovereignty and independence; internal wars are generally limited in area and in scope of military operation and therefore less terrible in their destructiveness.' (*Ibid*, at 547).

principles of humanitarian law on the use of weapons, and had summed up my painstaking perusal of State practice by concluding that these principles had not played any practical role in international relations to date and were thus pointless. Röling rightly assailed me (albeit in a most urbane manner), arguing that the importance of principles *per se* lies in their function as general legal standards, and even though they might be dormant or unutilised for some periods, they are nonetheless crucial to guide State behaviour. To discount their role, or *a fortiori* proclaim that they are dead, amounts to leaving States even freer to shape their policies based only on their national interests.[10] The methodological lesson I received at that roundtable from Röling had already been given in 1971 by Henkin to Tom Franck.

Henkin's two other major works relate to other areas of law: the role of international legal standards as restraints on foreign policy, which he addressed in *How Nations Behave: Law and Foreign Policy*[11]; and the interplay between international law and the US constitutional system as a regulator of foreign policy, covered in *Foreign Affairs and the US Constitution.*[12] Both are seminal books and extremely innovative in their own right. For one thing, they combine a sound positivist approach, including full respect for *lex lata* and its legal imperatives, with a perspicacious insight into the geo-political motivations of States and the reasons why, in some instances, they are ready to accept existing legal standards while, in others, they prefer to circumvent them.[13] *Foreign Affairs and the US Constitution* is the archetypal inquiry into the way democratic States structure their constitutional organs to deal with foreign relations and the way international legal rules (both treaty provisions and customary rules) operate at the domestic level. The analysis is not only exhaustive and in-depth, it is also critical. A notable illustration of the author's willingness to criticise his government is the remarks he makes with regard to US institutions' implementation of customary international rules.[14]

[10] The remarks by Röling, although somewhat softened in the final text, can be read in A Cassese (ed), *The New Humanitarian Law of Armed Conflict*, vol II (Naples, Editoriale Scientifica, 1980) at 77–79. My paper, as revised in light of Röling's comments, is 'Means of Warfare: the Traditional and the New Law' in A Cassese (ed), *The New Humanitarian Law of Armed Conflict*, vol I (Naples, Editoriale Scientifica, 1979) 161.

[11] L Henkin, *How Nations Behave: Law and Foreign Policy* (London, Pall Mall Press, 1968; 2nd edn, New York, Columbia University Press, 1979).

[12] L Henkin, *Foreign Affairs and the United States Constitution* (Mineola, The Foundation Press, 1972; 2nd edn, Oxford, Clarendon Press, 1996).

[13] Henkin also gave a general course at The Hague Academy, republished as L Henkin, *International Law: Politics and Values* (Dordrecht, Nijhoff, 1995).

[14] See Henkin, above n 11, 2nd edn, at 232–46. Among other things, he wrote (*ibid*, at 246): 'At the end of the twentieth century, customary international law, together with treaties which depend on customary law, remains the core of international governance and a pillar of US foreign relations. Like treaties, customary international law is law for the United States in relations with other nations, as well as law of the United States for its political institutions, its courts, and its citizens. Like treaties, customary international law must fit into the US constitutional framework and must find and keep its place in constitutional jurisprudence. Unlike treaties which have developed their part in the constitutional life of the United States, customary international law remains full of constitutional uncertainties. The Supreme Court has barely glanced at customary law in the twentieth century, and what the Court said in 1900, in

Without meaning to detract from Henkin's splendid argumentation and highly innovative analysis of the role of international law in the US domestic system, it bears noting that he seems to overlook a tendency which has progressively emerged in the last decades. Indeed, the rule of law, while it is considered a fundamental principle of *domestic* US law, has been demoted to a secondary concern when it comes to the US *external relations*. It would seem that at the level of its inter-State dealings, the American Government prefers to tread carefully: it endeavours to keep the crucial rules or principles of international law as vague as possible, avoids acceding to some major international treaties constraining the conduct of States in internal affairs or in areas of armed conflict, and also tends to incorporate and abide by international legal imperatives only to the extent that this suits its national interests.

How Nations Behave casts a new light on the impact of international legal rules on the actual conduct of States. Nevertheless, it is perhaps possible to argue that Henkin overestimates the role of law in international dealings. For instance, his broad statement that States comply with law most of the time is in my view overly optimistic.[15] One should not forget that *de maximis non curat ius*. In other words, with regard to matters which States deem 'existential' (such as the use of military or economic force, self-defence, the possible employment of nuclear and other mass-destruction weapons), international rules either do not exist at all, or are deliberately fuzzy and ambiguous. It naturally follows from this that a quest for legal standards inevitably leads one to rely on general principles, which, as correctly demonstrated by Schachter,[16] may prove in the end to contradict one another. In the area of these highly political matters, where the supreme interests of major powers are at stake, the restraining force of legal imperatives fades away. Notwithstanding all that, regardless of whether Henkin's sweeping appreciation of the *status quo* is correct, it remains of crucial importance that a leading US scholar should vigorously insist on the need for States to observe international rules.[17] His

opaque dictum and in outdated context, has only sown and harvested confusion. Surely, it is time for the Court "to say what the law is", beginning by revisiting the reverence of the Framers for the Law of Nations, and establish its clear and honorable place in our constitutional life.'

[15] 'Violations of law attract attention and the occasional important violation is dramatic; the daily, sober loyalty of nations to the law and their obligations is hardly noted. *It is probably the case that almost all nations observe almost all principles of international law and almost all their obligations almost all of the time.* Every day nations respect the borders of other nations, treat foreign diplomats and citizens and property as required by law, observe thousands of treaties with more than a hundred countries . . .'; Henkin, above n 11, 1st edn, at 47, emphasis in the original.

[16] O Schachter, *International Law in Theory and Practice* (Dordrecht, Nijhoff, 1991) at 20–23.

[17] It is notable that Henkin stated the following: 'In the [international] society we have, international law sustains what order we have and promises better. There is bound to be controversy about its application and interpretation, but that does not vitiate its significance or effectiveness. Nor is law destroyed by the fact that it is sometimes violated, even by the fact that it is sometimes hypocritically invoked by the violators. (We do not reject scripture merely because the devil may cite it.) *In regard to the law against force, there is no longer any doubt about its validity, its desirability, its necessity.*' Henkin, above n 11, 2nd edn, at 338 (emphasis added).

value-judgments should be embraced for their courage in emphasising the moral imperative for States to abide by the law.

Henkin's intellectual weight was no doubt enhanced by his open-mindedness and the balance he sought to achieve in his views. This receptivity to opinions and approaches different from his were visible at an international colloquium on 'The Right to Leave and to Return' which took place in Uppsala in 1972. The conference dealt with a burning issue which was relevant both to people from eastern countries, whom eastern governments prevented from travelling abroad, and to the Palestinian diaspora, which sought to assert its right to return to Palestine and the territories occupied by Israel. I had been asked to prepare a report on the international rules governing the matter, and had adopted a very critical stance on the current legal regulation.[18] Henkin was one of the major participants in the colloquium, and it was his legal and moral authority, as well as his balanced views, which prevented the conference from falling apart when Dr Musa Mazzawi, a Palestinian lawyer, withdrew, criticising the whole meeting as a 'put up job' intended to ignore Palestinian rights.[19] Henkin also was the most prominent member of a 'drafting committee' set up at the last moment to work out a sort of final declaration.[20] I remember having spent most of a night with him and a few other scholars or lawyers, trying to reach agreement on an acceptable text. During the conference, all the participants made an outing to visit a nearby town, and I was lucky to find myself sitting next to Henkin on the bus. He asked me many questions, not only on Italian legal culture, but also my personal history, a curiosity which was not doubt fuelled by the fact that he had been in Italy during the Second World War as an American soldier. He did not bat an eyelid when I told him how my father's academic interest in the history of peasants' revolutionary movements in Southern Italy in the 19th century had spurred him to move from a liberal anti-fascist attitude to embracing Communism in 1943. I was

[18] A Cassese, 'International Law and Implementation: On the Universal Level' in K Vasak and S Liskofsky (eds), *The Right to Leave and to Return, Paper and Recommendations of the International Colloquium Held in Uppsala, Sweden, 19–21 June 1972* (Ann Arbor, Mich, The American Jewish Committee, 1976) at 493–520. An American participant, S Liskofsky, commented in private that reading my pessimistic paper was akin to staying at the Wailing Wall. The paper had already been published in a revised form: 'The International Protection of the Right to Leave and to Return' in *Studi in onore di Manlio Udina*, vol 1 (Milan, Giuffré, 1975) 219–29.

[19] His frustration stemmed from the formal interpretation the conference's participants by and large adopted of the right of return, whereby only persons entitled to return to the country of which they are nationals could claim a right of return. This meant that Palestinian refugees could claim no such right. As he put it: 'The argument by Dr Weis that the reference in the Universal Declaration of Human Rights Art 13(2) to a person's right to return to "his country" as well as the later in the International Covenant on Civil and Political Rights Art 12(4) to a person's right to enter "his own country" should be interpreted to mean the right to enter the country of which the person is a national by the law of the state is, in my humble submission, unjustified . . . A person's "country" is that to which he is connected by a reasonable combination of such relevant criteria as race, religion, language, ancestry, birth prolonged domicile. Governments come and go, and their political fluctuations and vagaries should not affect the fundamental right of human beings, such as the right to return to one's own country and to have a homeland' (M Mazzawi, 'Comment on the Middle East' in Vasak and Liskofsky (eds), above n 18, at 343).

[20] For the text of the declaration, see Vasak and Liskofsky (eds), above n 18, at xxi–xxv.

expecting Henkin to be put off at the mere mention of a Communist connection, as was frequent in those years in the United States. Instead he listened with interest, and continued asking questions to grasp the reasons behind this state of affairs. No doubt his idealism prevented him from being prejudiced or boxed into pre-fabricated ideologies.

His wife Alice, herself a brilliant woman and the Director of the Aspen Institute's Justice and Society Program, amusingly once quipped: 'Lou once told me he'd heard that the world is divided between star-gazers and basket-weavers. I'm a basket-weaver, he's a star-gazer.'[21]

The last time I saw Henkin was in March 2007, when I received the Wolfgang Friedmann Award at Columbia University. Despite being in poor health, he was gracious enough to attend the ceremony, and lavished me with such praise that I began to think he was mistaking me for someone else.

As with Oscar Schachter, one may well wonder why the US establishment refrained from projecting this brilliant legal mind onto the international scene by nominating him as its candidate to the International Court of Justice. We can only speculate on the impact his idealism, moral integrity, a deep-seated belief in human rights and the rule of law, and his pursuit of more widely respected international legal standards might have had on international institutions, had he been offered the possibility to sit on the bench.

[21] S von Gutfeld, 'Columbia Celebrates the Human Rights Legacy of Professor Louis Henkin', *Columbia Law School Report*, Winter 2007, at 18; also available at <http://www.law.columbia.edu/law_school/communications/reports/winter07/louishenkin/fullstory> (last visited on 28 September 2010).

Interview with Louis Henkin

February 1995

I. The Formative Years

A. Early influences

Who was the international lawyer who most influenced your thinking at the beginning of your scholarly activity?

That is difficult to say because I came to international law late, and after I had finished my formal education and was professionally launched. When I studied law at Harvard, between 1937 and 1940, I was not interested in international law. The United States was not interested in international law. As a country, we were in our most isolationist mood. At that time, not many studied international law at Harvard. Manley Hudson was the professor and he was not very popular.

My interests were domestic, liberal and progressive. I was studying law in order to join the New Deal. It was not until World War II, which sent me to North Africa and Europe for four years, that I became interested in international matters.

When I came out of the war, I wished to work in international affairs, and to me the 'new deal' of the post-war [period] was the United Nations. So I came to international law through war, international politics and my interest in the new United Nations. My first professional job (other than my judicial clerkships) was as a foreign affairs officer, a civil servant, in the State Department, in UN affairs. My first 'boss' was Dean Rusk, who later became Secretary of State; at that time he was the Director of the Office, which was later called the Bureau of United Nations Affairs. I was not in the Legal Adviser's Office; I worked on UN matters as a foreign affairs officer.

I became interested in international law along two paths. Because I had been a Supreme Court law clerk, I was called on to work at what we now call 'foreign affairs and the Constitution', which included the place of treaties and of international law generally in US jurisprudence. The other path was through the United Nations as a force for peace, for the rule of law and for promoting human rights. Through those interests, I came to international law.

Now, to respond to your question. The people who influenced me most, I think, were Hersch Lauterpacht, Phil Jessup and later Wolfgang Friedmann, whom I came to know when I came to Columbia. Phil Jessup impressed me most. Later, the international lawyer I came to respect most is my colleague, Oscar Schachter, who is analytically acute, has breadth of knowledge and deep sensitivity.

Jessup influenced me in a different way. He was reasonable. He was practical. He was committed to law. And he understood its place in international affairs. Perhaps through him, I became interested in law and diplomacy, law as politics, law as international politics. International lawyers have too often treated their legal system as self-contained, having nothing to do with the world. I think that is a mistaken view. International law, like all law, is made by 'politicians', in the best sense of that word. Law is an element, a major element in international politics. One cannot understand the law except in the context of the international political system and international diplomacy.

So law and politics, law and diplomacy were my principal focus. If I've made any contribution to the field, it is in the small book published a long time ago called *How Nations Behave.*[22] It is that perspective on the law to which I contributed.

So I came to international law from law and politics. Also from an interest in what people mistakenly call, as you pointed out, 'monism' and 'dualism', the place of international law and international affairs in national constitutional systems. The second book I did, with which I am reasonably pleased, is *Foreign Affairs and the United States Constitution* (now being updated).[23] Those two books suggest my special interests.

Therefore you were mainly influenced by English or American international lawyers. But what about Europeans, say Lauterpacht?

Lauterpacht was my link to Europe. I was not influenced by other Europeans until later.

But later were there any other Europeans whom you regard as leading scholars, and who have in a way contributed to shaping your own views of international law?

Brierly[24] and his successors. At the beginning I found the French somewhat insular in their international law, a sort of French international law. More recently I have been impressed by Prosper Weil.[25]

Virally should be one closer to you.

Yes, he was, but I didn't get to know Virally[26] till much later. Virally was one of the best European international lawyers, but I didn't get to know him early, maybe because he was younger.

[22] Henkin, above n 11.
[23] Henkin, above n 12. The 2nd edn of this work was being prepared at the time of the interview.
[24] See 'Interview with Sir Robert Jennings', fn 18.
[25] See 'Interview with Eduardo Jiménez de Aréchaga', fn 19.
[26] See 'Interview with Sir Robert Jennings', fn 35.

What about the Austrian school, Kelsen?[27]

He was too formalistic for my taste.

Have you met him?

No, he went to California and I never got to know him. I read Kelsen and his disciples, but they didn't influence me much. Their approach to international law was jurisprudential, mine was political, diplomatic. The British and the French are in between. The British, through Lauterpacht, Brierly and their successors (eg, Fitzmaurice[28]), have had influence. Jennings came along later. Those of us who are older were not influenced by the young because when they came along we had already developed our way. We respect them, we work with them, but influence is a different concept.

B. On Positivism

Of course, labels are always wrong, but would you regard yourself as a positivist, not necessarily stricto sensu*?*

Not in the Kelsen sense, but I really am a positivist in that I recognise that the law has to be made by the politicians, I can't make it myself, and I cannot impose my values and declare them to be natural law. But I try to push the politicians towards human values, and to identify (and criticise) what they have done.

So you also stick to this famous distinction so greatly emphasised by the positivists between lege lata, lege ferenda*. Does it involve that one should only deal with the existing law and should not go into a future possible law, one should not make confusion with these two levels?*

One should not confuse them, but they are more fluid than some would like; and statesmen can make *ferenda* into *lata* by their actions, and lawyers even by their writing. I recognise the distinction, but I don't think it is as firm and fixed as some of my colleagues in the profession do.

C. Henkin's cultural background

Could we move to a further question. Leaving aside legal scholarship, what philosophical or ideological schools influenced your intellectual development?

I don't keep aloof from non-legal schools of thinking; my thinking is saturated with international politics. So-called 'realists' of a recent day, such as George

[27] See 'Interview with René-Jean Dupuy', fn 23.
[28] See 'Interview with Eduardo Jiménez de Aréchaga', fn 23.

Kennan[29] and Hans Morgenthau,[30] compelled me to ask myself 'Is international law real? Does it make any difference?' They influenced my thinking, if you will, negatively, responsively. I set myself to pointing out, as I think is the case, that the cause of the rule of law in international affairs, to which I am committed and which is my principal preoccupation, requires recognising and persuading others that international law is real, that it makes a difference. That requires us to point out to the 'realists' that when they fail to attend to international law they are not being very realistic. It is epitomised by the old story, when Stalin asked 'How many divisions does the Pope have?' The answer was he had lots of divisions, but Stalin didn't know how to recognise them.

That is my view of international law. I spend time on 'how nations behave' to demonstrate, as I think is the case, that international law shapes the behaviour of States, and therefore shapes international politics. To me, international law has no existence and little interest as some abstract system; if it is real, it matters. The fact that States devote huge wealth, and that hundreds of thousands of people spend their lives on it, is evidence that it matters. But it's important for us who care to show that the system works, and how it works and why law matters.

When I say that people such as Morgenthau and Kennan influenced me, I mean that they challenged me. In my view they failed to see the importance of international law in international politics; perhaps most important, they failed to see, surely they underestimated, the national interest (of the United States) in respect for law. They could see the national interest only in tangibles, in numbers of divisions. That respect for law in the national interest is a cause which I took on. So the realists influenced me because I spent lots of time reading them and thinking about them.

I've also been influenced by those who deal with 'ethics' in international affairs; in the United States, scholars such as Stanley Hoffmann[31] at Harvard. It's part of the same idea: that international law matters, is real; that it shapes and influences the system; that it is in the interest of all, of States as well as individual human beings, to promote the rule of law in international affairs.

[29] George Frost Kennan (1904–2005) was a distinguished US diplomat. In 1947–48, when George C Marshall was Secretary of State, he was most influential: Marshall valued his strategic vision, and had him set up and head what is now called the Policy Planning Staff, the State Department's internal think tank. Kennan became the first Director of Policy Planning. As an intellectual architect of the Marshall Plan, he helped launch the pillar of economic and political containment of the Soviet Union. Kennan's influence rapidly declined under Secretary of State Dean Acheson, in 1949 and 1950. In 1951–52 Kennan was US Ambassador to the Soviet Union and in 1961–63 US Ambassador to Yugoslavia.

[30] Hans Joachim Morgenthau (1904–80) was born into a Jewish family in Coburg, Germany, and educated at the universities of Berlin, Frankfurt and Munich. He pursued postgraduate work at the Graduate Institute of International Studies in Geneva. He taught and practised law in Frankfurt before emigrating to the United States in 1937. He taught at the University of Chicago, at the New School for Social Research and the City University of New York. He made landmark contributions to the theory of international relations and the study of international law. His major scholarly work is *Politics Among Nations: The Struggle for Power and Peace* (New York, Knopf, 1948).

[31] Stanley Hoffmann (born in Vienna in 1928) is the Paul and Catherine Buttenweiser University Professor at Harvard University.

But actually my question was also about whether or not you adhere to a particular philosophical school of thought.

No, I don't. I'm what I call a 'meliorist,' someone who believes in improving things. I am liberal, progressive and committed to the promotion of human welfare, and for me international law is an important, perhaps an essential, tool in that process.

Well, there is a question which is bound up with the ones you have already answered. Have you ever written in national or international newspapers, or taken part in talks or discussions on television? To what extent have you tried to bring to the fore your own theories and also to influence public opinion?

I have not appeared much in the public media. But I have testified before Congressional Committees, and I have written in legal and political-legal journals in support of what I believe in and favour. But I have not tried to be a news journalist.

You don't give talks on TV.

I've done it once or twice. I have no objection to others doing it, but I don't think such talks are intellectually satisfying either for the giver or the receiver, at least in the culture in which I live.

Why?

Because people don't listen. If I appear on TV, they give me 10 minutes, and then they edit out eight; I do not sense that I'm given an opportunity to get my message across. If I thought otherwise, I might feel differently. It's the character of the media.

As for the journals, I've written on foreign affairs, and on particular subjects, such as war powers in the United States. But I tend to be a private person, and don't relish appearing in public. I give speeches when invited but have never tried to develop a 'clientele'. I have no agent. I've given many speeches, and most of them were published, but in legal journals or quasi-legal journals, not in the popular press.

D. Participating in social or political activities

Do you consider that an international lawyer should get involved in social or political activities, or have what the French would call 'engagement'*?*

I am very much *engagé*, but you might not be able to tell that by looking at my activities. I lead a busy life but I generally speak as a lawyer, when I think I know something and am entitled to ask to be heard. I don't get involved in other aspects of national politics.

I am pleased to be identified as a liberal. When 'liberalism' became a pejorative word in the United States, I joined a group of people who placed a full-page ad in the *New York Times*—'We Are Liberals'. I care about these causes. But my principal activity has been the university and my students, my writing, and my speeches from a legal standpoint. I don't often speak about abstract legal questions. My speeches and writings are usually on legal questions that impinge on national and international affairs.

For example, during this past month I have spoken during four successive weekends on four different subjects. One was on refugees, a subject in which I have had some involvement. This past weekend, you and I were both involved in discussions of the place of international law in national courts. Next week I will participate in a panel on US war powers. Although it will be a constitutional discussion, it is an important political-international discussion; and we do become involved in the relationship between the UN Charter and the US Constitution. And the weekend after that, I will give a speech on collective intervention in support of human rights. I speak principally to legal audiences, university students.

I should have mentioned that, about 15 years ago, I became active in human rights, and that has become my principal international activity. I have written books and articles on the subject[32]; I am on the Board of the Lawyers Committee for Human Rights; I speak on that subject to anybody who asks me. So I'm definitely *engagé*, but not on the general political scene.

Have you ever been a member of a political party?

I am, nominally, but not actively. I register, I vote, I support progressive candidates.

Do you perceive yourself merely as a technician, or as a fully-fledged intellectual working in your country for a good cause?

I think of myself as an intellectual, not a technician.

You are an excellent technician in the sense of a professional scholar.

That's for you to say. Thank you. That takes us back to our earlier subject. My interest in international law is in how nations behave. Inevitably, that means I have to study the behaviour of States. My interest in human rights is not an abstract study of international covenants and conventions and institutions, but how they work, and how they influence the behaviour of States and the condition of human beings.

[32] See, eg, L Henkin, *The Rights of Man Today* (Londons, Stevens, 1978); L Henkin (ed), *The International Bill of Rights: The Covenant on Civil and Political Rights* (New York, Columbia University Press, 1981); L Henkin, *The Age of Rights* (New York, Columbia University Press, 1990); L Henkin, 'A Bill of Rights: And a Half' (1997) 32 *Texas International Law Journal* 483; L Henkin, 'The Universal Declaration at 50 and the Challenge of Global Markets' (1999) 25 *Brooklin Journal of International Law* 17.

II. Encounters with Other International Lawyers

Before we move on with our list of questions, there is one question which I normally put to all interviewees, namely, what scholars have you met in your life in the area of international law who have impressed you most, because of their personality, the richness of their ideas, or their approach to life or to international law? Could you mention a few names of people who have been very significant for you, whom you have met in the Institut de Droit international *in Europe, or in America?*

As I said, the person who impressed me most was probably Philip Jessup. But he was not one of those who made a major contribution to international law. Jessup was a highly intelligent, very decent human being, with excellent personal relations and fine human values. And he dedicated himself and the use of the law to those values. As you know, I became active in the international legal community later; when I was in the State Department I wasn't in that community; after I came to Columbia, Wolfgang Friedmann was my senior here. In a sense, I stayed in the background and worked in my own field, and I didn't get to know the Europeans and the British personally. I did meet and spent some time with Schwarzenberger,[33] who was engaging, and had a very good mind, but he and I did not always agree. There was another person whom we don't think of as an international lawyer who influenced and impressed me, Otto Kahn-Freund.[34] Probably international lawyers didn't think of him as an international lawyer.

He was a comparative lawyer and a labour lawyer.

Yes, but he worked on the bridges in the fields in which I worked. I liked Francis Mann[35]; he and I didn't have the same ideology, I suspect, but I had

[33] George Schwarzenberger (1908–91) was born in Heilbronn, Germany, and educated at the Universities of Heidelberg, Frankfurt, Berlin, Tübingen, Paris and London. He went to England in 1934 to become Secretary of the New Commonwealth Institute, which later became the London Institute of World Affairs. He was appointed to the Faculty of Laws at University College London in 1938, where he remained until his retirement in 1975. He was called to the English Bar by Gray's Inn in 1955. He was a strong believer in an interdisciplinary approach to international studies. In international law he used an inductive approach. His major contribution to international law is the four-volume work *International Law* (London, Stevens, 1945–86).

[34] Otto Kahn-Freund (German, 1900–79) became judge of the Berlin Labour Court in 1929. Dismissed by the Nazis in 1933, he fled to London. He was Professor of Comparative Law at the University of Oxford.

[35] Francis A Mann (1907–91) emigrated from Germany to the UK in 1938. He studied at the Universities of Geneva, Munich and Berlin, and worked as an assistant at the Faculty of Law of the Friedrich Wilhelm University in Berlin from 1930 to 1933. Mann re-established his life in London. He took an LLD at the University of London, presenting the first edition of *The Legal Aspect of Money* (London, Oxford University Press, 1938), later published as *The Legal Aspect of Money: With Special Reference to Comparative Private and Public International Law*, 5th edn (Oxford, Clarendon Press, 1992). His major works are *Studies in International Law* (Oxford, Clarendon Press, 1973) and *Further Studies in International Law* (Oxford, Clarendon Press, 1990). Schebwel wrote of him that he 'was a man of convictions, of strong views, and of a capacity for moral indignation. His writings were, if not opinionated, certainly combative. They were marked by an extraordinary acuity, which was as enlightening as it was stimulating. His conversation

respect for his intellect and his integrity. I have admired the European lawyers, but I think of them as in a special group (I'm distinguishing European Community and Union layers from the Madame Bastids[36] and the Rousseaus[37] and the Reuters[38] and Prosper Weil[39]). I have also admired the work of some of you people in Italy, and this is no idle compliment. I like what people such as Cappelletti[40] did, and my friend Eric Stein,[41] and Joe Weiler,[42] and Bruno Simma,[43] but they are classified as European and comparative rather than international. In the international field, I respect the work of Ago[44] but I never came to know him, because when I came over to Europe for a few days I did not have a chance to meet very many.

You didn't meet him at the Institut du Droit international*?*

I've been a member of the *Institut* for about 10 years. (I was over 60 years old when I became a member, a sort of 'new boy' on the block.) Schachter, when you talk to him, will give you a very different sense because Schachter has been part of that world through the United Nations. Before he became a professor, he was for 30 years in the United Nations and met all you lawyers in that context, and he was a member of the *Institut* ages before I was. As I told you earlier, I think Oscar is the leading international lawyer we have, and probably as good as any alive today, and he also knows the Community and has views on the subject which I am sure he will give you.

You mentioned Wolfgang Friedmann. Did he play any major role at Columbia University?

He did during the years he was here, but you know he died early, in 1972. Friedmann taught on every continent and wrote on jurisprudence, inter-

was no less enlivening.': S Schebwel, 'F A Mann (1907–1991)' (1992) 86 *American Journal of International Law* 102, at 103.

[36] See 'Interview with Sir Robert Jennings', fn 26.

[37] See 'Interview with Eduardo Jiménez de Aréchaga', fn 39.

[38] See 'Interview with René-Jean Dupuy', fn 18.

[39] See 'Interview with Eduardo Jiménez de Aréchaga', fn 19.

[40] Mauro Cappelletti (Italian, 1927–2004) was Professor of Comparative Law as well as at Stanford University Law School. He then became Professor of Law at the European University Institute in Florence.

[41] Erik Stein (*b* 1913) is Hessel E Yntema Professor of Law Emeritus at the University of Michigan Law School.

[42] Joseph Halevi Horowitz Weiler (Israeli, born in South Africa in 1951) is Joseph Straus Professor of Law and European Union Jean Monnet Chair at New York University Law School. Before getting a chair at NYU he was Professor of Law at the University of Michigan Law School (1985–92) and Manley Hudson Professor and Jean Monnet Chair at Harvard Law School (1992–2001). He is a Fellow of the American Academy of Arts and Sciences. He is currently the editor-in-chief of the *European Journal of International Law*. His major work is *The Constitution of Europe: Do the New Clothes Have an Emperor?* (Cambridge, Cambridge University Press, 1998).

[43] Bruno Simma (German, *b* 1941), Professor of International Law at the University of Munich (1973–2003) and at the Michigan University Law School (since 1987). He was a member of the UN International Law Commission (1996–2003) and since 2003 has been a member of the ICJ.

[44] See 'Interview with René-Jean Dupuy', fn 28.

national law, comparative law and administrative law. He was something of a Renaissance man in the law and had a powerful mind.

Would you regard his book on The Changing Structure of International Law[45] *as a major work?*

I think it is an important work. It is hard to say whether it was identifying something that had happened, or whether it was promoting it, hoping to help make it happen. Friedmann was identifying the changing law as a way of promoting it, and I think he had a significant influence in that respect. To that extent, he and I were on the same wave-length. We seek to identify—that's our positivism—as a way of promoting. We were not particular friends, but we were on the same wave-length.

III. The Role of the Jurist as Scholar and Practitioner

A. Some seminal books on international law

Before we move on to other questions, there are two questions which are not on the questionnaire. Would you mention a few seminal books on international law which, to your mind, are in a way ground-breaking, for they mark a turning point in the development of international law. I would of course include your own book on How Nations Behave,[46] *where you have opened new vistas in international law.*

Hersch Lauterpacht's writings generally. His book on *Human Rights*,[47] for example, and his edition of Oppenheim,[48] which I think has strong Lauterpacht elements; it is much more Lauterpacht than Oppenheim.

But why do you like those books? Is it because in a way he was not a strict positivist, he was infused with natural law? Well, his book on human rights was actually not a positivist book.

That is true. But then, I am interested in those who seek to promote international law as well as those who reflect it as is. I don't trust the wishful thinkers, I don't trust those who say 'this is the law because it ought to be'. But I support those, and I am one of those, who say 'this is what the law ought to be, and whether I'm not sure it's not, let me see to what extent it may be, or can be made to be'. I think Lauterpacht had something of that. Jessup is another.

[45] W Friedmann, *The Changing Structure of International Law* (London, Stevens and sons, 1964)
[46] Henkin, above n 11.
[47] H Lauterpacht, *International Law and Human Rights* (New York, Praeger, 1950).
[48] L Oppenheim, *International Law: A Treatise*, 5th edn, ed H Lauterpacht (London, Longmans, 1937).

As for Jessup, are you thinking of . . .

His small book, *A Modern Law of Nations*,[49] and the 'transnational law' concept, were insightful.

One of my troubles with international law positivists is that they tend to treat the law as hermetically sealed off from anything else, from both international politics and from national law and politics. Jessup pointed out that the real world is not like that. There is close interplay between national constitutional law and international law, and to see how they work in the real world you have to see them together.

Lauterpacht started with some natural law conceptions, but later he didn't talk natural law, because towards the end of his life, he was living in the age of positivism. It's 'the human rights business' that moved many of us positivists if not towards natural law, then towards something which I sometimes define as 'a common moral intuition' which is in the *Zeitgeist* at the second half of the 20th century, the time in which I've lived and worked. It is some such notion that explains the success of the human rights movement, insofar as it has succeeded. When I deal with 'cultural relativism' (which I deal with regularly), I challenge the world to tell me why we have succeeded in getting rid of apartheid; how come the whole world has agreed that apartheid is unacceptable? Some of that may have been cynical, some of it may have been hypocritical, some of it may have been instrumental (serving some other purposes), but we have created a political-legal universe in which the standards we identify with human dignity, and with notions of justice, are accepted.

But we don't wish to talk about natural law as their source because natural law has had a bad history. When Jeremy Bentham said that natural rights are nonsense, and natural and imprescriptible rights are 'nonsense upon stilts', he was right on one level. He was afraid of what had been done in the name of natural law, from the divine right of kings, to the inferiority of women, to the natural inferiority of slaves. But Bentham had a vision, he was a progressive; he knew where he was going. I would ask him, if he were here, 'Why do you think as you do, favour what you favour, why that rather than Hitler?' He would have had to come up with something like 'We all know what is decent and right.'

I have a similar feeling as to what international law should be. I think I can distinguish what is from what I would like it to be, but I like to work in those areas where there is some uncertainty as to whether it is or isn't, and to move it where I think it ought to be.

If we go on with the notion of books which you would select as seminal, would you include a book by Bert Röling, International Law in an Expanded World,[50] *where he for the first time took a very favorable stand to developing countries?*

[49] PC Jessup, *A Modern Law of the Nations: An Introduction* (New York, Macmillan, 1948).
[50] BVA Röling, *International Law in an Expanded World* (Amsterdam, Djambatan, 1960).

I am in that world through human rights. I believe in the human rights of all human beings, in their economic and social rights, as well as their political and civil rights. Development is essential to the enjoyment of both sets of rights. I think the international community should assume responsibility to protect and ensure all these rights, including the rights of the people and the peoples of the Third World. I've never considered myself a 'one-worlder'. (We used to have a one-world movement.) I believe in one world, but tempered by reality, which is the reality of nation-States. Therefore, as to the book you mentioned, *International Law in an Expanded World*, I sympathise with that perspective though I can't say I was influenced by it.

Going back, have you ever had the chance of reading a book which at that stage was seminal, again, by Politis, Les nouvelles tendances du droit international?[51] *It came out in 1926 I think. Are there similar books which in a way were of some value to you because they propounded new ideas, a new approach to international law?*

I don't think I've been deeply influenced by any particular book written in my time. Some wise things are said in some books or articles; I read the *Recueil des Cours* and I find good things in it. Some have no doubt influenced me, but I shall have to ponder which. For me, no one book has made a big 'splash' in modern times. I very much like my colleague Oscar Schachter's book deriving from his Hague lectures,[52] and I hope people will like my book, from my Hague lectures.[53]

That book will give you the idea of where I stand, and perhaps one could work back from it to look for antecedents and influences. In those lectures I was looking for values behind international law, and trying to identify the movement—I think the movement has been too slow—from what I call State-values to human-values. We care too much about *sovereignty*. I'm on a campaign to eliminate the word *sovereignty* (I know that's a Quixotic campaign). I think, first of all, that sovereignty is a mistake; 'they' took a domestic notion and gave it unwarranted international consequences it was not intended to have. Secondly, they are confused about its significance. A sovereign State, like a 'sovereign' human being, can agree to be governed; that is what the international system is about. So when someone says 'sovereignty', I say 'Yes, take your sovereignty and put it on the line here. We will all get together with our sovereignties and we'll have a UN Charter, and a UN organisation, and we'll have a UN human rights system.' I'm in favour of greater cooperation among States, but do not pretend that one can, or that I wish to, abolish States.

So I am involved these days in attacks on 'sovereignty' in favour of 'international governance'. I use that theme not only for human rights but for

[51] NE Politis, *Les nouvelles tendances du droit international* (Paris, Librairie Hachette, 1927).
[52] O Schachter, above n 16.
[53] Henkin, above n 11.

the environment, even for the things you and I are closest to, such as the International Court of Justice. I was appalled when—I think it was the late Judge Ruda[54]—I asked him one day, 'Why do you let those lawyers carry on for days and pile up thousands of pages of memorials when the Supreme Court of the United States, not an unimportant court, gives the most important people a half hour and limits the number of pages they can file to a very small number?' And he said to me, 'Well, you can't limit sovereign States.' I was appalled.

But I cannot trace my quest for values to any particular book or influence, other than those of Lauterpacht and Jessup, as I said.

B. The New Haven approach to international law

Can I move to two different questions. First of all, what do you think of the New Haven approach, I mean the McDougal's[55] view of international law? I think your approach is totally different.

Yes, it is different in two senses. On one level, it says what is obvious. (But we often need education in the obvious, as Holmes[56] said.) I agree with 'law as process'. But that idea has been abused by those who suggest that law is always in flux and therefore you can never have a confident answer to what the law is, and therefore nothing can be said to be illegal. I say, even if law is process, we who work in the real world have to be able to stop the process at a particular time and ask 'where are we?' Some of those committed to New Haven are reluctant to do that. And some of them used law as process as a pretext for coming up with whatever answer one may want. That is not my view of law. I am much more of a positivist.

A second problem is that too often what they thought about 'world order' coincided with the national policy of a particular State. And that is not my view. All States are subject to the international order, and even the best of States have to respect law, what I consider the law to be, or what others who have thought about it hard and *bona fide* consider the law to be at any given time. It would be interesting for someone to study what you call the New Haven School to see how often their prescriptions differed from the policies of their favourite governments.

[54] José María Ruda (Argentinian, 1924–94) was a member of the UN International Law Commission (1964–72). He also served as the Argentine Ambassador to the United Nations between 1966 and 1970. He then served as a judge in the ICJ (1973–91), presiding over the Court in 1988–91.

[55] See 'Interview with René-Jean Dupuy', fn 22.

[56] Oliver Wendell Holmes, Jr (1841–1935) was a Professor of Law at Harvard University, and later a great member of the US Supreme Court (1902 to 1932). Among the decisions he delivered for the Court some stand out, notably *Otis v Parker*, 187 US 606 (1903), and *Schenck v United States*, 249 US 47 (1919). He was also famous for his dissenting opinions, notably in *Northern Securities Co v United States*, 193 US 197 (1904), and *Abrams v United States*, 250 US 616 (1919).

So, in other words, you argue that they are ideologically biased?

Well, I don't know if they are, but that approach lends itself to ideological bias and has been in fact used to support ideological bias.

Also because normally the values propounded by most of them are the values of the US Government.

That's been said. In fairness, Nino, the US Government has in general been on the right side—but not always, and not in detail, and not specifically. And that's where the differences arise. That approach leads people to use the law to support US policy, rather than to hold US policy up for criticism in the light of the law. I have tended to be a critic of US policy when I considered it to be contrary to international law. I love the United States and I was a member of its Government, and I respect democracy, but I have sometimes seen it to be my job to provide friendly, constructive criticisms, because I think that is in the national interest of the United States to abide by and support the rule of law.

Do you feel that the Yale (or New Haven) School of international law is still powerful?

Well, Myres McDougal, for whose ability I have great respect, retired. There are different voices at Yale now. The principal proponent, I suppose, is Michael Reisman,[57] but he doesn't have the kind of influence or following that 'Mac' had. And Yale now has other voices—Harold Koh,[58] a young man mostly interested in national constitutional matters but moving into international law. He, I think, will be a very different influence.

And the various disciples such as Dick Falk?[59]

Dick Falk is probably the ablest of the people you call McDougal's disciples. But I think Falk split from McDougal. They differed on policy. Falk also recognised some of the abuses to which the Yale School could lend itself in the hands of people who wanted to use it.

Would you regard him as a lawyer? Because we in Europe regard Dick more as a visionary, as a sort of prophet.

That's not wholly inconsistent. One can be a visionary as well as a scholar. But until a certain time—during the years when he wrote, for example, about

[57] W Michael Reisman (*b* 1939) is Myres S McDougal Professor of International Law at Yale Law School, where he has been on the Faculty since 1965.

[58] Harold Hongju Koh (*b* 1954) has been Professor of International Law at the Yale Law School (1985–2009) and Dean of the Law School (2004–09). Assistant Secretary of State for Democracy, Human Rights and Labor (1998–2001). He currently serves as the Legal Adviser to the US Department of State.

[59] See 'Interview with Sir Robert Jennings', fn 77.

the theory of international law[60]—he was on the way to becoming the most powerful international law scholar in the United States. But then he turned into other fields. You are right. If one wishes to look for his scholarship, one ought to go to his early writings.

C. Acting as a practitioner

The next question is about the way you integrated, as it were, your activity as a scholar into your activity as a practitioner. You started off in the State Department as a legal counsellor?

No, not as a legal counsellor. In the State Department, I was a foreign affairs officer in the UN Bureau. I was never in the legal department of the State Department.

When I began to write, the first thing I published was on the US treaty power, an article which had some influence.[61] I found myself relating my intellectual work with my activities, but my activities were not legal but essentially 'general diplomatic', supporting the rule of law.

Later, I identified, and ploughed in, two fields. One was the Law of the Sea. I became involved in that quite early through the legal adviser who had been a friend of mine; and I became active in that field and have written on it.[62] Then, a little later, I got into human rights, and I began to relate my writing on human rights to 'activism.' I don't do any of this for pay, and I am not a practising lawyer in the sense your question might suggest, but I have worked *pro bono* for almost anybody who asked me to, for a cause I believe in. These days that includes mostly human rights work, though I have continued my interest in the Law of the Sea, trying to promote US adherence to the UN Law of the Sea Convention.

Those have been my two principal fields, that plus the rule of law in international affairs. As I said, I am not a practitioner, but I testify on 'the Hill', usually on invitation, before the Senate. I have been on advisory committees to the State Department, usually when the Democrats were in control. That's been my 'activism', but it's not 'practice' in the sense you were talking about.

Have you ever been a judge or an international judge?

No.

[60] See, eg, RA Falk, *The Role of Domestic Courts in the International Legal Order* (Syracuse, Syracuse University Press, 1964); RA Falk, *Legal Order in a Violent World* (Princeton, Princeton University Press, 1968); RA Falk, *The Status of Law in International Society* (Princeton, Princeton University Press, 1970).

[61] L Henkin, 'The Treaty Makers and the Law Makers: The Niagara Power Reservation' (1956) 56 *Columbia Law Review* 1151.

[62] See Henkin, *Law of the Sea's Mineral Resources* (New York, Institute for the Study of Science in Human Affairs, 1968).

Or legal counsel for a country before the ICJ?

No. The State Department usually has an advisory committee and I have been on that committee. The Department does have an institution called 'counsellor' on international law, and it was offered to me, but I did not wish to do that, partly for personal reasons (my family was in New York, my wife has a job and my children were growing); but also, I did not wish to work within the limitations of a bureaucracy. If they want my views, they get them; I give them freely.

So, you have never been a US delegate to the Third Committee of the General Assembly; they didn't ask you?

No, but I was an adviser to several US delegations in the early days.

I was an adviser to the US delegation to the General Assembly, to the Economic and Social Council, and to the Geneva Conference on Korea. During my stay in the State Department, I was actively involved in trying to bring about an armistice agreement in the Korean War. During that time, I went to Geneva with the 'Big Four'. While in the State Department, I was also the US representative on the committee that drafted the Refugee Convention.[63] When I came out of the State Department, I was always available to people wishing to do things which I believed in, to promote the rule of law. I was involved, for example, in the development of the Protocol to the Refugee Convention,[64] and in meetings in Montreal and elsewhere on human rights. But always as a free agent (and, I think, never for pay).

What were the primary motivations behind your non-scholarly career as a practitioner?

The primary motivations of my non-scholarly career were the same motivations as for my scholarly activities. I have seen international law not as a study of God-given or even history-given norms, but as a vehicle, perhaps *the* vehicle, for the rule of law in international affairs, for order in international affairs, for peace in international affairs, and for the promotion of individual values, human rights values, in both national and international affairs. I try to concentrate my scholarly work on those themes, and I have concentrated my 'practical', outside work on those themes.

[63] Reference is made here to the *United Nations Convention Relating to the Status of Refugees*, adopted on 28 July 1951 by the United Nations Conference of Plenipotentiaries on the Status of Refugees and Stateless Persons convened under General Assembly Resolution 429(V) of 14 December 1950. It entered into force on 22 April 1954.

[64] Reference is made here to the *United Nations Protocol Relating to the Status of Refugees*. The Protocol was taken note of with approval by the Economic and Social Council in Resolution 1186 (XLI) of 18 November 1966 and was taken note of by the General Assembly in Resolution 2198 (XXI) of 16 December 1966. It entered into force on 4 October 1967.

D. Contributing to international law

Now, we'll move to a different area. What would you consider as your major contribution to international law at a scholarly level? You mentioned already How Nations Behave[65] *and your book on the constitution.*

Foreign Affairs and the United States Constitution.[66] I like to think that my most recent book, which comes out of my Hague Lectures (it is called *International Law, Politics and Values*[67]) makes a contribution. It gives a different perspective on traditional issues. You can tell that from the title. It had three themes; I eliminated one from the title but not from the book. The first theme was that law is politics and has to be seen in the context of the political system; second, that law promotes values and that the system has moved, too slowly for my taste, but significantly, from what I call State values (those of the traditional 'Westphalian system' as you described it) toward human values; and the third is a movement from what I call conceptualism to functionalism. There I refer to a development such as the restrictive theory of sovereign immunity. It is a good example of movement which the system has made, recognising that sovereign immunity has little to do with notions of 'sovereignty'. If a government acts on the international scene, if it enters into a treaty, or joins an organisation, there is a derogation from its 'sovereignty', by definition. If a State wishes to have intercourse with others—other States, companies, individuals—it may do so, but other States may decide to subject such States to the jurisdiction of their courts. We have abandoned the notion that one cannot sue a sovereign State in the courts of another nation as a general principle, as though that were a logical impossibility. That is a good example of what I call a move from conceptualism to functionalism. There are other examples, suggested in that book.

E. The fight for human rights

Do you feel that the best way to achieve respect for human rights is through non-governmental organisations (NGOs), or by putting pressure on governments, or both ways? Are you not sceptical about the attitude of governments?

I am sceptical about governments and about their commitment to human rights, but I think almost all governments can be shamed and pressured. We need agreed norms, and therefore I am a strong supporter of the Universal Declaration and the Covenants and the Conventions. Therefore, I am strongly unhappy with reservations to those Covenants and Conventions, though I recognise one might sometimes be necessary (for example, for the United States, if a reservation were really required by the Constitution). I

[65] Henkin, above n 11.
[66] Henkin, above n 12.
[67] Henkin, above n 13.

am in favour of strengthening international machinery. I was for many years strongly in favour of a UN High Commissioner of Human Rights. It took 30 years to get there, but now it's here. I am in favour of governments giving *bona fide* support for human rights around the world, but not by use of force. As for NGOs, they work most successfully along with governments, and sometimes governments work through NGOs to promote respect for human rights in other countries.

The United States Government is not a bad example. When the Executive Branch has an activist human rights policy, it encourages NGOs to do things that governments don't feel as free to do. And vice versa; NGOs often try to get the government to do something. For example, NGOs might go to Congress and say 'Why don't you see to it that the Executive Branch carries out the law in which Congress said we will cut off arms sales to those guilty of gross human rights violations?' NGOs appear also before the agencies of government. In different degrees NGOs cooperate with the Executive Branch, but always from the outside, and they are very cautious and jealous [of] their independence. You have a kind of *pas de deux*, or *pas de trois*, if you will: the media, the NGOs and the government. And, in many ways, also, particular UN bodies. At different times, different UN bodies have been strongly supportive. For example, the United States has finally ratified the UN Covenant on Civil and Political Rights, but with reservations about which I am very unhappy (as you will see from the next issue of the *American Journal of International Law*).[68] The Human Rights Committee—not a UN body strictly, but a treaty body, supported by the UN—has tried to influence ratifying States both in respect of reservations and of compliance. Now the NGOs, I understand, go to the Human Rights Committee informally to suggest how the Committee might address reports of States. The United States report, for example, will be before the Human Rights Committee next month, and I'd be surprised if NGOs aren't suggesting questions to be asked, and what sort of examination or cross examination the Committee should engage in.

Governments don't feel free to disregard Amnesty International. In the United States, officials do not feel free to disregard Human Rights Watch and the Lawyers Committee for Human Rights, and other perhaps less well known groups. You might see this as a complex process of interaction. But it makes a big difference whether the governments are receptive or resistant, whether they wish to cooperate with the NGOs and even invite their cooperation, or whether they make it difficult for the NGOs to monitor governmental activities.

Of course, the attitude of the United States Government towards NGOs is different when the NGOs are criticising the United States [from] when the

[68] L Henkin, 'US Ratification of Human Rights Conventions: The Ghost of Senator Bricker' (1995) 89 *American Journal of International Law* 341.

NGOs are criticising other governments. The United States may not like it if NGOs criticise our friends abroad but they can't influence that, and usually don't try. What is more, the United States is engaged, as you know, in a very interesting process which the Carter[69] administration started, pursuant to Congressional command, producing annual 'country reports'. Think of that—the United States regularly appraises and criticises its friends (as well as anybody else)—and with the end of the Cold War, who is a friend and who isn't has changed character. And the NGOs contribute towards those reports. So there is a kind of interplay between the US Government and the NGOs in monitoring activities abroad, and there's going to be some interplay in monitoring human rights in the United States.

Is the State Department world report on human rights also prepared with the support of NGOs?

Well, the Department gets its material from embassies, but where do embassies get it? They read. Embassies don't obtain them entirely by personal monitoring. NGOs are involved in the process in various ways. Later NGOs are involved in the process in a different way. They evaluate and criticise those reports. Ten years ago you would find the Lawyers Committee and Human Rights Watch criticising the reports for being too friendly to some governments who didn't deserve it, and for not being sufficiently critical of our friends. Now it's different. The reports are better and therefore the human rights community is less critical, but the human rights community continues to monitor those country reports and makes suggestions for the future.

You said before that sometimes the US Government, or other governments for that matter, can't say a few things and then . . .

They are happy to have NGOs say that.

Can you give me an example?

Well, when I say 'the US government is happy', one has to ask, 'Who is the US government?' I know people who have worked on human rights inside the Government who, in certain administrations, didn't feel free to criticise certain foreign governments, and they were happy to have the NGOs do that. It's not an organised process, it's not coherent, but these are acts and attitudes that contribute to policy. The human rights community has been closer to the Government, or at least friendlier, during administrations that were themselves actively concerned with human rights, for example, the Carter administration, and more recently the Clinton administration. But in between, too, at different times, on working levels, there were friendly and

[69] James Earl 'Jimmy' Carter (*b* 1924) served as the 39th President of the United States from 1977 to 1981.

cooperative relations between the people who did human rights work in the State Department and the NGOs.

Also, as you know, Congress is full of committees, and committees hold hearings on subjects with human rights implications, for example, aid to African countries. And you will find requests by people from various parts of the NGO community testifying on what Congress should do—whether the Executive Branch likes it or not.

F. A school of international law?

Do you feel that you have been able to create a school by training and stimulating a number of disciples. What are in your view the features of this school, the Henkin school of international law?

Well, there isn't a Henkin school. And since you have posed a question as to whether I have any great regret, I confess my regret, I think my principal regret, that I did not do more to develop 'disciples'. This is in part a quality of personality. I am, as I said, a private person and I have not tried overtly to influence students or others. I say overtly; of course, I have always hoped that the things I wrote would influence people. If there is a 'Henkin school', it is not reflected in any particular, identifiable disciples, but it is a school dedicated to the following propositions, which I have already repeated: essentially, taking international law seriously, law as politics, and law as national interest.

G. The legal and political process

When you say law as politics, do you mean law as a political process, not as a set of legal rules only?

No, not only but also, law as a set of legal rules developed as part of a political process and operating within a political process. Like law in a national society, it is made by politicians. (Lawyers don't make that law: they become technicians at that stage.) That's one of the themes in *How Nations Behave.*[70] When my name is cited, it is often for that theme. So: how nations behave; law is politics and law has to be seen as part of the system. There are people who have picked up that theme, and you can call them Henkin 'disciples' though most of them didn't study with me.

Secondly, taking international law seriously, a separate theme: that international law matters. The most famous sentence I ever wrote, I think, says:

> It is probably the case that almost all nations observe almost all principles of international law and almost all of their obligations almost all of the time.[71]

[70] Henkin, above n 11.
[71] *Ibid*, 1st edn, at 47, emphasis in original.

That's been picked up by sceptics as well as others. I think it's true, and I think it's significant, although one shouldn't exaggerate its significance. There are other people committed to that proposition, though I would not call them my disciples.

Thirdly, respect for law is in the national interest. I've spent lots of time and effort 'banging that drum' in my country, and I hope that it has been accepted in other countries, that law and respect for law are in their national interest. I've often thought it ironic: if I say 'I act in my interest', I'm an egotist and selfish. If we say that a nation acts in its national interest, that's a truism. Well, on one level it's a truism; and it is perfectly fine for every State to act in its national interest, provided it recognises that the national interest includes respect for international law, that international order is an important element in the national interest. There is a paragraph on this in *How Nations Behave* which I have reproduced in our Casebook.[72] My answer to Kennan and to Morgenthau, the Americans who wrote on this, is that you fellows don't recognise how realist international law is. Morgenthau did take that view at different times of his life. Kennan has always remained more of a diplomat, sceptical of the restraints of law and morality (and I think blind to their importance). So there has been a 'Henkin school', if you will, on that.

And then, *Foreign Affairs and the United States Constitution*[73]: attention to constitutional norms as they govern the conduct of foreign affairs. Obviously, I'm talking about the United States, but I think others have tried to do the same in other countries, and I think I've had some influence in that respect. In fact, at this moment there is a Chinese scholar who is trying to use my book *Foreign Affairs and the United States Constitution* as a model for a book about foreign affairs and the Chinese Constitution. It's going to take a little stretching to do that, but you see what I mean. Looking at the constitutional system as it affects foreign affairs includes the subject you and I were talking about—the place of international law in the system, the later-in-time rule (between treaties and statutes); will the courts enforce international law—all that is part of a subject which I think I've made important here, as has my colleague, Professor Lori Damrosch.[74] She and I have been the principal 'sponsors' of that field, and now other people have followed. I think Harold Koh of Yale and Michael Glennon[75] at the University of California, Davis, would admit to having been influenced by this work, and there are others.

[72] L Henkin *et al, International Law: Cases and Materials*, 3rd edn (St Paul, Minn, West, 1993).

[73] Henkin, above n 12.

[74] Lori Fisler Damrosch (*b* 1953) is Henry L Moses Professor of Law and International Organization, Hamilton Fish Proferssor of International Law and Diplomacy at Columbia University Law School, and is a member of the Council on Foreign Relations, Department of State Advisory Committee on International Law.

[75] Michael J Glennon (*b* 1947) is Professor of International Law at the Fletcher School of Law and Diplomacy, Tufts University, in Medford, Massachusetts. Prior to going into teaching, he was Legal Counsel to the Senate Foreign Relations Committee (1977–80) and Assistant Counsel in the Office of the Legislative Counsel of the United States Senate (1973–77).

They are not disciples in the sense that I gave them PhDs and got them jobs but, I think, disciples in thought and spirit.

Another form of influence is of a different kind: what one might call 'imaginative lawyering'. That's where we began this interview, when we talked about how one can identify what is *ferenda* and what is *lata*. How one moves from *ferenda* to *lata* may take imaginative lawyering. That's something which good American lawyers have always known, and no doubt European lawyers do too, though I am not as well acquainted with them. We now think of re-opening questions such as the 'later-in-time' rule, and one tries to find the right case and get a lower court to pronounce on it. It required imaginative lawyering to get an important court to decide the *Filartiga* case.[76] And unimaginative lawyering can do harm to any cause; you bring the wrong case and you get a wrong decision, and it sets us back. We didn't do well in the Supreme Court on Haitian interdiction[77] or on Mexican abduction.[78] But every case is part of a long process, and we keep trying.

IV. A Look at the International Community

A. National interests and international law

If I can go back to one of your points. You said that States should be aware it is in the national interest to comply with international law. One could argue that, well, this may be a bit naive, because often in international law you don't have hard-and-fast rules; think of self-defence, the rules on the use of force and so on.

I don't agree. That's where I become very positivist. I don't think Article 2(4)[79] is ambiguous and I don't think Article 51[80] is ambiguous. I don't pay

[76] *Filartiga v Peña-Irala*, 630 F.2d 876 (2d Cir 1980).

[77] In May 1992, as many Haitians again began to flee to the US, the US Government adopted a policy of deliberate direct return of Haitian refugees to Haiti, in breach of the UN Refugee Convention (1951) and the US's Immigration and Nationality Act (1952). Many Haitians were held at Guantanamo, in Cuba. In 1993 the US Supreme Court pronounced on the matter in *Sale v Haitian Ctrs Council, Inc*, 113 S Ct 3028 (1993). As a result, more than 300 refugees held at Guantanamo were released. However, the President took immediate action to react to what he considered to be a serious foreign affairs crisis and the Supreme Court condoned the result. See on the matter HH Koh, 'The Human face of the Haitian Interdiction Program' (1993) 33 *Virginia Journal of International Law* 483; HH Koh, 'The "Haiti Paradigm" in United States Human Rights Policy' (1994) 103 *Yale Law Journal* 2391.

[78] Reference is made here to the decision of 15 June 1992 handed down by the US Supreme Court in *United States v Alvarez-Machain*, 504 US 655 (1992). The case concerned the abduction in Mexico by US enforcement agents of a Mexican accused of having killed a US official. The Court held had foreign citizens who commit crimes against US citizens outside US boundaries come under the jurisdiction of US courts even when forcibly abducted from their country over official protests of that nation. The Court, relying solely on US domestic law precedents, absent any reference to international law, held that international implications of the abduction were the concern of the executive branch.

[79] This is the text of Art 2(4) of the UN Charter: 'All members shall refrain in their international relations from the threat or use of force against the territorial integrity or political independence of any state, or in any other manner inconsistent with the Purposes of the United Nations.'

[80] This is the text of Art 51 of the UN Charter: 'Nothing in the present Charter shall impair the inherent right of individual or collective self-defence in an armed attack occurs against a Member of the

attention to Bowett[81] in this matter. And you know who else doesn't pay attention to Bowett? Governments!

I would disagree.

I know you do, Nino. The only government that pays attention to Bowett is a government which itself wants to violate at a particular time. So at Suez,[82] the British taught Bowett, and in Panama[83] . . .

If you go through the verbatim records of the Security Council, you very often find Bowett cited by the Americans, or the Israelis.

That's right, but that's not enough to persuade me. The lawyers for the violators will always argue whatever they can. You probably never saw an article I wrote about Panama, in which I attack the US position.[84] My position on the use of force is as positivist as can be, and I think 98 per cent of governments have agreed with me, not with Bowett. But occasionally a government is tempted. I like to think that the United States, which resisted that position for 45 years, until Panama (the only time its lawyers articulated a position in favor of 'free' self-defence), I like to think the United States doesn't mean it and will abandon that position for the long run. A lawyer succumbed to the immediate pressures of political forces, that is true. But to call that national interest? I say the contrary. I don't think it was in the national interest of the United States to go into Panama by force. I don't think it's in the national interest for the Legal Adviser to say what he said about the meaning of Article 51, and I will continue to insist on it till the end of time. That's what I mean.

You also wrote a persuasive rebuttal of Tom Franck's article 'Who Killed Article 2(4)'.[85]

I'm really quite a positivist. Where the international system has made great progress, I want to keep that progress. I think Article 2(4) is the most important norm of international law of our time. More important than human rights norms, if you will, though they are part of the same struggle for human values. And I've resisted every effort to weaken it. I don't think there is any

United Nations, until the Security Council has taken measures necessary to maintain peace and security. Measures taken by Members in the exercise of this right of self-defence shall be immediately reported to the Security Council and shall not in any way affect the authority and responsibility of the Security Council under the present Charter to take at any time such action as it deems necessary in order to maintain or restore international peace and security.'

[81] Reference is made here to D Bowett, *Self-Defence in International Law* (Manchester, Manchester University Press, 1958).

[82] Reference is made here to the UK intervention in Suez in 1956 (see C Gray, *International Law and the Use of Force*, 3rd edn (Oxford, Oxford University Press, 2008), at 158–59).

[83] Reference is made here to the US intervention in Panama in 1989 (see Gray, above n 82, at 57–58, 91–92, 157–58).

[84] L Henkin, 'The Invasion of Panama Under International Law: A Gross Violation' (1991) 29 *Columbia Journal of Transnational Law* 293.

[85] Above n 5.

basis in the language of Article 51 or in its history for the Bowett position. In the intervening years there have been efforts to weaken it, and I think they should be resisted—and my writing has been devoted to resisting it. There's a small book called *Right v Might*,[86] put out by the Council on Foreign Relations, where I have a piece, sort of on this theme, but it's not different from things I've said elsewhere.

You become a tough positivist when it is important.

When it is important, and when I think the system intended that the norm be important. We can afford to monkey around with the restrictive theory of immunity; we cannot afford to monkey around with what is self-defence and the use of force. That is the foundation of the post-World War II system.

By and large you feel that international law has developed in such a way that it can be used by a State to promote national interest but within the framework of the rule of law.

That's right. But we're engaged here in a discussion of what one might call hierarchies of national interest. As a basic proposition, which I don't think anybody would dispute, it is in the national interest of countries such as the United States (maybe not of Hitler) to maintain the rule of law in international affairs. We know it; we have no doubt about that. That's why we adhere to treaties, and that's why we continue to develop additional treaties, on trade or something else. And anybody who refuses to recognise that is blind. The problem always arises when a government confronts a particular temptation; how does it rank its general interest in the rule of law with its particular interest in violating a little bit or distorting a little bit. People like me rank the general interest very high. To some people the general interest is too subtle, too abstract: 'What is the rule of law?' And that, I think, is the key difference between some international lawyers and others. Those who see a particular national interest as very important worry less about the general national interest in the rule of law, and the Yale School, I think, was sometimes guilty of that.

In fairness to everybody, during the Cold War things were different. The period we are talking about, my lifetime as a lawyer, teacher, scholar—1947 to date—more than 40 years of this 50 year period, was Cold War, and our attitudes on international law were inevitably coloured by that fact. There were people who saw the Cold War in stark terms, as right and wrong, good and evil. Societies and their officials—and their lawyers—felt that victory in that war was the highest value, and therefore the rule of law was less important. I liked the Communists as little as others did, and I entertained no illusions about Stalin ever, but I also believed that it was important—above

[86] L Henkin *et al*, *Right v Might: International Law and the Use of Force* (New York, Council on Foreign Relations Press, 1989).

all—to keep the war cold, and secondly that there was plenty of room for the rule of law within the limits imposed by the Cold War. It is a nice exercise now for historians, but in those days for students, to see how much law operated between us and the Russians during the coldest parts of the Cold War. I do not refer only to the fact, say, that we didn't overfly each other's territory, that we were careful not to use force; even when we acted through surrogates, we were constrained and limited. And, in our legal posture and argumentation, we were careful not to talk self-defence too freely, because the Russians could then do so too. The Cuban missile crisis[87] is a very interesting example of that. The fact is the United States didn't drop bombs on Cuba, although there were suggestions that we should do so. The fact is that we didn't talk Article 51 to justify even the lesser measures we resorted to. We purposely didn't invoke Article 51, because we knew that if we did, it would be available to others ever after. Instead, we may have used a weak, unpersuasive argument. (Essentially, on the blockade, we confessed error, we might have said that what we did was so important to the survival of humanity that we were warranted in violating the law.)

The end of the Cold War has unleashed disruptive forces. It left a world in which political forces were not available to prevent the horrors of Yugoslavia from happening. In my view the West should have intervened to stop the ethnic cleansing from the beginning, with force if necessary, under the auspices of the Security Council. But no one was prepared or willing to do that. Six months later they said 'Well, maybe we should have done it six months ago, but it's too late.' Well, for five years now we've been saying 'six months ago; now it's too late'. That means that centrifugal forces, forces that break up the coherence of the system, have prevailed, and that is highly unfortunate. We must continue to try to keep the old/new UN order alive, hoping that the mood will pass and that we will get back to the spirit of 1945, which I think was not a bad spirit. It means something different today, but the ideas were the same.

B. Current concepts and institutions that are not worthy of being retained

What ideals or institutions of the present international community would you discard because they are not worthy of being kept?

To me, State sovereignty, in its archaic, abused sense. I don't like the term. What we really mean by that term is that there are areas of life over which States ought to have authority, control. I call them areas of State autonomy; in domestic law we call it privacy. I am a strong believer in State autonomy: I don't wish people in country X to tell me what my religion ought to be.

[87] Reference is made to the crisis between the US and the Soviet Union triggered by Cuba's decision to import nuclear missiles from the USSR, with the consequence that the US Government put in place a 'quarantine' of Cuba to prevent the Soviet ships from reaching Cuba's ports. See A Chayes, 'Law and the Quarantine of Cuba' (1963) 41 *Foreign Affairs* 550.

There ought to be large areas of State autonomy; some wish to call that State sovereignty, so be it. But there is no virtue in refusal to be governed by agreed norms and institutions, in refusal to cooperate, to be monitored. Instead of sovereignty, let's talk about 'international governance'. I am in favour of creating more cooperative institutions, for example for the environment; I am in favour of strengthening international human rights machinery; I am in favour of strengthening trade and financial arrangements. All these are areas in which the world has to be subject to international governance. So, I don't wish to abolish State autonomy, but I do wish to increase the areas of cooperation by more effective instrumentalities. Some will say: 'But more effective international norms, more instrumentalities, mean less sovereignty.' I say, that's your word, not mine; call it what you wish.

C. Concepts and institutions deserving to be enhanced

But do you think there is any future for jus cogens*?*

There is a future for *jus cogens*, but international lawyers have got carried away by the idea. I said earlier that the battle against apartheid revealed that there is an area of common conscience, a common moral intuition, which the world is prepared to recognise and give effect to. That includes, in addition to no apartheid, no genocide, no killings or torture, and a few other gross violations. (Note that I do not mention freedom of speech, and perhaps not even 'democracy'.) When I say that, I am saying, in effect, that's *jus cogens*. That is, those norms of fundamental, supreme value that the world, in our century, and in the coming century, is prepared to accept and live by. That's where my positivism moves over; I say, 'that's customary law'. So, I see *jus cogens* as substantially positivist, as is customary law generally. The concept is there, and is desirable and necessary; it is easier to work with, in regard to, say, apartheid, or even genocide, than to try to achieve the desired result by treaty. The trouble with the 1948 Convention on the Suppression of the Crime of Genocide, which I'm in favour of, is that the countries that commit genocide either aren't parties to it or don't pay attention to it, and the rest of the world isn't ready to attempt to enforce it. I'm happy to have the Genocide Convention, but I'm happy also to have genocide as *jus cogens*, for whatever uses can be made of it within our system.

Do you also think that there's a future for the notion of international crimes of States?

I think it's an interesting idea, and I am in favour of it, but not necessarily the way Ago used it.[88] What is the difference between a State delict and a

[88] Henkin is referring to Ago's Vth Report on State Responsibility, submitted in 1976 to the UN International Law Commission (UN doc A/CN.4/291 and Add 1 and 2, published in (1976) II (Part 1) *International Law Commission Yearbook* 3). In particular Henkin was referring to Art 18 of the Report, concerning international crimes of States.

State crime? Presumably the latter is a violation *erga omnes*, and individual perpetrators are subject to universal jurisdiction. I'm willing to extend *erga omnes* and universal jurisdiction selectively; do we need the notion of State crimes to do it?

Well, the notion of State crimes implies that the reaction of other States to the delinquent State is different from the one to a State which has committed a delict.

I agree. And if the idea of 'State crime' helps to achieve it, I see no objection, but I'm not sure it's necessary. I think many resisted the idea of States 'committing crimes'; it was too anthropomorphic and didn't fit with their intellectual, juristic systems. But we have moved in that direction, even though Ago's Article 19 hasn't got very far.[89] You know the *Barcelona Traction* paragraph[90]

[89] Henkin is referring to the Draft Art 19 (corresponding to Art 18 in Ago's Report, above n 88), on international crimes of States, as adopted by the UN International Law Commission. Art 19 provided as follows:

'1. An act of a State which constitutes a breach of an international obligation is an internationally wrongful act, regardless of the subject-matter of the obligation breached.
2. An internationally wrongful act which results from the breach by a State of an international obligation so essential for the protection of fundamental interests of the international community that its breach is recognized as a crime by that community as a whole constitutes an international crime.
3. Subject to paragraph 2, and on the basis of the rules of international law in force, an international crime may result, *inter alia,* from:

(a) a serious breach of an international obligation of essential importance for the maintenance of international peace and security, such as that prohibiting aggression;
(b) a serious breach of an international obligation of essential importance for safeguarding the right of self-determination of peoples, such as that prohibiting the establishment or maintenance by force of colonial domination;
(c) a serious breach on a widespread scale of an international obligation of essential importance for safeguarding the human being, such as those prohibiting slavery, genocide and *apartheid;*
(d) a serious breach of an international obligation of essential importance for the safeguarding and preservation of the human environment, such as those prohibiting massive pollution of the atmosphere or of the seas.

4. Any internationally wrongful act which is not an international crime in accordance with paragraph 2, constitutes an international delict.'

Text published in (1976) II (Part 2) *Yearbook of the International Law Commission* 75, at 81.

[90] In paras 33 and 34 of its Judgment of 5 February 1970 in the *Barcelona Traction Light and Power Company, Limited case (Belgium v Spain)* [1970] ICJ Rep 3, at 32, the ICJ stated as follows:

'33. When a State admits into its territory foreign investments or foreign nationals, whether natural or juristic persons, it is bound to extend to them the protection of the law and assumes obligations concerning the treatment to be afforded them. These obligations, however, are neither absolute nor unqualified. In particular, an essential distinction should be drawn between the obligations of a State towards the international community as a whole, and those arising vis-à-vis another State in the field of diplomatic protection. By their very nature the former are the concern of all States. In view of the importance of the rights involved, all States can be held to have a legal interest in their protection; they are obligations *erga omnes.*

34. Such obligations derive, for example, in contemporary international law, from the outlawing of acts of aggression, and of genocide, as also from the principles and rules concerning the basic rights of the human person, including protection from slavery and racial discrimination. Some of the corresponding rights of protection have entered into the body of general international law *(Reservations to the Convention on the Prevention and Punishment of the Crime of Genocide, Advisory Opinion,*

(which, I gather, Manfred Lachs[91] was behind). The reaction to terrorism may help; cooperation among States to help prevent or punish terrorism is happening. If Ago's use of the word 'crime' helps, I'm willing to support it. But the word is less important than spreading the concept.

D. Towards a world government?

If we moved to a more general area, to a sort of futuristic view, would you think the international community in the next 20 years was heading for a world government?

Not from my perspective. I think it is highly unlikely.

Then there is a scenario of a stronger UN, with a much stronger Security Council with real enforcement powers; and probably a scenario of a sort of horizontal integration, the spreading of various regional organisations at various levels. What do you think is the more realistic scenario for the next 30 or 50 years?

You should ask me about the next hundred years, because I would feel freer to prophesy. I'm more reluctant to guess about the next 20 years because I intend to be here to see whether I was right or wrong.

I dismiss world government. In the absence of world catastrophe, unforeseeable and even difficult to imagine, I don't think it's possible even in the form of a loose federation. I'm not sure it's desirable, because it might impinge too heavily on areas of State autonomy (which some people wish to call sovereignty). Of course, one could limit world government to certain areas of activity and jurisdiction, but then you do not have world government. Talk of world government requires us to ask: What will the world government govern? Will it govern only war and peace? The environment? And how will it tax? Also the words 'world government' scare people, so that it's not only probably undesirable but certainly unachievable.

So I favour the other two perspectives you offer, a stronger UN and more horizontal integration. I would support them, and though I am not optimistic, I am hopeful. We should move towards a stronger UN with better peace-keeping, and with peace-making by prevention, trying to intervene earlier to prevent threats to the peace. As I say, I am hopeful about achieving that, but the attitudes of major countries, such as the United States, do not make me optimistic. It's possible that even US attitudes might change—I hope so—but I have no reason to expect it.

We may have to work harder on the regional level. I am disappointed that you Europeans have not reorganised the Conference on Security and Cooperation in Europe (CSCE) into a peace-keeping, peace-making, human rights body of the kind it was promising to become. Western Europe's failure

ICJ Reports 1951, p 23); others are conferred by international instruments of a universal or quasi-universal character.'

[91] See 'Interview with Sir Robert Jennings', fn 99.

in Yugoslavia has set back that prospect. But sometimes some critical event happens, and something almost hopeless becomes possible, even easy to achieve.

I am in favour of that development and I think it's possible. It will depend to a large extent on Russia—on developments in the former Soviet Empire, but in Russia in particular, what kind of leadership it will have and where it will go; and on relations between Russia and Western Europe. If one could achieve some kind of European regional organisation to deal with peace and security, with human rights and development, and with the environment, it would be an important contribution to world peace. And the United States might be drawn in. I'd like to see such regional developments around the world, but that's very hard to achieve.

What about Asia?

Asia is not a continent; it's more than one continent. China is there, and we don't know where it is going. If we had a different China, or if Japan came out actively on the scene; if we had powerful governments leading and using their influence for benign purposes—for peace, stability, human rights, order—the regional arrangement I suggest could develop even in that part of Asia. India and Pakistan, to their shame, have continued their hostility all these years, and I do not see peace near. One has to hope and one has to work at it. As was said about religion, one believes although it's incredible. I feel that way about world order—it is incredible, but one must believe in it. Peace, however—like respect for human rights—is not achieved at one time for ever. It's a process, one has to keep working at it. Somebody once described a cook as having a harried look because he knew you can't feed people once and for all. You feed them once, then you have to feed them again six hours later. That's true about peace, and order, and human rights, and the environment—it has to be a continuous, unceasing process. And you have to build and maintain institutions that will encourage people within governments and across governments to dedicate themselves, and to work at it. That's what international law and an international legal system should be.

E. North–South

There is one more area which you are slightly playing down. Namely the question of north–south relations and the huge problem of development.

I don't play down its importance; but it's not an area in which I have been involved. Governments in the international system, like citizens in national systems, don't pay enough taxes. (That's a radical statement to make in the United States.) We don't contribute enough to foreign aid; we don't contribute enough to international causes. I believe we have to help the world develop. Unfortunately, isolationist trends in this country (and in some other countries) will lead to less money for foreign aid. Americans are a generous and sentimental people; if there's a flood or an earthquake, we go there and help. But the slow, long-term process of working on and helping development cuts across other values we have, including the principle of not paying 'too much' in taxes. The world has to commit itself to development, and the developed world has to commit itself to moving the world towards human rights-type development. I like to quote Julius Nyerere,[92] at one time the leading spokesman for the developing world: he said, 'you cannot have freedom without development, but you cannot have development without freedom'. The third world has to commit itself to peace and human rights, and to stopping environmental degradation. The first world should commit itself to full-fledged economic support for development.

F. The role of the Institut de Droit international

Before we move to some personal questions, I want to ask you a question which I forgot to put to you before. We mentioned the Institut de Droit international. *I gather you have been there for about 10 years. Do you think it is a useful institution? Robert Jennings, in his interview,[93] told me that in his view it's not playing a really major role, the role that it should play in the international community.*

I think there is some truth in that. I would seek and respect Oscar Schachter's views on that; he's been in the *Institut* much longer, and he knows its history and its people. I go to the *Institut* to meet colleagues, otherwise I don't get to meet them; I'm not in 'the circuit' as some people are.

What do you think of the debates there?

The debates, in general, are of marginal interest; on some subjects they are more useful than on others.

There are three different questions. One, is it a useful institution? The answer is, I think, that it is useful to have well-known international lawyers get together, bring in the younger people, and bring in third-world scholars and lawyers. The *Institut* has too long been a monopoly of the Europeans (and, if you will, the Americans). That is undesirable and unwarranted. I am not even sure that Europeans–Americans are, continue to be and will always be the leading international lawyers. In the past, there was a kind of arrogance about the institution. But most of the people in it are able, and nice and cooperative. So it's useful to perpetuate the *Institut*.

In the past, the *Institut* has done important intellectual work. Now there is competition in doing important intellectual work. Now much of it is done in universities, out of national societies such as the American Society of

[92] Julius Nyerere (1922–99) served as the first President of Tanzania and previously Tanganyika, from the country's founding in 1961 until his retirement in 1985.

[93] See 'Interview with Sir Robert Jennings', section III.A.

International Law. Recently, during the years in which I have been a member, I do not sense that the *Institut* has made many important jurisprudential, intellectual contributions. There have been some, but few: the rest have been marginal. I don't mean to suggest that it could not happen tomorrow. The process is slow, much is left to a rapporteur, and between sessions everybody goes back to his or her daily work. There's no sustained intense activity unless the rapporteur provides it, and there are different rapporteurs. So we've had spotty success.

I don't exclude the possibility that the *Institut* could become more important as some of us old-timers give way to younger people, and as international law and legal scholarship and influences become stronger in different parts of the world. With a kind of *noblesse oblige*, the *Institut* used to lay down the law from on high for the rest of the world to attend to. That won't work any more. But if the *Institut* achieves a broader base, if it becomes more cooperative, if it takes on the hard questions, I would be strongly in favour of keeping it going.

Has it had any influence on the shaping of international law? Actually resolutions adopted by the Institut *are hardly quoted in legal literature.*

I can think, for example, of an interesting and important contribution on external intervention in civil war.[94] But you're right, the resolutions are not cited often now. Sometimes reports of the *Institut* try to 'put things together'. We've been struggling with jurisdiction, for example, and I think there will be some useful things said before we're through. But I am in a strange position because I was Chief Reporter of the US *Restatement of Foreign Relations Law*,[95] which in many ways was doing the same kind of thing from an American perspective. I think we were more efficient, but we spent lots more time at it, and we didn't have a hundred countries to deal with.

G. The US Restatement of Foreign Relations

Of course I went through your Restatement, but there are some areas which are not covered. Why not?

Because we had limited time, we had to be selective.

What about the use of force?

Not covered. We could never have reached agreement on that subject.

[94] Reference is made here to the resolution *Le principe de non-intervention dans les guerres civiles*, adopted by the Institute on 14 August 1975 at the Wiesdbaden session of 1975. Text in (1975) 56 *Annuaire de l'Institut de Droit international* 544.

[95] Above n 1.

But I thought, well, here I will find all the most sensitive areas covered, and the use of force of course is the most sensitive.

You could not get agreement in the American community on a restatement of the law on that subject. Remember, the *Restatement* is done by American lawyers, not by American international lawyers. The entire American Law Institute would have to approve the text. With the State Department probably in opposition, it would not have approved what I would have proposed on the subject, and I'm not sure I could get even all my colleagues among the reporters to agree to my view of Article 2(4). It would be too 'political', too limiting of US freedom of action.

Also, the subjects to be restated are those of wide use and appeal to the legal community. Moreover, the subjects covered are the result of the accident of timing and personnel. We did lots of work on jurisdiction because Professor Andreas Lowenfeld[96] had a great interest in that subject; and jurisdiction is of interest to the practising lawyers and to judges. We addressed the foreign affairs and the Constitution because I was interested in that.

Does it have the official blessing of the State Department?

No—on the contrary. But it has a different kind of 'blessing' in our country; it is 'authoritative'. Lawyers cite it, the courts refer to it. The courts will cite it, first of all, because our judges don't know much about international law or the law of foreign affairs, and we provide a quick handbook on such international law as we covered. And the *Restatement* has prestige, and authority. So the judges use it and the lawyers use it. And even the State Department would be disposed to use it, generally. But the Restatement has no *imprimatur*. In fact, we reporters fought the State Department hard over a number of issues, and we fought them out in a public forum. In the end, the majority in the American Law Institute voted to approve our product. Of course, we compromised on some statements and modified some others. For example, on expropriation of foreign investments, and whether the law requires prompt, adequate and effective compensation. There were practising lawyers, indeed principally practising lawyers, in that audience. But we came out with something which we reporters were prepared to live with, and which the Institute was prepared to live with. In fact, we were pleased with the result.

Which are the areas which have been left out in addition to the use of force, because of lack of agreement? Did you cover State responsibility?

We covered State responsibility. Also sources of international law, subjects of international law; Law of the Sea; Environment; Remedies. Humanitarian law? No, we didn't do that.

96 Andreas F Lowenfeld (*b* 1930) is Rubin Professor Emeritus of International Law at New York University Law School, where he has been on the Faculty since 1967. He has taught, practised, and written on both public and private international law. He is frequently an arbitrator in international disputes.

And use of force?

No, those were the two big areas we didn't address.

And economic transactions?

Transactions, yes. Even there we were selective. We picked money, and GATT (General Agreement on Tariffs and Trade), and the IMF. There was a lot of law out there from all the specialised agencies which we didn't cover.

What did you say about compensation for expropriation? Is it a sore point?

Well it was a sore point at the time. It's amazing how it stopped being sore. Some wanted us to articulate, firmly, that compensation has to be prompt, adequate and effective, without exceptions. We said: 'We are not sure that that's the international law today.' In the end we said: 'Yes, in general, prompt and adequate and effective; but there might be some exceptions.' And in any event we prefer 'just compensation' as a standard, which gives a little more flexibility, although ordinarily just compensation might be prompt, adequate and effective. The number of months and years we spent arguing that! It helped us in our battles that the United States Constitution requires 'just compensation'.

H. On the theoretical approach to international law

It just crossed my mind that I should have asked you a question which has nothing to do now with your person. The question is as follows: are you interested in or familiar with theoretical works which have been produced recently; say, the famous book Eunomia *by Philip Allott?*[97] *Have you seen it?*

Yes, I have.

The various books by, say, Kennedy,[98] *books by Koskenniemi?*[99]

I read them without being persuaded. I read them without real interest. No. When I say 'without interest', I am pleased that people think in those terms, because most of us don't have time to sit back and look out on the world, but I have no particular interest in that, and I don't think any of them has 'spoken' to me. That is, I have not got up from a book and said 'Gee, that's right!'

So you don't get anything from those books?

No. I get more from books on the international political order. I mentioned Stanley Hoffmann[100] before. He's the kind of writer who speaks to me. I read

[97] P Allott, *Eunomia: New Order for a New World* (Oxford, Oxford University Press, 1990).
[98] See 'Interview with Sir Robert Jennings', fn 76.
[99] *Ibid*, fn 75.
[100] Above n 31.

the writings of political theorists who are engaged in life, from John Rawls[101] to Michael Walzer.[102] I am interested in political theory applied to life. I hasten to add that I often don't agree with some of these people and where they come out. But those are the questions that I'm interested in. My wife, as you know, runs a program called *Justice and Society*, for the Aspen Institute, and I have sometimes been a moderator there. But usually when I am there, I appear as a moderator for one day and talk about justice in international affairs. I lead discussion on questions such as: What is a just immigration policy for a just society? What is just international law? Is humanitarian intervention just in international affairs? I am interested in such questions, but I've not written any book on them. I read the Kennans and the Morgenthaus of an earlier generation, and Inis Claude[103] in international organisations, and my colleagues, John Ruggie[104] and Wolfgang Friedmann.[105] I didn't always agree with them, but they asked questions I have been interested in pursuing.

The end of the century—I don't know why the calendar is so important, why we are addicted to the decimal system—but it provides an occasion to reflect and to take inventory. The end of the Cold War has given us another opportunity, at least in the political-legal world, to reflect and take account. But the books you were talking about do it on too large a scale and from too speculative a perspective.

Incidentally, the international legal community has not done enough with the end of the Cold War. We have not studied the impact of 40 years of Cold War, and whether that impact has been dissipated or is permanent. Those of us who seek to participate in making law have not been asking whether new law is called for. Let me give you an example, human rights. We created a remarkable instrument in the 1948 Universal Declaration on Human Rights and not 'too bad' instruments in the two 1966 Covenants [on Civil and Political Rights, and on Economic, Social and Cultural Rights]. No one has stopped to ask: would those instruments have been different if Stalin had not been there, if we had no Cold War? They might not have been as good in some respects; the Cold War concentrated our attention and gave us focus. But the Universal Declaration and the Covenants papered over ambiguities,

[101] John B Rawls (1921–2002) taught moral and political philosophy at Harvard University (1962–95). His major book is *A Theory of Justice* (Cambridge, MA, Belknap Press of Harvard University Press, 1971).

[102] Michael Walzer (*b* 1935) was Professor of Political Philosophy at Harvard University (1966–80), and since 1980 has been professor at the Institute for Advanced Study in Princeton, New Jersey (currently emeritus). His major book is *Just and Unjust Wars: A Moral Argument with Historical Illustrations* (New York, Basic Books, 1977).

[103] Inis L Claude is the Edward R Stettinius Professor Emeritus of International Relations at the University of Virginia. His major work is *Swords into Plowshares: The Problems and Progress of International Organization* (New York, Random House, 1956).

[104] John Gerard Ruggie (*b* 1944) is Berthold Beitz Professor of International Affairs at the Kennedy School of Government, and an Affiliated Professor in International Legal Studies at Harvard Law School.

[105] See 'Interview with René-Jean Dupuy', fn 10.

such as the right to work, and matters we couldn't get agreement on, such as the right of asylum. Or look at the developments in fields such as aviation law, hijacking, etc. Would that law have been different had there been no Cold War?

That kind of study is, of course, speculative, but it might lead to: What opportunities does the end of the Cold War open for international law and international politics? What were the things we couldn't do before, which we might try to do now? That was what I had in mind when I spoke about what we might have done if we and the Russians had got together five years ago on the UN. But there may be new opportunities on nuclear weapons; we're struggling with non-proliferation again, but not very effectively. The Cold War being over, it changes the perspective on what one should and can do. So we have new challenges, new opportunities for lawyers interpreting old treaties, applying new treaties, helping promote additional treaties. The environment is obviously a field which calls for that. So there is beautiful work ahead for international lawyers, and one possible focus for that is to start with the significance of the Cold War and the end of it. Or one can start with 'Where are we today?', with disorder in the former Soviet Empire, with Rwanda and Bosnia. Let's take a fresh look. But my fresh look is not Kennedy's type of thing.

To go back to the theoretical books I mentioned, I should tell you that Sir Robert Jennings also took the same view.[106] *They are very interesting, but we can't get anything from them in practice. They are too abstract.*

I agree. Too high a level of generality.

It's a pity because probably we need a new theory of international law.

Well, you may need a new theory of international relations first, and a fresh look at the international system. We have to look at 'the market' and how it fits into, or reshapes or replaces a system of nation-States. In that sense, perhaps, the State system is dated, and a theory—and a law—that reflect the old system and do not attend to economic forces and institutions and to the communications revolution, are unreal.

I go back to my thesis, Nino. Law is part of international relations, inevitably. We have to establish the nature of international order, then we'll see what our international law is, and then put some theory under it. Unlike the Kelsens of the world, I start with life and put law and theory under it rather than the other way around. Kelsen had a very impressive mind, and a great spirit, but . . .

[106] See 'Interview with Sir Robert Jennings', section III.C.

And yet you didn't draw anything from his works?

No. Kelsen may have had influence. I have suffered from the fact that during those years when he might have influenced me, I was in your country fighting a war. I didn't look at the subject until much later. By that time, the UN was established and we were off in that direction. Oh yes, I'm in favour of that kind of writing, but his jurisprudence is too rigid for my taste. And perhaps I am not enough of a philosopher to appreciate that kind of theory.

V. Some Personal Questions

Shall we now move on? There are more personal questions.

Somebody once said, 'there are no indiscreet questions, only indiscreet answers'. I don't mind your asking. I don't know why you think you want this information, but I'm willing to try.

Because I think it's good to reflect in an interview not only the ideas of a scholar but also his personality. So my next question is whether you feel that you have heeded the commands of your demon and have fulfilled your mission.

I like to think so. But my demon doesn't always speak very clearly.

I think people might describe me as ideologically liberal, and as an enthusiast, and I lend my enthusiasm to the things I believe in. I guess I wanted to devote my energies and talents to trying to make the world a little better place, within the limits of what any single person can do, and also, I suppose, subject to the limitations of personality, opportunity, circumstance. I have therefore felt quite happy educating the young in the values that I promote, and in the use of the law to further those values. Obviously, every time something I propose is turned down, I am disappointed; that happens all the time.

Inevitably one has 'successes' and failures. But also one has the satisfaction of trying, and of the kind of life one leads. I have enjoyed teaching, so I don't intend to give it up until I am no longer able to do it. I enjoy speaking on subjects of the kind we have discussed: law, order, peace, human rights, etc, and I will speak to almost any audience, to educate, to try to persuade. I'm a kind of 'itinerant preacher'. And I have no regrets, I do not wish I had done something else with my life.

Those were my demons and I've heeded them, and I continue to heed them. You know, I used to be a mathematician. Sometimes, I thought, maybe I could have helped Einstein! But that's a sort of idle dream. Sometimes I hear a good cellist and I wish I could play like that. But those are different 'wishes'; they are not realistic ambitions or aspirations, but they tell you something of my values and what I might have liked to do. Like many a lawyer I might have liked to serve on the US Supreme Court, but it was not something I could aspire to, nor would I 'campaign' or do other uncongenial things that might have helped realise it. So, unlike Mr Freud . . .

You don't need palliatives.

No. I haven't been miserable. I have had the normal, ordinary frustrations and tragedies of human life. But my life has been quite happy. Maybe that's why I have not developed 'substitute gratifications' in your words. I happen to spend time reading poetry—I always have—and other literature in English or French (and a little in Hebrew, particularly *The Bible* and other classics). I read the *Times Literary Supplement* as my principal form of 'regular' reading: my second is the *New York Review of Books*. And I dip constantly into collections of poetry and literature. I don't have enough time even for that, because my demon says 'Why don't you write that speech you're going to give next week on armed conflict?' No, I don't need or use drugs; I don't have time for substitute gratifications.

Do you do any gardening?

No. I don't garden.

I have been interested in my Jewish roots. I identify and am interested in the Jewish tradition and its scholarship, and I play with that occasionally. I suppose it was Stendahl who said 'life is love and work'. And I have been very happy in my marriage and my family, and have been generally very happy in my work. And I continue to support humanitarian causes, with hope if not with optimism.

Thank you so much, Lou, for sharing your views with me. I hope that, by reading this interview, young scholars and practitioners will learn to be as courageous and optimistic as you.

Oscar Schachter

ONLY IN LATE 1994 did I meet Oscar Schachter. This occurred in New York, on the occasion of giving my first speech to the UN General Assembly in my capacity as President of the International Criminal Tribunal for the Former Yugoslavia. His friendly and very open-minded attitude prompted me to ask whether he would mind being interviewed for my future book of interviews. He promptly and gladly accepted. But it was in Lisbon, in September 1995, when I was admitted to the *Institut de Droit international* as an associate member, that I fully appreciated his great qualities. Schachter was a dominant figure within the *Institut*, highly respected and listened to by all the other members. What I had to do, therefore, was simply to learn from him (and many other outstanding international lawyers of the same calibre). He looked, generally speaking, austere, yet friendly and interested in talking to younger scholars. I was soon accepted among his admirers and followers, and then gradually acquired some degree of acquaintance with him. It was therefore no surprise to me that in November 1995, when I passed through New York, he gladly agreed to be interviewed. The next year I spent a couple of afternoons at his home in New York, asking him many questions, and now and then drinking coffee.

In a way Oscar Schachter's life (1915–2003) was professionally divided into two distinct parts: from 1944 to 1975 he worked for the United Nations; in 1975, at the age of 60, he retired from the UN and began a career as a professor of international law at the Columbia University Law School, concluding in 2003. In the first part of his professional life, he worked first for the United Nations Relief and Rehabilitation Administration (UNRRA). In 1945 he moved to the United Nations, where he worked initially in the Legal Division, of which he was Director from 1953 to 1966, and then at the United Nations Institute for Training and Research (UNITAR). This division of Schachter's career was not, however, watertight: in fact, during his spell at the UN, starting in 1955 and until 1970, he taught a seminar at Yale Law School with the two eminent leaders of the Yale School of international law: Myres McDougal and Harold Lasswell. There he had an opportunity to be exposed to and suggest criticism of the major tenets of that school of thought. In addition, he wrote many papers in major legal journals, chiefly the *American Journal of International Law*, and also gave a set of lectures at the Hague Academy in 1963.[1] It is, however, in the second half of his professional life that Schachter, besides continuing to contribute penetrating papers to legal journals, published his two major scholarly works: *Sharing the World's Resources*[2] and *International Law in Theory and Practice*,[3] the latter being based on his splendid general course at the Hague Academy.

Schachter was basically a positivist—but a very modern, open-minded and intelligent one—as is clear from his numerous writings, and as was expressly confirmed by him in an interview given in 1997, when he said:

> True, I am a positivist, at least in accepting the obligatory force of law with its own relative autonomy as distinct from politics or morality.[4]

His positivism was attenuated—or rather, I should say, enriched—by two important factors. First, his activity as a legal practitioner for 30 years. Clearly, in his job as a legal adviser he had to appraise new situations in the light of legal standards, but also to suggest courses of action or practical options that could reconcile respect for the rule of law with political or social demands. The position in which he thus found himself was illustrated by his recounting—it would seem many times—an episode from his early years. As he wrote in 1991, while discussing the 'policy-orientation of the practitioner':

> At one time in UNRRA, rather towards the end of my career there, I found myself the acting head of its legal department when a new Director-General came on the scene: Fiorello La Guardia, better known perhaps as a colourful reform mayor of the New York City.
>
> When I first met Mr La Guardia on business in his office, the first question to me in his office was: 'Sonny', he said (this was a long time ago) 'are you a hot lawyer or a cold lawyer?' I looked at him rather blankly, and he said, 'Well, if you are a hot lawyer, I am going to get myself a cold lawyer; and if you are a cold lawyer, I am going to get myself a hot lawyer.' This rather dumbfounded me, and I said, 'Does this mean I am through?'. He said, 'No, you are not through. But I need both of you. I need a hot lawyer to tell me that I can do what I want to do, and I need a cold lawyer to tell me I cannot do what I don't want to do.[5]

After recounting this episode, Schachter made the following illuminating comments:

> [L]et us first consider the unstated premises of La Guardia's attitude. One such premise, clearly, was that most legal questions permit at least two responses. A second was that it is the lawyer's role to serve his client, or in this case, to carry out the aims of the Director-General. It is apparent, too, that La Guardia's concern was not with rules of law but with the decisions that had to be taken.[6]

[1] O Schachter, 'The Relation of Law, Politics and Action in the United Nations' (1963-II) 109 *Recueil des Cours de l'Académie de Droit International de La Haye* ('*Recueil des cours*') 165.

[2] O Schachter, *Sharing the World's Resources* (New York, Columbia University Press, 1977)

[3] O Schachter, *International Law in Theory and Practice* (Dordrecht, Martinus Nijhoff, 1991).

[4] 'Conversation with Oscar Schachter' (transcript of interview by Brigitte Stern) (1997) 91 *American Society of International Law Proceedings* 343, at 347. The interviewer was Professor B Stern.

[5] Schachter, above n 3, at 19.

[6] *Ibid.*

How did Schachter solve the dilemma of a legal practitioner, split between the desire to comply with the wish of the client (a private company, a State, or an international organisation) and the need to take account of the law? The response he gave is a masterly example of his highly sophisticated legal knowledge coupled with wisdom and realism. In short, he notes that the practitioner should distinguish between three sets of parameters: rules, principles, and ends or policy. Rules, being specific provisions that 'dictated a specific result', constitute a major constraint for the practitioner. When rules are missing, however, he has greater leeway, for principles are general and abstract, lack definiteness and in addition are often in competition with other principles.[7] Schachter wisely notes that '[c]ontradictory principles are not seen as defects in the law but as reflections of complex social realities'.[8] Plainly, the practitioner can more easily opt for one principle rather than another. An even broader scope is left to him when he is able to have recourse to a third set of parameters, namely the objective underlying a legal rule or principle (such as peace, security, economic development, the dignity of person and so on). In this way Schachter shows that the practitioner has a wide range of choice in many cases, for law is not a compact, rigid and unambiguous set of prescriptions; it is instead a complex and polyvalent corpus of normative standards that need to be interpreted and offer some room for manipulation when a practitioner needs to serve the interests of his client. However, this may not necessarily lead to giving priority to those interests over the law. Schachter asks: 'Should policy or major purpose prevail over a rule that is clear and specific?' His answer is negative, and here can one discern his divergence from the Yale School of international law. This School—it may be submitted—in the event makes purposes prevail and thus, wittingly or unwittingly, gives pride of place to the interests and policy of major powers (chiefly the US), to the detriment of the values accepted by the world community as legal standards or yardsticks.

The second way in which Schachter's positivism was to some extent enriched is closely intertwined with the first one, and in a way derives from it. Schachter's constant awareness of the competing interests and demands of States, and of the multifarious translations of those interests and demands into conflicting principles, values and policies, led him to explore areas of law that could be improved upon, and in particular to devote much attention to crucial issues of the world community: the use of force, collective security, enforcement of the law, the dialectic between power and law. He thus devoted much reflection and innovative thinking to issues that are normally neglected or even ignored by pure positivists, as being extraneous to the legal inquiry and belonging more appropriately to the policy-maker.

[7] Schachter gives as examples 'non-use of force versus self-defence, self-determination versus territorial integrity, freedom of the seas versus historic rights': *ibid*, at 20.

[8] *Ibid*, at 21.

Let me add that Schachter also showed much courage and independence of thinking, in that he did not eschew the discussion of problems about which major powers (in particular, his own country, the US) are very sensitive and on which they therefore tend to avoid taking a clear-cut and definite position. It is a fact that the semi-official *Restatement of the Law Third—The Foreign Relations Law of the United States*,[9] in which Schachter took part, strikingly omits three crucial segments of the body of international law (the use of force; means of enforcing international legal standards; the law of State responsibility), while Schachter deals with all of these matters extensively in his writings and eventually in his Hague lectures.

The richness of his practical experience and profound reflection on major legal issues of the world community Schachter distilled into his masterpiece: *International Law in Theory and Practice*.[10] This book belongs to the small number of classical works on international law that will never die, for their authors condensed in them years of experience, wisdom and legal rigour, as well as a novel vision of the legal framework of the world community: I am thinking of the celebrated works by Anzilotti,[11] Brierly,[12] Verdross[13] and Kelsen.[14] Schachter's book stands out for its impeccable logical organisation of all the basic elements making up the body of international law, its exhaustive examination of the crucial problems of the world community, the profundity of its exploration of each set of problems, and the stringency of the argument. Schachter's book has another quality too, I believe: the beauty of the structure, the elegance of the style coupled with the sense of *finito* (refined and fully accomplished) to which the great painters so much aspire. Reading the book, I was once reminded of a long conversation I had sometime in 1960 with another distinguished international lawyer: Roberto Ago.[15] It took place in Geneva, where I was then attending the courses at the Graduate Institute of international Studies, and often had the chance of meeting him and listening to him at the International Law Commission. Once, discussing international law, or perhaps the writings of some of his fellow members of

[9] *Restatement of the Law (Third): The Foreign Relations Law of the United States*, 2 vols (St Paul, Minn, American Law Institute, 1986)

[10] Above n 3.

[11] D Anzilotti, *Corso di diritto internazionale (ad uso degli studenti dell'Università di Roma)*, 3rd edn (Rome, Athenaeum, 1928); French translation by GC Gidel: *Cours de droit international* (Paris, Recueil Sirey, 1929), re-edited by PM Dupuy and C Leben (Paris, Panthéon-Assas, 1999); *Opere di diritto internazionale*: vol 1, *Corso di diritto internazionale*, 4th edn (Padua, Cedam, 1955).

[12] JL Brierly, *The Law of Nations: An Introduction to the International Law of Peace* (Oxford, Oxford University Press, 1928); 6th edn edited by Sir Humphrey Waldock (Oxford, Clarendon Press, 1963).

[13] A Verdross, *Völkerrecht* (Berlin, J Springer, 1937). In 1957, in my third year as a university student, I wrote a detailed review of the 3rd edn of the *Völkerrecht* (Wien, Springer Verlag, 1955) in (1957) 40 *Rivista di diritto internazionale* 653. The most recent edition of this book, updated and re-elaborated by B Simma, is *Universelles Völkerecht: Theorie und Praxis*, 3rd edn (Berlin, Duncken und Humblot, 1984).

[14] H Kelsen, *Principles of International Law* (New York, Rinehart, 1952).

[15] See 'Interview with René-Jean Dupuy', fn 28.

the Commission, to my surprise he said that a legal book can exhibit features typical of a work of art, evincing some elements of beauty proper to the best paintings or pieces of music or architecture. At the time I was taken aback, and thought that this was a distorted view of the relations between art and other fields. (At that time I keenly believed in Hegel's proposition that art, philosophy and religion stand out and in a way take pride of place over any other human activity, for, unlike those other activities, they are about 'the absolute' and the 'eternal'. I now think that probably things are more complex than that.) At present I am led to think that Ago was right: Anzilotti's book might be compared to a harmonious and pure Romanesque church; Kelsen's book, with its gelid and austere concatenation of arguments, and its cascade of rigid propositions, has all the hallmarks of an impressive Gothic cathedral. Similar comparisons could be made for Schachter's book, which makes me think of a Mondrian painting, or one those magnificent sky-scrapers one can admire in New York, for instance the Chrysler Building.

Many will recall the distinction made by Saint-Exupéry in *Le petit prince*[16] between 'geographers' and 'explorers'. When the little prince travels to the Sixth Planet, he encounters the geographer, a man who never moves, for he is too important to leave his office; but he knows the location of all mountains, deserts, rivers, lakes and towns; he deals only with massive and stable things; he does not care about flowers, which are too ephemeral. However, his knowledge is based on what explorers tell him. Explorers go round to search for mountains, rivers and deserts, and report to the geographer. Without them the geographer cannot draw his maps. If one were allowed to distinguish between scholars on the basis of Saint-Exupéry's dichotomy, I would say that Schachter belongs to the category of the explorers: he has gone out to search for new ideas and concepts, and has also been curious about 'flowers'. He has enriched the legal landscape with his discoveries and provided us with new vistas.

After reading and rereading Schachter's writings, one is left with a troubling question: why was he never selected by the US State Department as a candidate for the International Law Commission or, even better, for the International Court of Justice? His unique scholarly stature, his moral integrity, his balance, his sagacity would have made him an outstanding commissioner or judge. Whatever the reasons for his failure to exercise his authority in one of those UN bodies, it is a fact that he remains one of the stars of international law of the 20th century.

[16] Antoine de Saint-Exupéry, *Le petit prince*, first published in 1943 (Paris, Gallimond, 2007).

Interview with Oscar Schachter

February 1995

I. The Beginning as a Scholar

Who was the international lawyer who most influenced your thinking at the beginning of your scholarly career?

The answer is probably Sir Hersch Lauterpacht,[17] on the assumption that my scholarly career began in 1948 when I wrote my first scholarly article on international law.[18] That article was requested by Lauterpacht, then editor-in-chief of the *British Yearbook of International Law*. At the time he was in New York as a 'consultant' to the UN Legal Department in its preparatory work for the new International Law Commission. Lauterpacht was then one of the most renowned figures in international law. During his short stay at the UN (then in Lake Success) he produced a survey of international law that covered the field comprehensively, with style and precision. By good luck, he and I were both on the *Queen Mary* on his trip to New York, and took our meals and walks together. His personal warmth, humour and directness made that trip memorable. Our friendship continued during his stay in New York, and thereafter until his death. I must say that although we had many conversations, we rarely discussed international law, but often the human side and idiosyncrasies of notable international lawyers. The great figures of European and British international law were 'humanised' by Lauterpacht's light-hearted stories.

His influence on my thinking came more from his writings than from our conversations. In particular, his magisterial work, *The Function of Law in the International Community*,[19] moved me to see international law not merely as rules, precedents and techniques, but also as a 'cause' epitomised by the 'rule of law' and the ideal of the international community embracing all of humanity. Lauterpacht's article on the 'Grotian Tradition' that appeared in the *British Yearbook* of 1946,[20] re-enforced this influence, and helped me to

[17] See 'Interview with Sir Robert Jennings', fn 20.

[18] 'The Development of International Law through the Legal Opinions of the United States Secretariat' (1948) 25 *British Yearbook of International Law* 91.

[19] H Lauterpacht, *The Function of Law in the International Community* (Oxford, Clarendon Press, 1933).

[20] H Lauterpacht, 'The Grotian Tradition in International Law' (1946) 23 *British Yearbook of International Law* 1.

comprehend more fully the conceptual richness of international law and its links to moral and political philosophy. My pre-law studies had emphasised philosophy and I maintained an interest in the subject. Lauterpacht's writings led me to read more widely in the philosophic commentaries and theories of international law. As a consequence, I came to view international law as more than a craft in my professional life; I saw it also as a 'calling' worthy of dedication beyond my official duties. Despite a heavy work-load, I began to respond to requests for scholarly articles.

I should add here that although Hersch Lauterpacht was an important influence for the reasons stated, my own ideas differed from his in some significant respects. This takes me beyond your question into a discussion of my own ideas. I will leave that for later so that I can mention two other individuals who influenced my 'scholarly career'. One was Abraham Feller, the second Myres McDougal.

Feller was the General Counsel of UNRRA (the United Nations Relief and Rehabilitation Administration), who asked me to join him as an Assistant General Counsel in 1944. I had been in the State Department for two years (1942–43) working mainly on economic warfare, but as a political officer rather than a legal adviser. My work in UNRRA under Feller involved a wide range of legal problems—drafting and interpreting regulations and agreements, giving legal opinions, negotiating with governments. UNRRA was operational, not a debating body. Its activities in newly-liberated areas—many under Communist control—raised novel legal issues. I drafted agreements with the USSR and the other Communist countries, and took part in their negotiation. I also advised on the many legal issues presented by activities involving rehabilitation of war-torn areas and displaced people, as well as on the procedures of UNRRA governing bodies. In January 1946 Feller was appointed General Counsel to the first Secretary-General of the United Nations, Trygve Lie.[21] (He was the first UN official to establish the United Nations in New York in February 1946.) In April, he (unexpectedly) asked me to assist him at the UN. I did not seek the job and only agreed to join for a short period, expecting to stay two or three months. (It turned out to be 30 years.) Feller was a remarkable man—scholar, litigator, teacher—and above all a counsellor who cut to the heart of complex issues and suggested

[21] Trygve Lie (Norwegian, 1886-1968) was Minister of Justice (1935–39), then Minister of Trade and Industries from July to September 1939 and, at the time of the outbreak of World War II, became Minister of Supply and Shipping. In that capacity he evolved the provisional measures that saved the Norwegian fleet for the Allies, after the German invasion in April 1940. He went to the UK and became acting Foreign Minister in December 1940, being appointed Foreign Minister of Norway in February 1941. He led the Norwegian delegation to the United Nations Conference on International Organization in San Francisco, in April 1945, and was Chairman of Commission III for drafting the Security Council provisions of the Charter. He was also Chairman of the Norwegian delegation to the United Nations General Assembly in London in January 1946. On 1 February 1946, Mr Lie was elected the first Secretary-General of the United Nations. The General Assembly, on 1 November 1950, confirmed Mr Lie in office for a further three years from 1 February 1951. He resigned as Secretary-General of the United Nations in November 1952.

solutions that were practical and acceptable. His learning was prodigious in international law, history and economics, but he carried it lightly and without any pretence. Unlike most high officials, he preferred to do his own research, write his own memos and letters. His counsel was sought daily by the Secretary-General, and by representatives of governments and senior officials. His practical approach and quick responses were greatly appreciated in the hectic pioneering days of the early UN. I admired the direct and unpretentious way he solved problems without requiring a large staff of lawyers. This must have had some effect on my own approach to legal counselling. I came to appreciate how law developed through responses to concrete problems. Our days in the UN were filled with challenges arising from the clash of interests, the lack of rules and the need to provide solutions. If and when acceptable solutions were reached, they usually gave rise to fresh problems that required new answers. The experience of the pragmatic evolution of law in international institutions was an important element in my later scholarly commentary.

A third influential figure in my international law scholarship was Myres McDougal. In 1955 McDougal persuaded me to join him and his intellectual partner, Harold Lasswell,[22] in teaching a graduate seminar at Yale Law School entitled 'World Public Order and International Organization'. It was held in the evening once a week for two hours, often spilling over into three or more hours. I participated for 16 years, from 1955 through 1970 (when Lasswell retired). I was expected to analyse UN law and related problems in the light of the categories and terminology that McDougal and Lasswell had proposed to describe the role of law in the 'world decision process'. They hoped that my discussion of the current problems in the UN would help to test their systematic 'policy science' approach and contribute to its further development. They also understandably expected me to be a convert to their crusade. I was pleased and flattered to be asked. My 16 years (1955–70)—over 200 sessions—proved to be enjoyable and intellectually challenging.

The seminars compelled me to examine UN problems in a more searching and profound way than I could otherwise have done. In line with McDougal's broad conception of law, we discussed current issues in the main substantive areas of UN activity—political conflicts, peacekeeping, human rights, economic and social programs—as well as issues of a more distinct juridical character, such as codification and treaty problems. Each week I faced McDougal's cross-examination; our spirited arguments delighted students (some remember those sharp exchanges more than what they were about). Most of the students were of high quality. Many turned out to be prominent as scholars, judges and in high government positions: for example, Judges Oda[23] and Rosalyn

[22] Harold Dwight Lasswell (1902–78) was Professor of Law and Political Sciences at Yale University (1946–70).

[23] See 'Interview with Sir Robert Jennings', fn 38.

Higgins[24] of the International Court. The seminars stimulated my thinking and made it much easier for me to undertake scholarly writing. During those years, invitations to lecture at academic conferences and to submit articles came in a steady stream. I felt able to respond more readily—and with more originality—because of my Yale experience.

A different aspect of McDougal's influence (and this includes Lasswell) came from my efforts to comprehend and apply their policy-science methodology. From a personal standpoint, it was natural in view of our seminar discussions and friendships for me to have a sympathetic attitude to their ideas. But it was not easy for me to apply their complex taxonomy and to provide answers to the many questions that their comprehensive framework posed. Lasswell's prodigious learning—especially in sociology, psychology and communications—stimulated my interest in these subjects. In later years, when I directed research at the United Nations Institute of Training and Research, I found that background valuable.

II. The Policy-Science Approach versus the Strictly Legal Approach

What is your assessment of the policy-science approach?

It is difficult to assess the policy-science approach in a few words. Myres McDougal has generously referred to me as 'one of the creators of the policy-oriented frame of jurisprudence', but added that I was later 'wavering between that frame and a paradigm of formalistic positivism'.[25] That may not be far off the mark, though I would not express it that way. My book, *International Law in Theory and Practice*[26] (originally my general course at the Hague Academy), presents my views more fully. The law-science approach should not be reduced to the simple, almost banal, proposition that law should serve policy ends. No one disagrees with that. The McDougal–Lasswell 'configurative jurisprudence' opens our eyes to the wide range of ends, conditioning factors, intellectual processes, social and psychological perspectives that enter into and influence decisions involving 'authority' and 'control' (ie, effectiveness). Within this broad—almost unlimited framework—they bring out various more specific insights of value. For example, they emphasise the importance of the 'observational standpoint' in reaching decisions (judges and advocates take different views). They also draw attention to the important difference between law as a 'myth system' and as an 'operational code'. A recognition of the complementary role of 'opposing' principles is another helpful—though not original—idea. Using 'human dignity' as a *summum*

[24] *Ibid*, fn 61.
[25] See (1985) *Proceedings of the American Society of International Law*, at 283.
[26] Above n 3.

bonum and specifying its components as 'goal values' is an attempt to provide a universal normative focus to legal decisions. Its generality is such that people of opposing views can always find support in one or more of the values.

As indicated, I have difficulty with some features of the policy-science approach and the way in which it has been applied. For one thing, the model or 'map' (as they called it) demands factual inquiry and answers in respect of an almost unlimited range of actions and attitudes ('subjectivities') on a global level. It would require a participant (eg a judge or government official) or an observer (eg professor) to ascertain the 'shared expectations' of peoples and how they are affected by their values, by state power, economic and social conditions, etc. Many questions are posed, few are answerable. One would have to be virtually omniscient to be able to fill in the contents of the numerous categories that are supposed to be applied.

One consequence, as shown by the positions McDougal and his followers have taken, is that their legal conclusions coincide with their 'politics' and predictable preferences. McDougal has a first-rate legal mind which often functions quite independently of the policy-science categories. However, when faced with controversial issues of legal policy (eg Act of State, use of force, the veto in the Security Council), McDougal's conclusions coincide with his politics (and generally the United States' position) but he feels constrained to justify them by asserting that they conform to the 'most intensely demanded' values and 'expectations' of humankind. I would refer to the 1985 *Proceedings of American Society of International Law*. For my observations on this as well as Richard Falk's.[27]

In my view, a more disciplined approach to 'policy' analysis is required if law is to be distinguished from politics. Basic values must be supported by legal criteria—that is, they must be demonstrated as values accepted in international law. Moreover, unlike politics, a State or any other entity subject to law cannot decide for itself in the last analysis whether and to what extent it is governed by a legal prescription.

How do you explain McDougal's enormous success with his students?

Several reasons come to mind. First of all, Mac took his students seriously. He saw them as potential disciples; he enjoyed intellectual exchange with them; and his personal warmth inspired loyalty and affection. On an intellectual level, he opened their eyes to a wide range of ideas beyond the law curriculum. Students from 'developing countries' were especially excited by the broad vista newly opened to them. Many saw his approach as an intellectual basis for reform in their countries. Even though very few of them continued to use his arcane vocabulary and adapted to the prevailing positivism of their communities, they were still inspired by his reformist vision.

[27] See 'Interview with Sir Robert Jennings', fn 77.

Mac also turned his theory into a crusade. He fiercely attacked the prevailing 'positivists'. At international law meetings, his characteristic opening sentence (in the 1950s and 1960s) was 'I never heard so much nonsense before'. Even Lasswell has noted (in writing) McDougal's 'furious tenacity', his 'use of intellectual bulldozing' and his 'love of verbal combat'.[28] McDougal's close friend, Eugene Rostow, a former Yale Law Dean, has written in an admiring mood of McDougal's skills as a 'politician', and his effectiveness in getting jobs for people and funds for his projects. All of these features played a role in his personal influence. For me personally, his personal warmth and affection, his down-to-earth qualities mattered a great deal—even as we differed on legal methodology and political positions.

What about Dick Falk?

I take it that you ask about his relation with McDougal? Falk was a student in the seminar I gave with McDougal and Lasswell and, as he has noted, he was much influenced by the McDougal–Lasswell approach. As a critic of US actions in many situations, Falk sharply differed with McDougal, but he paid tribute to what he recently described as McDougal–Lasswell 'configurative jurisprudence embedded in social context'. Falk's intellectual sources—as you know—range widely in contemporary political and social ideas, and except for his personal affection, he would not be considered a 'true believer' in the McDougal approach. In fact, in a recent review of the latest McDougal–Lasswell book,[29] Falk delicately concludes that 'the jurisprudence is conceptually troubled and unlikely to survive once the charismatic spell cast by its progenitors has passed'. It is evident that even international lawyers, who pay tribute in general terms to the 'policy-science' approach, do not apply its complex categories and terminology. Nonetheless, for many of them—as for me—immersion into their theories has contributed a great deal to our intellectual and moral approaches to international law. At the very least, it has brought home to us the advantage of viewing law as a many-sided process involving choices between alternative principles and ends, and requiring a profound knowledge of the relevant social and political contexts.

III. Encounters with Other International Lawyers

Did you ever meet Kelsen?[30]

Yes, in a curious way. When I was an Assistant General Counsel at UNRRA in 1944 or 1945 (located in Washington), I was asked by the Personnel Office

[28] See Lasswell's introduction to the book by HD Lasswell and MS McDougal, *Jurisprudence for a Free Society: Studies of Law, Science and Policies* (Dordrecht, Nijoff, 1992), at xxxvi.

[29] R Falk, 'Casting the Spell: The New Haven School of International Law' (1994-1995) 104 *Yale Law Journal* 1991 at 1994.

[30] See 'Interview with René-Jean Dupuy', fn 23.

to interview a job-seeker with a legal background. When he presented his card to me I said, in some astonishment, 'Are you the Hans Kelsen?' He then said: 'I have been looking for a job in Washington and you are the first person to recognise my name.' It was, of course, not surprising that government lawyers or officials did not know of Kelsen's eminence.

Did he get the job?

No. My chief, Abe Feller, did not think that it would be fitting to have Kelsen deal with our mundane legal questions, and that it would be undignified for him to have a librarian's post. Actually, Kelsen's problem arose because the law school at Berkeley—where he had been lecturing—had to 'downsize' because student enrolment in the war had been reduced.

You later reviewed Kelsen's book on the Law of the United Nations[31] *and criticised him strongly.*

Yes, in a sense I did, but I also praised the book. My main criticism was that Kelsen departed from his own stated doctrine—namely that if a provision of the UN Charter allowed for two (or more) different positions, the choice would properly be made by the competent political organs. However, in his book he treated several important disputes concerning the meaning of a provision as if only one interpretation was valid, even though in fact the governments were divided in their interpretations. My point was simply that his reading of provisions on which reasonable views were divided as though open only to one meaning, departed from his own theory of interpretation. I understand he was angry over my review. As I recall, I also praised the book for its impressive scholarship and close reading of texts. In fact, over the years I found it to be—to this day—a valuable exposition of the UN Charter. I might add that I also have a very high regard for Kelsen's general book on international law (which was edited for the English edition by Tucker[32]).

When you met Kelsen had you read his jurisprudential works?

I had read some of his writings on the 'Pure Theory of Law' for a college course on legal philosophy. At that time I regarded his approach as somewhat arid, for its sharp dichotomy between 'pure law' and policy. My own practical work as a legal adviser had impressed me with the importance of considering the purposes or functions of a legal rule in determining how it should be interpreted and applied. It also seems to me that this 'functional approach' (as it was once called) required a broad view of the aims of law, and in that sense

[31] H Kelsen, *The Law of the United Nations: A Critical Analysis of its Fundamental Problems* (London, Stevens and Sons, 1950).

[32] H Kelsen, *Principles of International Law*, 2nd edn, ed RW Tucker (New York, Holt, Rinehart and Winston, 1966).

was an aspect of the political process. This did not mean that law was reducible to politics; law had its sphere of autonomy that rested on the postulates of the legal system. However, choices had to be made between competing legal principles and rules, and that required recourse to the underlying reasons—in effect, the ends to be given preference. In this sense, I saw no sharp divide between law and policy; law in practice could not be 'pure'—and, in this respect, I did not follow Kelsen.

Still, I greatly respect Kelsen's contribution and admire his analytical power. I still often refer to his major works on international law and on United Nations law. And I still strongly reject a simplistic 'policy approach' that would reduce the process of law-making and application to political preferences and power.

It is interesting to me that Kelsen's theory has recently been invoked favourably by Koskenniemi,[33] usually regarded as something of an iconoclast on the basis of his influential work *From Apology to Utopia*.[34] In a talk to the American Society of International Law, Koskenniemi argued for treating the State in Kelsen's terms as pure juridical form. As a creature of 'pure law', the State would be neutral in respect to social policies, and would provide the structure of authority through which contending policies and demands could be resolved in a democratic way. I bring this up here to indicate that Kelsen is still influential, and that even a so-called 'post-modernist' finds value in his theory of pure law.

In addition to Lauterpacht, Kelsen and McDougal, what other great personality in international law have you met?

This question seems to call for a list of 'greats'. In my 50 years of work in international law, I have come to know virtually all the renowned figures in the field. Many of them took part in UN meetings in which I participated, and, of course, many were in the *Institut de Droit international* and at The Hague Academy. A century ago, it was easy to recognise the 'great' in our profession; the profession was fairly small, nearly all came from Western European and their writings could be—and were—in personal libraries. Today—and in recent decades—the profession has vastly expanded in numbers and in activities. It is no longer the province of the few, drawn largely from the upper classes of a few countries. The literature produced in bodies and journals is so vast that none of us can claim to be abreast of writings by even the most distinguished. Some years ago, I wrote an article entitled 'The Invisible College of International Lawyers'[35] in which, *inter alia*, I described the networks of communication and collaboration that link the profession in

[33] See 'Interview with Sir Robert Jennings', fn 75.
[34] M Koskenniemi, *From Apology to Utopia: The Structure of International Legal Argument* (Helsinki, Finnish Lawyers Publishing Company, 1989).
[35] (1977–78) 72 *Northwestern University Law Review* 217.

sharing and producing knowledge. We are an 'epistemic community', as well as a profession concerned with practical matters.

You ask me for 'great personalities' I have known. I will limit myself to those who have passed away. My list in alphabetical order would include Roberto Ago, Suzanne Bastid, Wolfgang Friedmann, Eduard Hambro, Philip Jessup, Eduardo Jiménez de Aréchaga, Lord McNair, Georges Scelle, Charles De Visscher, Michel Virally. With the exception of Scelle and De Visscher (whom I knew through meetings), I was well acquainted with all the others and considered them personal friends.

Did you ever meet Röling?

I knew him quite well, especially through his participation in the UN Legal Committee and the *Institut de Droit international.* As you know, he was a person of independent spirit and strong moral views. He did not hesitate to criticise this government's policy on colonialism and trusteeship.

He was let down by the Dutch Minister of Foreign Affairs, Luns,[36] *because he attacked the Dutch colonial policy. Did you see him later on?*

Yes, I saw him at meetings of the *Institut.* As I recall, he had become a strong supporter of world federalism and disarmament. He was outspoken in criticising those who did not agree with him on these issues. As I recall he resigned from the *Institut* because they did not go along with some of his proposals, a rather extraordinary action.

IV. The Theoretical Approach to International Law

Since you brought up Koskenniemi—and I would add David Kennedy[37] *and Philip Allott*[38]*—may I ask whether one can benefit from their theoretical approach?*

In general, I think that their writings are intellectually stimulating and pose some important questions. It is apparent that some, perhaps many, young scholars respond to their assault on traditional or established positions. Even as McDougal challenged the prevailing positivism 40 years ago (and indulged in vituperative attacks), the writers you mention also have attracted attention by their anti-establishment views. Parenthetically, I should say that I find them personally congenial and creative.

Koskenniemi's book, *From Apology to Utopia*, has apparently had a wide influence judging from the many references to it in current journals. It has

[36] Joseph Marie Antoine Hubert Luns (1911–2002) was a Dutch politician and diplomat. He was the longest-serving Minister of Foreign Affairs (1952–71). He also served as Secretary-General of NATO (1971–84).
[37] See 'Interview with Sir Robert Jennings', fn 76.
[38] *Ibid*, fn 71.

been seen as an 'exposé' that strips international law of its respectability by showing that legal argumentation rests inconsistently on both State consent (ie apologetic) and on a higher morality (ie utopian). His thesis was argued with copious material from respected sources, especially International Court of Justice cases. I did not find this upsetting. As a practitioner (legal adviser), my work almost always required me to support my conclusions by referring to both lines of support—namely, consent (ie precedent or agreement) and desirable ends. True, these arguments may be seen as resting on premises that are theoretically incompatible. For me they were—and are—two sides of social reality. Their persuasive force or validity depends on the context in which they are applied. I am certain that Koskenniemi in his practical role as a legal adviser to his Foreign Ministry had no intellectual hang-ups in arguing on grounds of both precedent and consent, on the one hand, and on desirable social ends, on the other. It is perhaps in point to mention that Koskenniemi's recent writings on law in the UN give rather more weight to the 'legal culture' (his term) and to the role of 'justice' through law. These are a far cry from the deconstructionist emphasis of his first book.

Others in the so-called 'new stream' including Kennedy are also moving in various ways to a more serious regard for the role of law. I believe this will also hold for the feminist critics, such as Shelley Wright and Christine Chinkin. Their writings have gained in depth and persuasiveness.

V. The Role of the Jurist as Scholar and Practitioner

A. Schachter's background

You have commented on many international lawyers and indirectly on your own approach. Would you care to say more about your own background?

Perhaps I should note that outside of law, my main intellectual training has been in philosophy and to a lesser degree economic theory. In philosophy, my interest ranged widely from, on the one side, logic and linguistic analysis and, on the other, social and political philosophy. As my writing on international law may show, I still have recourse to ideas of ethics and logic in my perceptions of law. You may perhaps note from my references in my book on *Sharing the World's Resources*[39] and in my *International Law in Theory and Practice*[40] the philosophers that I have found most helpful to my thinking. In general, they have helped me to find my way through the mine-field of the many factors influencing international law. I view international law (and indeed all law) not so much in terms of abstract concepts as in [terms of] actual human needs and interests, and the conflicts and obstacles they

39 Above n 2.
40 Above n 3.

encounter. I am not concerned with the eternal verities as much as I am with the changing procession of specific objectives, material conditions and attitudes of people in organised communities.

My experience in the practical role of a legal adviser and an administrator has greatly influenced my perspectives on international law. Above all, I have experienced legal activity as an exercise in problem-solving.

International law, as I see it, develops mainly in response to particular problems, problems that arise because wants and needs face obstacles in specific contexts. Thoughtful practising lawyers see that conflicts generate standards and rules; they also realise that solutions not only solve some problems, but [also] give rise to new problems and new ideas. They are usually aware of the role of power as a crucial factor in the creation of law and its observance. But many recognise, as I do, that power may be absorbed, so to speak, and in a degree transcended by institutions and practices based on law.

These comments, incomplete as they are, may help to give you some idea of my conception of law derived from my experience and reflection.

B. Ground-breaking books in international law

Would you regard Röling's book, International Law in the Expanded World,[41] *as a seminal work?*

I will now have to read it in the light of your implicit recommendation.

In your view, what would be the two or three books in this century that have been turning points in international law?

I do not think any book can be regarded as a turning-point in international law. A very influential book—at least in the US—was Jessup's *A Modern Law of Nations*,[42] which appeared in 1948 and was widely reviewed and praised in newspapers and by prominent figures. It was not a treatise but it covered major developments at the end of World War II, emphasising their practical value to security and economic benefits.

Lauterpacht's *Function of Law*[43] may well have been a factor in turning some international lawyers away from prevailing positivism toward more 'Grotian views'. Apart from that, its magisterial style and learning—as well as its idealism—gave it a high place in international law writing. On the Continental side, I would consider Charles De Visscher's *Theory and Reality in International Law*[44] as an outstanding contribution which certainly influenced my own thinking, at least as much as any other single book. I appreciate his judicious balancing of

[41] BVA Röling, *International Law in the Expanded World* (Amsterdam, Djambatan, 1960).
[42] PC Jessup, *A Modern Law of Nations: An Introduction* (New York, Macmillan, 1948).
[43] Above n 19.
[44] C de Visscher, *Theory and Reality in Public International Law* (Princeton, Princeton University Press, 1968).

conflicting values, and his perceptive insights as well as his sense of the drama of human affairs played out on the stage of international law. Looking at other areas, my first choice would clearly be Jimenez de Aréchaga's *International Law in the Past Third of a Century*[45], which was given as the general course in The Hague Academy in 1978. It deals with fundamental issues clearly and persuasively. It also reflects and clarifies positions of the developing countries in a way that commands respect.

Would you regard the book by Friedmann, The Changing Structure of International Law,[46] *as a seminal work?*

That book is a valuable contribution, going beyond the usual subjects of international law. It is a great contribution. It is a Friedmann product, expressing his own views on a vast array of topics, ranging beyond the usual subjects dealt with by contemporary writers. The distinction between the 'law of co-existence' and the 'law of cooperation' has been widely quoted, and might be regarded as 'seminal'. Friedmann's inclusion of economic development and international administrative law helped to bring these practical topics into international law scholarship. While his book was generally admired, it was strongly criticised in a review by McDougal in the *Columbia Law Review*.[47] Wolfgang was deeply wounded by this review (especially as it was in the *Journal* he inspired). The review is a sad example of a crusading approach that allowed for no merit in a different viewpoint.

Friedmann was not only a productive scholar but an admirable human being and an inspiring teacher. An opponent of Nazism and a refugee, he felt strongly that he should speak out against injustices and militarism. He often wrote letter to the *New York Times* and other journals. He was concerned about the under-dogs. He was scornful of academics who supported their government's positions to win favour. He treasured his students and spent far more time with them than was usual. His death was an enormous loss to Columbia University and to the profession. World-wide tributes were paid to him after his shocking murder. I am glad to have this opportunity to express once again my admiration and affection.[48]

Which is the one particular book you go back to now and then?

A hard question. It may be Charles De Visscher's *Theory and Reality* (which I mentioned earlier). Kelsen's *Principles of International Law* (Tucker ed)

[45] E Jiménez de Aréchaga, 'International Law in the Past Third of a Century' (1978-I) 159 *Recueil des cours* 1.

[46] W Friedmann, *The Changing Structure of International Law* (London, Stevens and Sons, 1964).

[47] MS McDougal, WM Reisman, 'The Changing Structure of International Law: Unchanging Theory for Inquiry' (1965) 65 *Columbia Law Review* 810.

[48] I have inserted into this paragraph on Friedmann passages from a letter Oscar Schachter sent to me on 21 February 1995, in which he clarified and elaborated upon the remarks he had made in his interview.

is probably in second place—despite my differences with his theory. I also return to Lauterpacht's classic works. Of course, Lou Henkin's many writings are high on my list.

C. The media

Can we move to a different area. Have you written for newspapers or taken part in TV talks?

In view of my UN position, I have been asked from time to time to take part in radio and TV 'talk' programmes on legal topics, and also to contribute to magazines of general interest. During the early years of the UN, the demand for UN participants was quite strong and I found it agreeable to respond to such invitations.

Was it because you felt the need to popularise international law?

It was really because I was asked, and I considered it an enjoyable and intellectually interesting activity. For example, in 1951, a popular magazine asked me to write on 'Who Owns the Moon'. The article I wrote (while I was in Paris for the UN General Assembly), entitled 'Who Owns the Universe?',[49] was the first legal article on outer space law. It was given very wide publicity in the American Press and in Europe, and led to many requests in the next few years for talks and articles on outer space.

At times of UN crises that involved legal issues, the UN Public Information Department asked me to speak in radio and TV discussions.

Subsequently, the media often sought my opinion as an 'expert' on international law issues that arose. My academic position, as well as positions in professional bodies (eg as the President of the American Society of International Law), led to numerous requests.

D. Politics, government, legal practice

Have you ever taken part in political activity?

When I was a student, I was quite active in political activities through student organisations. The international aspect of that centered on anti-fascist activities in the 1930s, including the major controversy in the US around 'collective security' versus neutrality. Most of our international law professors favoured neutrality in that period, whereas I strongly favoured collective security. My involvement brought me into the area of international law, though I was only marginally interested in that.

[49] First published in *Colliers*, 22 March 1952, at 36 and 70–71. Reprinted in C Ryan (ed), *Across the Space Frontier* (London, Sidgwick and Jackson, 1952).

In later years, my positions in the Government and in international bodies precluded partisan political activities. After leaving the UN for academic work, my political activity consisted in taking positions in professional and civic bodies in current issues.

Were you in academic posts in the Second World War?

No. From 1940 through 1943 I was in the US Government—mostly engaged on wartime problems. I dealt with wartime communication problems of a legal character and later, while in the State Department, with economic warfare and the economic problems of occupied Europe. In January 1944 I joined the newly-organised United Nations Relief and Rehabilitation Administration as an Assistant General Counsel. That brought me into an international organisation of a practical operational character. It also brought me to wartime Eastern Europe and into highly controversial problems relating to refugees and control over supplies for relief and rehabilitation. I left UNRRA in April 1946 to join the UN Legal Department.

Have you ever been a judge?

I was a judge on the arbitral tribunal in a case between France and Canada concerning the maritime boundaries of Saint-Pierre-et-Miquelon.[50] Our proceedings lasted for three years. I was one of the three neutral judges appointed by both parties. The others were Jiménez de Aréchaga (as President) and Gaetano Arangio-Ruiz. France appointed Prosper Weil, and Canada Alan Gotlieb. The tribunal was 'top-drawer'. It provided a memorable experience for me.

Were you ever a counsel before the International Court of Justice?

No. My principal links with the Court included, as part of my UN responsibilities, legal opinions relating to the election of judges and administrative issues. I also had some part in the preparation of the submissions by the Secretary-General in advisory proceedings (for example, *South West Africa*[51] and *Certain Expenses*[52]). A number of questions relating to the Court also arose in UN organs that called for legal opinions and studies in which I had a role. All in all, a substantial part of my work during my 20 years in the UN Legal Office related to the Court. After I retired from the UN in 1976,

[50] Reference is made here to the arbitration between Canada and France concerning the islands of Saint-Pierre-and-Miquelon (small French islands close to the shore of Newfoundland, Canada). See *Case Concerning the Delimitation of Maritime Areas between Canada and the French Republic (St Pierre and Miquelon)*, 10 June 1992 (see award in (1992) 31 *International Legal Materials* 1149).

[51] *Legal Consequences for States of the Continued Presence of South Africa in Namibia (South West Africa) Notwithstanding Security Council Resolution 276 (1970)*, 21 June 1971, [1971] ICJ Rep 16.

[52] *Certain Expenses of the United Nations (Article 17, Paragraph 2 of the Charter)*, 20 July 1962, [1962] ICJ Rep 151.

I was asked several times by governments to assist them in respect of the ICJ proceedings. I did not accept any of them—either because of their particular position, or because of the large commitment of time that would be involved.

You have never been a member of the International Law Commission?

No. I followed their work rather closely when I was in the UN, and subsequently I also, of course, have written a fair amount about their contributions.

Did you take part in any diplomatic conferences?

In my UN capacity I acted as a legal adviser, or in some cases as the Executive Secretary of conferences engaged in preparing multilateral treaties.

In several cases, the draft conventions were in fact initiated by us (ie, Secretariat), and carried through to completion by plenipotentiary conferences in which we had an active role. Although in most cases, these treaties were not central to UN politics, they had practical value. Two examples that come to mind are the Convention on Recognition and Enforcement of Arbitral Awards (referred to as the 'New York Convention')[53] and the Convention on Maintenance Obligations.[54] These are examples of an aspect of UN legal activity that is not given much publicity but which over time has resulted in substantial contribution to international law in the private as well as public domain. Above all, they have been of practical value, as have many other treaties of a specialised nature.

E. Contributing to international law

What would you consider your major contribution to international law on a scholarly level?

To my mind, at least, the answer is my principal work *International Law in Theory and Practice*,[55] which originated as my General Course in Public International Law at The Hague Academy in 1982. The book received the ASIL Prize for an outstanding scholarly achievement, and I am pleased that it continues to be referred to and cited often in current literature. Going back 20 years or so, I delivered lectures that resulted in my *Sharing the World's Resources*[56] which, as the title indicates, concerns some of the most controversial issues of economics, equity and environment that influence international law.

[53] Convention on the Recognition and Enforcement of Foreign Arbitral Awards, adopted on 10 June 1958, 21 UST 2517, 330 UNTS 38.

[54] Convention on the Law Applicable to Maintenance Obligations of 2 October 1973, published in (1973) 21 *American Journal of Comparative Law* 596.

[55] Above n 3.

[56] Above n 2.

VI. A Look at the International Community

A. The current state of international law

I would like to ask a few questions about your views on international law. What parts of the international community do you think are outmoded, and which parts should be retrieved? If you were to be a sort of world legislator, what would you promote and enhance, and what would you jettison?

Your question is challenging. It invites a utopian response, but I will resist that temptation. Two large problems trouble me at this time. The first is the explosion of micro-nationalism and 'particularism' in almost every part of the world, leading to conflicts and insecurity. I believe this may be (at least in part) a reaction to the manifestations of globalism and the anonymous markets that are felt by many to dominate their lives. In consequence, people turn to their own group, whether 'tribes' or localities, and ambitious leaders seek to create their separate domains, however small and weak. My response (as your hypothetical world legislator) would be first to understand the socio-psychological reasons for the negative reaction to globalism and to large conglomerates (whether private or public). Second, I would respond by broadening the role of non-State and sub-State organisations in the international decision processes. We already have evidence of some movement in that direction. Third, I would seek an institutional framework and practical rules for giving effect to the principle of 'subsidiarity' on the global, regional and national levels. The European Union debates on this would be pertinent.

Now that I am a world legislator I do not want to stop legislating. The second troubling problem is the plight of the United Nations. Let me suggest three practical measures. The first would be to provide more financial resources for the UN through levies on some international activities (such as transnational currency transfers and travel). Members would still control the budget and expenditures, but funds would be available beyond assessments that are frequently late or unpaid. I would also establish a small rapid deployment armed force, recruited by the UN to act under the authority of the Security-General pursuant to Security Council decisions. A third proposal would demand that the UN make a massive effort to improve the capabilities of people in the deprived areas of the world, especially through education for women and girls. Admittedly, these three goals will be hard to attain in the political climate that emphasises self-interest, markets and consumerism. Yet we cannot crawl into our own holes. Kant's phrase 'the unsocial sociability of man' reminds us that we have a realistic interest in combating violence and poverty that endangers all of us. These goals are not easy to achieve. But even if we are not world legislators, there is room for political and social action.

Finally, on a more technical level, let me say a few words in support of inter-disciplinary collaboration between international lawyers and related fields of study. Some lip-service is often paid to this idea, but in actuality little is done. In 1973 I made some specific proposals to the *Institut de Droit international* in my Special Report to its Centennial Session in Rome.[57] My suggestions for collaboration (eg joint commissions, questionnaires) received favourable comment in the debates, but they were not followed up by the *Institut*. I still hope that the *Institut* and the International Law Association (ILA) will see their way to collaboration with relevant non-legal bodies. My experience in UNITAR (1966–76) showed that seminars and research on interdisciplinary projects could be beneficial and break new ground. Today the UN University has fostered some such projects, but it has not paid much attention to international law. Perhaps Boutros-Ghali[58] can be persuaded to promote such joint efforts; he is certainly well qualified to take the lead in that direction. Some topics that come to my mind include the difficult problems (legal and otherwise) raised by new communication technology. A second area would be problems, earlier alluded to, of 'micro-nationalism' and diverse 'identities' that involve economic psychological and social aspects along with international law. There is surely a need for joint efforts on these as well as on other problems that transcend any single discipline.

B. The future of the international community

You mentioned UN accomplishments and your expectations. Now if we think of the future, the next 20, 30 or 40 years, how would you see the international community developing? I am thinking of three possible outcomes: world government; a much stronger UN; or a sort of horizontal integration of States. What in your view is the more realistic scenario?

Let me duck a little. Just the other day, I read a remark of Keynes[59]: 'The inevitable never happens; it is always the unexpected.' How wrong the forecasts about the UN have been! My own guess (for whatever it is worth) is that we will not have world government. As for the UN itself, my guess is that it will reflect a trend towards diffusion of power. The US will no longer be a 'sole superpower', and many more States will acquire a significant role. Moreover, I would expect a much-enhanced role for the non-governmental sectors, now called 'civil society'. Not all will be benign: many will favour narrow interests, but on the whole they will strengthen the UN in its varied roles. I would not exclude the possibility of replacing the UN by a new international organisation that would reflect changes in power and in attitudes of elites.

[57] *Institut de Droit international, Livre du Centenaire 1873–1973: Evolutions et perspectives du droit international* (Basel, Editions S Karger, 1973) at 447.

[58] See 'Interview with Sir Robert Jennings', fn 40.

[59] John Maynard Keynes (British, 1883–1946) was a great economist. His ideas and writings profoundly affected the theory and practice of modern macroeconomics, as well as the economic policies of governments.

Dag Hammerskjøld[60] wrote (around 1960) of the possibility of a 'third' world organisation succeeding the UN, just as the latter had succeeded the League. Whatever does happen is likely to be unexpected. It may be, as a poet wrote, that: 'The world is crazier than we think.' But that does not mean that we can abdicate our responsibility to humankind. We can still push for achieving our ideals through our profession. International law has its *grandeurs* as well as its frustrations. We can all share in both.

VII. The Jurist and Global Reality

Could we just wind up with personal questions? Have you been in need of palliatives because of the unbearable nature of life?

You put the question dramatically. Yes, I recognise the tragic aspect of human life and the impossibility of attaining many of our ideals. I must confess that over the years, many nights have been almost sleepless because of troubling problems or repressed anger. I sometimes console myself by thinking how lucky I have been to have achieved a fruitful career and high positions. I could not have imagined that, even in my day-dreams as a student. Doubtless luck played a role. I have been lucky in my family and in friendships. I often seek comfort in poetry (both old and new) and in philosophy (mostly old). My interest in the public affairs of the day is strong (perhaps excessive). I take sides on many issues and share the passions of my time. Living in New York keeps me in touch with all sorts of people—I walk its streets and parks frequently, and I feel enhanced when I do.

Do you have a sense of fulfilment?

Yes, to a degree. My 30 years in the UN were rewarding. I heard it often said that the UN could not function in that period because of the Cold War. Nonsense. Just think of its role in bringing colonialism to an end, in developing human rights law on a worldwide basis and in carrying out peacekeeping in many troubled areas. I had some part in all of these activities, as well as a part in the development of new law—a *corpus juris* that deals with almost every aspect of human activity. I must confess that I never expected that the

[60] Dag Hammerskjøld (Swedish, 1905–61) was Secretary-General of the United Nations 1953–61. In 1936, he was awarded the Nobel Peace Prize posthumously. He remains the only UN Secretary-General to die in office. Hammarskjöld had become a Secretary at the Bank of Sweden, and then Undersecretary of Finance. From 1941 to 1948, he served as Chairman of the Bank of Sweden. In 1945, he was appointed as adviser to the cabinet on financial and economic problems, and coordinated government plans to alleviate the economic problems of the post-war period. In 1947, Hammarskjöld was appointed to Sweden's Ministry for Foreign Affairs, and in 1949 he became the State Secretary for Foreign Affairs. He was a delegate to the Paris conference that established the Marshall Plan. In 1951, he became a cabinet minister without portfolio and in effect Deputy Foreign Minister. He became the chairman of the Swedish delegation to the General Assembly in New York in 1952.

UN could achieve what it did. The fact that I had a part surely gave me a sense of fulfilment. That feeling of accomplishment was enhanced greatly when, through my writings and teaching, I moved to the frontiers of international law. Both careers—official and scholarly—reinforced each other. Even with the inevitable disappointments, I feel fortunate in my dual career.

I agree with you, Oscar, about the importance of the UN. In spite of all the well-founded criticisms, it remains an indispensable machinery for peace. That it has worked fairly well is largely due to persons like you, to persons of integrity, of high ideals and tenacious attachment to the institution. How many people are aware of your crucial contribution to the good functioning of the UN? Thank you, Oscar, for both your efforts and this enlightening conversation.

Final Remarks

By Way of Conclusion

I. On the Limits of my Attempt to Highlight the Main Points of the Interviews

THE READER WHO has patiently gone through the various interviews has noticed, I am sure, how the unique personality, approach, vision and style of each interviewee shaped the dialogues and resulted in largely different end products. Before undertaking the interviews, it had been agreed that the questionnaire I had previously given to each of the participants should not be a strait-jacket for our conversations, but only a sort of skeleton or outline to be followed freely. Accordingly, within the general framework of the questionnaire, my questions varied, largely stimulated by the attitude and the responses of my interlocutors. The first interviewees, in particular, engaged in very interesting digressions; they thereby offered unique insights into their own lives and outlooks. The result, I believe, is refreshing and disarmingly candid at times, with each of the persons interviewed sharing a wealth of telling remarks, reflections and observations on facts, persons and institutions.

In this final chapter I shall not attempt a summation of the interviews, since they are too sapid and lively to be recycled with paraphrases. They also differ in vivacity and length as a result of the side-issues discussed and the tangential discussions some of interviewees did not shy away from launching. I will simply try to gather up the various threads emerging from the conversations and highlight some major ideas that may be drawn from them.

II. Basic Commonalities

Despite the more obvious differences between the interviewees, a few interesting elements did appear to be shared by all five scholars.

First, regardless of their nationality and country of origin, their training in the area of international law was made under the influence of a handful of great European scholars.

Secondly, they all embraced the same philosophy of law, namely legal positivism, although each one did so to a different degree and with notable nuances. One might say that while they all availed themselves of the same intellectual food, each seasoned it in a different way.

Thirdly, there is a significant factor which, although not explicitly articulated by any of my interlocutors, may be read between the lines of their respective interviews. Indeed, and unsurprisingly, they all were dramatically marked not only by the Second World War, but also by its aftermath, which was chiefly defined by a novel international ethos: the attempt to create a new Constitution for the world community upon the establishment of the United Nations, a Constitution proclaiming a set of values which should hold true universally and uniformly. The level of personal involvement of the interviewees in the war varied. While some of them managed to stay far from the actual belligerency or the political frontline, others found themselves in the eye of the storm. Jennings, for example, worked for British military intelligence. Henkin fought in Europe as a soldier in the US army. As for Schachter, he worked as a State Department adviser on wartime economic controls and the liberated European areas. The diverse wartime experiences of my interviewees nonetheless caused them to share a strong belief in the new fundamental values of today's world community: peace, human rights, the rule of law and the peaceful settlement of disputes. They also strongly believed in the right to self-determination, with only Jennings adopting a tepid, if not critical, attitude towards it.[1]

Fourthly, all these scholars appeared to harbour a sort of instinctive distrust of—or, at the very least, a lack of interest in—general jurisprudential works on international law. This was to a large extent reflected in their reactions to Kelsen's pure theory of law (*Reine Rechtslehre*), in which only Jiménez de Aréchaga showed some interest,[2] although it was clear that he preferred Kelsen's general approach to international law to the grandiose edifice that is the 'pure theory of law'. The lack of interest in jurisprudential works held true for the more recent publications by Richard Falk, David Kennedy, Philip Allott and Martti Koskenniemi. In essence, the interviewees felt that, however original and profound the works of these authors might be, not much could be drawn from them that could prove useful to a lawyer's daily tasks.

Fifthly, and most importantly, all of them belonged to that class of persons that Hegel categorised as 'men of passions' (*Menschen von Leidenschaften*[3]), that is, persons who strongly will and accomplish something great, who unhesitatingly and unflinchingly pursue some goals and devote all their energies to those goals; men who have an insight into the 'requirements of the time', in what 'is ripe for development', and fall in with the needs of the age. The interviewees were all animated by passion for research and teaching. They were keen to put their scholarship into practice, in order to contribute to the common good (while admittedly simultaneously pursuing in some instances their private purposes as well). According to Hegel, 'passion is the

[1] See 'Interview with Sir Robert Jennings', section IV.I.

[2] See 'Interview with Eduardo Jiménez de Aréchaga', section I.

[3] Georg Wilhelm Friedrich Hegel, *Vorlesungen über die Philosophie der Weltgeschichte,* in GWF Hegel, *Sämtliche Werke* (ed Georg Lasson), vol VIII (Leipzig, Verlag von Felix Meiner, 1920) at 79.

necessary condition for men to beget something of value'.[4] The interviewees were all moved by 'passion', and most of their works were momentous contributions to scholarship and to the development of law.

In addition, they were all members of the prestigious and highly influential *Institut de Droit international*, a cosmopolitan body set up in the 19th century not only to create a *koiné*, that is a common ethos and a common vision of international law, but also to promote a joint effort to further the development and progress of the law regulating inter-State dealings.

Lastly, by no coincidence, all the interviewees delivered general courses on international law at The Hague Academy of International Law. The Academy was concretely set up in 1923 as one of many reactions to the First World War, with the aims, *inter alia*, of instilling a universalist and cosmopolitan outlook in budding jurists, as well as disseminating among trained professionals an internationalist approach to problem-solving.[5]

In sum, it can safely be said that the five scholars interviewed here represent the core of the internationally-educated and internationally-minded leading personalities who contributed in the second part of the 20th century to shaping the mindset and the cultural vision of generations of aspiring jurists.

I shall expand on these points in the following sections.

III. The European Kernel in the Education of the Interviewees

Not surprisingly, all save one of the interviewees were strongly influenced in their formative years by scholars who were also their countrymen: Dupuy fell for Georges Scelle's intellectual charm, and was for a long time under his legal ascendancy; Jennings' mentor from the outset was Lord McNair; Henkin's early influences were a European international lawyer, Sir Hersch

[4] '*Die Leidenschaft ist die Bedingung, dass aus dem Menschen etwas Tüchtiges hervorkommt*' (*ibid*, at 80).

[5] It is indeed striking that the Academy, the foundation of which was first proposed at the 1899 Hague Peace Conference with a view to 'dealing with a broader development of international law', initially was closely linked to the *Institut de Droit international*, for it was the *Institut* which in 1913 adopted the Academy's Statute. In 1923, the year when the Academy began its teaching, its governing body, the Curatorium, adopted a declaration which, *inter alia*, stated the following: 'L'Académie ne se présente pas comme une doublure, encore moins comme une concurrente des universités. Elle ambitionne au contraire la même oeuvre de lumière et de progrès sur un terrain et avec des moyens d'action qui ne sont pas les leurs. Par son personnel, ses auditoires, ses tendances, ses résultats, elle sera essentiellement internationale . . . Mis en contact, dans un commerce quotidien, les représentants des diverses écoles nationals parviendront à mieux comprendre les raisons des divergences doctrinales et pratiques des autres pays. Leurs vues particularistes finiront par faire place à une conception commune internationale.' (cited by S Verosta, 'L'historie de l'Académie de droit international de La Haye', *Livre jubilaire de l'Académie* (Leyden, Sijthoff, 1973) at 41). On the history of the Academy, see also EN van Kleffens, 'The Hague Academy of International Law: An Aid to the Diffusion and to a Clearer Notion of the Law of Nations' (1925) 6 *British Yearbook of International Law* 172; R-J Dupuy, 'La contribution de l'Académie au développement du droit international' (1973-I) 138 *Recueil des cours de l'Academie de Droit International de la Haye* ('*Recueil des cours*') 45.

Lauterpacht, and the US professor and judge, Philip Jessup; Lauterpacht, along with the American academics Abraham Feller and Myres McDougal, also mentored Schachter. Jiménez de Aréchaga was an exception: he was not influenced by any Latin American scholar but by European international lawyers, chiefly the Austrian Kelsen and the Italian Anzilotti.

As the five international lawyers interviewed are highly representative of the legal scholarship of that period, one can probably conclude that European legal thought had the greatest impact on nearly all of them. The assertion is thus warranted that, at least until the end of the 20th century, Western Europe still yielded great intellectual authority in the field of international law. In contrast, neither the North American legal traditions, such as the Yale School of Myres McDougal (1906–98), nor, *a fortiori*, the schools of thought of socialist countries (think in particular of the Soviet Grigory Tunkin (1906–93) and the East-German Bernhard Graefrath (1928–2006)), had any enduring impact on the intellectual development of most scholars or practitioners.

What is more important, however, is the fact that in their later years, all the interviewees became more inclined to turn to the doctrinal contributions of European international lawyers: the British Hersch Lauterpacht, Gerald Fitzmaurice and Humphrey Waldock, the French Paul Reuter and Michel Virally, the Belgian Henry Rolin, the Dutch BVA Röling, the Italian Roberto Ago. There was thus a steady cross-fertilisation of ideas and legal approaches. This occurred, in particular, within two bodies: the UN International Law Commission (although only one of the interviewees, namely Jiménez de Aréchaga, was a member of this body and took an active role in it, the Commission's debates deeply influenced the others) and the *Institut de Droit international* (of which instead all five were active members).

The UN International Law Commission in past years was, much more than at present, a forum where great experts from across the world met and freely discussed proposals and drafts, without being pre-conditioned by political leanings or restrained by (informal) instructions from their governments. The Commission was really an organ where there was mutual intellectual respect and a free confrontation of ideas. There, the new international law could be shaped in a balanced manner as a result of critical and constructive exchanges of views. I recall that in 1960, when I was spending a year in Geneva to attend courses in international law at the Graduate Institute of International Relations, I had the chance of being invited by Ago to attend a few sittings of the Commission. Watching the free-wheeling debates between masters like Ago, the Yugoslav Bartoš, the British Fitzmaurice, the Uruguayan Jiménez de Aréchaga, the Soviet Tunkin, the Austrian Verdross, the Iraqi Yasseen, the Czechoslovak Žourek was awe-inspiring. None of them had a prepared text, all spoke off the cuff. They dazzled me with their quick wit and the profoundness of their contributions. Based on this visit, the Commission came to epitomise for me the collective thought process behind international law-making.

The other body which was instrumental in innovating the law (and in which, as I have already noted, all the interviewees played a very significant role) was the *Institut de Droit international.* Its membership is composed of distinguished scholars and practitioners, chiefly international judges, who get together every other year to attend meetings and to debate important legal problems, but who also socialise during dinners and excursions. In the 19th and 20th century, the *Institut* played a leading role in promoting the formation or evolution of new rules on international law. During that period, the debates were genuine exchanges of views, unfettered by political or ideological conditionings. There, the younger members got to meet and appreciate the senior members, and were stimulated to learn from them. I am afraid in the last decades the *Institut* has become somewhat too vulnerable to ideological leanings, political affiliations or diplomacy to be able significantly to contribute to the progressive development of international law. Still, it remains a body where many international lawyers, coming from different areas of the world, have a chance to meet and exchange views (if only in Commissions which deal with specific issues, or on a private basis), and in addition can listen to, and learn from, leading academics or judges.

IV. Legal Positivism

As I noted in the Preface to this book, one of the subjects on which I laid much emphasis in the questionnaire was the influence of any given legal philosophy on the interviewees. Naturally, this entailed sustained probing of their stand on positivism.

It clearly emerged from their answers that all of them embraced the main postulates of legal positivism and were therefore eager to distinguish between *lex lata* and *lex ferenda*. They also unanimously held that the main task of an international lawyer is to interpret international legal rules, as well as to propound legal constructs based on existing law. For all of them, a good lawyer should refrain from projecting his or her own values onto the existing legal framework of the world community. Nevertheless, they were all sensitive to the need for international lawyers to also be critical of the current rules and institutions whenever these do not satisfy the socio-political needs of the international community. Neither did they have any qualms about lawyers trying to innovate by suggesting new ways to surmount old problems, or proposing new rules to fill in gaps in the existing law. This, however, was predicated on the notion that one should be aware of the marked distinction between this *propositive* approach and the *interpretative* method that a lawyer should normally opt for. It may suffice to quote Henkin:

> I really am a positivist in that I recognise that the law has to be made by the politicians, I can't make it myself and I cannot impose my values and declare them to be

> natural law. But I try to push the politicians towards human values, and to identify (and criticise) what they have done.[6]

A similar attitude was shown by Dupuy. Although he was a European scholar deeply versed in the European tradition, he eventually adopted the same view as Henkin:

> They [international lawyers] should be revisionist positivists. They should be positivists in the sense that they can't discard the law in order to evade reality through theories, because this evasion would betray their vocation. The jurist must be a positivist in order to correctly measure the law, but he cannot bow down to the law. He always has to examine it with a critical eye. I think that's what great jurists have always done.[7]

While formally all the interviewees adopted this position, it is safe to say that, when pressed, their views betrayed a slightly different underlying opinion. The three lawyers whose legal education was basically European, or at least inspired by European thinkers (Dupuy, Jiménez de Aréchaga and Jennings) shared a general feeling that one should go beyond *lex lata*. They were nevertheless more inclined to give priority to the interpretation of *existing law* and to tone down both the socio-political dimension of legal rules and the necessity to change inadequate rules. In contrast, the two US scholars I interviewed (Henkin and Schachter), although they upheld the basic postulates of positivism, appeared to be very alert to the extra-legal context of law, as well as sensitive to the moral duty for lawyers to propose reform of rules and regulations whenever this proved necessary.

It is interesting to note that both Henkin and Schachter managed to define their approach to law largely by opposing it to the legal philosophy embraced by the so-called New Haven school of thought (whose main representatives were McDougal and Lasswell). The difference between the approaches taken by that school, on the one hand, and our two international lawyers on the other, was illustrated most starkly by Henkin's response to my question about the degree to which he differed from the New Haven school. He noted that some members of the school used law as process, 'as a pretext for coming up with whatever answer one may want'. In addition, according to Henkin. 'too often what they thought about "world order" coincided with the national policy of a particular State'.[8] Also Schachter, in his interview, emphasised what he considered to be the flaws of the New Haven school. He had 'difficulty with some features of the policy-science approach' and the way in which it had been applied. Furthermore, according to Schachter, their legal conclusions coincided with their 'politics' and predictable preferences:

[6] See 'Interview with Louis Henkin', section I.B.
[7] See 'Interview with René-Jean Dupuy', section IV.D.
[8] See 'Interview with Louis Henkin', section III.B.

> When faced with controversial issues of legal policy (eg Act of State, use of force, the veto in the Security Council) McDougal's conclusions coincide with his politics (and generally the United States' position) but he feels constrained to justify them by asserting that they conform to the 'most intensely demanded' values and 'expectations' of humankind.[9]

While Henkin and Schachter had in common a critical view of the McDougal school, the attitude to positivism taken by each of them differed in some respects. The fundamental reason why Henkin held the view that law must be seen in its context, as part of a human socio-historical process, resided in his conception of the role of law. For him, law was not an abstract set of rules removed from the fabric of life but an integral part of the social process, a corpus of behavioural standards put in place by politicians and legislators to allow a relatively smooth unfolding of social intercourse. For him, law was essentially a piece of social engineering. He pointed out:

> International lawyers have too often treated their legal system as self-contained, having nothing to do with the world. I think that is a mistaken view. International law, like all law, is made by 'politicians', in the best sense of that word. Law is an element, a major element in international politics. One cannot understand the law except in the context of the international political system and international diplomacy.[10]

Responding to a question about the weight of the dichotomy between *lex ferenda* and *lex lata*, Henkin explained:

> One should not confuse them, but they are more fluid than some would like; and statesmen can make *ferenda* into *lata* by their actions, and lawyers even by their writing. I recognise the distinction, but I don't think it is as firm and fixed as some of my colleagues in the profession do.[11]

In short, Henkin was inclined to do what he colourfully labelled as 'imaginative lawyering', namely utilising the capacity to construe existing law correctly, to discern its weaknesses, limitations and loopholes, and to supplement them with an interpretation of existing rules which slowly nudges them towards some amelioration. Henkin rightly cited the famous *Filártiga* case[12] as illustrative of this approach.[13]

[9] See 'Interview with Oscar Schachter', section II.
[10] See 'Interview with Louis Henkin', section I.A.
[11] *Ibid*, section I.B.
[12] *Filártiga* v *Peña-Irala*, 630 F.2d 876 (2d Cir 1980).
[13] 'How one moves from *ferenda* to *lata* may take imaginative lawyering. That's something which good American lawyers have always known, and no doubt European lawyers do too, though I am not as well acquainted with them. We now think of re-opening questions such as the "later-in-time" rule, and one tries to find the right case and get a lower court to pronounce on it. It required imaginative lawyering to get an important court to decide the *Filartiga* case. And unimaginative lawyering can do harm to any cause; you bring the wrong case and you get a wrong decision, and it sets us back. We didn't do well in the Supreme Court on Haitian interdiction or on Mexican abduction. But every case is part of a long process, and we keep trying.' See 'Interview with Louis Henkin', section III.G.

Schachter's methodology seems to me to be even more sophisticated. In his interview, after spelling out in what respects he felt he differed from the New Haven school, Schachter stated:

> In my view, a more disciplined approach to 'policy' analysis is required if law is to be distinguished from politics. Basic values must be supported by legal criteria—that is, they must be demonstrated as values accepted in international law.

As Schachter showed in a masterful way in his *International Law in Theory and Practice*,[14] a positivist lawyer does have some leeway whenever confronted with what Hart termed 'penumbral situations'[15] (as opposed to clearly set out law). He is free to trace rules or principles all the way back to the original policies or objectives which spawned them (these policies or objectives I would call 'values'). Once this 'genealogical' investigation is completed, the positivist lawyer can decide which principles should prevail in the interpretation of a particular norm, as well as which policies or objectives (values), as embodied in law, should be given precedence. By breaking down positivism this manner, Schachter successfully laid out the entire range of options available to a scholar who is conscious of the conflicting principles governing the world community and of the values enshrined in the legal framework of that community. This sophisticated approach is a far cry from the orthodox positivist outlook, according to which the jurist is confined to the selection of the interpretation of the applicable legal rules which he considers to be the best for the situation at hand.

I believe that the various scholars interviewed, and in particular Henkin and Schachter, paved the way for a new positivism free from the fetters of the traditional positivist philosophy of law.[16] In short, a new approach to law, which one could call *critical positivism*, might be predicated on the following assumptions:

a) The investigation of legal rules and institutions must not be carried out without a proper contextualisation, both socio-politically and ideologically, in order fully to understand the dynamics which spurred their adoption or establishment. This will enable lawyers to understand the *raison d'être* of a rule (that is, its primary philosophy) or the motivation behind the creation of a legal institution.

[14] O Schachter, *International Law in Theory and Practice* (Dordrecht, Martinus Nijhoff, 1991) at 18–31.

[15] HLA Hart, *Essay in Jurisprudence and Philosophy* (Oxford, Clarendon Press, 1983) at 64–65, 71–72.

[16] I should note that a critical look at positivism was also taken by another distinguished French international lawyer, Michel Virally. In the major work on jurisprudence he wrote in his early years, namely *La pensée juridique* (Paris, Editions LGDJ, 1960), he limited himself to emphasising the 'inadequacies of positivism' (*les insufficances du positivisme juridique*), at xii–xxii. In a later publication he stressed that jurisprudence must rely on other disciplines interested in the same realities as the ones that are the subject of legal doctrine, stressing that there are two reasons for that: the extraordinary progress of social sciences in modern times; and the huge transformations that law in modern societies has gone through ('Le juriste et la science du droit' (1964) 80 *Revue du droit public et de la science politique en France et a l'etranger* 591 at 608–19).

b) When reconstructing the content of the rule or outlining the powers of the institution, the strict methodology for legal interpretation and the conceptual construction of legal notions should be respected. Normally, this task can be discharged along the lines of 'pure' legal conceptualisation. But how often is one faced with hard-and-fast written rules in real life? Especially in international law, where custom plays such an extensive role, there exist many 'penumbral situations' (to borrow Hart's terminology again). In that situation, traditional legal hermeneutics may not suffice. It may prove necessary, as suggested by Schachter, to draw upon general principles consecrating universal values upheld in the world community (as noted above, they include the pursuit of peace, human rights—and chiefly respect for human dignity—self-determination of peoples, the rule of law, democracy). Resort to these principles can make it possible to engage in a teleological interpretation, that is, an interpretation which emphasises the sought objective of a rule or an institution within the general framework of the values underpinning the current legal structure of the world community. What, then, if those universal values turn out to be in conflict with each other (for instance, if in a particular situation, respect for human rights or the right to self-determination is at odds with the maintenance of peace and international order)? At that stage, in the choice between values, the interpreter will necessarily have to rely upon his or her personal ideological or political leanings. What matters, however, is that he or she should make it explicit and clear that the choice between two conflicting values is grounded in a personal slant or bias, and not in any 'objective' legal precedence of one value over the other.
c) Once the scope, content and purport of the legal rule or institution are determined, along with all the related legal ramifications, the critical positivist should feel free critically to appraise the rule or institution not in light of his or her own values or political or ideological leanings, but in light of the aforementioned general values upheld in the international community. He or she should thus determine to what extent the rule or institution complies with those values, or in what respects it fails to do so.
d) The critical positivist could thus be in a position to criticise the existing law and suggest new legal alternatives which would better meet the existing demands.

If the above is correct, one could even go so far as to apply to legal interpretation—*cum grano salis* (with a grain of salt)—Bertolt Brecht's and Roland Barthes'[17] suggestion for literature: instead of letting the reader or the spectator enjoy a literary work with empathetic identification or a relatively passive

[17] See Brecht's writings in J Willet (ed), *Brecht on Theater* (New York, Hill and Wang, 1992) at 39–41, 91–99, 143–45, 191–95 (as is well-known, Brecht, in criticising the traditional approach to art conceived as a form of mere entertainment, spoke of a 'culinary' approach: see *ibid*, at 40–41, 52); R Barthes, *Essais critiques* (Paris, Éditions du Seuil, 1964) at 48–49, 260.

emotional attitude, they advocated a literature or drama where the reader or the spectator was actively involved and reacted to what they read or heard with a critical mind, or even with outrage. Similarly, legal interpretation, instead of remaining neutral and impassive, primarily aiming at enriching the legal knowledge of the reader, could stimulate the scholar to cast a critical eye over existing law and suggest new ways of implementing the universal values of the international community.

V. Scholar versus Practitioner

It sounds obvious to say that one cannot be a good lawyer without having, at some point or other, practised law. This, *a fortiori*, applies to international lawyers, who handle rules and legal institutions which exist outside their habitual domestic world and with which lawyers therefore do not have the same familiarity as with domestic rules and institutions. It is hence no surprise that the interviewees, all brilliant jurists, in one manner or another were also (or had been at various intervals in their careers) practitioners. One of the reasons for such practical engagement was wittily hinted at by Jiménez de Aréchaga: '[L]aw professors and the crocodile are alike, in that they have to eat while they swim. The idea is that you have to work while you teach.'[18]

The degree of their participation in international institutions varied, of course. Two of the interviewees (Jiménez de Aréchaga and Jennings) sat as judges on the International Court of Justice, and presided over the Court for one term of three years each. Dupuy often appeared as counsel before the same Court, presided over arbitral tribunals and also acted several times as a State delegate in international conferences. Schachter spent 30 years in the UN system. Henkin held various national posts, sat on the UN Human Rights Committee and was principal Reporter for the US Third Restatement of International Law.

Their involvement in international affairs depended in a large measure either on personal inclination, or on external circumstances. But all of them had some form of practical experience, and no doubt this broadened their understanding of the law governing international dealings. Most of the interviewees confirmed that engaging in diplomatic or judicial practice, or in international advocacy had proved extremely useful to their scholarly activity, and had given them a perspective academia alone could never offer.

Besides these practical motivations, there were also deeper and less professional reasons behind their involvement in the practice of law. An idealistic motivation was particularly manifest in the attitude of Henkin, who remarked:

> The primary motivations of my non-scholarly career were the same motivations as for my scholarly activities. I have seen international law not as a study of God-given or even history-given norms, but as a vehicle, perhaps *the* vehicle, for the rule of law

[18] See 'Interview with Eduardo Jiménez de Aréchaga', section III.A.

in international affairs, for order in international affairs, for peace in international affairs, and for the promotion of individual values, human rights values, in both national and international affairs. I try to concentrate my scholarly work on those themes, and I have concentrated my 'practical', outside work on those themes.[19]

Interestingly, at least one of the interviewees, again Henkin, stated in so many words that he had deliberately refused to take on certain functions, such as that of legal adviser or legal counsellor, or international judge nominated by a government. In response to whether he had acted at any point on behalf of the State Department, he answered that he refused to accept an offer to become 'counsellor on international'(legal affairs) because he 'did not wish to work within the limitations of a bureaucracy', adding that 'if they want my views, they get them; I give them freely'.[20]

VI. Political Involvement

Only Jiménez de Aréchaga took part in politics and played a major role, if limited in time, in the government of his country. The others felt that their abstention from any political activity was a natural consequence of their duty to be neutral and refrain from taking sides. In other words, it derived from their need for independence. They also stressed that they had refrained on purpose, but perhaps also as a consequence of their character, a reticence towards 'going public' through national or international media, accepting only to speak on the radio whenever strictly necessary. Sir Robert Jennings' answer to my questions about his possible involvement in politics is telling. After noting that he never engaged in political activities, he pointed out:

> I would say that really all lawyers, even international lawyers, are citizens of their country and in that capacity they may or may not feel that they ought to take part in politics. There's no particular reason why international lawyers should be different from anybody else in this respect. It is important that good and important people are concerned with politics. I'm concerned of course with the government of my country. One has to be. But I have no great stomach for party politics of any hue.[21]

As for Jiménez de Aréchaga, he was far from enthusiastic about his experience in politics. Lamentably for him, he did not take pride in his involvement, and even came to regret it. True, he noted that engaging in politics 'enriches your experience', and he also pointed out that 'it is desirable that one should participate in the political activity in one's country'. However, he added that he soon withdrew from the political scene. In response to my question about whether politics had been important for his intellectual thought and development, he answered:

[19] See 'Interview with Louis Henkin', section III.C.
[20] *Ibid.*
[21] See 'Interview with Sir Robert Jennings', section III.A.

> Well, it was important in the sense that I gave up politics entirely as a result of that experience and the consequences I have suffered, because of the attitude of the people who gained control of the university. I decided I was not made for politics. I did not want to be a politician. So I support the party, but I am not active.[22]

Furthermore, to my question about whether his political experience had had any influence on his legal thinking or on his approach to international law, or whether the two had remained separate, he answered that 'they remained completely separate', adding: 'The only thing I learned was to keep away from politics.'

VII. The Evils of the Current International Community

The interviewees shared the feeling that, in spite of all its limitations, international law is an indispensable tool in inter-State relations. Without the normative infrastructure it offers, States would encounter more frictions and tensions than they do now. This feeling was well set out by Dupuy:

> We have become so used to seeing the pathological violations suffered by international law that we increasingly ignore the fact that it is applied every day, at every moment. Many international treaties, conventions and institutions function very well and allow life to continue in front of our very eyes. The world exists, in large part, thanks to international cooperation in the scientific, technical and also political domains.[23]

This qualified optimism does not equate to turning a blind eye to international law's defects. For one thing, it is high time to revisit and call into question the notion of State sovereignty, which has always been and continues to be a linchpin of the international community. Among the interviewees, Henkin was the most critical of sovereignty. He noted that 'we care too much about *sovereignty*',[24] adding that he was in favour of 'international governance',[25] of 'creating more cooperative institutions, for example for the environment'.[26] He supported 'the strengthening of international human rights machinery' as well as 'trade and financial arrangements.'[27]

While it is easy to agree with these comments in theory, the problem of how *concretely* and *specifically* to dislodge sovereignty from atop its perch is an altogether different story. The solution probably lies in increasing the powers of international mechanisms capable of restraining the freedom of States. Dispute settlement bodies should perhaps be granted broader juris-

[22] See 'Interview with Eduardo Jiménez de Aréchaga', section III.A.
[23] See 'Interview with René-Jean Dupuy', section IV.C.
[24] See 'Interview with Louis Henkin', section III.A.
[25] *Ibid.*
[26] *Ibid*, section IV.B.
[27] *Ibid.*

diction. Monitoring institutions should be rendered more incisive. Devices should be worked out for the purpose of facilitating the formation or updating of general rules applicable to all States. In this respect, the International Law Commission, the International Court of Justice and the *Institut de Droit international* could become more proactive, forward-looking and firm in helping to crystallise nascent (or incipient) international customs. In tandem, domestic courts should be prompted to play a greater role in ensuring the national implementation of international rules, under the 'role-splitting' doctrine (*théorie du dédoublement fonctionnel*) suggested by George Scelle in the 1930s.[28]

The awareness that international law suffers from too many deficiencies was apparent in the interviews with all five scholars. Dupuy drew attention to the gap between the norms accepted in principle by the world community, and their arbitrary implementation by States and other international actors in practice. He delineated this gap by drawing upon his own set of conceptual tools, namely the conflict between the 'historical' community and the 'mythical' community:

> The gap is created because of contradictions. It's a gap between two contrasting visions of the international community which I have labelled the 'historical community' and the 'mythical community'. The historical community is burdened with all the sin in the world and all its misery. The mythical community is what men conceive as an ideal of reconciliation, understanding and cooperation.[29]

Jiménez de Aréchaga saw the main flaws of the current world community as being the unsatisfactory regulation of the use of force by States, the way in which the Security Council powers are governed by law, and the use of the veto by the Big Five in the Security Council. When prodded about which elements of the present international community gave rise to anxiety and could possibly disrupt the current fabric of the world community, he answered:

> The interpretation of Article 2(4); the interpretation of Article 51; the interpretation of Article 25; the fact that control by the five Permanent Members through this veto has disappeared; the temptation to use Chapter VII of the Charter; and the compulsory effect of Security Council resolutions as an instrument for exercising power over the international community. These are disquieting factors. Another factor relates, for instance, to the *Lockerbie* case.[30]

He restated his concern about the role of the Security Council when he discussed the way in which that body had reacted to the political and military crisis in the former Yugoslavia by establishing the International Criminal Tribunal for the former Yugoslavia:

[28] I commented on Scelle's theory in my paper 'Remarks on Scelle's Theory of "Role Splitting" (*Dédoublement fonctionnel*) in International Law' (1990) 1 *European Journal of International Law* 210.

[29] See 'Interview with René-Jean Dupuy', section IV.B.

[30] See 'Interview with Eduardo Jiménez de Aréchaga', section IV.C.

> You see, you have another example of the strange function of the Security Council: establishing a tribunal. Normally tribunals are set up by a treaty between States. Here you have the Security Council setting up a tribunal, appointing the members. I think it's a new development which, in this case, is good, progressive, very much needed. On the other hand, it shows to an extreme how the powers of the Security Council can be exercised.[31]

Despite their misgivings about the current state of affairs, however, it is safe to say that, by and large, none of my interviewees proposed any concrete measure or corrective to improve upon the current legal structure and functioning of the world community.

VIII. The Outlook for the World Community

In any inquiry into the paths the international community might take in the coming decades, a logical point of departure is Henkin's proposition that 'the international legal system remains primitive and its radical development is not in sight'.[32] In addition, to assess the prospects of development of the world community and try to anticipate in what direction it may evolve, one must perforce look upon this community in a historical context. It is a fact that the present Westphalian model has evolved from a rather closed and primitive society comprising a handful of States, into a larger society where States, while still playing a major role, are no longer the exclusive actors and where communitarian values have emerged which try gradually to erode the traditional bilateral, sovereignty-orientated features of the society. Henkin tellingly spelled out this notion in 1995 in a book based on his Hague lectures:

> [T]he values of the [international] system are still strongly state values in a liberal system—state independence and autonomy, the impermeability of state territories and societies, state egoism in the pursuit of national interest. But those values are increasingly in tension with human values, as both individual states and the system extend and deepen their concern for individual welfare—for individual human rights and individual basic needs.[33]

Based on these premises, it is notable that the interviewees seemed to agree upon four main postulates:

a) dismissal of any forecasts of radical change in the international community in the near future;
b) the ruling out of the creation of a world government;
c) the unlikelihood of any significant reform of the United Nations; and
d) a gravitation towards regionalism.

[31] *Ibid*, section IV.D.
[32] L Henkin, *How Nations Behave: Law and Foreign Policy*, 2nd edn (New York, Columbia University Press, 1979) at 314.
[33] L Henkin, *International Law: Politics and Values* (Dordrecht, M Nijhoff, 1995) at 279.

They all dismissed the idea of a world government, predicting instead that the world community will endure in its present configuration, although some improvements may be introduced gradually. For instance, Schachter said:

> My own guess (for whatever it is worth) is that we will not have world government. As for the UN itself, my guess is that it will reflect a trend towards diffusion of power. The US will no longer be a 'sole superpower', and many more States will acquire a significant role. Moreover, I would expect a much-enhanced role for the non-governmental sectors, now called 'civil society'. . . . I would not exclude the possibility of replacing the UN by a new international organisation that would reflect changes in power and in attitudes of elites.[34]

Another point on which all the interviewees (including Schachter, judging from the proposition I have just quoted) agreed, was that there is no hope to reform the United Nations. This was best articulated by Jiménez de Aréchaga:

> The problem is that any revision of the Charter would create enormous difficulties. One cannot be certain that, if a reform of the Charter is attempted, we will end with a better instrument than the one existing now. There will be great difficulty. . . . This was said with respect to recent attempts by Germany and Japan to become permanent or quasi-permanent members of the Security Council. It is very difficult, in realistic terms, to embark on a revision of the provision of the Charter. Of course, it would be better to have resolutions of the General Assembly interpreting the terms of the Charter; like, for instance, Resolution 2625 (XX), which has been given a prominent position by the International Court in the *Nicaragua* case, stating that it represents the law of the Charter, which has also become customary law.[35]

Others suggested that regionalism could be one of the directions the world community might take. This belief was held in particular by Jiménez de Aréchaga and Jennings. As the former put it:

> You need what you have in Europe, a commission of independent people, who are devoted to integration and also a Court which implements and ensures a uniform interpretation of the rules adopted by the Community.[36]

On the whole, it is apparent that all the interviewees were substantially North-orientated in their approach to the world community. Even Jiménez de Aréchaga, despite being from a developing country, manifestly shared the mindset of scholars and practitioners from the North, although he was alert to many of the problems of developing countries. This feature could perhaps explain why, to some extent, the interviewees seemed unprepared to perceive the importance of some new trends which had emerged in the 1980s and 1990s, and suggest ways to come to grips with them. I am referring, of

34 See 'Interview with Oscar Schachter', section VI.B.
35 See 'Interview with Eduardo Jiménez de Aréchaga', section IV.B.
36 *Ibid*, section IV.D.

course, to a few well-known historical phenomena, notably the multiplication of internal armed conflicts motivated by ethnic, social or religious tension, the dramatic appearance of terrorism, the festering of the Middle East's problems along with the incapacity of the UN to impose a solution to the Palestinian conundrum, the worsening of the North–South gap despite the increasing role of some developing countries such as China, India and Brazil, the spreading of non-State actors that are politically and militarily organised and possess a State-like structure, the gradual emergence in the world community of the notion of individual accountability for heinous crimes, and the accompanying crystallisation of mechanisms enforcing international criminal justice.

To be sure, the interviewees were not blind to these problems. Jiménez de Aréchaga, Henkin and Schachter, in particular, tackled some of these issues in their writings. Nevertheless, even these three scholars were too much a product of their own time to be able to view their world with sufficient detachment. Probably they were too steeped in their disappointment in the United Nations as a global institution, to have a heightened sensitivity to these new problems and the consequent need for effective solutions at the legal level.

Some might criticise me for being too demanding of international lawyers who, after all, like all lawyers, are perforce tuned to the present and the past more than they are to the future and, what is more, feel impotent in the face of all the huge evils of society. In *Le Colonel Chabert*, Derville, one of Balzac's characters, famously mused on the role of lawyers. Complaining that there are three vocations which cannot regard men with esteem—the priest, the doctor and the lawyer—he explains:

> They are dressed in black for they wear mourning for all the virtues and all the illusions lost. The most unfortunate of the three is the lawyer. When a person calls on a priest, he is led by repentance, by remorse, by a faith that makes him interesting, enhances him and also consoles the mindset of the go-between in a task that is not deprived of pleasure: the priest purifies, reconciles and mends. But we lawyers, we see all over again the same wicked feelings; nothing can remedy them; and our legal practice is a sink that cannot be drained.[37]

I, for one, although keenly aware of the limitations of lawyers, do not share this extreme view: I strongly believe that one should be driven in one's work by the desire (and the moral imperative) to try to improve the existing situation even at the legal level.

[37] H Balzac, *Le Colonel Chabert* (1835) (Paris, Librio, 1994) at 95 (translation mine): 'Savez-vous … qu'il existe dans notre société trois hommes, le Prêtre, le Médecin et l'Homme de justice, qui ne peuvent pas estimer le monde? Ils ont des robes noires, peut-être parce qu'ils portent le deuil de toutes les vertus, de toutes les illusions. Le plus malheureux des trois est l'avoué. Quand l'homme vient trouver le prêtre, il arrive poussé par le repentir, par les remords, par des croyances qui le rendent intéressant, qui le grandissent, et consolent l'âme du médiateur, dont la tâche ne va pas sans une sorte de jouissance; il purifie, il répare, il réconcilie. Mais nous autres avoués, nous voyons se répéter les mêmes sentiments mauvais, rien ne les corrige, nos études sont des égouts qu'on ne peut pas curer.'

As I have noted above, all five scholars shared the desire to see improvements to the current international community. Some of them also felt that lawyers are under a moral obligation to take action to this end. Nonetheless, it was evident that none of them had given much thought to how this could be achieved in practice. They all resorted to citing vague and grand formulas, no doubt due both to the inherent difficulties of the task and to the fact that they never felt compelled to focus their minds on legal predictions, or on how the international community could better attain some of the objectives it had already formulated and accepted 'in the abstract'. Dupuy saw the task as an effort to build Utopia. As he put it:

> People need Utopia. I have always distinguished utopian means from utopian ends. Utopia is bad when it is reduced to means. Such as, for example, the belief in a perfect constitution which would suit all countries in all epochs. A utopian end, in contrast, is the aspiration towards an ultimate goal. Of course, it can't be achieved without the appropriate means. But these means can never be definitive, they can only be provisional: they are temporary, interim and can be corrected or discarded.[38]

Probably the best way to go about all these efforts was formulated by Henkin:

> Peace, however—like respect for human rights—is not achieved at one time for ever. It's a process, one has to keep working at it. Somebody once described a cook as having a harried look because he knew you can't feed people once and for all. You feed them once, then you have to feed them again six hours later. That's true about peace, and order, and human rights, and the environment – it has to be a continuous unceasing process. And you have to build and maintain institutions that will encourage people within governments and across governments to dedicate themselves, and to work at it. That's what international law and an international legal system should be.[39]

It was also deemed crucial for scholars to speak out whenever governments fail to abide by international legal standards in their policies and behaviour. Scholars should not shun attacking their own national authorities when the latter stray from the observance of imperative legal norms. While this sentiment was clearly and unanimously shared by the interviewees, Henkin best spelled it out, when he said:

> In fairness, . . . the US Government has in general been on the right side—but not always, and not in detail, and not specifically. . . . I have tended to be a critic of US policy when I considered it to be contrary to international law. I love the United States and I was a member of its government, and I respect democracy, but I have sometimes seen it to be my job to provide friendly, constructive criticisms, because I think that is in the national interest of the United States to abide by and support the rule of law.[40]

38 See 'Interview with René-Jean Dupuy', section IV.B.
39 See 'Interview with Louis Henkin', section IV.D.
40 *Ibid*, section III.B.

IX. Personal Matters

In the Preface to this book, I explained that I was interested in the interviewees not only as legal professionals. I also wanted to learn more about their human dimension, their hopes, expectations and idiosyncrasies. I was keen to know how they had grappled with what the Italian poet Eugenio Montale called '*il male del vivere*' (the agony of living), that is, all the infelicities we confront on a daily basis. I was reassured that my curiosity was not unwarranted when Oscar Schachter recounted a journey by ship from the United Kingdom to New York, during which his travel companion was Hersch Lauterpacht. Their conversations at sea dealt with the same human dimension of international lawyers in which I myself was interested:

> I must say that although we had many conversations, we rarely discussed international law, but often the human side and idiosyncrasies of notable international lawyers. The great figures of European and British international law were 'humanised' by Lauterpacht's light-hearted stories.[41]

It was perhaps naive of me to include the questions about whether they felt they had heeded their 'inner demon', and whether they needed gratifications, diversions or any other 'palliatives' to make life more bearable. I had underestimated the natural reticence of anybody to talk to an acquaintance about intimate matters and, indeed, those matters most crucial to each of us: Do we feel we have accomplished something good in life, thus proving to ourselves and others that the 'grace' has put us among the 'elect' and not among the 'reprobate'? How do we manage to cope with the myriad problems of life? Are we profoundly unhappy and, if so, why?

A further reason for the relative serenity of the interviewees is that, I believe, they all took comfort from religion. This can be of great psychological help in life. For those, like the present writer, who are radically secular, life can be more troublesome. Those who have no belief system think that *homo sapiens*, having reason, has become aware of two things of which all other animals have no consciousness, ie the great complexity and the mysterious nature of our world, and the ineluctable finitude of each individual's life; hence the dread of death. To cope with these two things and achieve relative peace of mind, human beings had to invent splendid tales (including religion) about the creation of the world, about the reason for our existence and about the afterlife. If a secular 'pocket philosophy' is chosen instead, life and work become more haphazard. Luckily, as I said, the interviewees were not beset by these problems.

In addition, I was talking to eminent scholars and practitioners who had been exceedingly successful in their lives and careers. I should therefore have taken for granted that the answer to my first question about their 'inner demons' would be generally affirmative. I thought I would find some form of disquiet or anxiety. Some people might be existentially tormented knowing

[41] See 'Interview with Oscar Schachter', section I.

that 'the universe is a safe of which humanity seeks the combination'.[42] I am afraid I was at that time still unaware that the search for the safe's combination is illusory and wrong: it is pointless to look for a combination, because solving small and specific problems suffices to provide personal fulfilment. Consciously or unwittingly, the scholars to whom I spoke applied Spinoza's wise proposition that 'the more we understand specific matters, the more we understand God'.[43] Delving deeply into a specific problem, regardless of the capacity in which this is done, enables one better to understand the intricate web of social and, more generally, human relations: the macrocosm itself is reflected in the microcosm of a specific problem, just as the sun's rays reflect in a pond. It is natural then to feel content and fulfilled after a lifetime spent mulling over individual problems and in the search for specific solutions. To all this, one should also add the sense of gratification obtained from professional success, and the attendant monetary rewards.

Among the responses concerning the joy and the sense of fulfilment derived from their profession, probably that given by Dupuy was the most illuminating:

> There is scientific activity, but there is above all teaching activity. Teaching has brought me extraordinary joy. I always went up to the lectern feeling an intense happiness.[44]

This satisfaction with their jobs and professional successes also explains why none of the interviewees felt, or at least voiced out loud, the belief that life is inherently tragic (*spirat tragicum*, as Horace said[45])—a belief that appears to be enhanced in those who look at reality also or primarily through the prism of criminal justice. This is why, if the interviewees often indulged in 'powerful diversions' (in the form of gardening, mountaineering, intellectual companionship, friendship and so on) or in 'substitute gratifications' (in the form of art, music, or poetry), it was only to while away their leisure time during what Hegel would call 'the Sunday of life'. These diversions or gratifications were in no way substitutes for their daily labours; they were simply complementary to otherwise fulfilling professional lives.

I did, however, sense a tinge of melancholy in Jiménez de Aréchaga's interview, when he noted that a few times he felt the need to find solace—with moderation—in Bacchus' gifts. And in Schachter, one could find more than a hint of sound pessimism (or, better, of a realistic vision of life), when he said:

> I recognise the tragic aspect of human life and the impossibility of attaining many of our ideals. I must confess that over the years, many nights have been almost sleepless because of troubling problems or repressed anger.[46]

[42] R Barthes, *Mythologies*, first published in 1957 (London, Vintage Books, 2009) at 78 first published in 1957 (London, Vintage Books, 2009) at 78.

[43] '*Quo magis res singulares intelligimus eo magis Deum intelligimus*': Spinoza, *Ethica geometrico more demonstrata*, propositio XXV.

[44] See 'Interview with René-Jean Dupuy', section V.D.

[45] Horace, *Epistles*, II,166.

[46] See 'Interview with Oscar Schachter', section VII.

However, he quickly added:

> I sometimes console myself by thinking how lucky I have been to have achieved a fruitful career and high positions. I could not have imagined that, even in my day-dreams as a student. Doubtless luck played a role. I have been lucky in my family and in friendships. I often seek comfort in poetry (both old and new) and in philosophy (mostly old).[47]

X. Final Observations

In retrospect, I think it is fair to say that these five interviews provide us with a lively insight into the legal thinking of a few prominent scholars and practitioners at the turn of the 20th century. While each of them possessed unique traits and idiosyncrasies, they all shared a common legal philosophy and embraced a common vision of the world community. They also resorted to the same conceptual tools to decipher the legal reality of the inter-State society, although each of them used those tools according to his own intellectual inclination and temperament. They also entertained respect for and showed appreciation of one another.

I believe that new generations of lawyers would find it interesting to become acquainted with the vision of international lawyers from the old generation. It should also be interesting to see how those 'old scholars' regarded and appreciated the great lawyers who had preceded them in time. In this respect, I think the reader will find revealing not only the comments on Hans Kelsen by Jiménez de Aréchaga, Schachter and Jennings (as well as those published in the *European Journal of International Law* by Gaetano Arangio-Ruiz[48]), but also the brief observations by Jennings. Similarly of great interest are the remarks by Dupuy and Jiménez de Aréchaga on Röling, those by Jennings on Lauterpacht, McNair and Virally, the remarks by Jiménez de Aréchaga on Fitzmaurice and Rolin, the observations by Dupuy, Henkin and Schachter on Friedmann, as well as those by Dupuy on Scelle (I have already discussed above the critical comments by Henkin and Schachter on the doctrines of Myres McDougal).

Can we draw any inference from this overview of several generations of international lawyers? Perhaps one might note that there has been a gradual abandonment of the traditional normativism which prevailed in Europe at the beginning of the 20th century. The approach to law embraced in the United States, which is essentially immune from legal formalism, has no doubt been beneficial to European scholarship. Legal scholars in the US have insisted that law is an indispensable organisational factor in the social functioning of any community. Albeit gradually, this notion has led European lawyers to depart from the traditional view of law as a self-contained body of rules, to

[47] *Ibid.*

[48] See G Arangio-Ruiz, E Jiménez de Aréchaga and O Schachter, 'Kelsen, Personal Recollections' (1998) 9 *European Journal of International Law* 386. The interview with Arangio-Ruiz is at 386–87.

be investigated with special conceptual tools; in short, as a subject per se, disconnected from any other social institution. On the other hand, the Anglo-American scholarship has benefited from the European tradition's emphasis on rigorous conceptualisation. Thus, the new generations of international lawyers now have at their disposal a vast array of methodological tools and general concepts. On the whole, I think it can be safely maintained that there has been progress towards a more multi-faceted, as well as insightful, overall understanding of international legal institutions.

Let me end by noting that however appalling the man-made evils of the world community may be (unfortunately men are 'naturally enemies'—*sunt ergo homines ex natura hostes*, as Spinoza wrote[49]), we can feel a minimum of reassurance at the thought that we are in a position to benefit from some outstanding scholars. It is heartening to know there are highly sophisticated professionals who, while coming from different countries, still manage to have a few things in common: they share the same fundamental values (peace, human rights, the rule of law, justice), operate for the promotion of international legal standards and aim at translating those values into living reality. Of course, international lawyers, however good they may be, will not 'save the world'. Like any lawyer, they suffer from a double disadvantage. They do not deal with the fundamentals (as Hegel once wrote, only philosophy, religion and art are involved in the universal and the eternal, all the other disciplines being therefore destined to discuss only the transient). Furthermore, for lawyers—more than for any other social scientist—this drawback is accentuated by the fact that any patiently built legal construct is bound to collapse as soon as the rules in which it was grounded are changed by the lawmakers—the 'three words of the legislature' mentioned by Kirchmann.[50]

Plainly, the key to the principal problems of the world community is in the hands of politicians, diplomats and military leaders. Nevertheless, legal scholars may suggest ideas and advance solutions—without, however, harbouring too many illusions. One can also find a reason for hope in the presence of lawyers who (like the five scholars interviewed in this book) positively show that they shun taking either of two positions common to so many scholars: (i) indifference to the plight of others, or (ii) the keen and exclusive pursuit of one's own interests. One can graphically illustrate these two attitudes by drawing on the literature. For the first stance the most telling metaphor is that conjured up by Lucretius: that of the man who gazes from the shore at a shipwreck at sea and the suffering of those persons fighting against the waves; he is joyful not because others' afflictions are in themselves a source of delight, but because to be free from troubles is itself a joy (*quibus ipse malis careas quia cernere suave est*).[51] That

[49] *Tractatus politicus*, Chapter II, Section 14.

[50] JH von Kirchmann, *Die Wertlosigkeit der Jurisprudenz als Wissenschaft: Ein Vortrag* (Berlin, Nachdrunk der Ausg, 1848) at 29.

[51] Lucretius, *De rerum natura*, II, 1–5; see Lucretius, *On the Nature of the Universe*, tr and introduced by RE Latham (London, Penguin, 1951) at 60.

position is—of course—fallacious: how can one keep aloof in the midst of so many tragedies occurring in the world around us? The other questionable stand is best illustrated by the utterances of that extraordinary character depicted by Voltaire—Candide. Faced with the evils of life he has just experienced, Candide in the event suggests that each should confine himself to 'cultivating his own garden', that is, to pursuing his own interests—which, in the case of lawyers, chiefly means chasing monetary success.

Our five interviewees primarily devoted themselves to pursuing the interests of the world community at large. This is one further reason for our admiration. I believe that we would be warranted in applying to them the last words of the leading Russian politician and diplomat Adolph Abramovich Joffe (a man in whom international lawyers should be interested, for he, amongst other things, was crucial in the drafting of the Brest-Litovsk ceasefire agreement and forcefully suggested an important notion of self-determination of peoples in 1917).[52] I am referring to the words Joffe wrote in the farewell letter left for his friend Leon Trotsky before committing suicide to put an end to the excruciating suffering caused by his illness:

> Human life has meaning only to the extent that, and as long as, it serves the infinite, which for us is humanity.[53]

[52] Adolf Abramovich Joffe (1823–1927) was a Russian politician and diplomat. From 30 November 1917 until January 1918, Joffe was the head of the Soviet delegation that was sent to Brest-Litovsk to negotiate an end to the hostilities with Germany. On 22 December 1917, Joffe announced the following Bolshevik pre-conditions for a peace treaty: 1) No forcible annexation of territories seized in the war; 2) Restore national independence where it was terminated during war; 3) National groups independent before the war should be allowed by referendum to decide question of independence; 4) Multi-cultural regions should be administered so as to allow all possible cultural independence and self-regulation; 5) No indemnities. Personal losses should be compensated out of international fund; 6) Colonial questions should be decided in accordance with points 1–4. Although Joffe had signed a ceasefire agreement with the Central Powers on 2 December 1917, he supported Trotsky in the latter's refusal to sign a permanent peace treaty in February 1918. Once the Bolshevik Central Committee decided to sign the Treaty of Brest-Litovsk on 23 February 1918, Joffe remained a member of the Soviet delegation only under protest and in a purely consultative capacity. Joffe, although he no longer played a political role—among other things because he was too close to Trotsky—was very active as a diplomat. He negotiated a ceasefire with Poland in October 1920 and peace treaties with Estonia, Latvia and Lithuania in late 1920. In 1921 he signed the Peace of Riga with Poland, ending the Polish–Soviet War. Joffe was one of the Soviet delegates at the Genoa Conference in February 1922 and, after the Soviet walkout, was made ambassador to China. In 1923, he signed an agreement with Sun Yat-Sen in Shanghai on aid to Kuomintang, on the assumption that the latter would cooperate with Chinese Communists, presumably with Lenin's approval. While in China, Joffe travelled to Japan in June 1923 to settle Soviet–Japanese relations. The negotiations proved long and difficult, and were aborted when he became gravely ill and had to be sent back to Moscow. After a partial recovery, he served as a member of the Soviet delegation to Great Britain in 1924 and as Soviet representative in Austria in 1924–26. In 1926 his declining health and disagreements with the ruling Bolshevik faction forced his semi-retirement. He committed suicide in 1927.

[53] This letter of 15 November 1927 may be read in its entirety in an English translation by Nadezhda A Joffe, *Back in Time: My Life, My Fate, My Epoch* (Oak Park, Mich, Labor Publications, 1995), at 55–63. The passage I have quoted above is at 56. Nadezhda A Joffe was Adolf Joffe's daughter.

I keep and cherish the tapes of all the interviews in this book, as well as the first transcripts of them, in some cases with handwritten additions and corrections by the interviewees. As I consider this material valuable, I shall deposit it with the Library of the Special Tribunal for Lebanon.

Index of Names

Index

www.ingramcontent.com/pod-product-compliance
Ingram Content Group UK Ltd.
Pitfield, Milton Keynes, MK11 3LW, UK
UKHW020135290926
15471UKWH00003B/497

9 781849 461207